**Nature and nurture during infancy
and early childhood**

Nature and nurture during infancy and early childhood

ROBERT PLOMIN
The Pennsylvania State University

JOHN C. DeFRIES
University of Colorado

DAVID W. FULKER
University of Colorado

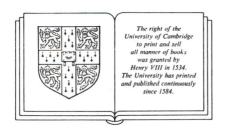

The right of the
University of Cambridge
to print and sell
all manner of books
was granted by
Henry VIII in 1534.
The University has printed
and published continuously
since 1584.

CAMBRIDGE UNIVERSITY PRESS

Cambridge
New York   New Rochelle   Melbourne   Sydney

Published by the Press Syndicate of the University of Cambridge
The Pitt Building, Trumpington Street, Cambridge CB2 1RP
32 East 57th Street, New York, NY 10022, USA
10 Stamford Road, Oakleigh, Melbourne 3166, Australia

First published 1988

Printed in the United States of America

Library of Congress Cataloging-in-Publication Data
Plomin, Robert, 1948–
Nature and nurture during infancy and early childhood.
Bibliography: p.
Includes indexes.
1. Nature   and   nurture.   2. Behavior   genetics.   3. Difference   (Psychol-
ogy)   4. Child psychology.
I. DeFries, J. C., 1934– .   II. Fulker, David W.
III. Title. [DNLM: 1. Environment. 2. Genetics, Behavioral – in infancy & child-
hood. QH 457 P729n]
BF701.P55   1988   155.4'22   87-38222

British Library Cataloguing in Publication Data
Plomin, Robert
Nature and nuture during infancy and early childhood.
1. Children. Behaviour. Environmental factors & genetic factors
I. Title
155.4

ISBN 0 521 34370 4

To the memory of Ronald S. Wilson

Contents

Preface

Behavioral genetic theory, methods, and research provide a unique perspective on nature and nurture during infancy and early childhood, that is, on the genetic and environmental origins of individual differences in behavioral development. The words "nature" and "nurture" each have warm associations until they are brought together. One of our goals is to emphasize the conjunction "and" rather than the projective test provided by the dash in "nature–nurture" or the explicit hostility in the phrase "nature versus nurture." We believe that the perspective of behavioral genetics is as useful for understanding environmental influences in development as it is for exploring the role of heredity, and we hope that this book will convince developmentalists of the importance of both genetic and experiential factors in the origins of behavioral differences during infancy and early childhood. At the simplest level, the components-of-variance approach – which we explore in terms of simple correlations as well as by means of model-fitting analyses – often indicates that genetic variance is significant and invariably shows that nongenetic factors are important.

The decomposition of phenotypic variance into genetic and environmental components of variance is the standard fare of behavioral genetic research. Somewhat newer is an emphasis on the decomposition of the environmental component of variance into two components, one shared by family members, which increases their phenotypic resemblance, and the other not shared; correlations for genetically unrelated children reared together in the same adoptive homes are especially powerful for detecting the "bottom line" influence of growing up in the same family. The importance of the distinction between shared and nonshared environmental influences becomes clear when we show that shared environmental influences increase in importance for cognitive abilities during infancy and early childhood but that nonshared environmental influences predominate for all other domains of development. Behavioral genetic analyses that incorporate specific measures of the environment can be used to go beyond the decomposition of variance in order to explore such topics as the impact of environmental influences in adoptive families in which family members share environment but not heredity, genetic influence on measures of the family environment and on environment–development associations, and genotype–environment interaction and correlation. Some of the results of this research are surprising. For example, genetic influences on measures of the family environment appear to be substantial, at least in infancy. This finding has great implications for our study of the family environment, especially when we study family members who share heredity as well as family environment.

In addition to its emphasis on nurture as well as nature, another special feature of this book is its focus on the etiology of change as well as continuity during the first four years of life. The essential point is that genetics contributes to change as well as to continuity during development. The life-blood of research on developmental change and continuity is the longitudinal study, and our contribution to longitudinal behavioral genetic research is the Colorado Adoption Project, which we refer to extensively in this book to illustrate issues of the genetic and environmental etiology of individual differences, change, and continuity during infancy and early childhood.

We dedicate this book to the memory of Ronald S. Wilson (1933–86), one of the founders of the subdiscipline of developmental behavioral genetics. His lasting memorial is the longitudinal Louisville Twin Study, the premier study in the field of human developmental behavioral genetics. Professor Wilson directed the project for nearly 20 years, during which time nearly 500 pairs of twins were studied in more than 5,000 test sessions from the first year of life through adolescence. This single study has been the major source of knowledge about nature and nurture during infancy and early childhood, and our book relies heavily on its results. Although Professor Wilson's work on physical development and temperament has been influential, he is perhaps most well known for his concept of genetic influence on "spurts and lags" in mental development, a concept depicted vividly in his frequently reprinted figures of longitudinal profiles of scores for individual pairs of identical twins and pairs of fraternal twins. Infants and young children often show dramatic changes from year to year in their scores on mental tests; however, identical twins change in tandem, more so than fraternal twins. Professor Wilson's work on this topic has succeeded in convincing many developmentalists of the possibility of genetic change as well as continuity during development. He had the vision to see the importance of a large-scale longitudinal twin study – longitudinal behavioral genetic studies alone can answer questions about change and continuity during development – and the determination, courage, and tenacity to fulfill that grand aim. It is a striking achievement that has been a model for us and, we hope, will be for future generations of behavioral geneticists.

Acknowledgments

Because there are so few behavioral genetic studies on infancy and early childhood, this book relies heavily on the two major longitudinal behavioral genetic studies carried out during infancy and early childhood: the Louisville Twin Study and the Colorado Adoption Project (CAP). The Colorado Adoption Project, begun in 1974, involves 245 adoptive and 245 nonadoptive families in which adopted and nonadopted children have been studied in their homes at 1, 2, 3, and 4 years of age; the biological and adoptive parents of the adopted children and the parents of the nonadopted children have been administered a 3-hour battery of tests and questionnaires. The long-term, large-scale nature of this project has led to a lengthy list of people to whom we are indebted. We are deeply grateful to the parents and children for their participation, cooperation, and encouragement. Two adoption agencies and their administrators – John Califf and Jodi McElhinny of Lutheran Social Services of Colorado and James Mauck and Dolores Schmidt of Denver Catholic Community Services – made the study possible. We greatly appreciate Salley-Anne Rhea's efforts in coordinating the project, Diane Perry's work in conducting the home visits, and the diverse efforts of Anne Boland and Beth Shafer. As this book was being written, four students who worked on the study during their entire graduate careers received their doctorate degrees for dissertations based on analyses of CAP data: Robin Corley, Denise Daniels, Treva Rice, and Lee Thompson. Several other graduate students who contributed to analyses described in this book continue to be involved in the CAP research enterprise: Cindy Bergeman, Hilary Coon, Michele LaBuda, and Kay Phillips. The Institute for Behavioral Genetics has subsidized the project financially and, most importantly, with the day-to-day assistance of its excellent staff; we especially thank Agnes Conley, Dianne Johnson, and Rebecca Miles. We have profited from interactions with our colleagues at the Institute, especially from Steven Vandenberg, whose experience was very helpful in planning for the study. Our gratitude to many other individuals who contributed earlier to the CAP was acknowledged in a book that reported CAP results in infancy (Plomin & DeFries, 1985a) – their contributions, and our appreciation, have been compounded during the 13 years of the CAP.

We are grateful for the continuous support of the National Institute of Child Health and Human Development since 1977 for the collection of CAP data at 1, 2, 3, and 4 years of age (HD-10333); NICHD also supports an extension of CAP to middle childhood (HD-18426). Since 1978, the National Science Foundation has awarded grants (BNS-7826204, BNS-8200310, BNS-8505692, BNS-8643938) that enabled us to collect video-taped recordings of mother–infant interaction at 1, 2, and 3 years of age and to study interactions among adoptive and nonadoptive siblings. The CAP was launched in 1976 with the aid of funds from the University of Colorado's Biomedical Research Support Grant and a small grant from the National Institute of Mental Health (MH-28076); the project was supported in 1977 by the William T. Grant Foundation. The Spencer Foundation provided support from 1982 to 1985 for the purpose of testing younger adopted and nonadopted siblings of the probands at 5 and 7 months of age on a measure of novelty preference; the Spencer Foundation also launched an extension of the study into early adolescence. Finally, our research and thinking about nature and nurture during infancy and early childhood has profited immensely from our participation since 1982 in the Transition from Infancy to Early Childhood Research Network of the John D. and Catherine T. MacArthur Foundation.

1   Introduction

The goal of this book is to explore the origins of individual differences in behavioral development during infancy and early childhood. A key phrase is "individual differences." When developmentalists look at infancy and early childhood, they are usually absorbed by the dramatic changes that members of our species undergo during this fast-moving period of development. For example, Jean Piaget, the most influential figure in developmental psychology since the 1960s, described cognitive changes in terms of the transition from the sensorimotor actions of infancy to the representational abilities of early childhood, seen most clearly in the blossoming of language. However, Piaget was concerned only with average developmental trends, not with differences among children.

In contrast, when we look at children, we see children, not the child. That is, our interest centers on the development of individual differences among children rather than universal or normative (average) aspects of our species' development. A powerful theory of development must be able to explain individual differences, if for no other reason than that such differences exist – individual differences represent a major part of the phenomenon to be explained. There are, however, other reasons for studying individual differences: Descriptions and explanations of normative aspects of development bear no necessary relationship to those of individual differences; questions concerning the origins of individual differences are more easily answered than questions concerning the etiology of normative aspects of development; and the developmental issues of greatest relevance to society are issues of individual differences. A discussion of these topics can be found in Chapter 2.

A second key word is "origins." Because our perspective is quantitative genetics, the word "origins" implies an interest in understanding the role played by genetic as well as environmental factors in the development of individual differences. As explained in Chapter 3, quantitative genetics provides a general theory of the development of individual differences that

1

leads to novel concepts, methods, and research. Emphatically, it is more than the study of nature versus nurture. For example, a current research focus is the "nature of nurture," the developmental interface between genetic and environmental influences. Relevant research addresses such topics as genotype–environment interaction, genotype–environment correlation, and genetic mediation of "environmental" influences, discussed in Chapters 9, 10, and 11, respectively.

Another important example of the extension of quantitative genetics beyond the nature–nurture question is the study of the role of genetics in developmental change as well as continuity. The realization that genetic influences contribute to change has broad implications for the study of development, beginning with a conceptual reorientation away from the old notion of genes as static, unchanging influences and leading to new methods and research that address genetic etiologies of developmental transitions and changes, the topic of Chapters 5 and 6 and the focus of a new sub-discipline, developmental behavioral genetics (Plomin, 1986a).

The lifeblood of research on developmental change and continuity is the longitudinal study, and research on genetic transitions and changes in development requires longitudinal quantitative genetic designs. The difficulties of conducting longitudinal studies are legion, and these difficulties are magnified many times in developmental behavioral genetic research by the need for special samples such as twins and adoptees. For this reason, in addition to Skodak and Skeels's (1949) classic longitudinal adoption study of IQ, there are only two long-term longitudinal quantitative genetic studies of behavioral development. One is the Louisville Twin Study, a 20-year study of twins from infancy through adolescence (Wilson, 1983). The focus of this work has been IQ, although during the past decade, temperament has become central to the study.

The other major study is the Colorado Adoption Project (CAP). One of the aims of this book is to present new data from the CAP that address the origins of individual differences during infancy and early childhood, especially changes and continuities. The CAP history, design, measures, and basic results in infancy were described in an earlier book (Plomin & DeFries, 1985a); these infancy analyses were based on data from a sample of 182 adopted infants and 165 nonadopted infants who were studied at both 12 and 24 months of age. The background of the CAP is briefly described in Chapter 4, and in later chapters we update the infancy results for the complete CAP sample of 245 adoptive and 245 nonadoptive families. However, we focus primarily on issues of change and continuity during infancy and early childhood; in addition to the infancy data for the complete CAP sample, we present data for 186 adopted and 151 nonadopted CAP children at 3 years and 162 adopted and 134 nonadopted children at 4 years.

Until now, CAP analyses have relied on parent–offspring comparisons – the biological and adoptive parents of the adopted children and the parents of the nonadopted children were also tested as part of the CAP. Parent–offspring comparisons are especially interesting when offspring are studied in childhood because genetic sources of change during development lead to differences between parents and their young offspring. In this genetic sense, the CAP design can be seen as an "instant" longitudinal study from childhood to adulthood. Viewed from this perspective, the CAP parent–offspring data have yielded some surprising results, as described in Chapters 6 and 8. An important complement to the parent–offspring data is the sibling adoption design, which compares adoptive and nonadoptive siblings. The contemporaneous relationship of siblings as compared with the developmentally distant relationship of parents and young offspring adds a new dimension to the CAP results. The present book describes this first longitudinal study of adoptive and nonadoptive siblings for the following sample of adoptive and nonadoptive siblings: 67 and 82 pairs, respectively, at 1 year of age; 61 and 70 pairs at 2 years; 50 and 54 pairs at 3 years; and 42 and 43 pairs at 4 years.

One of the major advances in quantitative genetic techniques during the past decade has been the development of model fitting, in which family resemblance is expressed in terms of an underlying model consisting of several unobserved genetic and environmental parameters and this model is compared with, or "fit" to, the observed correlations. The CAP design is sufficiently powerful that simple correlations for the various genetically related and unrelated family members can be meaningfully compared – and these simple data are presented throughout the book. The advantages of model fitting include the following. It makes assumptions explicit; it tests the fit of a specific model and compares different models; it provides standard errors of estimates; and it can incorporate into a single analysis different types of data – such as data from nonadoptive as well as adoptive families and parent–offspring data as well as sibling data – rather than considering each type of data separately. The main disadvantage of model fitting is the relative inaccessibility of models to people who have not learned the model's special language and the accompanying feeling that models are black hats from which estimates magically appear. For this reason, in Chapter 7 we introduce model fitting and develop simple parent–offspring models for CAP.

In Chapter 8, these simple models are applied cross sectionally to the basic CAP data for adopted and nonadopted children at 1, 2, 3, and 4 years of age. The parent–offspring model and a combined parent–offspring and sibling model are also extended to the analysis of longitudinal data. All of these models are univariate, although longitudinal analysis is conceptually similar to multivariate analysis (Plomin, 1986b). A new development in model fitting is multivariate analysis (DeFries & Fulker, 1986); multivariate extensions of the CAP sibling and parent–offspring models are also presented in Chapter 8 and applied to the analysis of interrelationships among temperament and cognitive measures at 2 and 3 years of age and to the developmental differentiation of specific cognitive abilities in early childhood.

In summary, the purpose of this book is to consider the development of individual differences in behavioral development during infancy and early childhood as illuminated by quantitative genetic theory and research, emphasizing developmental change as well as continuity. We begin in the next chapter by contrasting individual-differences and group-differences approaches to the study of development and discuss the advantages and disadvantages of the two approaches. In Chapter 3, we suggest that quantitative genetics provides the basis for a general theory of the etiology of individual differences, a theory of a scope and power rarely seen in the behavioral sciences. Chapter 4 describes the design and measures of the Colorado Adoption Project, the data of which provide the foundation for much of what we know about the origins of individual differences from infancy to childhood.

We then discuss issues and evidence concerning developmental transitions and changes, specifically in relation to infancy and early childhood. The focus of Chapter 5 is the description and prediction of developmental change from the perspective of individual differences, not from the usual normative perspective. In Chapter 6, we turn to an explanation of these changes, considering both genetic and environmental etiologies.

The next two chapters form a section on model fitting. Chapter 7 is a didactic chapter that provides an elementary introduction to model-fitting approaches used in quantitative genetics. The chapter builds toward the basic univariate sibling and parent–offspring models employed in CAP. In Chapter 8, these models are used to analyze the major CAP sibling and parent–offspring data at each year. Chapter 8 also presents a longitudinal parent–offspring and twin model that considers genetic correlations from childhood to adulthood. The final topic of Chapter 8 is the extension of the parent–offspring models to the multivariate case; the multivariate sibling model is applied to the relationship between temperament and cognition at 2 and 3 years of age, and the multivariate parent–offspring model is applied to data on specific cognitive abilities at 3 and 4.

The next three chapters address the developmental interface between nature and nurture. Interaction is the focus of Chapter 9. We emphasize genotype–environment interaction because adoption data alone permit an exploration of this type of interaction. In addition, however, we examine three other types of interactions: interactions involving parent–offspring resemblance, longitudinal interactions (specifically, longitudinal changes in IQ), and temperament–environment interactions. Developmentalists' concerns with genotype–environment interaction are often better represented by the concept of genotype–environment correlation, which refers to the correlation rather than interaction between environmental influences and genetic propensities. In Chapter 10, three types of genotype–environment correlation are discussed and attempts to assess each type are presented. Finally, the issue of genetic mediation of "environmental" influences is the focus of Chapter 11. In other words, heredity can contribute to the variance of measures of family environment and to the covariation between environmental measures and measures of development; these issues are addressed using sibling and parent–offspring comparisons in the adoptive and nonadoptive families of the CAP.

The purpose of the final chapter is to summarize what we know as well as what we need to learn about the origins of individual differences during infancy and early childhood. It will come as no surprise that the ratio of what we know to what we do not know is small indeed. Nonetheless, the ratio is more impressive when we consider how few studies have addressed these issues. Moreover, the numerator of the ratio contains some exciting findings, and we hope that these will fuel further research on the origins of individual differences.

2 Individual differences and group differences

Interest in as well as understanding and acceptance of behavioral genetics are often hindered by a single issue: confusion between individual differences and group differences. That is, behavioral genetic theory and research address individual differences (variance), whereas most psychological research involves group comparisons (means). In this chapter, we contrast these two approaches and then discuss the advantages and disadvantages of an individual-differences perspective. In part, the relative neglect of an individual-differences approach is due to its apparent atheoretical orientation. For this reason, the next chapter considers quantitative genetics as the basis for a general theory of the origins of individual differences.

The group-differences approach focuses on average differences, such as gender, age, cultural, or species differences, among groups of individuals within a population. In contrast, the etiology of differences among individuals in a population is the focus of individual-differences research. The point of this chapter is not that the individual-differences approach is better than the group-differences approach. The two approaches are perspectives, and perspectives are neither right nor wrong, only more or less useful for a particular purpose. However, we do argue that the two approaches differ in important ways that affect theories and research. In the following section, the basic distinction between the two approaches is examined more closely.

Individuals and groups

The term "individual differences" usually refers to continuous variation among individuals in a population. Variance, an index of individual differences, is the average squared deviation from the mean. Group differences such as differences between the means of boys and girls or groups of children of different ages are clearly not individual differences. Therefore, at first glance, it seems straightforward to distinguish between

6

individual-differences and group-differences approaches. However, the distinction requires closer examination.

Experiments

The mere mention of these two approaches in psychology will no doubt trigger associations with the distinction drawn 30 years ago between the experimental and correlational "disciplines of scientific psychology" (Cronbach, 1957):

> While the experimenter is interested only in the variation he himself creates, the correlator finds his interest in the already existing variation between individuals, social groups, and species. (p. 671)

> Individual differences have been an annoyance rather than a challenge to the experimenter. His goal is to control behavior, and variation within treatments is proof that he has not succeeded. Individual variation is cast into that outer darkness known as "error variance." . . . whatever your device, your goal in the experimental tradition is to get those embarrassing differential variables out of sight. (p. 674)

In terms of the present issue, experimenters usually focus on group differences. However, experiments are only a small subset of studies of group differences. As indicated in the first quotation, Cronbach compares experiments with all other research on group differences as well as individual differences. Further complicating the relationship between the experimental –correlational distinction and the distinction between group differences and individual differences is the fact that the experimental method is not limited to the study of group differences. It can be applied to the study of individual differences, as in analyses of aptitude-by-treatment interactions, which was the thrust of Cronbach's prescription for the integration of experimental and correlational approaches.

Nonetheless, the primary focus of experimental research is usually on group differences, the group membership being considered an independent variable. Experiments are discussed again later in this chapter when we consider analyses of the etiology of group differences and individual differences.

Dichotomies

Another problem of classifying research in terms of the distinction between individual differences and group differences occurs when a trait is defined and measured as a dichotomy. In psychopathology, the disease model borrowed from medical pathology leads to dichotomous diagnoses – for example, children are diagnosed as autistic or not. Is this a group difference or an individual difference? We suggest that when individuals can be assessed only dichotomously, as in the presence or absence of a disorder, the dichotomy can be viewed as either a group difference or an individual difference.

The problem is further complicated because psychopathology rarely involves true dichotomies; continuously distributed differences among individuals are the rule (e.g., Rutter & Garmezy, 1983). For example, children's attentional problems and conduct problems are not distributed as dichotomies. In such cases, when the normal distribution for problem behavior is divided at some threshold, information is lost because we pretend that every individual above the threshold has the disorder and everyone below does not. The assignment of dichotomous scores in such cases is analogous to having an extremely crude measure of height in which we diagnose individuals as either "normal" or "tall." However, until we are able to measure the individual variability that exists in nature, these cases, for all practical purposes, must be treated as dichotomous individual differences, like autism. For the same reason, nonclinical studies that divide their samples at some point such as the mean are best considered crude studies of individual differences.

Extremes

A second problematic category leads to a different conclusion: mean comparisons involving the high or low extremes of a distribution. Analysis of extremes cannot lead to generalizations concerning the normal distribution of individual differences for the simple fact that only the extremes of the distribution are studied. This is not merely a semantic argument: Descriptions and explanations of extreme groups bear no necessary relation to the description and explanation of the normal continuum of individual differences.

Within the analysis of extreme groups, an individual-differences approach can be taken. For example, the genetic and environmental etiologies of individual differences at the low or high ends of the IQ distribution – mental retardation and genius – could be explored. More often, however, membership in extreme groups is considered an independent variable. For example, children selected to be shy are brought to the laboratory and compared with a group of children selected for their lack of shyness (Kagan, Reznick, & Snidman, 1986). Another category of examples comes from "at-risk" studies: Children are selected whose parents are extreme for some problem behavior; the mean performance of the children at risk is compared with the mean performance of a control group of children (Watt, Anthony, Wynne, & Rolf, 1984). Results of such studies are limited to the extreme groups studied and cannot be generalized to the distribution of differences among individuals within the normal range.

Naturally occurring groups

A third possible confusion involves naturally occurring categories such as gender, age, and ethnic group. Given that children are either girls or boys, is gender an individual-differences variable? The answer is no. Psychologists may assess a dependent behavioral measure, one that is nearly always continuously distributed, and then compare girls and boys for that measure. For example, the average verbal abilities of boys and girls have often been compared. As argued later, such group differences are usually trivial compared with individual differences within the groups and, again, description and explanation of differences between groups are not necessarily related to those within groups. For example, if the average difference in verbal ability between girls and boys were found to be due to hormonal differences, it could not be assumed that individual differences among boys' or girls' verbal ability are also due to hormonal differences.

As in the case of extreme groups, individual differences can be studied within groups. In this book, for example, parent–offspring resemblance and associations between environmental and behavioral measures are compared for infants and children in order to detect possible differences in the etiology of individual differences during the transition from infancy to early childhood.

Universals

Another complication in distinguishing between individual-differences and group-differences approaches concerns "universal" theories, such as theories of why the human species talks or walks. Clearly, these are not studies of individual differences. The focus is on the average behavior of a group – the group in this case is the human species. Because the behavior of a single group is studied, such research does not literally involve group differences; nonetheless, all of the issues relevant to the study of group differences are relevant to the study of a single group.

Within-individual differences

Finally, we reserve the term "individual differences" to refer to differences between individuals, not to ipsative approaches that study within-individual variability. Unless ipsative approaches are meant to be strictly idiographic, their generalizability depends on studying within-individual variables in a between-individual context. In this book, we analyze longitudinal change and continuity within individuals; however, these issues are considered in a between-individuals framework.

The neglect of individual differences

Despite the exceptions just described, it is generally not difficult to make the distinction between group-differences and individual-differences research. When research is seen from this perspective, a surprising imbalance emerges: Far more contemporary research in psychology, and in developmental psychology in particular, focuses on group differences than on individual differences.

For example, the *Handbook of Child Psychology* (Mussen, 1983) presents a recent and representative sampling of theory and research in the field of developmental psychology. Of the 2,926 pages of text (excluding references, outlines, and notes), 78% are devoted predominantly (i.e., more than half the page) to group differences. Of the 48 chapters, 41 include more pages on group differences than on individual differences. Moreover, 19 chapters include not a single page on individual differences, and 4 other chapters consider individual differences on 2% or fewer of their pages. The topics of these 23 chapters are instructive because they point to areas most likely to profit conceptually and empirically from an individual-differences approach. The 23 chapters fall into two major categories and two minor ones. Six chapters involve the oldest fields of psychology: perception and learning. Nine chapters consider cognition and language. In addition, there are two chapters on brain development and three chapters on intervention. The three remaining chapters involve history, systems theory, and cross-cultural research.

Only eight chapters in the *Handbook* devote more than 50% of their pages to individual differences. A list of these chapters follows:

> "The Evolution of Environmental Models in Developmental Research"
> "Design and Analysis in Developmental Psychology"
> "Assessment of Children"
> "Developmental Behavioral Genetics"
> "Morality"
> "Stylistic Variation in Childhood and Adolescence"
> "Socialization in the Context of the Family"
> "Developmental Psychopathology"

Between the lines of this hodgepodge list lie several stories about trends in developmental research on individual differences. First, research on psychopathology is almost by definition concerned with individual differences (Rutter & Garmezy, 1983). Second, the chapters on variation in styles and morality are included in the volume of the *Handbook* devoted to cognitive development, yet of the 13 chapters in the volume, these are the only two that devote the majority of their pages to individual differences. Moreover, cognitive styles and morality are least central to the study of cognitive development. It will surprise most psychologists not familiar with the influence of Piaget on contemporary developmental psychology that this cognitive volume of 728 pages of text includes only 15 pages on individual differences in mental development.

An interesting trend emerges in these 8 chapters and in the other chapters of the *Handbook* that consider both individual differences and group differences: The theoretical part of the chapters often involves a group perspective, whereas the empirical portion emphasizes individual differences. For example, a chapter on self-esteem and self-control begins by describing psychoanalytic, ethological, and other theories of the development of self in the human species. However, the rest of the chapter focuses on research attempting to describe individual differences in self-esteem and self-control and to explore their correlates and causes. The significance of this observation is twofold. As described later, dangers lie in mixing theories about group differences and data about individual-differences research. Second, the absence of theories of individual differences implies that there is a need for such a theory, a point addressed in detail in the next chapter.

Why study individual differences?

As indicated in the preceding section, there is clearly an imbalance in the relative amount of theory and research on individual differences and group differences. However, it is reasonable to ask why psychologists should be concerned about individual differences – and also why they are not. These two issues are the topics of this section and the following one. This section contains five general answers to the question Why study individual differences? It also includes a case study of a research area that was rejuvenated when it adopted an individual-differences perspective.

Individual differences exist and thus theories must be able to account for such variability

Although it may sound facetious, one important reason for studying individual differences is that they are there: For nearly all physical, physiological, and psychological phenomena, differences among individuals loom large, if we choose to see them. For example, differences in height are obvious. Eliminating the highest and lowest individuals per thousand in order to avoid including extreme scores, the range ratio for adult height is 1.3:1, roughly 6.5 feet to 5 feet. Although height is noticeably variable, range ratios for other characteristics are even greater: 2.4:1 for adult weight, 2.0:1 for adult pulse rate, 2.2:1 for simple reaction time, 2.5:1 for memory span, and 2.9:1 for IQ scores (Wechsler, 1952). Within the normal CAP sample, the range ratios for Stanford–Binet IQs of children 4 years of age is 1.6:1 (i.e., 139:84) after the lowest and highest IQs are eliminated. The range ratios for some other measures are extremely large; for example, the Sequenced Inventory of Communication Development yields range ratios of 8:1 at 2 years and 11:1 at 3 years; the range ratios for total scores on the Child Behavior Checklist is 34:1; many children had scores in the 60s, and other children had scores of 2 or 3. Clearly, a powerful science of developmental psychology needs to explain variation as well as central tendency.

When we see infants and young children, we are more impressed in our adult egocentrism by the extent to which they differ, on average, from us than we are by individual differences among them. Nonetheless, when carefully studied, infants and children differ substantially in most domains such as language, mental and motor development, and temperament. An important, but unexplored feature of the transition from infancy to early childhood is the marked increase in obvious differences among children as well as the increased long-term predictiveness of these differences, issues to which we shall return in comparing CAP results in infancy and in early childhood.

Psychological issues of greatest relevance to society are issues of individual differences

Although we have no solid evidence to support this assertion, it seems to us that individual differences are more socially relevant than group differences or developmental universals. For example, although it would be interesting to know why human infants are natural language users, the following questions are of greater concern: To what extent is some children's use of language delayed? Do individual differences in language acquisition make a difference later in life – for example, in reading performance? Why is the use of language of some children delayed or disabled? Can language disabilities be prevented or remediated? Societal interest in psychology comes from the study of things that make a difference

– the description, prediction, explanation, and alteration of individual differences.

Differences between groups are relatively unimportant compared with individual differences within groups

It is easier to think about average differences between groups, such as those between boys and girls, than it is to conceptualize individual differences. However, the ease with which group differences can be conceptualized is beguiling because we tend to think about differences between groups in terms of nonoverlapping distributions when in fact the distributions for the two groups may show substantial overlap. For example, one of the most thoroughly documented gender differences in cognition is the superior performance of girls over that of boys on tests of verbal ability (Maccoby & Jacklin, 1974). This average difference, however, is less than one-fifth of a standard deviation, which implies that less than 1% of the variance of verbal ability is explained by gender (Plomin & Foch, 1981). This mean difference is equivalent to a point biserial correlation of less than .10; distributions of the two groups overlap by more than 85% (Cohen, 1977). In other words, if the only thing known about a particular child is gender, relatively little is known about the child's verbal ability. The small effect size for average differences between the genders is now widely acknowledged (e.g., Jacklin & Maccoby, 1983).

The description and explanation of group differences bear no necessary relationship to those of individual differences

The most important reason for studying individual differences is that we learn relatively little about such differences from studies of group differences. As an example of descriptive discrepancies, consider physical development. From early childhood to adulthood, height more than doubles and weight more than quadruples. Despite these large mean differences between ages for both height and weight, the rank orders of individuals remain remarkably stable from childhood to adulthood.

As an instance of explanatory differences, consider mental development. The rapid average increases in mental development in infancy seems likely to be due to maturational events highly canalized at the species level, yet individual differences in infant mental development are apparently due largely to environmental influences (Plomin & DeFries, 1985a).

*Questions concerning the origins of individual differences are
more easily answered than questions about the etiology of
group differences*

Although average group differences can easily be established, going beyond descriptions to explanations is more difficult. Group-differences research does not usually extend beyond significance testing for a single variable or for the relationship between two variables. Although elaborate theories are often proposed to explain observed group differences, the core explanatory constructs are seldom tested or even testable. For Piaget, for example, the essential explanatory processes of development are assimilation and accommodation. But how can we test whether these processes explain the dramatic leaps in mental development that occur during the transition from infancy to early childhood? Attempts to explain average differences between groups usually involve the use of experiments, cross-cultural comparisons, other group comparisons, and inappropriate individual-differences data.

Experiments. When explanation is sought, psychologists' thoughts naturally turn to experimentation. However, experimental studies such as those involving training or deprivation experiments cannot provide definitive explanations of group differences:

The results of experimental research tend to answer the question of whether X can cause Y, but do not directly answer the question of whether X does cause Y in society. Adults can learn nonsense syllables, for example, but they rarely do; children can be classically conditioned, but this may or may not be the process by which they learn most or even many behaviors; and children can be made to display more aggressive actions by viewing violent television programs, but television may or may not play a major role in producing violent crime in society or even aggressive behavior in nursery schools. (Appelbaum & McCall, 1983, p. 419)

Factors responsible for producing differences in experiments may not be important in producing variation in the world outside the laboratory; conversely, factors responsible for individual differences au naturel may be difficult to test in the laboratory. In developmental research, age is the prime variable and it cannot be manipulated, which attenuates the usefulness of experimental analyses of developmental phenomena (Wohlwill, 1973).

Two other issues concerning experiments should be mentioned. First, the experimenters' ability to address causality has nothing to do with the use of analysis of variance as opposed to correlation. Covariance, standardized in the form of correlation or unstandardized as regression, is the mainstay of all inferential statistics, including analysis of variance, which is a computational short-cut for computing regressions (Cohen, 1968). Correlation/regression is the only parametric statistic available for describing associations, regardless of whether the association is between an experimental treatment and an outcome variable or between measures of parental treatment and children's development. Can correlations imply causality? They can, if we have some purchase on causal interpretations as in experiments, longitudinal studies, and behavioral genetic studies.

The second issue is the relationship between experiments and other research. In an article with the tantalizing title "Individual Differences as a Crucible in Theory Construction," the experimentalist Benton Underwood (1975) proposed: "We should formulate our nomothetic theories in a way that will allow an immediate individual-differences test. I am proposing this because, among other benefits, I believe this approach will make individual differences a crucible in theory construction" (p. 128). Because the causes of average differences between groups need not be related to the causes of individual differences, individual-differences research cannot test theories involving experimentally induced differences between groups. However, individual-differences research can test the generalizability of experimental research and theory. Underwood used his own research on frequency theory as an example. After performing 50 experiments on the relationship between frequency of words and recognition memory, Underwood conducted a study of individual differences that yielded a substantial correlation between frequency discrimination and recognition memory. Underwood concluded: "Suppose we had found a zero correlation between measures of frequency discrimination and measures of recognition memory? The theory would simply have to be dropped" (p. 129). This conclusion would be more appropriate if it were phrased in terms of generalization: If the correlation between the two measures were zero, we would conclude that the factors responsible for producing an association between word frequency and recognition in the laboratory were not important sources of covariance between the two measures outside the laboratory. Moreover, playing the devil's advocate, finding a correlation between the two measures does not prove that the same factors produce the correlation inside and outside the laboratory.

Cross-cultural comparisons. Comparisons between cultures tell us little about etiology. For example, in *Coming of Age in Samoa*, Margaret Mead (1928) described adolescence as much more tranquil in Samoa than in other cultures. She ascribed this difference to another group difference: greater sexual permissiveness of parents. However, even if we accept Mead's description (cf. Freeman, 1983), we cannot safely conclude that the average difference between the Samoan culture and other cultures is environmental in origin, because isolated groups differ genetically as well as environmentally. Conversely, finding universals of development across cultures does not prove that nature dominates nurture, because universal environmental contingencies could shape development similarly in all cultures.

Other group comparisons. Research on average group differences often involves descriptive associations – for example, relating one behavioral difference to another behavioral difference. Occasionally, attempts are made to explain a behavioral difference between groups by relating it to a group difference of another kind. For example, on the average, the vocabulary of 4-year-olds is markedly superior to that of 3-year-olds in quantity and quality. If parents of 4-year-olds are shown to use more complex language structures than parents of 3-year-olds, we cannot conclude that the language-learning environment is responsible for language acquisition. Such studies essentially produce correlations based on two differences; even if the results prove to be replicable, it is not possible to make causal inferences.

Individual differences. Another attempt to explain group differences involves the inappropriate use of individual-differences data to address the etiology of group differences, as had happened, for example, in language acquisition research (see Hardy-Brown, 1983). As discussed earlier, the universal use of language in our species could be hard-wired by natural selection and yet individual differences in the rate of language development could be due entirely to environmental differences experienced by children.

In contrast to the difficulty of explaining average differences between groups stands the tractability of individual differences. As described in the next chapter, quantitative genetics provides a powerful theory and methods with which to explore the origins of individual differences.

A case study: infant novelty preference

One implication of this emphasis on group differences is that some domains in psychology – including some of the oldest domains such as perception – have rarely been studied from an individual-differences perspective. Individual differences in these domains have not yet been shown to be important in a predictive sense. The relative disregard of individual differences is unfortunate because experimental psychologists have developed especially sensitive and process-oriented measures that could be profitably applied to the study of individual differences. We predict that areas that have neglected individual differences may find their major avenues of advance in that direction.

A recent example comes from the heartland of experimental research, perception. Three relevant chapters in the *Handbook of Child Psychology* – those devoted to visual perception, auditory and speech perception, and attention, learning, and memory – contain a total of 189 pages of text and yet include not a single page on individual differences. However, one of the most important advances in the field is the discovery during the past decade of the long-term predictiveness of individual differences in infant novelty preference.

After using Fantz's novelty preference technique for several years to study normative perceptual development, Joseph Fagan of Case Western Reserve University began to consider individual differences (Fagan & McGrath, 1981; Fagan & Singer, 1983). He obtained vocabulary scores from children whom he had tested for novelty preference several years earlier in the first half-year of life and found significant correlations. In a review of 12 studies from his group and from other researchers in which novelty preference was assessed at 3 to 7 months and cognitive test scores were obtained at 2 to 7 years, the correlations ranged from .33 to .66, with a mean of .44 (Fagan, 1985). This exciting result provides the first evidence of any behavioral characteristic in the first half-year of life that predicts later cognitive ability. The mean correlation of .44 is particularly dramatic because the novelty preference tests were not designed to be used as measures of individual differences – the tests included only 1 to 5 items and their reliabilities are likely to be less than .50 (Fagan, 1985). Thus, the mean correlation of .44 between infant novelty preference and later cognitive ability is likely to be considerably attenuated compared with the correlation that could be obtained with psychometrically stronger tests, which Fagan is now developing. Recent work with one of these tests indicates substantial resemblance between the Fagan measure at 7 and 9 months and parental IQ (Fulker et al., 1987).

In addition to enriching research on infant perception, the work on individual differences has led Fagan (1985) to formulate a theory of the development of intellectual functioning that hypothesizes that "*g*," a general factor of basic cognitive processes, represents the core of continuity from infancy to childhood. Moreover, beyond these advances in research and theory, Fagan's individual-differences work has obvious practical utility: It can be used to assess individual risks for infants in perinatal risk conditions, to provide early assessments of the results of intervention, and to test individuals such as profoundly retarded children for whom conventional tests of cognitive ability are inappropriate.

Other domains of psychology are also likely to profit by moving in the direction of individual differences. Consider, for example, some of the chapters in the *Handbook of Child Psychology* that do not address individual differences: information processing, language, Piagetian theory, brain development, and cross-cultural research. In the past ten years, the most notable shift to an individual-differences perspective has occurred in the area of adult information processing, which has made substantial gains toward bridging the gap with psychometric research on intelligence (e.g., Hunt, 1985). However, the shift to individual differences has not yet occurred in information-processing studies in childhood.

Interest in variability and awareness of the important distinctions between the two perspectives is beginning to emerge among language researchers (e.g., Hardy-Brown, 1983; Nelson, 1981). In contrast, Piagetian researchers show little interest in individual differences. However, an important and unanswered challenge has emerged from some research on individual differences: Piagetian measures correlate highly (i.e., near their reliability) with standard psychometric measures of intelligence (e.g., Gottfried & Brody, 1975).

Brain research and cross-cultural research can profit as much as any other domain from an individual-differences perspective. Although brain research tends to be limited to normative descriptions of anatomy and physiology, neural phenomena are likely to be no less variable than behavior. Cross-cultural research might seem to depend on a group-oriented approach; nonetheless, it is important to recognize that variation among individuals within cultures exceeds variation between cultures.

To summarize this section, individual differences are important, they lead to testable questions, and some results have indicated the kind of excitement that can be generated when a traditional area of psychology turns to the study of individual differences. Why, then, do psychologists so often overlook the "very standard deviation" (Levine, Carey, Crocker, & Gross, 1983)?

Why is the study of individual differences neglected?

Despite the importance of individual differences, research and theory on group differences clearly prevails in psychology. Why should this be? One reason involves historical happenstance.

William James

William James's (1890) *Principles of Psychology* has had a strong influence on psychologists' categories of thought. Unfortunately, James seldom wrote about individual differences. His 1,278-page tome ranges across most of the domains of psychology, including habits, instincts, emotions, will, thought, self, attention, cognition, reasoning, perception, learning, time perception, memory, and imagination. Nonetheless, there is only one brief section on individual differences, and this section merely presents Galton's work on individual differences in visual imagination. In terms of mental ability, James recognized only a distinction between genius and normal analytic thinking. Other than these scattered bits, James essentially ignored individual differences.

James's neglect of individual differences is especially curious because, in the last few pages of *Principles*, he wrote vigorously against Lamarck's notion of the inheritance of acquired characteristics as espoused by Spencer, and he championed Darwin's theory: "... 'accidental variation,' as Mr. Darwin termed it, in which certain young are born with peculiarities that help them and their progeny to survive. That variations of this sort become hereditary, no one doubts" (p. 626).

Founders of developmental psychology other than Binet also neglected individual differences. Although the middle, golden age of developmental psychology (1913–46) was marked by a concern for the description, prediction, and explanation of individual differences, this focus was lost in the modern era, with the hegemony of learning theory that dominated until the 1960s. Piaget's theory filled the void left by learning theory, and Piaget rarely considered individual differences, as indicated by three chapters on his work in the 1983 *Handbook*, one by Piaget himself, that contain not a single page concerning individual differences.

Developmental rate

One reason that developmentalists in particular neglect variability is that differences among children are often thought to be "just" differences in the rate of development, especially in the area of cognitive development. Although one 3-year-old can identify a picture of a fence and another cannot, nearly all children eventually understand the meaning of the word "fence." The fact that most children learn the meaning of simple words does not imply that differences among children at a particular age are unimportant. For example, it is possible that the 3-year-old who understands the word "fence" also has a larger vocabulary as a 30-year-old.

However, individual differences in childhood need not be predictive of differences later in life in order to be of interest to developmentalists, for two reasons. First, development is as much the study of change as of continuity, and this is just as true for the study of individual differences as it is for the normative perspective on development. Second, differences among children describe their current status, and this information can be useful in terms of fostering children's development, for example, maximizing their strengths and minimizing their weaknesses.

Moreover, the issue of developmental rate may be more apparent than real. Developmental rate is most obvious when we emphasize outcome rather than process. For example, a vocabulary test can be thought of simply as a list of words that a child knows or does not know, and as in the example of the word "fence," many words that differentiate children at one age are known by nearly all children at a later age. However, a vocabulary test can also be considered an index of cognitive processes required to abstract, categorize, and retain the meaning of new words. Defined in this way, differences among children are not simply differences in rate of development, although the items used as an index of variability in vocabulary must be changed to accommodate the increasing verbal expertise of children.

Learning to play a sport provides an analogy. During the few days of practice before the first game, a Little League baseball coach must decide who should play shortstop and who should bat first. With first-time players, the coach will look for very basic skills – which children can catch, throw, and hit the ball at all. As the season progresses, all children learn these basic skills, and more sophisticated criteria begin to enter into the coach's decisions. For example, how quickly can a child move to the ball when catching? How accurately can a child throw? How well can a child place the ball when batting? As in development, variation among children on an index of skill early in the season may or may not be related to a skill index late in the season or in later seasons. However, the value of the index during the first days of practice does not rest on its capacity to predict later performance. From the first day of practice, the coach must evaluate children's strengths and weaknesses in order to help each child improve as much as possible during the practice sessions.

In addition, there are many areas of development in which developmental rate is unimportant because average changes during development are not nearly as impressive as are individual differences among children. For example, consider temperament: Some children are more emotional, active, or shy than others. These differences are not differences in developmental rate; in the case of temperament, the differences happen to show some stability during infancy and even more stability during early childhood (McDevitt, 1986).

Sample size, psychometrics, and statistics

A practical reason for the neglect of individual differences is that the study of individual differences is more demanding in terms of psychometrics and statistics than is the study of group differences.

The major psychometric issue is reliability of measurement. Because calculation of an average dilutes the impact of errors of measurement, reliability is not of major concern in studies of group differences. In contrast, reliability of measurement is of paramount concern in the study of individual differences. For example, the upper limit of an observed correlation is the square root of the product of the reliabilities of the two measures involved in the correlation. Although it may appear as if larger sample sizes are needed for individual-differences research, in fact, for a given reliability and effect size (which is expressed in terms of variance explained), the same number of individuals is needed to reach statistical significance for two independent samples in a mean differences analysis and for a correlation between subjects for two variables (Cohen, 1977).

A more subtle, and paradoxical, obstacle to the study of individual differences is that the statistics of individual differences are readily translated into the amount of variance explained. In contrast, analyses of group differences focus on statistical significance. The focus on variance explained is often depressing because it rudely reminds us, for example, that the ubiquitous correlation of .30 explains less than 10% of the variance. However, despite its bitter taste, this is important medicine. Psychology's preoccupation with statistical significance has left a mountain of statistically ‘significant results that are insignificant by any definition of societal relevance. The emphasis on variance explained is a virtue of individual-differences analyses: Any mean group difference can also be converted to a statement of effect size (Cohen, 1977) and often, as in the case of gender differences in verbal ability, these group differences account for less than 10% of the variance.

Another major impediment to the study of individual differences is that it requires different and more sophisticated statistical tools than does research on group differences. Because group differences can be readily visualized, psychologists are not as dependent on statistics to guide inferences. Individual differences, however, are much less easily visualized and thus require more dependence on statistical maps to draw inferences from research results. Some sophisticated individual-differences techniques, such as factor analysis and structural equation models, are especially formidable to researchers who study group differences.

Inequality

Another barrier to the study of individual differences is the concern that individual differences violate the fundamental belief that all persons are created equal. Of course, our forefathers were not so naive as to think that all people are identical. Even the seventeenth-century philosopher John Locke, whose treatise played a key role in the American Revolution and in educational thought, had a more balanced view than is usually recognized. By "equality," Locke clearly meant political equality – equality in opportunity and before the law – not an absence of individual differences (Loehlin, 1983). A democracy does not treat people equally because they are identical; there would be no need for principles of equality if all people were identical. The essence of democracy is to treat people equally despite their differences.

Individuality is a fact. It is also the foundation for the dignity of humankind: We are not interchangeable. The real danger lies in treating people on the basis of group membership – ethnic group, gender, age – when individual differences within these groups far exceed average differences among the groups.

Absence of theories of individual differences

A final impediment to studying individual differences is that individual-differences research often seems atheoretical. Without a theory, data gathering can lead to a collection of inconsequential facts. The issue, however, is not a dichotomy between theory and data but rather the balance between them. Researchers interested in individual differences tend to start with data and stay close to their data; their theories often remain implicit. Sometimes minitheories are developed that organize individual-differences data and make new predictions, as in the example of Fagan's work on novelty preference that led to a g theory of infant mental development. However, to date psychologists have attempted to formulate relatively few general theories of individual differences.

Although psychologists have not developed a general theory of individual differences, the basis for one exists in another discipline: quantitative genetics. Quantitative genetic theory has been extant for more than 50 years, but its potential application to theory in psychology has gone largely unrecognized. The next chapter describes quantitative genetics as the basis for a general theory of individual differences.

3   Quantitative genetics as the basis for a general theory of individual differences

One reason for the relative disregard of individual differences in psychology is that research on this subject appears atheoretical and usually addresses correlation rather than causation. In this chapter, we suggest that quantitative genetics provides the basis for a general theory of the etiology of individual differences of scope and power rarely seen in the behavioral sciences. After a brief overview of quantitative genetics, we describe a general theory of individual differences in terms of 10 propositions and then consider the theory in the context of current trends in the philosophy of science.

We will not concern ourselves with the philosophical intricacies of the word "theory." The term obviously means different things to different psychologists, as illustrated by formal differences among the best-known theories in psychology, such as learning theories, personality theories, and Piagetian theory. Nonetheless, from the pragmatic view of a behavioral researcher, theories should clarify our thinking by describing, predicting, and explaining behavior. At the very least, theories should be descriptive, organizing and condensing existing facts in a reasonable, internally consistent manner. However, they should also make predictions concerning phenomena not yet investigated and allow clear tests of these predictions to be made. At their best, theories explain phenomena as well as describe and predict them.

Is there any theory that meets these criteria? In all the life sciences, no theory is grander than evolutionary theory. Before the new synthesis (Mayr, 1982), however, evolutionary theory was largely descriptive. Once evolutionary theory had assimilated the methodology and theory of quantitative genetics, it became predictive and explanatory as well.

Background

Quantitative genetic theory emerged in the early 1900s from disagreements between the Mendelians, who rediscovered Mendel's laws of inheritance,

24

and the biometricians, who believed that Mendel's laws, derived from experiments with qualitative characteristics in lower organisms, were not applicable to the complex characteristics of higher organisms, which are nearly always distributed quantitatively in a normal, bell-shaped curve. When Ronald Fisher (1918) and Sewall Wright (1931) used the postulates of Mendelian inheritance to deduce the biometric relationships among various relatives, quantitative genetic theory was born.

Quantitative genetics is a theory of the etiology of individual differences in a population – specifically, the genetic and environmental differences among individuals that underlie phenotypic variability. It is applicable to any individual-differences variable – physical, physiological, or psychological. Much of the current research in quantitative genetics is based on applications to the study of behavior.

The essence of quantitative genetic theory is that Mendel's laws of discrete inheritance also apply to normally distributed complex characteristics if we assume that many genes, each with a small effect, combine to produce observable differences among individuals in a population. If more than three or four genes affect a trait, the observed distribution cannot be distinguished from a normal curve. For example, a trait influenced by two alleles at each of three loci yields 27 different genotypes. Even if there are equal and additive effects at each locus and no environmental variation, seven different phenotypes will be observed and their distribution will approximate a normal curve. Psychological phenomena demand a polygenic (multigene) approach because the complexity of these phenotypes makes it unlikely that any single gene accounts for a substantial portion of the variance in the population. Although single-gene mutations can be devastating for affected individuals, as in the case of the severe retardation caused by untreated phenylketonuria, no single gene has been shown to account for a detectable amount of variance in the normal range of individual differences.

Environmental variation is always potentially important as well. The value of quantitative genetics is that it represents a balanced view that considers nurture as well as nature in the etiology of individual differences. In this sense, the term "quantitative genetics" is somewhat misleading because the theory and its methods are as informative about environmental components of variance as they are about genetic factors. As discussed later, the most important contributions of human behavioral genetic research to date involve nurture as well as nature.

Quantitative genetic theory is unlike most contemporary theories in psychology in that it is not limited to a particular substantive domain. It is analogous in this respect to learning theory, which predicts not what is learned but rather the processes by which learning occurs. Quantitative genetics is also formally similar to learning theory in that neither specifies molecular mechanisms. That is, learning theory does not predict which neurotransmitters are involved in the learning process, nor does it predict that neurotransmitters are involved at all. Although quantitative genetics is based on the proposition that variation in DNA leads to phenotypic variation, it does not specify which genes are responsible for phenotypic variance. By the end of this century, however, it may be possible to identify DNA segments responsible for genetic sources of variance even for psychological traits to which each of hundreds of genes may contribute miniscule portions of variance. Although the identification of specific environmental factors is not part of the theory, quantitative genetics provides some important tools for the exploration of environmental influences, as will be discussed later.

One other preliminary point must be emphasized: The theory and its methods apply largely to the study of individual differences; it has little to say about average differences between groups. The most well known example of the confusion that results when the two approaches are not distinguished is the argument that genetic influence within ethnic groups implies that average differences between ethnic groups are also due to genetic factors (Mackenzie, 1985). Another example is the frequently read statement that the effects of nature and nurture cannot be disentangled because "there can be no behavior without an organism and there can be no organism without genes" (e.g., Gottlieb, 1983, p. 5). Quantitative genetic theory does not apply to an organism or the organism; its focus is on variance, differences among individual organisms in a population. We can assess the extent to which observed variance for a characteristic is due to environmental factors, as legions of environmental studies have attempted to do, and we can estimate the contribution of genetic differences among individuals.

The remainder of this overview of quantitative genetic theory will be presented in terms of somewhat formal propositions in order to emphasize the descriptive, predictive, and especially the explanatory power of the theory. The approach is expository; more detailed presentations can be found in Chapter 7 and in textbooks (e.g., Falconer, 1981; Hay, 1985; Plomin, DeFries, & McClearn, 1980).

Genetic differences among individuals can lead to phenotypic individual differences

The fundamental tenet of quantitative genetic theory is that genetic differences among individuals can lead to phenotypic differences among individuals. The theory leads directly to methods by which one can identify genetic and environmental components of variance. Even the most vociferous critics of behavioral genetic research now admit that the theory of quantitative genetics and its methods are valid. For example:

The total variation in phenotype in a population of individuals arises from two interacting sources. First, individuals with the same genes still differ from each other in phenotype because they have experienced different developmental environments. Second, there are different genotypes in the population which differ from each other on the average even in the same array of environments. The phenotype of an individual cannot be broken down into the separate contributions of genotype and of environment, because the two interact to produce the organism; but the total variation of any phenotype in the population can be broken down into the variation between the average of the different genotypes and the variation among individuals with the same genotype. (Lewontin, Rose, & Kamin, 1984, pp. 96–7)

These authors continue to deny that the case has been made for genetic influence on intelligence and schizophrenia. Nonetheless, outside of these circles, the past decade has seen increasing acceptance of the evidence of genetic influence on such complex psychological characteristics (Herrnstein, 1982).

The term "genetic influence" does not imply that the environment is unnecessary for development, nor does it imply genetic determinism in the sense of a direct or close relationship between genes and their effects on behavior. The pathways from gene expression through cells, tissues, and organs to the effect of genes on behavior are likely to be incredibly complex. As mentioned earlier, it may soon be possible to isolate specific sequences of DNA as they relate to phenotypic variance. In some few cases, physiological pathways from genes to behavior may be understood. For now, however, "genetic influence" means only that genetic differences among individuals are related to behavioral differences observed among them – no specific genetic mechanisms or gene-behavior pathways are implied.

A related issue involves the "new" molecular genetics, the explosion of knowledge that has come from recombinant DNA techniques developed in the early 1970s. The new concepts such as split genes, transposable genes, and temporal genes do not vitiate the theory of quantitative genetics that is based on the postulates of classical Mendelian genetics. Quantitative genetics represents the "bottom line" of genetic variability as it affects phenotypic variability. That is, quantitative genetic methods assess the total impact of genetic variability of any kind, regardless of its molecular source (Plomin, 1986a).

The expected phenotypic similarity among relatives is a function
of their genetic similarity to the extent that heredity is important

Quantitative genetics quantifies the degree of resemblance expected for different types of family relationships. For example, if genetic differences among individuals completely account for observed differences among individuals for a particular trait, first-degree relatives – parents and their offspring and siblings – are expected to yield a correlation of about .50. Half-siblings, who have only one parent in common, and other second-degree relatives are expected to yield a correlation of about .25. The expected correlation for identical twins, who are essentially clones from the genetic point of view, is 1.0. Pairs of genetically unrelated individuals, even when adopted into the same family early in life, are expected to yield a correlation of .00 for a trait whose variance is completely accounted for by heredity.

In psychology, however, we have no examples of traits with heritabilities near unity. If heredity accounts for half the variance for a trait (and sharing the same family environment does not lead to similarity), the expected correlations would be half those listed above: .25 for first-degree relatives, .125 for half-siblings, .50 for identical twins, and .00 for genetically unrelated individuals adopted together into the same family. If familial correlations are near zero, heredity is unimportant in the etiology of individual differences.

The theory recognizes that family environment can augment familial resemblance when family members share environment as well as heredity. However, all the relationships just described share family environment but differ in their hereditary similarity. Thus, if heredity is important, full siblings should be more similar than half-siblings and even more similar than adoptive siblings. Similarly, in the classical twin design, identical twins should be more similar than fraternal twins.

The power of the adoption design comes from its capacity to separate the influence of shared environment from the influence of heredity. The resemblance between genetically unrelated individuals reared in the same family directly assesses the contribution of shared environment; similarity between pairs of genetically related individuals adopted apart provides a direct assessment of the contribution of heredity. In the full adoption design of the CAP, shared environment is estimated from the similarity between adoptive parents and their adopted children, and the influence of heredity is assessed from the correlation between biological parents and their adopted-away offspring. In addition, the CAP includes nonadoptive families matched to the adoptive families; in these families, parents and offspring share heredity as well as family environment and thus provide a useful comparison group.

Quantitative genetic theory involves many refinements of these expectations of familial resemblance. For example, identical twins will be more than twice as similar as fraternal twins if nonadditive genetic variance is important, that is, if genes interact in a nonlinear manner rather than merely add up in their cumulative effect on the phenotype. (The model postulates that genetic variance consists of additive genetic variance and two types of nonadditive variance: dominance and epistasis.) Another example is assortative mating, a positive correlation between spouses for particular traits, which increases genetic resemblance among first-degree relatives. The classic explication of quantative genetic theory was written by Falconer (1960, revised 1981; for a simpler presentation, see Plomin et al., 1980).

Because quantitative genetics is applicable largely to the study of individual differences, it employs the statistics of individual differences such as covariances and correlations. Two frequently confused points regarding correlations should be mentioned briefly. First, correlations can be used to imply causation, despite the revered rule to the contrary. As mentioned in Chapter 2, data from experiments are in fact analyzed in terms of correlations – more specifically, regressions – using the computational shortcut analysis of variance. We do not hesitate to impute causation to these correlations. Correlations in behavioral genetic research can also imply causation. For example, the correlation for identical twins adopted apart into uncorrelated environments estimates genetic influence. The correlation is not squared because at issue is the percentage of variance common to the twins rather than the percentage of variance of the twins' scores that can be predicted by the co-twins' scores (Ozer, 1985). If the correlation is zero for a particular trait, we can only conclude that genetic factors are unimportant in the etiology of the trait. If the correlation is significant and substantial, genetic influence is implied.

In addition to genetic influence, quantitative genetic theory postulates that phenotypic variance can be caused by environmental influences, genotype–environment interaction, and genotype–environment correlation, which are discussed next.

Environmental differences among individuals can lead to phenotypic individual differences

This proposition seems more nearly a definition because no psychologist needs to be convinced that environmental differences can make a difference in behavior. Nonetheless, this aspect of quantitative genetic theory is noteworthy because quantitative genetics employs a much broader definition of environment than is usual in psychology. "Environment" in this context literally means "nongenetic," in the sense that it is that portion of variance that cannot be accounted for by heredity. This definition of environment thus includes biological factors such as anoxia at birth, prenatal effects of drugs, and even environmental influences on DNA, as well as traditional environmental factors such as childrearing, school environment, and peers.

It should be emphasized that behavioral genetic research yields the best evidence for the importance of the environment for all psychological traits – including schizophrenia and IQ – while at the same time pointing to significant genetic influence for many traits.

Quantitative genetic parameters change when genetic and
environmental sources of variance change

As in any research, conclusions based on quantitative genetic research are limited to the particular populations sampled. Populations with different blends of genetic and environmental influences yield different estimates of quantitative genetic parameters. In addition, historical change can produce different results across time. For example, genetic change is expected when natural selection, migration, or miscegenation occur. Quantitative genetics, in this instance referred to as population genetics, makes precise predictions about the effect of such population changes (e.g., Crow & Kimura, 1970), although psychologists rarely consider them.

Environmental change across generations, cohort effects, have been brought to the attention of psychologists by researchers interested in life-span development (e.g., Baltes, Reese, & Lipsitt, 1980; Elder, 1985). The dramatic changes in our society even during the past three decades – such as the widespread availability of radio and television and educational op-portunities – are all likely to affect the etiology of individual differences in industrial societies.

For developmentalists, the major marker of genetic and environmental change is age. That is, the contributions of genetic and environmental factors can differ from age to age. For example, one might expect that the relative importance of environmental variation increases during childhood, as children experience increasingly diverse environments. Also, the specific environmental correlates of development might be expected to change during development. Throughout this book, we examine such develop-mental changes from infancy to early childhood.

The environmental component of variance for a particular trait
can be decomposed into two subcomponents, one shared by
family members, the other not shared

The central issue in human behavioral genetic methodology is to disen-tangle two major sources of covariance among relatives: family environment and heredity. For example, resemblance between parents and offspring could be due to the fact that they have the same family environment or that they share heredity. In the CAP, the influence of family environment shared by parents and offspring is assessed by the correlation within pairs of adoptive parents and their adopted children. The remainder of the environmental variance, the portion not shared by family members, is nonshared environment plus error.

One of the most important findings in the field is that shared environmental influences are unimportant in the development of personality, psychopathology, and perhaps intelligence (Fulker, 1981; Plomin, 1988; Plomin & Daniels, 1987; Rowe & Plomin, 1981; Scarr, Webber, Weinberg, & Wittig, 1981; Scarr & Weinberg, 1978). Given that environmental variance is important but shared environment is not, critical environmental influences must be of the nonshared variety, making parents and children in the same family as different from one another as are pairs of parents and children selected randomly from the population. The importance of this finding lies in the fact that previous environmental research has been misguided: Environmental factors relevant to psychological development lie not *between* families, but *within* families.

Genes can affect measures of the environment and the relationship between environmental measures and psychological measures

Measures of the environment often indirectly assess behavior. Some environmental measures, such as the Family Environment Scales (FES; Moos & Moos, 1981), involve perceptions of the environment; ratings on such self-report questionnaires could easily filter through genetically influenced characteristics of individuals. In two studies of adolescent twins employing different self-report measures of the environment, David Rowe (1981, 1983) found that adolescents' perceptions of parental affection are significantly influenced by heredity, whereas perceptions of parental control are not.

Heredity can also affect the relationship between environmental measures and psychological measures. For example, the most widely used environmental measure in studies of cognitive development is the Home Observation for Measurement of the Environment (HOME; Caldwell & Bradley, 1978), an observation and interview measure that assesses such dimensions as maternal responsiveness, involvement, and restrictiveness. If parental behavior involved in such dimensions is influenced by genes that also affect children's development, relationships between the HOME and children's development in nonadoptive families could be mediated genetically. However, in the absence of selective placement, such relationships in adoptive families should not be confounded by hereditary influences. Comparisons between the HOME and FES and measures of development in CAP adoptive and nonadoptive homes suggest that, at least in infancy, relationships between these putative environmental measures and psychological measures are substantially mediated by heredity (Plomin, Loehlin, & DeFries, 1985). This topic is discussed in detail in Chapter 11.

In addition to genetic and environmental "main effects,"
phenotypic variance may be due to
genotype–environment interaction

Genotype–environment interaction denotes an interaction in the statistical sense of a conditional relationship: The effect of environmental factors differs depending on genotype. In other words, genotype–environment interaction refers to nonlinear combinations of genetic and environmental influences. Although it is difficult to assess the overall importance of genotype–environment interaction for human variation, adoption studies can isolate specific interactions between genotypes and measures of the environment, using biological parents' scores to estimate the genotype of their adopted-away offspring and using any measure of the adoptive home environment or characteristic of the adoptive parents as an environmental measure (Plomin, DeFries, & Loehlin, 1977). Although research to date has not uncovered many genotype–environment interactions in human behavior (Plomin, 1986a), we consider genotype–environment interaction in Chapter 9.

Phenotypic variance may also be due to genotype–environment
correlation

Genotype–environment correlation literally refers to a correlation between genetic deviations and environmental deviations as they affect a particular trait. In other words, it describes the extent to which individuals are exposed to environments as a function of their genetic propensities. It represents variance that is neither solely genetic nor solely environmental, but both. Even when genetic deviations and environmental deviations are perfectly correlated, however, genetic variance and environmental variance remain; genotype–environment correlation contributes additional phenotypic variance. In fact, the correlation between genetic and environmental deviations can contribute substantially to phenotypic variance only when both genetic variance and environmental variance are substantial (Jensen, 1976).

Three types of genotype–environment correlation have been described (Plomin et al., 1977). *Passive* genotype–environment correlation occurs because children share heredity as well as environmental influences with members of their family and can thus passively inherit environments correlated with their genetic predispositions. *Reactive* or evocative genotype–environment correlation refers to experiences of the child that derive from other people's reactions to the child's genetic propensities. *Active* genotype–environment correlation occurs when, for example, children actively select or even create environments that are correlated with their genetic propensities. This has been called niche building or niche picking (Scarr & McCartney, 1983). Genotype–environment correlations can be negative as well as positive (Cattell, 1973).

Adoption studies can be used to isolate specific genotype–environment correlations, as described in Chapter 10. An important spur for research in this field is Scarr and McCartney's (1983) theory based on the three types of genotype–environment correlation as processes by which genotypes transact with environments during development.

Correlations among traits can be mediated genetically as well as environmentally

Work during the past decade has extended behavioral genetics from a univariate analysis of the variance of traits considered one at a time to a multivariate analysis of the covariance among traits (e.g., DeFries & Fulker, 1986). Rather than assuming that separate sets of genes or separate sets of environmental factors affect each phenotype, the overlap of etiological factors can be studied as they affect the covariance among traits. Genetic correlations indicate the extent to which a set of genes that affects one trait overlaps with the set of genes that affects another trait. Any quantitative genetic analysis of the variance of a single characteristic can be applied to the covariance among characteristics. In the CAP, all parent–offspring analyses must be viewed as multivariate analyses in the sense that we cannot assume that the characteristic assessed for parents is the same as that of the children even when the adult and child measures have the same name. In addition, we can intentionally explore the relationship between different traits in parents and children. For example, we can use multivariate analysis to study the differentiation of cognitive abilities, as discussed in Chapters 6 and 8.

Although multivariate genetic–environmental analysis has only rarely been applied to human data, the approach has considerable potential for explaining, not merely describing, the relationship among traits. For example, to what extent are individual differences in mental development and the development of language influenced by the same genetic factors? Another category of examples explores the etiology of associations between physiological variables and behavioral variables. One cannot assume that associations between behavioral and physiological variables such as heart rate, evoked potentials, hormones, and levels of neurotransmitters are mediated genetically – the etiology of such associations must be studied empirically.

A third profitable area for the application of multivariate genetic–environmental analysis will be longitudinal analysis of change and continuity in development, as indicated by the following proposition.

Genes can cause change as well as continuity in development

Individual differences in the regulation of developmental processes are due in part to the influence of developmental control genes (Sternberg & Horritz, 1984). Genetic sources of change in development are a major focus of contemporary molecular genetic research, which seeks to solve the mystery of how we begin life as a single cell and develop into a highly differentiated organism with trillions of cells, each with the same DNA. The proposition that control genes can induce change in development is the essence of a new field within behavioral genetics, developmental behavioral genetics, which considers change as well as continuity in development (Plomin, 1986a). By applying the methods of multivariate genetic–environmental analysis to longitudinal data, it is possible to analyze the extent of age-to-age genetic correlations and environmental correlations, as discussed in Chapters 6 and 8.

Quantitative genetics as a progressive theory of individual differences

In summary, the theory of quantitative genetics attempts to explain the origins of variance and covariance, a goal that must be the essence of any theory of individual differences. The theory begins by partitioning phenotypic variance into genetic and environmental components. Although the nature–nurture question is a reasonable first step in understanding the variance of a particular trait, the theory also leads to novel individual-differences concepts: shared and nonshared environmental variance; genetic influence on environmental measures and on relationships between environmental measures and behavioral measures; genotype–environment interaction and correlation; multivariate genetic and environmental influences on the covariance among traits; and genetic and environmental sources of change as well as continuity in development.

Quantitative genetics is a powerful theory of individual differences. At its most general level, the theory provides an expectation that individuals will differ in the complex behavioral traits that interest psychologists. In this way, quantitative genetics organizes a welter of data on individual differences so that they are no longer viewed as imperfections in the species type or as nuisance error in analysis of variance, but rather as the quintessence of evolution.

An attractive feature of quantitative genetic theory is that, in philosophy of science jargon, the theory is progressive (Lakatos, 1970). That is, it leads to new predictions that can be verified empirically; potential problems with the theory are examined rather than ignored. The most recent example of the heuristic value of the theory was mentioned earlier: Once one realizes that measures of environment that are used in psychological research are, indirectly at least, measures of behavior, the prediction emerges that environmental measures as well as their relationship with measures of children's development can show genetic influence. Quantitative genetic methods exist to test this prediction empirically, for example, by comparing environment–development relationships in nonadoptive and adoptive families (Plomin et al., 1985).

Because the theory is explicit and powerful, it also leads to an open interest in its potential shortcomings. For example, consider the possible problem of the equal-environments assumption of the twin method. If identical twins are treated more similarly than are fraternal twins for nongenetic reasons, then greater resemblance of identical twins could be due to environment rather than to heredity. Behavioral genetic researchers identified this issue and have attempted to ascertain the extent of the bias. In this case, the assumption of equal environments has been found to be reasonable (e.g., Plomin et al., 1980). In other cases, however, further examination of aspects of the theory have uncovered problems that must be taken into account in behavioral genetic research. For example, twins, whether identical or fraternal, share environmental influences to a greater extent than do nontwin siblings, which means that twin studies will overestimate the importance of shared environment (Plomin, 1986a). Similarly, selective placement is the major potential problem with the adoption design – if adoptees' biological and adoptive parents are similar, genetic influence will inflate the correlation between adoptive parents and their adopted children, and environmental influence will inflate the correlation between biological parents and their adopted-away children. The biasing effects of selective placement have been discussed (DeFries & Plomin, 1978) and can be taken into account in structural equation models (e.g., Fulker & DeFries, 1983). A major advantage of the CAP is that selective placement is negligible (Plomin & DeFries, 1985a), as discussed in Chapter 4.

Quantitative genetic theory leads directly to an armamentarium of research methods that create the strong empirical grounding of behavioral genetics. Attacks on traditional empirical and rational approaches to science, including the subjectivity of the classical hermeneutics of Heidegger (1962; Packer, 1985), Gadamer's (1975) more radical hermeneutics, which emphasizes engagement in the existential sense, and Kuhn's attack on rationalism (Kuhn, 1962), are subsiding (Skinner, 1985). For example, Kuhn's view of science removes empirical evidence from its role as the final arbiter among competing research programs, resulting in a relativity of scientific truth that has been eagerly accepted by some psychologists. More recent views, however, such as those of Lakatos (1978) and Laudan (1981), attempt to return empirical evidence to its role as judge of scientific truth (Gholson & Barker, 1985). According to this view, successful theory maximizes empirical successes and minimizes conceptual liabilities. To the extent that this view becomes accepted in psychology, quantitative genetics is likely to be seen as the basis for a powerful theory of the origins of individual differences.

4   The Colorado Adoption Project

As mentioned in the preceding chapter, quantitative genetic theory
recognizes that genetic and environmental influences change during development, and it proposes new concepts and methods for exploring developmental change as well as continuity. This is the core
of a new subdiscipline, developmental behavioral genetics. When the
field of behavioral genetics is surveyed from a developmental perspective, it is clear that the relative roles of genetic and environmental influences change during development (Plomin, 1986a). If this were not
the case, there would be no need for the field of developmental behavioral genetics – the story in childhood would be just the same as that in
adulthood.

The conclusion that the relative magnitudes of genetic and environmental
influences change during development is founded primarily on cross-
sectional comparisons across studies, for the obvious reason that
most behavioral genetic studies are cross-sectional. Although the cross-
sectional design can be illuminating, the lifeblood of developmental
analysis of change and continuity is the longitudinal design (McCall,
1977; see also Chapter 5). The few longitudinal behavioral genetic studies, discussed below, add disproportionately to the weight of these conclusions because the same subjects are studied at different ages and,
at each age, subjects are usually studied within a relatively narrow age
band. In contrast, not only do cross-sectional studies use different subjects and often different measures, but the subjects usually span a
wide age range. In addition to these benefits of the longitudinal design,
it has a special advantage in developmental behavioral genetics over
the cross-sectional design: It can explore genetic and environmental
etiologies of age-to-age change and continuity, as emphasized in Chapters 6 and 9.

Longitudinal behavioral genetic studies

Because there are few longitudinal studies of any kind, it comes as no surprise that there are few long-term longitudinal behavioral genetic studies. Longitudinal behavioral genetic studies compound the usual hardships of mounting a longitudinal study with the burden of obtaining and maintaining special samples such as twins and adoptees. In this section, the major longitudinal behavioral genetic studies are described because these studies are frequently mentioned in later chapters.

The major longitudinal twin study is the exemplary Louisville Twin Study, which was initiated more than 25 years ago (Wilson, 1983). Approximately 25 to 35 pairs of twins have been recruited each year since 1963, resulting in a sample of about 500 pairs of twins now participating in the longitudinal research program, in which the twins are studied from the age of 3 months to 15 years. The twins are tested at 3, 6, 9, 12, 18, 24, 30, and 36 months and annually thereafter to 9 years of age. A final test session is administered when the twins are 15 years old. Until recently, the focus of the Louisville Twin Study was IQ and physical growth, although some data relevant to temperament were collected by means of maternal interviews concerning behavioral differences within twin pairs and the Infant Behavior Record, a 30-item rating scale that is completed by the examiner following administration of the Bayley Scales of Infant Development (Bayley, 1969). Since 1976, however, the focus has turned to the temperament of infant twins, which is studied by means of a structured laboratory assessment sequence that is videotaped and rated later using a modification of the Infant Behavior Record (Wilson & Matheny, 1986).

Two other longitudinal twin studies should be mentioned. One is a study of 39 pairs of identical twins and 56 pairs of fraternal twins administered tests of specific cognitive abilities at 12 years and again at 18 years (Fischbein, 1981). The other is an ongoing study in Australia that uses a mixed-longitudinal design in which twins from 3 to 15 years of age are accepted into the project and studied repeatedly (Hay & O'Brien, 1983).

By far the most well known longitudinal adoption study is that of Marie Skodak and Harold Skeels (1949). A group of 100 illegitimate children adopted before 6 months of age were administered IQ tests on at least four different occasions, at the average ages of 2, 3, 7, and 13 years. IQ tests were also administered to 63 of the biological mothers of these adopted-away children. Although this is a landmark study, it is not without problems. Most important from the perspective of developmental behavioral genetics is the fact that the children were tested at widely varying ages – for example, the first testing at the average age of 26 months included children from 6 months to 6 years of age. Moreover, significant selective placement occurred – the correlation between educational level of the birth mothers and the average educational level of the adoptive parents was .30. The effect of selective placement is to raise estimates both of genetic influence and of the influence of family environment (DeFries & Plomin, 1978). Finally, the study missed an important opportunity to study environmental influences unconfounded by heredity because neither adoptive parent IQ nor the adoptive family environment was assessed; also missing were measures other than IQ of children and their parents.

Only five other adoption studies followed adoptees longitudinally. In one of these studies (Casler, 1976), 151 adopted children were tested five times from 2 to 27 months of age; Gessell tests were administered and the adoptees' scores were compared with the IQ scores of their birth mothers. One shortcoming of this study is that selective placement for IQ was intentionally practiced. In another longitudinal adoption study (Fisch, Bilek, Deinard, & Chang, 1976), IQ was assessed at 4 and 7 years of age for 94 adopted children and their adoptive parents and for 50 nonadoptive children and their parents. No data were available for birth parents. The three remaining longitudinal adoption studies are problematic. In one interesting study in which adoptees were tested twice during the first year of life, only educational and occupational information were obtained for the parents; moreover, the sample consisted of only 24 adoptees (Beckwith, 1971). In another study, 53 adoptees were tested in infancy and at 10 years of age, and extensive environmental information was obtained; however, no information was obtained for birth parents or for nonadoptive families, which vitiates the study's capacity to estimate genetic influence (Yarrow, Goodwin, Manheimer, & Milowe, 1973). A similar shortcoming is apparent in another longitudinal study of adoptees from infancy through early adolescence, a study designed primarily to study developmental outcomes of the adoption process (Hoopes, 1982).

Design of the Colorado Adoption Project

A review of 19 familial adoption studies of normal development is included in the first CAP book (Plomin & DeFries, 1985a). In summary, only three of these studies collected information other than education and occupation for biological parents; only one large study considered infants; sample sizes were quite small in some studies; IQ has clearly been the focus of previous studies; only 7 of the 19 studies obtained measures of the environment other than parental education or occupation; all but three of the studies showed some selective placement; and nearly all of the studies were retrospective. The major prospective, longitudinal study is that of Skodak and Skeels; although, as described above, most of its subjects were past infancy at first testing, the sample consisted of only 63 pairs of birth mothers and adoptees tested for IQ, the focus of the study was IQ, no environmental measures were obtained, and selective placement was considerable.

In 1974, Plomin and DeFries formulated a plan to conduct an adoption study that was large, longitudinal, prospective, and multivariate, with minimal selective placement; that tested birth parents; that included non-adoptive families matched to adoptive families; and that assessed the home environment. With the cooperation of the two largest adoption agencies in the Rocky Mountain area, Lutheran Social Services of Colorado and Denver Catholic Community Services, birth parents were tested beginning in 1975, which marked the launching of the Colorado Adoption Project. Steven G. Vandenberg, who had directed the Louisville Twin Study in the 1960s, participated in the planning. David W. Fulker became involved several years later in terms of developing models for analysis of the full adoption design (e.g., Fulker & DeFries, 1983) and assumed a more active role in the CAP in 1983 when he left the Institute of Psychiatry, University of London, and became a faculty member at the Institute for Behavioral Genetics. It was fortunate that the CAP began by 1975. The availability of contraceptives, legalized abortions, and an increase in the number of unmarried mothers who kept their children had combined to lower drastically the number of infants available for adoption (Sklar & Berkov, 1974). The decrease was most dramatic for white neonates, the primary group of adoptees in the Rocky Mountain area. The number of available adoptees has steadily decreased since the CAP began, from more than 100 per year to fewer than 20 per year. As a result, it was necessary to extend the number of years of the project in order to obtain the necessary sample size. This actually added another strength to the design, however, in that cohort effects can be analyzed to determine the generalizability of our results across a decade, as discussed later in this chapter.

CAP's goal was to include 250 adoptive families and 250 nonadoptive families, with the adoptive and nonadoptive probands and their younger siblings tested in their homes at 1, 2, 3, and 4 years of age. The children are tested again in the laboratory in middle childhood at 7 years of age, and an early-adolescence project involves testing at 9, 10, and 11. CAP's long-term plan is to study this unique sample through adolescence to 16 years of age, when the children will be able to complete the same tests their parents completed more than a decade and a half earlier.

Three factors augured well for the project. First, the two Denver adoption agencies participating in the CAP, like other progressive agencies, do not attempt to match birth parents and adoptive parents. The only exceptions concern geographical area and height: Infants are not placed in the geographical area in which their birth parents reside, and social workers intentionally avoid large mismatches in height. Second, the biological and adoptive parents are representative of the Denver metropolitan area in terms of socioeconomic status, although nearly 90% of the biological parents and more than 95% of the adoptive parents are white. The adoption agencies eliminate very few prospective parents and do not use wealth as a criterion. Data concerning selective placement and representativeness are presented later in this chapter. Third, some of the biological fathers were available; about 20% of the biological fathers of the adopted children in the CAP have been tested. In 1972, the Supreme Court (*Stanley* v. *Illinois*) ruled that biological fathers had the same rights as biological mothers concerning relinquishment and required that the biological father sign a release to facilitate the adoption of the child. After a couple of years, however, it became apparent that the decision was unworkable and unenforceable; nonetheless, agency policies and attitudes toward biological fathers had changed. In the CAP, biological parents were not asked for blood samples to exclude paternity because of legal implications as well as the negative effect such a request would have on participation rates. Biological paternity is presumed on the basis of reports by the social worker, the birth mother, and the putative father. Although CAP test data are available for only a relatively small percentage of biological fathers, they represent the first test data for biological fathers in an adoption study, data that are essential to determining birth parents' assortative mating, the tendency for like to mate with like. Assortative mating affects estimates of genetic parameters and cannot be presumed to be the same for unwed parents as for married couples.

The CAP design is a "full" adoption design, including data from both biological and adoptive parents of adopted children. In addition, nonadoptive families are matched to the adoptive families. In other words, the CAP includes "genetic" parents (biological parents and their adopted-away children), "environmental" parents (adoptive parents and their adopted children), and "genetic-plus-environmental" parents (nonadoptive or control parents and their children). Comparisons among the three family types can disentangle the causes of familial resemblance. That is, in nonadoptive families, parents share both heredity and environment and thus parent–offspring resemblance could be due to either factor. In the absence of selective placement, resemblance between biological parents and their adopted-away offspring can be due only to shared heredity; resemblance between adoptive parents and their adopted children can be due only to shared environment. Thus, the CAP design can be seen as a simple quasi-experimental design in which family environment is randomized in comparisons between biological parents and their adopted-away offspring, and in the other prong of the two-pronged thrust of the full adoption design, heredity is randomized in comparisons between adoptive parents and their adopted children.

In later chapters, the basic parent–offspring design is specified and expanded in terms of path diagrams and causal modeling. However, a few additional design issues should be mentioned at this point. Assortative mating between mothers and fathers inflates mother–offspring and father–offspring correlations. Thus, assortative mating inflates genetic estimates if biological parents mate assortatively, and it also inflates estimates of shared environment if adoptive parents mate assortatively. Parent–off-spring correlations are also affected by selective placement: Covariance between the phenotypes of biological and adoptive parents inflates correlations between biological parents and their offspring as well as between adoptive parents and their adopted children, thus inflating both genetic and environmental estimates in the full adoption design.

In terms of environment, it should be emphasized that resemblance between adoptive parents and their adopted children does not estimate all forms of parental influence on children – it estimates only that component of parent–offspring resemblance due to shared environment. For example, parents affect their children through direct tuition as well as modeling, but these environmental effects are assessed as shared environmental influences only if they contribute to phenotypic similarity between adoptive parents and their adopted children. All other environmental influences are estimated as "nonshared" influences – that is, variance not explained by heredity or by shared environment. However, in addition to this components-of-variance approach, the parent–offspring adoption design is particularly useful for identifying specific environmental factors that affect development in adoptive families, in which environmental influences are not conflated by hereditary similarity between parents and offspring.

A particularly important point concerning genetic estimates from the parent–offspring adoption design is that parents and offspring cannot be viewed as resembling each other 50% genetically when the parents are adults and the offspring are children. As explained in Chapters 6 and 9, genetic effects on a phenotype can change from childhood to adulthood; for this reason, genetic resemblance between offspring and their parents is a function not only of their coefficient of genetic relationship, which is .50 when mating is at random, but also of the magnitude of genetic influence in childhood, the magnitude of genetic influence in adulthood, and the extent to which genetic effects in childhood are correlated with genetic effects in adulthood. Although this fact makes it difficult to detect genetic influence in childhood using the parent–offspring design, its benefit is that, from a genetic perspective, the parent–offspring design is like an "instant" longitudinal study from childhood to adulthood. That is, significant resemblance between biological parents and their adopted-away children will be found only when all three conditions are met: Heritability is substantial in childhood and in adulthood and the genetic correlation between childhood and adulthood is substantial. This is the core concept of developmental behavioral genetics – genetically mediated age-to-age change and continuity. Although much more will be said about this in Chapters 6 and 9, it should be noted that if the genetic correlation is low between childhood and adulthood, this suggests genetic change during development. The genetic correlation between childhood and adulthood could be low even though the heritabilities at both ages are high.

Another valuable feature of the CAP design is that younger siblings of the adopted and nonadopted probands are studied in the same manner as the probands. Adoptive siblings are genetically unrelated children reared in the same family. The addition of the developmentally contemporaneous relationship of adoptive and nonadoptive siblings tested at the same age is important because it provides estimates of heritability in childhood, which, in combination with parent–offspring comparisons and estimates of heritability in adulthood, can yield estimates of genetic correlations between childhood and adulthood. In addition, adoptive siblings provide a direct estimate of the sum of all environmental influences shared by two children reared in the same family that affect a particular trait. No longitudinal study of adoptive siblings has previously been reported. In this book, data are reported for 67 adoptive and 82 nonadoptive sibling pairs in which both members of the pair were tested at the age of 12 months; 61 adoptive and 70 nonadoptive pairs tested at 2 years; 50 and 54 pairs at 3 years; and 42 and 43 pairs at 4 years. A path model describing the CAP sibling adoption design is presented in Chapter 7 and applied to the major CAP measures in Chapter 8; a combined parent–offspring and sibling design is discussed in Chapter 9.

CAP sample

The CAP sample includes 245 adoptive families and 245 nonadoptive families matched to the adoptive families. Analyses presented in this book are based on 241 adopted and 245 nonadopted probands at 12 months, 212 adopted and 229 nonadopted probands at 2 years, 203 adopted and 195 nonadopted at 3 years and 183 adopted and 166 nonadopted at 4 years. The adopted probands number fewer than 245 at 1 year because data were used only if a child had reasonably complete data at an age and the testers indicated that the quality of the testing was adequate. The sample size drops further at 2 years for the same reason and because some families had moved or no longer wished to participate. The decline in sample size at 3 and 4 years is due to these reasons plus the fact that some children have not yet been tested at 3 and 4. As just mentioned, in addition to these probands, younger siblings of the adopted and nonadopted probands have also been tested at 1, 2, 3, and 4 years of age.

The biological mothers and the adoptive mothers and fathers of the adopted probands and the mothers and fathers of the nonadoptive probands have been tested on a 3-hour battery of behavioral measures. In addition, 50 biological fathers of the adopted probands have been tested. Nearly 90% of the biological parents and more than 95% of the adoptive and nonadoptive parents report that they are Caucasian; the rest are primarily Hispanic and Oriental.

In this section, the procedure by which parents were selected is discussed, and data concerning the representativeness of the sample and the issue of selective placement are presented. The description of these topics is brief; a fuller discussion can be found in an earlier book (Plomin & DeFries, 1985a).

Sample selection

Biological parents were solicited through two Denver adoption agencies, typically when the biological mother was in the last trimester of pregnancy. Biological parents were usually tested in small groups and were paid for their participation.

For adoptive parents, the adoption process is lengthy, usually about 3 years. Fewer than 10% of potential adoptive parents are denied a placement. General guidelines exist concerning age of the couple, religion, number of years the couple has been married, number of other children in the family, and a medical factor making it undesirable or impossible for the couple to have their own child. Although the ability of the couple to meet financial obligations is considered, income per se is not a criterion, nor is homeownership. Adoptive parents who happened to adopt a child whose biological mother was tested as part of the CAP were asked to participate after the adoption was finalized, typically when the child was 7 months old. Adoptive couples were usually tested together in groups, and they were paid an honorarium.

At the average age of 4.1 days, the adopted infants were taken by a social worker from the hospital to a foster family, usually older parents with children of their own. The infants remained with the foster family until the legal requirements concerning relinquishment were fulfilled. The children were placed in their adoptive homes at the average of 28.5 days. None of the placements of CAP adoptees into adoptive families has been terminated.

Nonadoptive (control) families were ascertained through local hospitals. Families with newborn children received a letter describing the project and a return postcard on which they could request a telephone call to discuss the project in greater detail. Parents who returned the postcard were contacted by phone, and information was obtained to decide whether the family could be matched to an adoptive family based on the following criteria: gender of proband, number of children in family, age of father (± 5 years), National Opinion Research Center (NORC) rating of occupational status of father (± 8 points), and total years of the father's education (± 2 years). This matching procedure was designed to ensure comparability between adoptive and nonadoptive families; it was not undertaken for the purpose of statistical analyses based on paired observations. After a match between adoptive and nonadoptive families was confirmed, nonadoptive couples were tested in small groups, usually at the Institute for Behavioral Genetics, and were paid an honorarium for their participation.

Adopted and nonadopted probands, their younger siblings, and their home environments were assessed primarily during 2- to 3-hour visits in their homes by a full-time home tester at 1, 2, 3, and 4 years of age. The CAP children were tested at the average age of 1.02 years (SD = .04), 2.01 years (SD = .05), 3.01 years (SD = .03), and 4.01 years (SD = .04).

Representativeness

For the complete CAP sample of 245 adoptive and 245 nonadoptive families, Table 4.1 presents descriptive statistics concerning education, occupational status, and age of CAP parents. As a result of the matching procedures, adoptive and nonadoptive parents are similar with regard to education and occupational status. However, adoptive parents are somewhat older than nonadoptive parents, and both are considerably older than biological parents. Because many biological parents are teenagers, their years of education and occupational status are lower than those of adoptive and nonadoptive parents. However, the data for the grandparents – that is, the parents of the CAP parents – indicate that the average years of

Table 4.1. *Means and standard deviations for education, occupational status, and age of CAP parents*

	Biological mother (N = 247)		Biological father (N = 45)		Adoptive mother (N = 245)		Adoptive father (N = 245)		Nonadoptive mother (N = 244)		Nonadoptive father (N = 245)	
	Mean	SD	Mean	SD	Mean	SD	Mean	SD	Mean	SD	Mean	SD
Education	12.1	1.8	12.3	1.8	14.7	2.1	15.7	2.5	14.9	2.1	15.6	2.3
Occupational SEI[a]	—	—	33.4	22.4	—	—	62.5	20.8	—	—	60.3	18.7
Age	19.8	3.6	21.3	4.8	32.6	3.5	34.0	4.0	29.7	4.1	31.5	4.3

[a]Revised SEI (Hauser & Featherman, 1977) based on occupational titles from the 1970 census.

education and occupational status of the biological grandparents are comparable to those of the adoptive and nonadoptive grandparents, as indicated in Table 4.2.

Thus, these demographic data support the internal coherence of the CAP design. However, the issue of representativeness extends also to comparisons with other samples. As discussed in detail in the first CAP book, occupational status of the CAP adoptive and nonadoptive families compares favorably both in means and in variances to a stratified random sample from a Denver suburban area taken from 1970 census data. On the basis of national norms for the U.S. white labor force, the CAP sample was found to be somewhat above the national average in occupational status, although the CAP sample is nearly representative in terms of variance.

Selective placement

Positive selective placement will inflate estimates of both heredity and shared environment. As mentioned earlier, one of the reasons that the two Denver adoption agencies were so appealing as a source of participants was that they, like other progressive agencies, do not attempt to match adoptees to adoptive parents, because they believe that this sets up false expectations for adoptive parents and that the agency's resources are better spent counseling adoptive parents about the differences that are likely to occur.

Later in this chapter, selective placement correlations are examined for behavioral traits. However, social workers do not have access to behavioral test data; any selective placement they attempt would have to be based on demographic characteristics such as education and occupational status. Educational attainment of biological mothers correlates $-.13$ with that of adoptive mothers and $.04$ with that of adoptive fathers. For the revised Socioeconomic Index (SEI) (Hauser & Featherman, 1977), biological mothers' occupational status correlates $-.05$ with occupational status of adoptive mothers and $.18$ with that of adoptive fathers. As mentioned earlier, biological mothers are young, and their educational attainment and occupations might not adequately describe their social status. For these reasons, the most informative selective placement information compares the biological mothers' fathers with the adoptive fathers and the fathers of adoptive mothers and fathers. Education level of the fathers of the CAP biological mothers correlates $.07$ with the adoptive fathers' education, $.07$ with education of the fathers of the adoptive mothers, and $.03$ with education of the fathers of adoptive fathers. For SEI, the correlations are $.02$,

Table 4.2. *Means and standard deviations for education and occupational status of CAP "grandfathers"*

	Biological mothers' fathers (N = 218)		Biological fathers' fathers (N = 42)		Adoptive mothers' fathers (N = 204)		Adoptive fathers' fathers (N = 189)		Nonadoptive mothers' fathers (N = 204)		Nonadoptive fathers' fathers (N = 203)	
	Mean	SD	Mean	SD	Mean	SD	Mean	SD	Mean	SD	Mean	SD
Education	13.5	3.0	13.5	4.1	12.4	3.7	11.7	3.6	13.4	3.5	13.0	3.2
Occupational SEI[a]	54.6	23.3	58.7	21.0	54.1	22.4	49.8	21.9	56.0	22.4	54.7	23.1

[a]Revised SEI (Hauser & Featherman, 1977) based on occupational titles from the 1970 census.

− .10, and .03, respectively. Overall, the median selective placement correlation is .04 for education and .02 for SEI, indicating negligible selective placement for those demographic variables most accessible to social workers.

CAP measures

The selection of measures in the CAP was guided by an advisory committee including L. Heston, J. C. Loehlin, R. B. McCall, W. Meredith, and S. Scarr, with additional advice provided by J. Block, W. Charlesworth, J. Kagan, and M. Weir. The goal was to collect as many valid and reliable data as possible during relatively brief testing periods, sampling extensively and broadly rather than intensively and narrowly.

The measures used in the CAP to test parents and to assess infants and their home environments at 12 and 24 months are described in the first CAP book (Plomin & DeFries, 1985a); copies of the unpublished measures are included in the appendix of that book. For this reason, parental measures and measures employed in infancy will be described very briefly. New measures used in the 3- and 4-year home visits will be characterized in greater detail. For all measures, individuals missing 20% or more of the data for a scale were treated as missing the entire scale. In our previous analyses, we had eliminated outliers whose scores on a scale were three standard deviations above or below the mean. However, further analyses indicated that removal of such outliers scarcely affected the results, and for this reason the present analyses do not remove outlying scores.

Parental measures

The CAP biological, adoptive, and nonadoptive parents complete the same 3-hour test battery; tape-recorded instructions standardize the administration of tests across sessions and set time limits. The domains assessed include general and specific cognitive abilities, personality, interests and talents, common behavioral problems, commonly used drugs, and miscellaneous information.

Cognitive abilities. The CAP cognitive battery is modified from the tests used in the Hawaii Family Study of Cognition (DeFries et al., 1974), which yield a stable factor structure across ethnic groups, gender, and age from adolescence to middle age that includes spatial, verbal, perceptual speed, and memory abilities. The 13 test scores derived from the CAP cognitive abilities battery yielded a median internal reliability of .86 and a median test–retest reliability of .80. The scores were adjusted for age, age squared, and gender separately for each group of parents because age is significantly related to cognitive scores and is confounded with parental type in that the biological parents are about 10 years younger than the other parents.

Factor analyses yielded highly congruent first principal components for the three types of parents, with all tests loading substantially. In the Hawaii Family Study of Cognition, a first principal component based on similar cognitive measures correlated .73 with WAIS full-scale IQ, a correlation that is comparable to correlations reported between WAIS IQ and other standard tests of intelligence (Kuse, 1977). In the CAP, nonadoptive and adoptive parents are being tested on the WAIS when their children are 7 years old. The correlation between the first-principal-component scores and WAIS IQ more than 6 years later coincidentally is also .73 for 183 CAP parents. Thus, we consider the first-principal-component score to be a measure of general cognitive ability and it will be referred to as IQ.

Varimax rotation following a principal-component analysis yielded four factors accounting for 61% of the total variance. The Verbal factor has its highest loadings on Educational Testing Service (ETS) Things Categories Test, Vocabulary (a combination of Primary Mental Abilities [PMA] and ETS vocabulary tests), and ETS Word Beginnings and Endings. The Spatial factor is defined largely by the Minnesota Paper Form Board Test, ETS Card Rotations, ETS Hidden Patterns, and ETS Identical Pictures. Two tests, ETS Subtraction and Multiplication and Colorado Perceptual Speed, account primarily for the Perceptual Speed factor. Finally, the Memory factor is defined almost completely by Hawaii Family Study of Cognition (HFSC) Picture Memory and Colorado Names and Faces. PMA Pedigrees and an abbreviated Raven's Progressive Matrices assess less specific abilities, yielding moderate loadings on the Verbal, Spatial, and Perceptual Speed dimensions. Rotated principal-component scores for Verbal, Spatial, Perceptual, and Memory are used in the CAP as measures of specific cognitive abilities.

As described earlier, selective placement in the CAP is negligible for those variables about which social workers have the best knowledge: socioeconomic status and education. Is there selective placement for cognitive abilities? For IQ in the full sample, biological mothers' scores correlate .00 with adoptive mothers' IQ (243 pairs) and .00 with adoptive fathers' IQ (237 pairs). Biological fathers' IQ correlates − .04 (50 pairs) and .01 (45 pairs) with the adoptive mothers' and fathers' IQ, respectively. Specific cognitive abilities show no greater selective placement: Biological mothers' Verbal scores correlate .01 and .04 with adoptive mothers' and fathers' Verbal scores, respectively; for the Spatial factor, the selective placement correlations are .05 and − .01; for Perceptual Speed, the correlations are − .07 and − .01; and for Memory, the correlations are − .11 and − .01.

Personality. Measures of parental personality consist primarily of two self-report measures. Form A of Cattell's Sixteen Personality Factor Questionnaire (16PF; Cattell, Eber, & Tatsuoka, 1970) yields 16 primary scales and two second-order factors that assess extraversion and neuroticism. An adaptation of a temperament survey developed by Buss and Plomin (1975) is used to obtain self-report and "mate ratings" of personality. Means, variances, and factor structures in the CAP are discussed at length in the first CAP book, which concluded that the CAP sample is reasonably similar to the standardization sample.

Similar to the results for demographic variables and cognitive abilities, selective placement is negligible for personality. For the two second-order 16PF factors, biological mothers' scores correlate with adoptive mothers' and adoptive fathers' scores as follows: − .12 (246 pairs) and − .03 (240 pairs) for Extraversion and .06 and .15 for Neuroticism. The median selective placement correlations for the five EASI scales are .00 for adoptive mothers and .03 for adoptive fathers.

Interests and talents. The test booklet includes 40 items that assess interests and abilities. Separate scores are derived for interests and talents in the following areas: artistic, group sports, individual sports, mechanical, and domestic. Other interest scores obtained in the CAP include the amount of television viewing, reading, and religiosity.

Common behavioral problems. Frequently occurring behavioral problems are assessed for the CAP parents: depression, hysteria, sociopathy, phobias, compulsive behavior, sleep problems, motion sickness, menstrual problems, headaches, and speech problems. Depression was assessed using three items; for hysteria (nine items) and sociopathy (three items), items were modified from the Iowa 500 project (Tsuang, Crowe, Winokur, & Clancy, 1977).

Commonly used drugs. Detailed questions concerning the parents' smoking history are included in the parents' test battery, and questions are also asked about alcohol consumption and coffee drinking.

Miscellaneous measures. Demographic information such as education, occupation, and ethnicity is obtained. The CAP test booklet also contains an 11-item questionnaire on handedness, questions about family history of handedness, a 21-item questionnaire concerning food preferences, and additional questions concerning hours of sleep, frequency of colds, height, and weight. Finally, parents are asked to read aloud a section of the Gray Oral Reading Test, which is tape-recorded for possible use as a screening tool for major reading problems.

Not all of these parental measures have as yet been analyzed in relation to measures of children's development. Some parental measures, such as drug use and the tape-recorded reading sample, are not as relevant to infancy and early childhood as they will be later in development. This rich data set permits the exploration of many interesting possibilities; however, in an effort to curb the temptation to present an overwhelming amount of data, we have focused our presentation of CAP results on relatively straightforward comparisons between parents and their children.

Child measures

The information obtained during the 2- to 3-hour home visits at 1, 2, 3, and 4 years of age includes measures of mental development, communication, personality, behavioral problems, motor development, and miscellaneous measures, such as the child's health, interests in toys and other objects, and handedness. These data are collected via standardized tests, tester ratings, parental ratings, interviews, and videotaped observations of mother–child interaction. Because test–retest reliability is generally not known for these measures, we obtained 2-week test–retest reliability correlations for twenty-six 1-year-olds for all measures and for thirty-two 3-year-olds for all measures except for questionnaires used at earlier ages.

Mental development. The Bayley Mental Scale (Bayley, 1969) is administered at 1 and 2 years of age, and Form L–M of the Stanford–Binet Intelligence Scale (Terman & Merrill, 1973) is employed during the home visits at 3 and 4 years. Test–retest correlations in the CAP are .80 for the Bayley at 1, .82 for the Stanford–Binet at 3, and .84 at 4 years. Four of the seven Uzgiris–Hunt Ordinal Scales of Psychological Development (Uzgiris & Hunt, 1975) were administered at 12 months; however, this test is not as reliable as the Bayley – the test–retest reliability for the total score is .52 – and it appears to correlate near its reliability with the Bayley test.

In an attempt to assess specific cognitive abilities in infancy, we used factor analyses reported by Lewis (1983; see also Lewis, Jaskir, & Enright, 1986) to create three scales of Bayley items at 12 months (Means–End, Imitation, Verbal Skill) and four scales at 24 months (Lexical, Spatial, Verbal, Imitation). The test–retest reliabilities of the 12-month scales are

.61, .75, and − .04. We have no explanation for the lack of reliability for the Verbal Skill scale; this result suggests caution in interpreting its results.

A major CAP research effort during early childhood was directed toward the development of batteries of specific cognitive abilities for 3-year-olds (Singer, Corley, Guiffrida, & Plomin, 1984) and for 4-year-olds (Rice, Corley, Fulker, & Plomin, 1986). Each battery was piloted on a nursery school sample and then fine-tuned for use in the CAP. The verbal tests include a picture vocabulary test and a test of word fluency (e.g., naming things that make noise); the spatial tests include a simplified version of a block design test and a figure–ground test in which the child is asked to point to animals embedded in a complex background; and the perceptual speed tests involve a form-discrimination test in which the child points to the picture in a row of four that is identical to the target stimulus item at the left end of the row and a test in which the child finds a standard stimulus (a cow) in rows of line drawings of five animals. At 3 years, a recognition memory test is employed in which children are asked to remember line drawings of familiar objects. (An associative memory task developed by Singer et al. was not used in the CAP.) At 4 years, immediate and delayed versions of the recognition memory test are used. In addition, an associative memory task is employed at 4 years in which the child is shown pairs of animals and then asked to recall the other member of the pair when only one member is displayed. Each battery requires 30 to 40 minutes to administer.

For both test batteries, factor analyses supported the a priori placement of the tests on four factors: Verbal, Spatial, Perceptual Speed, and Memory. The factor structures conform to simple structure in that each test loads most highly on the conceptually appropriate factor and has low loadings on the remaining factors. Confirmatory factor analyses of the 4-year battery suggests that the best model is a simple correlated factor model with equal loadings and equal correlations among the factors (Rice et al., 1986). The average intercorrelation among the four scales is .23 for the 3-year battery and .33 for the 4-year battery, suggesting that the CAP battery assesses relatively differentiated cognitive abilities. In contrast, intercorrelations for the McCarthy Scales of Children's Abilities (McCarthy, 1972) are considerably higher – the average intercorrelation among the verbal, perceptual, quantitative, and memory scales of the McCarthy test is .71 at 3 years and .64 at 4 years.

Test–retest reliabilities for an unrotated first-principal-component score is .75 at 3 years in the CAP sample, .77 at 4 years for a sample of 54 nursery school children, and .90 in a separate sample of 29 nursery school children. The unrotated first-principal-component score correlates .61 and

.51 with Stanford–Binet IQ scores at 3 and 4 years, respectively; these correlations compare favorably, for example, with the correlation of .47 between the Bayley Mental Index and the Stanford–Binet at 30 months reported by Bayley (1970). Test–retest reliabilities of the Verbal, Spatial, Perceptual Speed, and Memory scales, respectively, are .67, .40, .68, and .64 at 3 years and .81, .78, .77, and .56 at 4 years.

Communication. At the 2- and 3-year home visits, age-appropriate items from the Sequenced Inventory of Communication Development (SICD; Hedrick, Prather, & Tobin, 1975) are administered in order to provide standardized measures of language production and comprehension. Items that were not age appropriate, that were too difficult to administer, or that closely resembled items from the 24-month Bayley Mental Scale or the 3-year Stanford–Binet Intelligence Scale were not included. At age 2, 19 expressive items and 13 receptive items were used, and at age 3, 9 expressive and 6 receptive items were included. Test–retest reliabilities of the Expressive, Receptive, and total scores at 3 years are .73, .70, and .79, respectively.

The home visits at 1, 2, and 3 years include 15-minute videotaped observations of mothers and their children interacting in three situations – free play; a semistructured situation, which is feeding at 1, playing with dollhouse at 2, and playing with a toy picnic set at 3; and a structured teaching task. Despite their brevity, the videotaped situations have proved to be behaviorally rich. For example, even at 12 months, about 45 vocalizations of infants and 225 vocalizations of mothers occur during the 15-minute videotape. Transcripts and 12 hours of coding per 15-minute videotape yielded a dozen communication measures, such as communicative gestures, syllable structure, and true words at 12 months (Hardy-Brown & Plomin, 1985; Hardy-Brown, Plomin, & DeFries, 1981). The various communicative measures intercorrelate and yield an unrotated principal component of communicative competence, which correlates .59 with a scale composed of language items from the Bayley test (Plomin & DeFries, 1985a). The laboriousness of these ratings have limited our analyses to a subsample of 50 adopted and 50 nonadopted children at 1 year; these results were reported in the first CAP book.

Personality and temperament. The CAP measures in this domain were planned with the goal of permitting aggregation of ratings across items, across situations, and across sources of information (Rushton, Brainerd, & Pressley, 1983). Information is obtained from three sources: testers, parents, and videotaped observations. At the 1- and 2-year home visits, testers use the 30 items of the Infant Behavior Record (IBR; Bayley, 1969) to rate the children's behavior during administration of the mental tests. The IBR is a promising measure of infant behavior, because children are rated on the basis of their reaction to a standard, somewhat stressful situation. The CAP data replicate the major factors Affect–Extraversion, Task Orientation, and Activity reported by Matheny (1980) for infants. Scale scores representing these three factors were constructed; test–retest reliabilities for the three scales at 12 months are .76 for Affect–Extraversion, .60 for Task Orientation, and only .06 for Activity.

At 3 and 4 years, the IBR was revised to include 17 items with 5-point ratings: interest in persons, amount of cooperativeness, resistant behavior, fearfulness, activity level, persistence, attention span, frustration level, happiness, independence, reactivity, expressiveness, person orientation, object orientation, gross coordination, fine coordination, and deviant behavior (rated yes or no). The items were rated twice, once for the child's behavior during administration of the Stanford–Binet and again during the rest of the home visit. Rotated factor analyses yielded a Social Responsiveness dimension composed of the interest-in-persons and person-orientation items as rated both during the Stanford–Binet testing and during the rest of the visit. Two other factors, Cooperativeness and Reactivity, yielded separate factors for ratings during the Stanford–Binet testing and ratings during the rest of the home visit. For both types of ratings, however, the same items were involved: The cooperativeness dimension consisted of cooperativeness, resistant behavior (reversed), persistence, attention span, frustration level, and happiness. Reactivity included the following items: fearfulness (reversed), activity level, independence, reactivity, and expressiveness. Because independent factors emerged for these two factors during the two rating sessions, separate scales were constructed for cooperativeness and reactivity as rated during the Stanford–Binet testing and during the rest of the home visit.

The test–retest reliabilities of these scales are modest at 3 years: .46 for Social Responsiveness, .51 for Stanford–Binet Cooperativeness, .60 for Home-Visit Cooperativeness, .74 for Stanford–Binet Reactivity, and .71 for Home-Visit Reactivity. If these scales were used exclusively, longitudinal comparisons across infancy and early childhood would be lost, because the nature of the factors at 3 and 4 differs from the factors at 1 and 2. For this reason, analogs of the IBR factors in infancy were created from the revised IBR items used at 3 and 4. A scale of Affect–Extraversion was created summing interest in persons, cooperativeness, fearfulness, and happiness; Activity was assessed by an activity item; and a Task Orientation scale was composed of items assessing concentration, attention span, and frustration level.

The Colorado Childhood Temperament Inventory (CCTI; Rowe & Plomin, 1977) is a parental rating instrument employed at each age, with ratings obtained from fathers as well as mothers at 1, 2, and 3 years. The CCTI is an amalgamation of the EAS temperament dimensions described by Buss and Plomin (1975, 1984) and the nine dimensions of temperament postulated by the New York Longitudinal Study (NYLS; Chess & Thomas, 1984). Average ratings of mothers and fathers are used at 1, 2, and 3 years to improve the reliability of the ratings; at 4, mothers' ratings are used alone because fathers were not asked to complete the CCTI at 4 years. The same six scales are constructed from each year's data: Emotionality, Activity, Sociability, Attention Span-Persistence, Reaction to Food, and Soothability. The median alpha reliability of the six scales is .80, and the median 1-week test–retest reliability of children 2 to 6 years of age has been reported to be .73 (Rowe & Plomin, 1977). In the CAP, the median test–retest reliability is .66 for 1-year-olds.

A third source of information comes from the videotaped observations at 1 and 2 years. The rating instrument is one modified from the work of Matheny and Wilson (1981). Seven analogs of IBR ratings are used to create three scales comparable to the three IBR factors at 1 and 2 years. Analyses of videotapes from the 3-year home visit are in progress.

Behavioral problems. At each year, parents are asked to rate their children on 10 scales representing the nine NYLS dimensions of temperament and a general item of how difficult they perceive their child to be. A first principal component of these items yields a dimension of difficult temperament similar to other measures of this construct (Daniels, Plomin, & Greenhalgh, 1984). In infancy, parents were also asked to rate infants' specific behavioral problems with daily events such as sleeping, eating, and elimination; similar items were included at 3 years, but not at 4.

At 4, the parent rating version of the Child Behavior Checklist (CBC; Achenbach & Edelbrock, 1983) was added to the battery in order to obtain a standard measure of behavioral problems. The CBC consists of 118 3-point items that are scored on two second-order factors, Internalizing and Externalizing, and a total score, which yield 1-week test–retest reliabilities of .88, .95, and .92, respectively, for a sample of children 4 and 5 years of age. At 4 and 5 years, internalizing scores consist of the following behavior problem scales for both boys and girls: social withdrawal (e.g., "withdrawn," "won't talk," "stares blankly"), somatic complaints ("nausea," "stomach problems," "pains"), and depressed ("feels guilty," "worrying," "feels worthless"). In addition, internalizing problems include an immaturity scale for boys ("acts too young," "clumsy," "accident prone") and a schizoid/anxious scale for girls ("can't sleep," "hears things," "anxious"). Externalizing scales include an aggressive scale for both genders ("cruel to others," "disobeys at home," "destroys others' things"); in addition, for boys, a delinquent scale ("sets fires," "vandalism," "bad friends") and a schizoid scale ("sees things," "runs away," "sleeps little") are included; and additional scales for girls are a hyperactive scale ("hyperactive," "disobeys at school," "shows off") and a sex problem scale ("sex preoccupation," "wishes to be opposite sex," "plays with sex parts too much"). Norms for nonclinical as well as clinical samples are available.

Motor development. Motor development was assessed at 1 and 2 years by the Bayley Motor Scale (Bayley, 1969) and at 3 years using an extension of the Bayley Motor Scale developed by the CAP staff. The 3-year test includes drawing (vertical line, circle, horizontal line, 90-degree angle, asterisk), stacking blocks, stringing beads, throwing and catching a 3-inch-diameter ball, kicking a ball, jumping (both feet off floor, from bottom step, distance), walking (straight line, on tiptoe), standing (on left foot, on right foot), hopping, and balance beam (standing with both feet, attempting step, alternating steps, walking sideways, walking backward). The items were standardized and two motor scales, suggested by factor analyses of the items, were created: fine motor skills (drawing, stacking blocks, stringing beads, throwing, and catching) and gross motor skills (walking straight line, walking on tiptoe, standing on left foot, standing on right foot, and the balance beam items).

Miscellaneous. A 10-minute interview with the parent and a form for the child's pediatrician cover major health-related aspects of development. A simple rating of general health yielded a test–retest reliability of .55 at 1 year and .73 at 3 years. Height and weight are also assessed each year; test–retest reliabilities for height and weight are .94 and .96 at 1, respectively, and .92 and .90 at 3.

Each year, mothers are interviewed concerning the children's liking of general categories of objects such as gross motor, fine motor, and musical toys. Unfortunately, test–retest reliabilities at 3 years are low for a general scale of interest in artistic objects ($r = .40$) and interest in other objects ($r = .37$). At age 4, an attempt was made to develop scales of talents as well as interests that were more similar to those obtained from the parents. On the basis of the social competency items of the CBC and additional interview items, the children's favorite hobbies and activities were categorized and used as an expression of interests; talent for each of these was assessed by parental ratings of the child's relative ability. Six categories of interests and talents were employed: outdoor activities (other than the following), individual sports, team sports, performing arts, arts and crafts, and literary arts.

Finally, the videotapes at 1 and 2 years have been used to rate relative and absolute strength of hand preference (Rice, Plomin, & DeFries, 1984). Also, at 3 years, testers record hand preference during the testing of motor development, a scale that yields a test–retest reliability of .78.

Environmental measures

As mentioned earlier, the inclusion of measures of specific environmental factors within a longitudinal adoption design facilitates novel approaches to the analysis of environmental influences. CAP environmental data come from interviews and observations in the home and from parental questionnaires.

Home Observation for Measurement of the Environment. The core environmental measure is the HOME (Caldwell & Bradley, 1978), a semi-structured instrument appropriate for 1- and 2-year-olds that consists of 45 items, two-thirds of which are based on observations in the home and the remainder on parental reports. CAP 2-week test–retest reliability at 12 months for the HOME total score is .74.

The HOME was developed primarily for use in lower-class families; the HOME manual reports psychometric characteristics of the HOME for 174 Arkansas families in which 66% were black, 34% on welfare, and 29% with no father present. In order to increase its sensitivity in middle-class homes, a quantitative scoring system for the HOME was developed that can be used in place of the traditional dichotomous scoring, as described in the first CAP book. (A copy of the instrument used in CAP is included in the appendix of that book). Item scores were transformed by natural log and square root transforms as needed to improve their distributional characteristics; items with insufficient variance – that is, when a single score occurred more frequently than 90% – were eliminated from analysis. The quantitative scoring system was found to be superior to the usual dichotomous scoring, especially in terms of stability from 1 to 2 years.

Because the factor structure of the HOME does not correspond closely to the six scales that are traditionally scored for the HOME, CAP analyses rely primarily on scales derived from factor analysis of the quantitatively scored items. These variables include an unrotated principal component representing a general HOME factor and four scales representing rotated factors referred to as Toys, Maternal Involvement, Encouraging Developmental Advance, and Restriction-Punishment. The test–retest reliability at 12 months for the HOME general factor is .86; the reliabilities of the four rotated factors are .84, .74, .79, and .69, respectively.

The CAP required a HOME-like measure at 3 years before the preschool version of the HOME (Caldwell & Bradley, 1978) was generally available. For this reason, the CAP staff developed a toddler extension of the HOME, which is quite similar to the HOME used in infancy. A few HOME items were deleted, primarily because they did not yield sufficient variability: items 3, 4, 5, 6, 24, 25, 35, 36. Three items were added to provide more details concerning mothers' provision of structured learning experiences, formal instruction by others, and number of family members present at meals. Total number of hours child watches television was obtained by asking mothers whether and how frequently the child watched each of the major children's programs.

Quantitatively scored items yielded an unrotated first principal component that was dominated by items about toys, although other items also loaded moderately, such as amount of caregiving by father, frequency with which child gets away from house, and affectionateness of mother. We refer to factor scores based on this dimension as the HOME general factor. Its test–retest reliability is .79.

Rotated factors were also similar to those obtained in infancy, except that a Restriction-Punishment factor – which was a weak factor even in infancy – did not emerge in analyses of the 3-year HOME. The highest-loading items on the Toys factor were cuddly or role-playing toys, eye–hand coordination toys, and books and musical toys. The Encouraging Developmental Advance factor was defined by such items as mother consciously encourages developmental advance; mother provides structured learning experiences such as teaching colors, letters, and numbers; and mother provides toys or interesting activities for the child during the interview. The third HOME factor, Maternal Involvement, consists primarily of the following items: mother spontaneously praises child's qualities or behavior during visit; when mother speaks of or to child, her voice conveys positive feeling; mother shows positive emotional responses to praise of child offered by visitor; amount of time spent with child looking at books; and formal instruction. Scales were constructed by summing the highest-loading items on each factor, after all items were transformed to z scores in order to weight them equally. Although the test–retest reliability of the Toys scale was high ($r = .92$), the other two scales, Maternal Involvement and Encouraging Developmental Advance, yielded only moderate test–retest reliabilities ($r = .63$ and $.43$, respectively).

For the 4-year home visit, items from the preschool version of the HOME were used (Caldwell & Bradley, 1978), with some CAP additions. The only items that remain from the HOME used in infancy are items 8 (mother spontaneously praises child's qualities or behavior during visit), 9 (when mother speaks of child, her voice conveys positive feeling), 10 (mother caresses or kisses child during visit), 14 (mother slaps or spanks child during visit), 15 (mother reports that physical punishment occurred during the past week), 16 (mother scolds or derogates child during visit), and 41 (amount of caregiving by father). Twelve items were added to assess stimulation through toys and games. These items include counting the number of toys that facilitate the learning of colors and shapes such as pegboards; jigsaw puzzles; record player and children's records; artistic toys for free expression such as crayons and Play-doh; toys such as paper dolls, dot books, and coloring books; toys that facilitate the learning of numbers, such as blocks with numbers and books about numbers; children's books; toys for learning names and other information about animals; real or toy musical instruments; gross motor toys; role-playing or fantasy-play toys; and construction toys. In each case, the number of toys is assessed; the other items in the preschool HOME are also scored quantitatively, as counts or 5-point ratings, unless otherwise indicated.

Two items assess parental attempts to teach social skills: parent teaches child simple manners (rated yes or no); parent tries to get child to pick up and put away toys after play session. Other items assess maternal responsiveness and involvement (parent encourages child to relate experiences or takes time to listen to child relate experiences; mother converses with child during visit – scolding and suspicious comments not counted; mother answers child's questions or requests verbally); pride (the extent to which the mother encourages child to show off during visit; child's art work is displayed – scored as yes or no), and affection (the extent to which parents cuddle child). Other related items attempt to assess permissiveness: child is permitted some choice in lunch or breakfast menu; the extent to which child snacks, expresses negative feelings without harsh reprisal, is permitted to hit parent without harsh reprisal, and is physically restrained by parent during visit. The number of meals the child eats with mother and father present and the number of other people present at meals are also assessed.

Finally, a series of questions in the 4-year HOME assesses structured learning: the extent to which the parent encourages the child to distinguish shapes and teaches the child numbers and letters (unlike the preschool HOME, separate questions were not included to assess learning of colors,

Descriptive statistics

In this section, means and standard deviations are compared for the major parental, child, and environmental measures among the three types of parents, the adopted and nonadopted children, and the adoptive and non-adoptive homes. This presentation will free us in later chapters to focus on issues of individual differences.

Parental measures

Raw means and variances for the 13 cognitive test scores for adoptive, biological, and nonadoptive parents are presented in Table 4.3. Significant differences in variance occurred only for Paper Form Board and Picture Memory. Means differ significantly for most tests, biological parents generally scoring lower than the other two types of parents, especially on verbal tests. Other than a large difference on vocabulary, most of the other significant differences between biological parents and adoptive and non-adoptive parents account for only one-quarter of a standard deviation. Age is significantly related to cognitive scores and is confounded with parental type because the biological parents are about 10 years younger than the other parents. In addition, fathers scored higher than mothers on spatial tests and mothers outperformed fathers on the memory tests. Again, however, the largest differences amount to only half of a standard deviation. Nonetheless, the 13 scores were adjusted for age, age squared, and gender separately for each group of parents. The resulting standard scores – and the factor scores representing IQ (scores for the unrotated first principal component) and the four specific cognitive ability measures – thus do not differ in terms of means or variances for the three types of parents or for mothers and fathers.

Descriptive statistics for the EASI self-ratings and mate ratings are presented in Table 4.4, and similar information for the 16PF can be found in Table 4.5. As described in our previous book, the CAP parents are quite representative of the 16PF norms in terms of means and variances.

For the six groups of parents (mothers and fathers of each of the three types), a multivariate test for homogeneity of dispersion matrices indicated significant heterogeneity of variance for EASI self-ratings and mate ratings and for the 16PF primary and second-order scales; univariate tests for homogeneity of variance also indicated significant heterogeneity for most measures. However, with large samples, significant heterogeneity will be detected when differences among the group variances is very small; in the

Table 4.3. *Means and standard deviations for 13 cognitive test scores for parents*

Test	Biological mother (N = 243)		Biological father (N = 48)		Adoptive mother (N = 240)		Adoptive father (N = 232)		Nonadoptive mother (N = 234)		Nonadoptive father (N = 235)	
	Mean	SD	Mean	SD	Mean	SD	Mean	SD	Mean	SD	Mean	SD
Paper Form Board[a,b]	10.3	3.4	11.3	3.1	10.7	3.8	12.6	4.2	11.4	3.7	12.7	4.0
Card Rotations[a]	92.5	36.6	104.9	30.4	90.9	31.7	111.3	30.6	91.8	30.0	114.6	31.7
Hidden Patterns[a,b]	65.4	21.6	71.7	19.2	75.3	20.2	83.2	21.1	80.1	19.1	84.4	22.9
Identical Pictures	80.0	11.6	81.3	10.7	80.4	11.9	81.1	11.9	83.7	10.4	83.1	11.2
Progressive Matrices[a,b]	20.0	4.1	20.9	3.5	20.6	3.8	21.6	4.5	21.1	3.8	22.1	4.1
Things[b]	27.4	8.6	27.3	8.8	32.4	9.8	35.2	10.2	34.8	9.6	36.1	10.2
Vocabulary[b]	33.2	14.3	32.0	15.3	48.9	12.7	47.3	13.7	50.2	12.6	50.4	13.2
Word Beginnings and Endings[b]	17.6	6.4	16.3	5.2	19.5	6.8	18.3	7.3	20.9	6.7	19.9	6.9
Subtraction and Multiplication[b]	47.5	18.7	48.4	20.2	61.7	20.7	65.4	21.6	60.8	19.7	61.4	19.6
Colorado Perceptual Speed[a,b]	36.5	7.1	33.4	7.0	39.3	6.4	36.7	7.5	41.2	6.5	38.1	7.5
Pedigrees[a,b]	28.1	7.9	24.5	7.2	28.6	7.7	27.3	7.7	32.0	5.8	29.9	6.9
Picture Memory[a]	25.4	6.0	25.0	7.0	26.3	5.6	24.4	5.3	27.1	4.9	25.2	5.7
Names and Faces[a,b]	13.0	6.0	11.5	5.5	15.7	6.1	12.3	5.9	15.1	5.9	12.5	6.2

[a]Significant gender difference ($p < .01$).
[b]Significant difference among biological, adoptive, and nonadoptive parents ($p < .01$).

Table 4.4. *Means and standard deviations for the EASI Temperament Survey for CAP parents*

Measure	Biological mother		Biological father		Adoptive mother		Adoptive father		Nonadoptive mother		Nonadoptive father	
	Mean	SD	Mean	SD	Mean	SD	Mean	SD	Mean	SD	Mean	SD
EASI (self-rating)												
Emotionality-Fear[a,b]	13.7	3.6	11.7	3.0	12.4	3.1	10.3	2.6	12.9	3.4	10.2	2.8
Emotionality-Anger[b]	12.0	3.8	12.7	3.7	11.5	3.3	11.3	3.4	12.0	3.7	11.7	3.4
Activity[b]	16.0	3.1	17.7	3.6	17.0	3.2	17.2	3.1	16.2	3.3	17.6	3.3
Sociability[a,b]	17.9	4.3	16.6	3.6	18.6	3.6	16.3	3.7	17.5	3.9	16.2	3.9
Impulsivity[b]	13.2	3.1	14.2	3.0	11.7	2.8	11.8	2.7	12.4	2.8	12.6	2.9
EASI (mate rating)												
Emotionality-Fear[a,b]	15.5	3.3	11.2	3.3	14.5	3.4	8.9	2.8	14.5	3.5	9.3	2.9
Emotionality-Anger[a,b]	14.4	3.4	14.9	4.4	13.3	3.5	10.8	4.1	13.4	4.0	11.8	4.7
Activity	16.0	3.5	16.1	3.9	16.5	3.4	16.8	3.7	16.0	3.7	16.6	4.1
Sociability[a]	18.2	3.2	18.0	4.2	18.9	3.5	18.0	4.2	18.5	3.9	17.5	4.5
Impulsivity[b]	14.0	2.3	16.7	3.7	12.6	2.9	12.8	3.5	13.0	3.0	13.5	3.5

[a]Significant gender difference ($p < .01$).
[b]Significant difference among biological, adoptive, and nonadoptive parents ($p < .01$).

Table 4.5. *Means and standard deviations for the 16PF Questionnaire for CAP parents*

Measure	Biological mother Mean	SD	Biological father Mean	SD	Adoptive mother Mean	SD	Adoptive father Mean	SD	Nonadoptive mother Mean	SD	Nonadoptive father Mean	SD
Primary scales												
A. Outgoing[a]	9.6	3.1	7.3	3.0	10.1	3.3	7.9	3.5	9.5	3.1	7.7	3.4
B. Bright[b]	8.0	2.1	8.0	2.4	8.4	2.0	8.8	1.9	9.0	1.9	9.2	2.0
C. Emotionally Stable	16.0	2.8	15.1	3.7	16.4	3.7	17.2	3.8	15.8	3.9	16.7	3.7
E. Assertive[a,b]	11.4	3.9	14.0	3.3	11.3	4.9	14.1	4.4	12.6	4.5	15.7	4.2
F. Happy-go-lucky[b]	16.5	4.4	16.6	4.0	13.9	4.2	13.0	4.1	13.9	4.4	13.6	4.5
G. Conscientious[b]	11.7	3.4	11.3	3.7	13.9	2.8	14.3	2.9	12.8	3.4	13.3	3.4
H. Venturesome[b]	13.1	5.9	13.6	5.3	14.5	6.0	13.8	5.8	13.3	6.1	14.6	6.1
I. Tender-minded[a,b]	13.2	2.8	9.2	3.3	14.1	2.9	8.1	3.5	13.4	3.3	8.6	3.7
L. Suspicious[b]	8.0	3.1	9.7	3.3	6.7	3.1	7.3	3.5	7.2	3.4	7.6	3.5
M. Imaginative[a,b]	11.5	3.4	11.2	4.0	12.6	3.5	13.4	3.4	12.9	3.3	13.8	3.3
N. Astute[a]	9.5	2.7	8.6	2.2	9.2	2.9	8.5	3.0	9.2	2.9	8.1	2.8
O. Apprehensive[a,b]	12.1	3.6	10.9	4.0	10.6	4.2	8.5	3.7	10.8	3.9	8.6	3.8
Q1. Experimenting[a,b]	8.3	2.9	10.5	2.6	6.3	2.7	8.9	3.1	7.7	3.3	9.9	3.3
Q2. Self-sufficient	10.7	3.7	12.1	3.2	11.1	3.8	12.0	3.2	11.7	3.6	12.3	3.7
Q3. Controlled[a,b]	11.9	3.1	11.6	2.4	13.3	2.9	14.2	2.7	12.5	3.0	13.0	3.1
Q4. Tense[a]	14.2	2.8	14.0	4.5	14.0	4.9	11.9	4.9	14.7	4.8	12.3	5.0
Second-order factors												
QI. Extraversion[a,b]	48.8	17.7	53.8	13.1	57.2	19.8	50.8	17.1	53.5	19.4	52.7	16.9
QII. Neuroticism	51.8	18.5	57.2	15.4	56.5	18.2	55.3	16.0	56.2	17.1	55.5	16.0

[a]Significant gender difference ($p < .01$).
[b]Significant difference among biological, adoptive, and nonadoptive parents ($p < .01$).

66

present case, significant heterogeneity is detected when standard deviations differ on average by as little as 1%.

As indicated in the tables, numerous significant mean differences for gender and for parental type emerged, although it should be remembered that samples of this size provide statistical power to detect mean differences that account for only a small amount of variance. The largest mean difference (greater EASI Emotionality-Fear for females) is about three-quarters of a standard deviation for the self-report measure and about one and a half standard deviations for the mate-rating measure. Most of the other significant group differences represent less than half a standard deviation mean difference. For the 16PF second-order factors that are used in many of the analyses reported in this book, no significant mean differences for gender or for parental type were found for Neuroticism, although significant differences were found for Extraversion, accounting for .23 and .13 of a standard deviation for gender and parental type, respectively.

Common behavioral problems of parents were assessed using brief scales of depression, hysteria, and sociopathy. Means and standard deviations for these three scales are listed in Table 4.6. The sample size is lower for hysteria and sociopathy (about half the sample of biological parents and about two-thirds the sample of adopted and nonadopted parents) than for depression because these items were not added until after half of the biological parents had been tested. As expected, females had lower scores than males on sociopathy and higher scores on hysteria; however, no significant gender differences emerged for depression. Biological parents report more sociopathy and depression than do other parents; the differences represent less than half a standard deviation, however.

Child measures

Descriptive statistics for the Bayley Mental Development Index (MDI) at 1 and 2 years and the Stanford–Binet at 3 and 4 years are included in Table 4.7. Variances for the groups were not significantly heterogeneous in MANOVA analyses of adoptive status, gender, and their interaction. It is not clear why variances on the Stanford–Binet increase from 1 to 2 years on the MDI or why they decrease from 3 to 4. The variances at 2 and 3 years are nearly as high as those of the standardization samples. No significant mean effects were found for adoptive status except at age 4; at 2 and at 4, girls scored higher than boys, by about one-quarter of a standard deviation. The CAP means are about half a standard deviation above the standardization samples for the MDI and Stanford–Binet, which are based on samples stratified on the basis of urban–rural, race, and educational

Table 4.6. *Means and standard deviations for behavioral problems of CAP parents*

Measure	Biological mother		Biological father		Adoptive mother		Adoptive father		Nonadoptive mother		Nonadoptive father	
	Mean	SD	Mean	SD	Mean	SD	Mean	SD	Mean	SD	Mean	SD
Sociopathy[a,b]	0.98	0.37	1.2	0.45	0.71	0.14	1.1	0.29	0.79	0.24	1.1	0.34
Depression[b]	2.3	0.74	2.3	0.78	2.0	0.58	2.0	0.60	2.1	0.62	2.1	0.64
Hysteria[b]	1.9	0.77	1.7	0.82	1.8	0.58	1.6	0.61	1.9	0.61	1.6	0.58

Note: Means and variances differ from an earlier report (Plomin & DeFries, 1985a) because the summed scores for each scale have been divided by the number of items for each scale in the present analysis.

[a]Significant gender difference ($p < .01$).
[b]Significant difference among biological, adoptive, and nonadoptive parents ($p < .01$).

Table 4.7. *Means and standard deviations for IQ from 1 to 4 years*

Measure	Age	Adopted			Nonadopted		
		Mean	SD	N	Mean	SD	N
Bayley MDI	1	106.5	11.6	241	108.5	12.3	245
Bayley MDI[a]	2	107.3	14.7	212	108.4	16.0	229
Stanford–Binet IQ	3	104.4	14.0	203	107.3	14.2	195
Stanford–Binet IQ[a,b]	4	106.6	11.8	183	109.7	11.9	166

[a]Significant gender difference ($p < .05$).
[b]Significant difference between adopted and nonadopted children ($p < .05$).

Table 4.8. *Means and standard deviations for Bayley scales at 1 and 2 years*

Age	Measure	Adopted			Nonadopted		
		Mean	SD	N	Mean	SD	N
1	Means–End[a]	1.8	1.2	241	1.8	1.2	245
	Imitation[a,b]	1.9	1.5	241	2.4	1.7	245
	Verbal Skill[a]	1.7	1.1	241	1.7	1.1	245
2	Lexical[a]	8.5	3.2	215	8.6	3.0	229
	Spatial	0.8	2.0	215	0.9	2.1	229
	Verbal[a]	8.0	1.7	215	8.0	1.8	229
	Imitation	2.6	1.1	215	2.4	1.2	229

[a]Significant gender difference ($p < .05$).
[b]Significant difference between adopted and nonadopted children ($p < .05$).

attainment of the head of the household. For the Bayley MDI at 12 months, for example, the standardization sample consists of 94 children, 16% of whom lived in rural residences and 13% of whom were nonwhite; for 24% of the infants, the head of the household had had an eighth-grade education or less. With these differences in mind, it again appears that the CAP sample is reasonably representative of the white, urban–suburban, middle-class population.

Included in Table 4.8 are means and standard deviations for scales derived from the Bayley items. MANOVA analyses yielded significant gender differences for all three scales at 12 months; boys received higher scores than girls on the Means–End and Imitation scales, and girls outperformed boys on the Verbal Skill scale. At 24 months, genders did not differ significantly on the Spatial and Imitation scales; however, means for girls were significantly greater than means for boys for the Lexical and Verbal

Table 4.9. *Means and standard deviations for specific cognitive abilities at 3 and 4 years*

		Adopted			Nonadopted		
Age	Measure	Mean	SD	N	Mean	SD	N
3	Verbal	−0.05	0.79	201	0.08	0.81	194
	Spatial[a]	−0.09	0.82	201	0.10	0.79	194
	Perceptual Speed	−0.06	0.81	194	0.01	0.81	192
	Memory[a]	−0.18	0.93	198	0.15	1.04	192
4	Verbal[a,b]	−0.09	0.71	182	0.08	0.67	165
	Spatial	−0.07	0.86	182	0.00	0.84	165
	Perceptual Speed[b]	−0.11	0.94	177	−0.02	0.89	165
	Memory	−0.12	0.87	179	0.10	0.84	165

[a]Significant difference between adopted and nonadopted children ($p < .05$).
[b]Significant gender difference ($p < .05$).

scales. Only one significant difference emerged between adopted and non-adopted infants: The nonadopted infants scored higher than the adopted infants on the Imitation scale at 12 months. However, the 24-month Imitation scale revealed no such difference. Some significant heterogeneity of variance among the four groups of adopted and nonadopted boys and girls was detected; a multivariate test of the homogeneity of the variance–covariance matrices was nonsignificant.

Table 4.9 lists means and standard deviations for factor scores derived from the CAP batteries of specific cognitive abilities at 3 and 4 years. Variances for the groups were not significantly heterogeneous. No significant gender differences emerged at 3 years; at 4, girls scored higher on the Verbal factor and the Perceptual Speed factor. Nonadopted children scored higher than adopted children on the Spatial and Memory scales at 3 years and on the Verbal and Memory scales at 4 years. The unrotated first principal component also yielded higher scores for nonadopted than adopted at 3 and 4 years. Consistent with these results suggesting gender differences in verbal ability are the results for the SICD. At both 3 and 4 years and for both the Expressive and Receptive scales, girls outperformed boys; the mean differences account for about half a standard deviation at 2 and about one-third of a standard deviation at 3. No differences between adopted and nonadopted children were observed. The personality measures include testers' ratings on the IBR at 1 and 2 years and on a modification of the IBR suitable for use with 3- and 4-year-olds. Means and standard deviations for these scales are listed in Table 4.10; the results at 3 and 4 years are based on the IBR scales that employ analogs of the IBR

Table 4.10. *Means and standard deviations for the Infant Behavior Record*

Age	Scale	Adopted			Nonadopted		
		Mean	SD	N	Mean	SD	N
1	Affect-Extraversion	35.7	4.8	239	35.0	5.9	239
	Activity	17.8	3.2	234	17.6	3.1	238
	Task Orientation	21.7	3.5	237	22.0	3.5	237
2	Affect-Extraversion	35.7	6.8	216	35.6	6.9	229
	Activity	16.2	3.3	215	16.0	3.5	227
	Task Orientation	23.6	3.5	216	23.7	3.3	227
3	Affect-Extraversion	9.3	2.5	209	9.1	2.6	197
	Activity[a]	3.2	0.6	209	3.0	0.7	197
	Task Orientation	9.2	1.7	208	9.4	1.5	196
4	Affect-Extraversion	10.0	2.2	199	10.4	2.0	166
	Activity[a,b]	3.1	0.6	200	2.8	0.6	166
	Task Orientation[a,b]	9.7	1.5	200	10.1	1.2	166

Note: Because the factors at 3 and 4 years differ from those at 1 and 2, data are presented for 3- and 4-year analogs of the infancy factors from tester ratings during the administration of the Stanford–Binet; these are the scores used in longitudinal analyses.
[a]Significant gender difference ($p < .05$).
[b]Significant differences between adopted and nonadopted children ($p < .05$).

factors in infancy. None of the means differed significantly for boys and girls or for adopted and nonadopted children at 1 and 2. At 3 and 4, slight but significant mean gender differences emerged for activity; surprisingly, girls were rated more active than boys. At 4, adopted children were rated significantly higher in activity level and lower in task orientation than nonadopted children.

Table 4.11 lists means and standard deviations for CCTI ratings in which mothers' and fathers' scores have been averaged at 1, 2, and 3 years in order to increase the reliability of the measures. Two types of significant mean gender differences emerged: Boys were rated more active than girls at 1, 2, and 4 years, and parents rated girls more emotional than boys at 3 and 4 years. Adopted children were rated less emotional than nonadopted children at 1, 2, and 4 years; also, at 3 years only, adopted children were rated more sociable than nonadopted children.

Table 4.12 contains means and standard deviations for Difficult Temperament at all four years and, at 4 years of age, for total scores and for Internalizing and Externalizing scales of the CBC. For difficult temperament, no mean gender differences emerged; adopted children were rated less difficult than nonadopted children at 12 months only. For the CBC

Table 4.11. *Means and standard deviations for midparent ratings on the Colorado Childhood Temperament Inventory*

Age	Scale	Adopted			Nonadopted		
		Mean	SD	N	Mean	SD	N
1	Emotionality[a]	11.9	3.1	228	12.9	3.4	235
	Activity[b]	20.9	2.7	228	21.1	2.3	235
	Sociability	19.7	3.8	228	19.1	3.7	235
	Attention Span	17.3	2.4	228	17.4	2.2	235
2	Emotionality[a]	12.9	2.9	224	14.0	3.1	223
	Activity[b]	21.1	2.4	224	21.1	2.3	223
	Sociability	19.6	3.7	224	19.2	3.5	223
	Attention Span	17.7	2.7	224	17.4	2.7	223
3	Emotionality[b]	13.7	3.2	211	14.3	3.2	196
	Activity	20.5	2.6	211	20.3	2.6	196
	Sociability[a]	19.9	3.6	211	18.8	3.5	196
	Attention Span	17.6	2.8	211	17.7	2.8	196
4	Emotionality[a,b]	13.2	4.0	205	14.4	3.7	167
	Activity[b]	20.0	3.3	205	19.6	3.1	167
	Sociability	19.6	4.4	205	18.6	4.5	167
	Attention Span	17.9	3.3	204	18.0	2.9	166

[a]Significant difference between adopted and nonadopted children ($p < .05$).
[b]Significant gender difference ($p < .05$).

Table 4.12. *Means and standard deviations for parental ratings of behavioral problems*

Age	Measure	Adopted			Nonadopted		
		Mean	SD	N	Mean	SD	N
1[a]	Difficult Temperament	−0.09	0.97	226	0.10	0.98	232
2		−0.04	0.99	222	0.08	1.00	222
3		−0.11	0.97	204	−0.01	0.96	189
4		−0.05	0.94	203	0.06	0.99	165
4	Child Behavior Checklist:						
	Internalizing, boys	10.1	7.9	88	11.7	7.8	86
	Internalizing, girls	10.4	8.5	76	12.2	9.8	62
	Externalizing, boys	11.1	7.9	88	12.4	7.8	86
	Externalizing, girls	9.2	7.6	76	8.4	7.4	62
	Total problems	23.0	14.8	164	25.4	15.3	148

[a]Significant difference between adopted and nonadopted children ($p < .05$).

Table 4.13. *Means and standard deviations for Home Observation for Measurement of the Environment from 1 to 4 years*

Age	Measure	Adopted			Nonadopted		
		Mean	SD	N	Mean	SD	N
1	General factor[a]	0.05	1.1	239	0.22	1.0	241
	Toys[a]	−0.21	4.9	240	1.19	5.3	241
	Maternal Involvement[a,b]	0.43	3.1	210	−0.39	3.3	235
	Encouraging Developmental Advance	0.18	4.3	240	0.36	4.6	241
	Restriction-Punishment[a,b]	0.03	1.9	220	−0.55	1.8	222
2	General factor	0.09	1.0	213	−0.02	1.0	228
	Toys	0.14	4.8	214	0.95	5.1	228
	Maternal Involvement[b]	0.28	3.5	194	−0.17	3.1	220
	Encouraging Developmental Advance	0.45	4.5	212	−0.48	4.4	229
	Restriction-Punishment[a]	0.26	2.1	210	−0.36	1.8	229
3	General factor[a]	−0.25	1.0	202	−0.05	0.9	192
	Toys	−1.33	5.1	204	−0.51	4.5	190
	Maternal Involvement	0.47	3.2	209	0.04	3.2	200
	Encouraging Developmental Advance[b]	0.24	3.0	202	−0.14	2.7	193
4	General factor	−0.12	1.0	174	−0.01	0.9	159
	Toys	−0.94	7.3	176	−0.08	7.1	155
	Maternal Involvement	0.21	4.5	184	−0.29	4.1	165

[a]Significant difference for homes of boys and girls ($p < .05$).
[b]Significant difference between adoptive and nonadoptive families ($p < .05$).

Internalizing and Externalizing scales, means and standard deviations are presented separately for boys and girls because the scales include different items for boys and girls. Means for these scales and the total problems scores did not differ significantly for adopted and nonadopted children or for boys and girls.

Environmental measures

The two major environmental measures are the HOME, assessed at each year, and the FES, obtained at 1 and 3 years. Means and standard deviations for the HOME general factor and the scales derived from rotated factors are listed in Table 4.13. Significant variance differences emerged, but as indicated in Table 4.13, the differences are small and inconsistent; for example, although significant heterogeneity of variance was indicated for Maternal Involvement and Encouraging Developmental Advance at 1 and 2 years, nonadoptive families showed greater variance than adoptive families on these two scales at 1, but at 2, adoptive families had the greater variance.

In terms of mean differences on the HOME general factor, MANOVA analyses revealed no gender differences; at years 1 and 3, adoptive families obtained lower scores than nonadoptive families, although the differences were less than one-fifth of a standard deviation. For the rotated factors, more mean differences for gender and adoptive status occurred in year 1 than in the other years combined. At 12 months, adoptive scores were higher than nonadoptive scores for Maternal Involvement and Restriction-Punishment, and the reverse was the case for the Toys scale. Families with girls obtained higher scores than families with boys for Maternal Involvement; the reverse occurred for Restriction-Punishment. At 2 years, adoptive families continued to score more highly than nonadoptive families on the Restriction-Punishment scale; families with girls again scored higher on the Maternal Involvement scale. At year 3, only one significant group difference emerged: Families with boys obtained higher scores on the Encouraging Developmental Advance scale than families with girls. At 4, no significant group differences were observed. None of the group differences are large, however; the mean differences account for about one-quarter of a standard deviation.

Table 4.14 lists means and standard deviations for the 10 FES dimensions at 1 and 3 years. Families of boys and girls do not differ significantly for any of the scales at either year. At both 1 and 3 years adoptive parents reported less Conflict, less Intellectual-Cultural Orientation, and more Moral-Religious Emphasis than did nonadoptive parents. Of these, the only large difference concerns Moral-Religious Emphasis – for which adoptive families are also less variable than nonadoptive families – which is not surprising given the religious affiliations of the two adoption agencies. Even so, the difference is only about two-thirds of a standard deviation.

As expected from these group differences on the FES, the second-order FES factor, Personal Growth, yielded no significant difference between adoptive and nonadoptive families. Traditional Organization – which is composed primarily of the Moral-Religious, Organization, and Control dimensions – shows significantly greater scores for adoptive families. The difference accounts for one-half of a standard deviation at 1 year and one-third of a standard deviation at 3 years.

Cohort effects

During the past decade, interest in cohort effects has increased, due primarily to the life-span development movement (e.g., Baltes, Reese, &

Table 4.14. *Means and standard deviations for the Family Environment Scale at 1 and 3 years*

Age	Scale	Adopted			Nonadopted		
		Mean	SD	N	Mean	SD	N
1	*Relationship Dimensions*						
	Cohesion	37.9	3.8	220	37.3	4.1	235
	Expressiveness	32.1	3.8	220	32.3	4.1	235
	Conflict[a]	18.8	4.2	220	19.9	5.1	235
	Personal Growth						
	Independence	32.7	3.5	220	32.5	3.5	235
	Achievement Orientation	29.7	3.8	220	29.7	3.7	235
	Intellectual-Cultural Orientation[a]	29.9	5.3	220	31.3	5.0	235
	Active-Recreational Orientation	30.7	5.1	220	30.3	5.2	235
	Moral-Religious Emphasis[a]	34.2	5.8	220	29.2	8.1	235
	System Maintenance						
	Organization[a]	33.3	4.3	220	30.9	4.9	235
	Control[a]	26.5	4.1	220	25.3	4.7	235
3	*Relationship Dimensions*						
	Cohesion	36.8	4.4	209	36.3	4.7	195
	Expressiveness	31.7	4.0	209	32.0	4.0	195
	Conflict[a]	20.3	4.3	209	21.7	4.9	195
	Personal Growth						
	Independence	32.0	3.2	209	32.2	3.7	195
	Achievement Orientation	29.5	3.8	209	29.2	3.8	195
	Intellectual-Cultural Orientation[a]	30.4	5.4	209	31.7	5.0	195
	Active-Recreational Orientation	30.1	5.4	209	30.4	5.1	195
	Moral-Religious Emphasis[a]	34.5	5.7	209	30.2	7.6	195
	System Maintenance						
	Organization	32.8	4.2	209	31.3	5.0	195
	Control	28.1	3.6	209	27.2	4.3	195

[a]Significant difference between adopted and nonadopted families ($p < .05$).

Lipsitt, 1980; Elder, 1985). As mentioned earlier, the CAP probands were born during an 8-year period, which permits some limited exploration of cohort effects. Year of birth showed little relationship to cognitive variables. For example, the correlations with IQ at 1, 2, 3, and 4 years, respectively, were .09, $-.01$, $-.01$, and $-.04$. No systematic pattern emerged for specific cognitive abilities at 3 and 4 years. Although the SICD showed a significant effect for the expressive scale at 2 years ($r = .14$) and for the receptive scale at 3 years ($r = .13$), the total SICD score was not significantly related to year of birth.

Correlations between year of birth and gross motor development at 1, 2, and 3 years were .05, .19, and .25, respectively, suggesting that children born later (in the 1980s) achieved higher motor scores than children born earlier (in the 1970s). Even more surprising was that the largest correlation we observed in our cohort analyses was a negative correlation ($r = -.35$) for a scale of fine motor development at 3 years. (Fine motor development was assessed only at the 3-year home visit.)

Finally, a modest but systematic pattern of negative correlations emerged between year of birth and Attention Span at 2, 3, and 4 years and Soothability at 3 and 4 years; a positive correlation with Difficult Temperament was observed at 3 and 4 years. We have no hypotheses as to why the later birth cohorts were rated by their parents as lower in attention span, less soothable, and more difficult. It is noteworthy that the magnitude of these relationships is low (correlations of about .12); moreover, total problems on the CBC at 4 years showed no relationship to year of birth ($r = .01$). It seems likely that this is an effect of parental ratings, because tester ratings on the IBR showed no effects for Task Orientation at 3 years ($r = -.03$) and a positive correlation at 4 years ($r = .15$). A significant positive correlation with year of birth also emerged for IBR ratings of Affect-Extraversion at 4 ($r = .22$).

In sum, there are a few hints of relationships to year of birth, but the magnitude of these relationships is quite small; most variables show no cohort effect within the narrow range of birth years represented in the CAP.

Now that the Colorado Adoption Project and its measures have been introduced, subsequent chapters will turn to issues of greater substance. The next two chapters discuss developmental transitions and changes, specifically those in infancy and early childhood.

5 Transitions and changes: description and prediction

Infancy blossoms into childhood with the dramatic changes of the second and third years of life. These average changes from infancy to early childhood are so marked that one of the founders of developmental psychology, James Mark Baldwin (1894), suggested that, during the first year, infants possess only the properties of lower vertebrates; during the second year, they employ processes of higher vertebrates; not until the third year of life, however, do children begin to use cognitive processes characteristic of the human species. Although Baldwin's ontogeny-recapitulates-phylogeny interpretation of the changes from infancy to early childhood would find few adherents today, no one would deny that the average changes from infancy to early childhood are considerable. It is critical, however, to recognize that what we know about the transition from infancy to early childhood is limited primarily to average age differences rather than to individual differences.

This chapter discusses what is meant by developmental change in terms of individual differences rather than average age differences. Developmental change in terms of individual differences can be quite different from normative change because, as discussed in Chapter 2, the description and explanation of group differences are not necessarily related to individual differences. Indeed, it has been suggested that "there may be an inverse relationship between the suitability of a dimension as an expression of individual differences and its status as a dimension of major developmental change" (Wohlwill, 1973, p. 335).

In thinking about developmental changes and transitions in terms of individual differences, issues of variance and covariance, rather than means, are the focus of attention. We suggest that there are three major individual-differences issues relevant to the description of developmental change: (1) changes in variances of characteristics as a function of age, (2) changes in covariances among variables (factor structures), and (3) changes in age-to-age covariances. Only the last-named have received attention

77

from developmentalists – indeed, the lack of substantial age-to-age correlations has been the impetus for the shift from a model of constancy to
a model that emphasizes change as a proper focus of developmental research (Brim & Kagan, 1980; Wohlwill, 1973). At the outset, we should
state that we do not view change and continuity as a dichotomy (Hinde &
Bateson, 1984). In this chapter, we focus on change as an antidote to
decades of research on continuity; however, the methods and data described in this chapter consider both change and continuity.

Descriptive and predictive issues relevant to change and continuity during infancy and early childhood are the topic of the present chapter. The
following chapter considers genetic and environmental underpinnings of
developmental change. Etiological categories of developmental changes
mirror the descriptive changes: changes in variance (heritability and environmentality), changes in covariance structure within an age (genetic and
environmental correlations among measures), and changes in age-to-age
covariance (genetic and environmental correlations between the same
measures at different ages).

Because so little is known about developmental change from an individual-differences perspective, the primary goal of these two chapters is
merely to introduce these issues and to consider the forms that developmental change can take. We do not hope to provide definitive answers to
questions such as whether a transition from infancy to childhood occurs
or when and why it occurs, questions that will no doubt have different
answers for the various domains of development.

The word "transition" connotes something more than developmental
change; it suggests marked change – that is, discontinuity – from one state
or plateau to another. The distinction is somewhat semantic and researchers
are not consistent in their use of the term, especially with regard to individual differences. For example, if the prediction of a certain trait from
childhood to adulthood were substantial at 3 and 4 years but not at 2 years,
that period would probably be referred to as a transition. If, however,
long-term stability correlations increased linearly at 1, 2, 3, and 4 years,
the word "transition" might not be used even though developmental change
is evident. What is the magnitude of change and the time course needed
to qualify as a transition? In this chapter, we reserve the word "transition"
for statistically significant, nonlinear changes that occur within a year or
less during infancy and early childhood. Changes that are more gradual
are referred to as developmental changes, but not transitions.

One other preliminary remark is in order. A problem arises in comparing
variances and covariances (as well as means) across ages: Because many
new abilities emerge during the first few years of life, the content of be-

havioral measures often changes substantially, especially for ability measures such as cognition, language, and motor development. For example, there is little overlap between the items used on the 12- and 24-month Bayley tests. This is not so great a problem for nonability domains – temperament, for example – although, even for these domains, changes in motoric, linguistic, and cognitive capabilities must at least affect the choice of behaviors assessed before and after the transition (Dunn, 1986). When measures change, it is difficult to make comparisons across ages.

Nearly 40 years ago, Nancy Bayley (1949) described this problem in relation to cognitive development:

Ideally, for purposes of measuring the rates of intellectual growth in individual children, we should be able to measure the same children from birth to maturity on a single test which is applicable over the entire age range. Such a test, furthermore, should be calibrated in absolute units, so that velocities of growth in individuals and over different segments of the span may be compared directly. However, in spite of repeated efforts to produce them there are no existing intelligence tests which meet either of these criteria. It now seems unlikely, from the very nature of the growth of intellectual abilities, that such a test can ever be devised. The mental behaviors which are developing during the first year of life are very different from those developing in the three-year-old who has learned to talk fluently, and these in turn are very different from the complex mental functions of later ages. (pp. 165–6)

The most blatant case involves the emergence of language abilities during the second year of life. If a test of infant mental development contained no language items at 12 months and added numerous language items at 24 months, it would not be surprising to find change in the factor structure from 12 to 24 months. Our answer to this problem is pragmatic: It is important to know the extent to which a general factor of infant cognitive functioning correlates with a general factor at 24 months. It is also important to know the extent to which the general factor as we measure it at 12 and 24 months represents linguistic content as well as other abilities. If language items at 12 months were intentionally excluded, low correlations between 12 and 24 months or different factor structures are artifactual. However, if linguistic processes become increasingly important during the second year for all children, the effect of this normative change on individual differences is not without interest.

Changes in variance

The most basic developmental change relevant to individual differences is a change in variance. Changes in variance are important because they implicate changes in genetic or environmental influences, as discussed in the next chapter. A temporary increase in variance will occur, for example, if individual differences in timing of the developmental change are important. During the period of change, variance due to differences in the timing of the onset of a normative change could add to variance existing before and after the transition.

More permanent changes in variance might be observed if different processes affect a trait before and after a transition. Increases in variance seem more likely than decreases because new processes brought to bear on traits are likely to magnify extant differences among children. For example, individual differences in older children's shyness presumably involve cognitive, symbolic processes in addition to whatever processes are responsible for individual differences in shyness among younger children. Moreover, increases in variance might be expected simply because older children can do more than younger children, which means that there is greater opportunity to observe differences among older children. For example, productive vocabulary is not likely to differentiate children much at 14 months, when, on the average, children say two words, as compared to later in childhood, when children's vocabularies include hundreds of words.

Nancy Bayley (1949) was especially interested in developmental changes in variance for mental age:

> More significant than the means, it seems to me, is the trend of the standard deviations of mental ages. . . . The SD's are too small during most of the first year and too large after seven years, and especially at 9, 10, and 11 years. These variations cannot be attributed to inequalities in the sampling of cases, as they are based on essentially the same cases throughout.

In particular, Bayley (1949) explored a sharp drop in variance toward the end of the first year of life and concluded:

> For all tests and samples, and for different methods of scoring, there is decreased variability in scores at or near one year of age, with the SD's increasing as we go either up or down the age scale from there. The consistency of these trends suggests that children are less variable in their behavior-maturity patterns at one year than earlier or later. (p. 176)

Bayley speculated that the restricted variability is "due to the approach to maturity of the particular processes being measured" (p. 178), a "ceiling" effect hypothesis.

Increases in variance during early childhood have been posited on theoretical grounds. For example, Robert McCall (1981, 1983) proposed a "scoop" model of mental development, at the core of which lies the hypothesis that variance increases substantially beginning at about 2 years of age and continuing to about 6 years. This hypothesis follows from the assumption that mental development during infancy is strongly canalized:

When development is less canalized, the self-righting tendency is weaker, individuals differ from one another to a greater extent, and individual differences are more likely to persist through time because there is less pull by nature to keep her children in single file. (McCall, 1983, p. 114)

Sandra Scarr (1983) has made a similar argument from an evolutionary perspective in which she suggests "that infant intelligence is phenotypically less variable than later intelligent behavior because it has been subjected to longer and stronger natural selection" (p. 193).

Assessing changes in variance

Many statistics are available for assessing the significance of differences in variances for two independent samples, as in cross-sectional studies. The most widely used statistics are Hartley's F-max, Bartlett's test, and Cochran's C, although numerous other tests are available (O'Brien, 1978). F-max, for example, is simply the ratio of the largest variance over the smallest variance. Cochran's test uses information in addition to the largest and smallest variances. Bartlett's test yields a chi-square distribution and, although widely used, is not recommended (Winer, 1971). Because all of these tests are sensitive to departures from normality, significant differences in variances should be interpreted cautiously for non-normal distributions.

For longitudinal comparisons, tests assuming independent samples will underestimate differences between variances at different ages. An adjustment is needed for the correlation between the ages. McNemar (1969) suggests a formula that is essentially the difference in variances divided by the pooled variance corrected for covariance. This yields a t with $N - 2$ degrees of freedom:

$$t = \frac{(s_1^2 - s_2^2)/(N - 2)}{\sqrt{4s_1^2 s_2^2(1 - r_{12}^2)}}$$

However, this formula does not take mean changes into account, nor do model-fitting approaches in which a variance–covariance matrix of measures at different ages is analyzed to test whether the fit of the model is significantly reduced when variances are equated. As mentioned earlier, when measures or means change across age, it is difficult to compare variances. One simple solution, by no means completely satisfactory, is to employ the coefficient of variation (CV), dividing the standard deviation by the mean (e.g., Snedecor & Cochran, 1980), although no test of differences in CVs is available.

A special problem occurs with measures such as IQ tests that yield deviation scores based on standardization samples at each age, which elim-

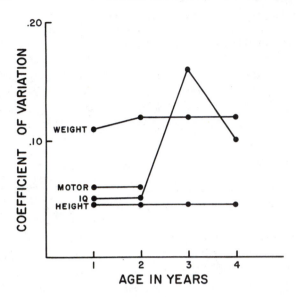

Figure 5.1. Coefficients of variation for CAP physical, cognitive, and motor measures.

inates age differences in variance. A similar problem ensues when scores are standardized, such as are factor scores, for example. In these cases, unstandardized scores must be used. Another problem is that variances are correlated with means. For example, from 12 to 24 months, mean height increases from 29.8 inches to 34.1 inches; the standard deviation also increases from 1.4 to 1.6. However, the CV – dividing the standard deviation by the mean – remains unchanged from 12 to 24 months for height. In the Berkeley Growth Study, the CVs for mental age at 6-month intervals from 6 months to 60 months are .133, .068 (the drop in variance at 12 months noted by Bayley), .120, .118, .121, .121, .111, .127, .129, and .140.

CAP changes in variance

Because of the paucity of data on the topic of changes in variance from infancy to early childhood, we examined the CAP data at 1, 2, 3, and 4 years from this perspective. Figures 5.1, 5.2, and 5.3 depict CVs for selected CAP measures. Results for height, weight, and cognitive measures in Figure 5.1 indicate that CVs for height and weight are unchanging from 1 to 4 years; the CV for weight is twice as great as the CV for height. CVs for

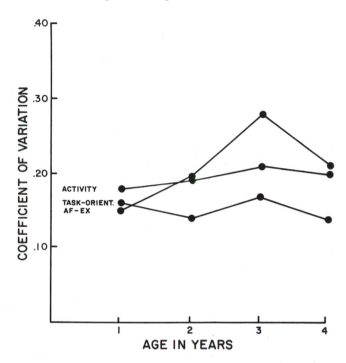

Figure 5.2. Coefficients of variation for CAP Infant Behavior Record measures (AF-EX, Affect-Extraversion).

Bayley mental and motor scores at 1 and 2 are low; it should be noted that the CAP data do not replicate the Berkeley Growth Study finding that CVs for Bayley scores dip at 12 months. CVs for Stanford–Binet scores at 3 and 4 years (.13 and .10, respectively) are twice as large as CVs for Bayley scores for 1 and 2 (.05 and .05, respectively). Although it is not possible to evaluate the statistical significance of this developmental change in variance, the twofold increase in the CV for IQ in early childhood is noteworthy.

Figure 5.2 indicates that CVs for Infant Behavior Record (IBR) tester ratings of personality are generally higher than CVs for height, weight, and IQ. CVs are similar for the three IBR dimensions and for the four ages, ranging only from .14 to .28. Parental ratings on the Colorado Childhood Temperament Inventory (CCTI) suggest some differentiation among the CCTI scales, as shown in Figure 5.3. Similar to the IBR, CVs do not change substantially across infancy and early childhood.

In general, this first examination of CVs during infancy and early childhood reveals little evidence for developmental change in variance although

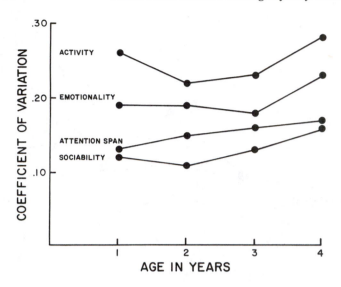

Figure 5.3. Coefficients of variation for CAP Colorado Childhood Temperament Inventory scales.

CAP results provide some support for the generally accepted hypothesis that variance for cognitive measures increases from infancy to early childhood. An absence of change in phenotypic variance, however, does not necessarily imply that similar results will be found for other descriptors of developmental change – changes in factor structures and changes in covariance between ages.

Changes in factor structure

Transitions can be marked by changes in covariances among variables, which might be expected if constituent processes change during development. For example, language items might correlate highly with nonverbal cognitive items during the transition from infancy to early childhood as language begins to assume its symbolic role in communication and becomes an important component of *g*, general cognitive ability. When more than a few measures are involved, factor analysis can be used to summarize the pattern of intercorrelations. This facet of developmental change implies an important aspect of transitions: reorganization or restructuring of processes.

Two aspects of developmental change in factor structure can be examined: differences in the strength of factors – the amount of variance they explain – and differences in the nature of the factors, seen in the pattern of factor loadings.

Werner's (1948) orthogenetic principle states that development is marked by differentiation. Although the principle is phrased in terms of normative developmental changes, from an individual-differences perspective, differentiation is seen as a decline in the magnitude of intercorrelations among measures. In a multivariate context, this can be expressed as a decrease in the amount of variance explained by an unrotated first principal component. For example, items on tests of infant mental development would intercorrelate to a greater degree in infancy than in early childhood if cognitive abilities differentiate during the transition. As an example from the realm of temperament, it has been hypothesized that fear and anger differentiate from primordial distress during infancy (Buss & Plomin, 1984); thus, we would expect to see less variance explained by a general distress factor following differentiation. We could also examine developmental changes in the strength of rotated factors, although this is complicated by the order in which rotated factors are extracted and it shades into the next issue, changes in the nature of factors.

A second aspect of developmental change in factor structure involves changes in the pattern of unrotated and rotated factor loadings. For example, does the nature of general cognitive ability change during the transition from infancy to early childhood? Do relationships among receptive and expressive language abilities change during the transition? Does the organization of temperament change?

Changes in the strength of factors

Cognitive development. The CAP data have been utilized to explore the factor structure of the Bayley Mental Scale in infancy (Plomin & DeFries, 1985a). The task is complicated by the fact that many items on the Bayley are interdependent. For example, at 12 months, three separate items involve putting 1, 3 or more, or 9 cubes in a cup. We managed this problem by sorting such interdependent items into scales. Items and scales were deleted from factor analysis if they showed less than 10% variability. For 12-month-olds, this procedure resulted in the selection of 16 items and 6 scales; for 24-month-olds, 4 items and 12 scales were selected. At 12 months, the unrotated first principal component accounted for 18% of the variance; at 24 months, the general factor accounted for 23% of the variance.

We examined the factor structure of the Stanford–Binet items for the CAP children at 3 and 4 years using a similar procedure. At 3 years, 13 items and 2 scales yielded an unrotated first principal component that accounted for 18% of the variance; at 4 years, 10 items and 1 scale yielded a principal component that accounted for 21% of the variance.

In addition, as described later, we developed batteries of specific cognitive abilities for 3- and 4-year-olds in the CAP. Using similar tests at 3 and 4 years, we found that the first principal component at 3 and 4 accounted for approximately 30% of the variance, which is much greater than the variance explained by the unrotated first principal components for Bayley items and scales; it is also similar in magnitude to the amount of variance explained by *g* in studies of adults (Jensen, 1980). For the CAP parents, the first principal component accounts for 36% of the variance.

Thus, these results suggest some developmental change in that the first principal component, *g*, accounts for an increasing amount of variance from 1 to 4. Contrary to the differentiation hypothesis, no decreases in intercorrelations are indicated. Although some developmentalists deny any important role for *g* in infancy (e.g., Lewis, 1983), we suggest that it plays a modest role during infancy and early childhood. This does not imply that all aspects of cognitive functioning can be described by a single factor; specific cognitive abilities are discussed later.

Temperament. The hypothesis of differentiation seems more reasonable for noncognitive domains such as temperament. Moreover, it is somewhat easier to assess similar behaviors in infancy and early childhood for temperament characteristics than it is for mental development. Thus, comparisons of factor structures across ages for temperament are less likely to be affected by artifacts of measurement.

A recent report of parental rating and videotape observation data from the Louisville Twin Study (LTS) included data relevant to the issue of developmental changes in factor structures (Wilson & Matheny, 1986). For parental ratings of temperament, an unrotated first principal component at 9, 12, 18, and 24 months accounted for 31, 27, 28, and 29% of the variance, respectively. Videotapes of children reacting to standardized situations in the laboratory were rated for emotional tone, activity, attentiveness, and orientation to staff. The first principal component for these four ratings at 9, 12, 18, and 24 months, respectively, accounted for 40, 47, 46, and 45% of the variance. Thus, these results do not suggest that the LTS temperament ratings based on parental ratings or videotape observations differentiate during the first two years. In the LTS, tester ratings on the IBR have also been obtained, but the variance explained by an unrotated first principal component has not been reported.

Tester ratings and parental ratings from the CAP at 1, 2, 3, and 4 years were used to explore this issue further. For the parental ratings on the CCTI, the percentages of variance accounted for by an unrotated first principal component at 1, 2, 3, and 4 years were 22, 19, 22, and 19, respectively. For the tester ratings on the IBR, the corresponding variance percentages were 18, 18, 24, and 25. Finally, factor analysis of the videotape ratings yielded 41 and 45% variance at 1 and 2 years.

These initial analyses yield no evidence of developmental differentiation of temperament during infancy and early childhood. For mental development, we suggest that convergence rather than divergence prevails in the transition from infancy to early childhood.

Changes in the nature of cognitive factors

In addition to developmental changes in the strength of factors, we can compare patterns of loadings as a function of age for both unrotated and rotated factors.

Changes in the unrotated first principal component. Does the pattern of loadings of items on the first principal component of infant mental test items change during infancy and early childhood? McCall and his colleagues have used this approach in analyses of Gesell items from the Fels study (McCall, Hogarty, & Hurlburt, 1972) and in analyses of the Berkeley Growth Study for the California First-Year Test, the precursor of the Bayley test (McCall, Eichorn, & Hogarty, 1977). In the latter study, comparisons of factor loadings for first principal components for 25 ages from 1 month to 5 years led to the conclusion that the most marked changes occur at 8, 13, and 21 months. The nature of the first principal component at the three ages, respectively, was described as separation of means from ends, entity–entity relations, and symbolic relationships (McCall, 1979). Although the first principal components are not easily interpreted, it is clear that unrotated first principal components at 12 months largely involve fine motor and gross motor skills; at 24 months, the general factor is primarily verbal in nature; the 18- month principal component is intermediate.

Similar results were obtained in the CAP at 12 and 24 months (Plomin & DeFries, 1985a). At 12 months, all but six of the items/scales described earlier load above .30 on the first principal component. The scale scores for Pegboard, Cubes in Cup, Scribbles, and Blueboard load above .50; language items such as "imitates words" and "says two words" load less highly, .43 and .39, respectively. At 24 months, the principal component is marked primarily by verbal items. The highest-loading scales are "names pictures" (.86), "names objects" (.75), "points to pictures" (.71), and "names watch" (.56).

CAP analyses of 3- and 4-year Stanford–Binet items also indicate that the nature of *g* is substantially verbal. At 3, the highest-loading items include a scale of comprehension items (.63), definitions (.62), an analogies scale (.58), picture vocabulary (.51), and picture comparisons (.50). The highest-loading items at 4 years involve an analogies scale (.67), vocabulary (.57), number concepts (.54), and copying a square (.51). It is interesting that, although number concepts and figure-copying items are included at 3 years, these items loaded only .37 and .25, respectively, on the first principal component at 3. Although *g* at both 3 and 4 years is without doubt dominated by verbal items, the appearance of nonverbal items at 4 years is noteworthy, suggesting that *g* may come to encompass increasingly varied abilities.

A persistent problem in such comparisons is that items of a different nature are used at different ages. For example, few language items appear until the second half of the second year. The old saw that "you get out of factor analysis only what you put in" raises the distinct possibility that factor analyses find greater loadings of language items during the second half of the second year simply because it was not possible to include language items earlier. This objection does not make the finding trivial, however, as mentioned earlier. Although the number of language items is greater in tests toward the end of the second year, these items might not have loaded so highly on the *g* factor – indeed, the few language items included at 12 months do not load highly on that factor.

Changes in rotated factors. The nature of rotated factors may also change during infancy and early childhood. It would seem reasonable, for example, to posit that specific cognitive abilities differentiate during childhood in the sense that verbal, spatial, and memory abilities become more distinct. However, factor-analytic work of this type has rarely been conducted because infant tests have emphasized *g*.

Stott and Ball (1965) summarized the results of rotated factor solutions for various infant tests administered to a total of 1,926 infants and young children. The California First-Year Scale was used only at 6 and 12 months, as was the Gesell test. The Merrill–Palmer was employed at 24, 30, 36, and 48 months, and the Stanford–Binet was used at 36 and 48 months. Comparisons among the factors at different ages was complicated by the necessity of using different tests; the Merrill–Palmer, for example, assesses motor function to a greater extent and language function to a lesser extent than does the California First Year or the Stanford–Binet. Nonetheless,

Stott and Ball (1965) concluded that factor structures change with age, although specifics of these developmental changes remained elusive.

In the CAP, factor analyses of Bayley and Stanford–Binet items/scales were conducted. As mentioned earlier, interdependent items were sorted into scales; items and scales showing less than 10% variability were eliminated. For the Bayley test, 16 independent items and 6 scales were analyzed for 12-month-olds, and 4 items and 12 scales were used for 24-month-olds. Details of these analyses were presented in our earlier book (Plomin & DeFries, 1985a). At 12 months, three factors were rotated. The first factor correlated with the Pinkboard, Blueboard, and Pegboard scales; the second factor involved imitation somewhat more, in that it included high loadings for cubes in cup and puts beads in box, measures that involve modeling; and the third was a lexical factor involving two items, imitates words and says two words.

The factor-analytic results for the 24-month-olds were not much more satisfactory. Four factors were rotated. The first factor is clearly lexical, with its highest loadings for sentence of two words, names objects, names pictures, and names watch. The second factor also involves language, perhaps reception more than production, with high loadings for discriminates three and points to pictures. The third factor, similar to the first factor at 12 months, has high loadings for the Pinkboard and Blueboard scales, which may require spatial ability. Also similar to a 12-month factor is the fourth factor, which involves tower of cubes, folds paper, and scribbles, measures that involve imitation.

Alternative approaches – such as rotating more factors, using tetrachoric correlations for the dichotomous items, and different methods of factor extraction and rotation – did not substantially improve the solutions at 12 and 24 months. In summary, the rotated factors for the Bayley items suggest increasing differentiation of language-related measures from 12 to 24 months. Similar results using Bayley items have been reported by Michael Lewis (1983; Lewis, Jaskir, & Enright, 1986).

Stanford–Binet items and scales for the CAP 3- and 4-year-olds were submitted to factor analysis. The factor structure at 3 years yielded only single-item factors, except that one factor consisted of two comprehension language items: comprehension and definitions. The structure at 4 years was somewhat more interesting, consisting of a verbal factor with loadings on analogies, definitions, and vocabulary, and a spatial-like factor with loadings on copying a square, rectangles, and number concepts. It is interesting that the same types of items loaded on the first principal component at 4 years but not at 3. One possible explanation of these results is that *g* comes to encompass increasingly complex abilities at 4, while at the same time specific cognitive abilities begin to diverge. However, interpretations of such item analyses are complicated by the fact that the Stanford–Binet was not designed to assess specific cognitive abilities.

CAP battery of specific cognitive abilities. Although the items of the Bayley and Stanford–Binet yield some relevant information concerning developmental changes in the factor structure of cognitive processes, these tests were designed to assess g rather than specific cognitive abilities. In infancy, several attempts have been made to assess Piagetian features of development (Uzgiris, 1983), although the most notable is the Uzgiris–Hunt (1975) Ordinal Scales of Psychological Development in Infancy. Even though the seven scales scarcely intercorrelate (King & Seegmiller, 1973), factor analyses of the scales have been conducted; the factor structure shows some differences at 14, 18, and 22 months (Wachs & Hubert, 1981).

The McCarthy Scales of Children's Abilities (McCarthy, 1972) is the only commercially available test designed to assess specific abilities in children younger than 5 years of age. However, a factor analysis of the tests revealed the presence of only three factors in early childhood: General Cognitive, Motor, and Memory (McCarthy, 1972); only the last factor would be regarded as a specific cognitive ability. The intercorrelations among the tests are so high – the average correlation among the verbal, perceptual, quantitative, and memory tests at 4 years is .62 – that the McCarthy scales are not useful for assessing distinct cognitive abilities.

As part of the CAP, batteries of tests were constructed to assess Verbal, Spatial, Perceptual Speed, and Memory factors, using similar tests at 3 and 4 years, as described in Chapter 4. The factor structures at 3 and 4 years were quite similar. At both ages, four rotated factors emerged with eigenvalues greater than 1.0, each of the four factors accounted for about 10% of the total variance, and the loadings indicated that the four factors were clearly the hypothesized factors Verbal, Spatial, Perceptual Speed, and Memory. The only difference between the two ages was that the structure at 4 years was somewhat simpler in that tests hypothesized to load on a factor loaded higher on that factor and lower on the other factors. Nonetheless, confirmatory factor analysis of the 4-year data indicates that the best-fitting model involves correlated rather than orthogonal factors. Thus, the similarities between the factor structure of cognitive abilities at 3 and 4 by far outweigh any differences.

In summary, all we can say with confidence at this time about changes in factor structure for cognitive abilities is that individual differences in language development play an increasingly important role in mental development. The increased presence of verbal items on unrotated first principal components and on rotated factors emerges primarily during the second year of life. However, we are also confident that there is much more to learn about changes in the organization of specific cognitive abilities during infancy and early childhood. For example, our analyses of Stanford–Binet items in early childhood suggest that *g* encompasses increasingly diverse cognitive functions while, at the same time, cognitive abilities begin to diverge.

Changes in the nature of temperament factors

Does the factor structure of temperament shift during infancy and early childhood? As mentioned earlier, the comparison of factor structures across age for temperament has an advantage over comparisons involving cognitive development because similar items can be used to assess temperament in infancy and early childhood.

Factor analyses from the Louisville Twin Study. Data from the LTS are relevant to the first two years of life (Wilson & Matheny, 1986). Three types of temperament data have been obtained: parental ratings, tester ratings on the IBR, and ratings from videotapes of children reacting to standardized situations in the laboratory. For parental ratings and videotape ratings, only a first principal component was examined. For both parental rating and videotape rating data, the patterns of loadings on the first principal component were similar at 9, 12, 18, and 24 months, providing little support for the hypothesis that the organization of temperament is transformed during the first two years.

One of the best comparisons of factor structures for temperament during the first two years involves the IBR data from the LTS, as reported by Adam Matheny (1980). For a sample of 300 to 400 infants at 3, 6, 9, 12, 18, and 24 months, 25 rating scales were submitted to factor analysis with rotation. Matheny concluded that "the analyses provided 5 major factors and 2 minor factors that were considerably consistent at all ages" (p. 1157). The only notable developmental changes were changes in the amount of variance accounted for by the factors; these changes, however, appear to be due to the order in which the rotated factors were extracted.

Factor analyses from the CAP. Tester ratings on the IBR and parental ratings on the CCTI were included in the CAP assessments at 1, 2, 3, and 4 years. As reported in the CAP book on infancy, the rotated factor structures of these two measures changed little from 1 to 2 years. Comparisons between infancy and early childhood are weakened for the IBR

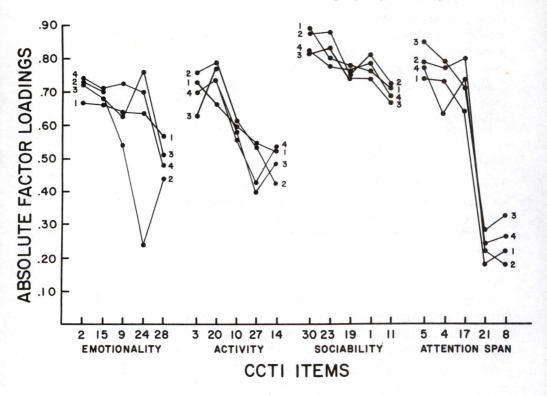

Figure 5.4. Absolute factor loadings for Colorado Childhood Temperament Inventory items at years 1, 2, 3, and 4 in CAP.

by the fact that fewer items were used in the early childhood version. As described in Chapter 4, the IBR factors in early childhood are different from those in infancy, although the results at 3 and 4 years are similar. A general factor in infancy that involved emotionality and social responsiveness is differentiated at 3 and 4 years into separate factors of Social Responsiveness, Reactivity, and Cooperativeness. An Activity factor seen in infancy does not emerge in early childhood, although this is an artifact because only one activity item was included in the early childhood measure. In contrast to the infancy data, no clear Task Orientation factor emerged in early childhood – persistence and attention span load on the Cooperativeness factor.

Not much can be made of these differences in IBR factor structure, however, because of the differences in items used in infancy and early childhood. For the CCTI, the same items were used at all four ages and the factor structures are similar across the ages. As indicated in Figure 5.4, the factor structure of these items is remarkably similar from 1 to 4 years of age. The only exception to nearly complete similarity is item 24 on the Emotionality scale, which shows much lower loadings on the scale at 2 years of age than at other years; this could be a real difference in that the item is "child gets upset easily," which shows reduced variance at 2, perhaps because during the "terrible twos" most children are easily upset.

Nonetheless, the overwhelming impression from Figure 5.4 is substantial similarity of factor structure across all four years for the CCTI. It is possible that the similarity of structure for these parental ratings of temperament resides in the minds of parents rather than in the behavior of children; it is interesting, nonetheless, that the factor structures of parental ratings on the CCTI are so similar throughout infancy and early childhood. The CCTI primarily assesses emotionality, activity, and sociability, traits that show the greatest heritability and stability in childhood (Buss & Plomin, 1984); other dimensions of personality might show greater developmental change in factor structure.

In summary, although some changes in factor structure are observed during infancy and early childhood, no sharp transitions occur. Changes are seen primarily in cognitive development rather than temperament. The clearest finding concerns the nature of the unrotated first principal component: Language items become increasingly important, especially from 1 to 2 years of age. Rotated factors suggest some differentiation of language-related and spatial abilities in early childhood.

Age-to-age correlations

That age-to-age stability increases from infancy to early childhood has been elevated to the status of a basic law of individual differences in development. For example, Clarke and Clarke (1984) conclude:

Hundreds of reports illustrate two general laws originally advanced in relation only to IQ but which, with very rare exceptions, also apply to the development of all psychological characteristics (e.g., temperament, attainments, personality). First, measures of infant behavior scarcely predict later ordinal position within a group. There are probably two reasons for this: these scores must inevitably relate to qualities which have little overlap with those exhibited in later childhood or adult life. Moreover, many important characteristics have not yet emerged, even incipiently, and so are not available for predictive measurement.

The second law (as noted) is that, regardless of age, the longer the period over which assessments take place, the lower the correlation is likely to be, that is, the greater the change in ordinal position of individuals within a group. (p. 197)

The second law is usually referred to as the simplex pattern of longitudinal correlations. The simplex pattern bears on the issue of age-to-age correlations during the transition because it raises the question of whether changes in stability from infancy to early childhood are disordinal. That is, the simplex pattern implies that predictions to adulthood will increase year by year during infancy and early childhood. The word "transition," however, implies a marked change, greater than expected on the basis of the simplex pattern.

Although such a transition from infancy to early childhood is generally accepted, the evidence has not been carefully examined. Do age-to-age correlations change during infancy and childhood for physical characteristics, temperament, and behavioral problems in addition to mental development? Are the developmental changes in age-to-age correlations abrupt or linear? When do the changes occur?

In the following sections, we review longitudinal data, including new data from the CAP, on height and weight, cognition, temperament, and behavioral problems. Three types of data are relevant. The first type relies on age-to-age correlations during infancy and childhood. In the arena of individual differences, this type of developmental change has received the most attention. Although the problems of interpreting differences in age-to-age correlations are considerable (Bateson, 1978), the basic idea is that, if an individual-differences transition exists, correlations during early childhood should exceed those that cross the transition from infancy to early childhood. McCall (1983) refers to this as "dips in cross-age stabilities of individual differences:"

It is quite possible that individual differences become rearranged at the advent of new skills, a phenomenon that would be reflected in reduced cross-age stabilities at points in development where major discontinuities in the developmental function occur. Consequently, cross-age stabilities should be higher for periods that do not span a discontinuity, and lower for comparable periods that do embrace a discontinuity in developmental function. (p. 120)

Using the CAP as an example, if a transition occurs after 24 months, correlations from 3 to 4 years should exceed those from 2 to 3; if the transition occurs before 24 months, correlations from 2 to 3 years and from 3 to 4 should exceed those from 1 to 2. Figure 5.5 illustrates a case in which individual differences in developmental timing alone scramble the rank ordering of individual differences during a transitional period. Correlations among ages, 1, 1.5, 3.5, and 4 years are 1.0; however, correlations from 2 to 3 years are low.

The second approach involves long-term correlations, such as those found in the birth-to-maturity Berkeley and Fels studies. In terms of developmental change, we are interested in changes in long-term predictiveness during infancy and early childhood.

The CAP provides a novel alternative to studying infant-to-adult continuity because, from a genetic perspective, the CAP parent–offspring de-

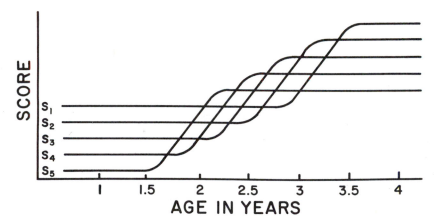

Figure 5.5. Change in age-to-age correlations as a result of individual differences in the timing of a transition.

sign provides an instant longitudinal study from infancy to adulthood. Significant relationships between biological mothers and their adopted-away infants can be found only if three conditions are met: The measures are substantially heritable in infancy and in adulthood, and the genetic correlation between the measures in infancy and adulthood is substantial. Thus, if significant associations are found between biological mothers' scores and scores of their adopted-away infants, some genetic continuity between infancy and adulthood is implied. Because this approach to studying the infant-to-adult continuity is so central to the behavioral genetics' focus of the CAP, these data are included in the following chapter, which considers etiological changes during development.

Height and weight

Discussions of transitions do not often mention height and weight, perhaps because mean developmental changes are obvious. In the CAP, for example, average heights in inches at 1, 2, 3, and 4 years of age are 29.8, 34.1, 37.2, and 40.2, respectively. For weight in pounds, the averages are 20.5, 26.3, 30.9, and 35.5. In terms of individual differences, height and weight provide a useful comparison for psychological development because they are more heritable and stable than psychological traits.

Do age-to-age correlations for height and weight change during infancy and early childhood? In the CAP, correlations for height from 1 to 2, 2 to 3, and 3 to 4 years are .56, .62, and .75, respectively; for weight, the correlations are .76, .87, and .84. Other studies provide support for two

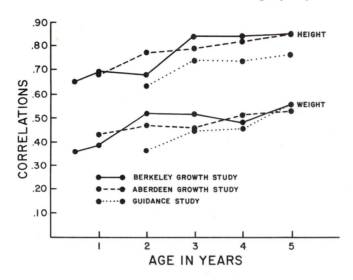

Figure 5.6. Correlations for height and weight from childhood to adulthood in three studies.

features of these results: slightly but steadily increasing age-to-age correlations for height and age-to-age correlations for weight that do not show systematic change during infancy and early childhood. For example, for 80 children in the Aberdeen Growth Study (Tanner, Healy, Lockhart, Mackenzie, & Whitehouse, 1956), the comparable correlations were .81, .87, and .92 for height and .81, .75, and .85 for weight. For 136 children in the Guidance Study (Tuddenham & Snyder, 1954), correlations for height were .85 from 2 to 3 years and .93 from 3 to 4 years; for weight, the correlations were .89 and .90. Although the developmental trends in age-to-age correlations are similar in the CAP, it is not clear why the CAP correlations for height but not for weight are lower than those reported in these other studies. In summary, there is some indication of developmental change in the form of increasing stability for height – nonetheless, height shows no sharp discontinuities in age-to-age correlations during infancy and early childhood.

Correlations between childhood and adulthood support these conclusions. Figure 5.6 presents data for 80 individuals in the Aberdeen Growth Study (Tanner et al., 1956), 50 individuals in the Berkeley Growth Study (Bayley, 1954), and 136 individuals in the Guidance Study (Tuddenham & Snyder, 1954). The results are remarkably consistent among the three studies. Stability increases only slightly, about .10, for weight as well as height from 1 to 5 years. The most noticeable features of Figure 5.6 are

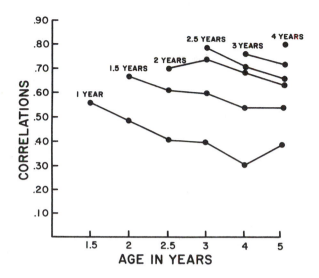

Figure 5.7. Age-to-age IQ correlations in the Louisville Twin Study (Wilson, 1983).

the generally large magnitude of the correlations from infancy and child-hood to adulthood and the greater correlations for height than for weight.

Together, these data provide some evidence of slight increases in year-to-year correlations for height and in long-term correlations for both height and weight during infancy and early childhood. However, developmental changes in these correlations are not nearly as impressive as the overall magnitude of the correlations.

Cognitive development

Developmental trends in age-to-age correlations for IQ are quite different from those for height and weight. The results of one of the most recent studies, the Louisville Twin Study (Wilson, 1983), are illustrated in Figure 5.7. One-year correlations from 1 to 2, 2 to 3, and 3 to 4 years are .48, .74, and .76, respectively. The correlation from 1 to 2 years is significantly lower than the correlation from 2 to 3, suggesting a transition during the second year of life. Moreover, the correlations based on 6-month intervals suggest that the transition occurs during the first half of the second year; the correlation from 12 to 18 months is significantly lower than the correlation from 18 to 24 months.

This conclusion receives some support from a review of nine studies conducted in the 1930s (Thorndike, 1940). The average correlation was .50 from 1 to 2 years, .68 from 2 to 3, and .66 from 3 to 4. The 6-month

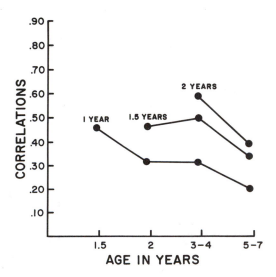

Figure 5.8. Age-to-age IQ correlations from major longitudinal studies as summarized by McCall (1979).

correlations, however, do not support the hypothesis of a transition; the correlations were .66 from 12 to 18 months, .68 from 18 to 24 months, and .74 from 24 to 30 months. Figure 5.8 summarizes the results from six major longitudinal studies as reviewed by McCall (1979). The correlations are .10 to .20 lower than in the LTS, perhaps due to the greater variance in the latter study, which might result from its inclusion of different ethnic groups. Nonetheless, the pattern of results is similar in that the correlation from 1 to 2 years ($r = .32$) is substantially lower than the correlation from 2 to 3–4 years ($r = .59$). The CAP also yields correlations that are about .20 lower than those of the LTS. The CAP data suggest a steady increase in age-to-age correlations from 1 to 4 years: The correlations are .39, .46, and .58, respectively, from 1 to 2, 2 to 3, and 3 to 4 years. The only significant difference is between the correlation from 1 to 2 and the correlation from 3 to 4.

Although all studies show that stability increases during infancy and early childhood, it is uncertain whether an abrupt change in IQ stability occurs. The most parsimonious view may be that stability increases linearly. In 1938, Marjorie Honzik, one of the major workers in this area, suggested that increases in stability were sufficiently linear that the size of age-to-age correlations could be reasonably estimated up to 5 years of age by dividing the age at the first test by the age at the second test – for example, estimating

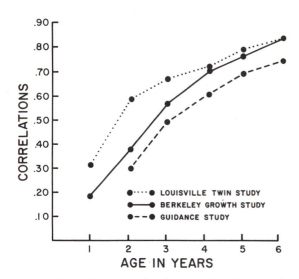

Figure 5.9. Correlations between IQ at 8 years and earlier IQ scores in three studies.

correlations of about .50 between 1 and 2 years of age, about .66 between 2 and 3, and about .33 between 1 and 3.

These differences in age-to-age correlations could be due to increases in reliability. For example, if the 12-month Bayley were less reliable than the 24-month Bayley, the correlation from 12 to 24 months would be lower than the correlation from 24 to 36 months. However, in the CAP, the 2-week test–retest correlation for the 12-month Mental Developmental Index (MDI) is quite high, .80. We are not aware of other reports of test–retest reliability of the MDI. Split-half reliability for the Bayley test during the first year has been reported to be .93 (Werner & Bayley, 1966). Thus, lower age-to-age correlations at 12 months do not appear to be caused by low reliability.

A second type of data relevant to changes in age-to-age correlations involves longer-term correlations. Figure 5.9 depicts correlations between IQ at 8 years of age and earlier IQ scores in the LTS, Berkeley Growth Study (Bayley, 1949), and Guidance Study (Honzik, Macfarlane, & Allen, 1948). In the LTS, the correlation from 12 months is significantly lower than the correlation from 18 months, suggesting again that a transition occurs before 18 months; the increase in correlations from 18 to 24 months is not statistically significant. However, in the Berkeley Growth Study, the correlation increases as much from 2 to 3 years as it does from 1 to 2, and the increase from 2 to 3 is also considerable in the Guidance Study. On balance, these data suggest that stability correlations increase linearly to

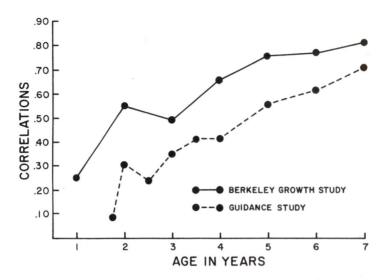

Figure 5.10. Correlations between IQ at 18 years and earlier IQ scores in two studies.

about 3 years of age. This conclusion is also consistent with the infancy-to-adulthood correlations from the Berkeley Growth Study and the Guidance Study, as shown in Figure 5.10.

In summary, for IQ, both short-term and long-term correlations increase during the first four years of life; the increase appears to be linear.

Much less is known about cognitive measures other than IQ. The data of the CAP are not particularly useful in this context because natural language use was assessed from videotaped observations only at 1 and 2 years, the Sequenced Inventory of Communication Development was employed only at 2 and 3, and specific cognitive abilities were assessed only at 3 and 4. Two data points are not sufficient to assess developmental trends in age-to-age correlations.

Three studies have suggested that vocalization in infancy yields significant long-term correlations with IQ, at least for females (Cameron, Livson, & Bayley, 1967; Kagan, 1971; Moore, 1967). In the Berkeley Growth Study (Cameron et al., 1967), the age at which a child first passed each test item was used for these analyses and is thus not applicable to the question of transitions in stability during infancy and early childhood. Moore (1967) reported correlations between language scores at 6 and 18 months and various outcome measures at 3, 5, and 8 years. Although correlations increased from 6 to 18 months for nearly all measures, two data points at 6 and 18 months are not sufficient to assess developmental trends during infancy and early childhood. Another group of studies relevant to specific cognitive abilities utilize the seven scales of the Uzgiris–Hunt test. Significant age-to-age correlations are rarely found for the seven scales (King & Seegmiller, 1973; Wachs, 1979), a result that may be due to low reliability. An absence of age-to-age correlations has also been reported for Escalona and Corman's Object Permanence Scale (Lewis & McGurk, 1972). In short, we cannot begin to answer questions concerning developmental changes in age-to-age correlations for specific cognitive abilities.

Temperament

Despite the surge of interest in temperament, research tends to focus either on infancy or on childhood and, with the exception of the New York Longitudinal Study, does not span infancy and early childhood. A review of longitudinal studies from a life-span perspective with an excellent discussion of problems in the field has been written by Moss and Susman (1980).

Two studies using parental ratings in early childhood revealed evidence of increasing stability from 3 to 6 years (Fox, 1979; Matheny, in McDevitt, 1986). These one-year correlations tend to be higher than those found in other studies in infancy, thus providing some indirect support for increasing stability from infancy to early childhood. In a review of continuity and discontinuity in temperament, McDevitt (1986, p. 35) concluded that "the magnitude and duration of stability appears to increase dramatically after the age of three but the trajectory of this developmental function is not precisely defined." However, stability in infancy was low primarily because of the inclusion of neonatal studies; as McDevitt (1986) pointed out, "in the first 3 months of life there is insufficient reliable variance in temperament measures to detect many of the possible links" (p. 36). Thus, questions remain as to whether and when changes in age-to-age correlations occur for temperament during infancy and early childhood. Also, the diverse behaviors subsumed under the rubric of temperament make it unlikely that the if-and-when story will be the same for all temperaments.

New York Longitudinal Study. A book by Kagan and Moss (1962) presented personality data from birth through adulthood for the Fels longitudinal study; however, the data are not relevant here because ratings during the first three years of life were combined. An important source of longitudinal information on temperament is the New York Longitudinal Study (NYLS; Thomas & Chess, 1986), a study of 133 subjects from infancy to adulthood that began in 1956. Parents were interviewed twice per year

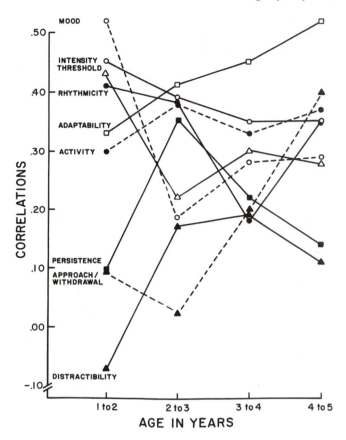

Figure 5.11. Year-to-year correlations for temperament in infancy and early childhood in the New York Longitudinal Study (Thomas & Chess, 1986).

during the infancy and childhood of their offspring, and nine dimensions of temperament were rated from the interview protocols. Figure 5.11 shows the results for the nine NYLS traits. The correlations from 1 to 2 years range from − .07 to .52; however, from 2 to 3, 3 to 4, and 4 to 5 years, the range of correlations is narrower and centers around .30. The most stable trait was Adaptability, the ability to change in response to new or altered situations. This trait suggests linearly increasing one-year stability from infancy to early childhood, although even the correlations of .33 and .52 are not significantly different. Longer-term stability is low, .14 from 1 to 5 years.

Approach/Withdrawal shows the most sharply increasing pattern of correlations, a finding that might deserve further investigation because of the centrality of this dimension in the NYLS and in other approaches to temperament. In factor analyses of items designed to assess the NYLS dimensions, Approach/Withdrawal accounts for more variance than other NYLS dimensions, although the factor appears to involve approach and withdrawal to people, that is, sociability and shyness (Buss & Plomin, 1984). The NYLS Approach/Withdrawal dimension is also the starting point for the work of Kagan and his colleagues on "behavioral inhibition" (Kagan, Reznick, & Snidman, 1986). Laboratory observations of interactions with unfamiliar persons and objects were collected at 21, 48, and 67 months in one study and at 31, 43, and 60 months in another. For 46 children, the correlation for a composite index of behavioral inhibition is .41 from 21 to 48 months and .66 from 48 months to 60 months, a difference in correlations that is not nearly significant. Moreover, extreme groups of inhibited and uninhibited children were selected for this study, which may have inflated these age-to-age correlations.

In summary, the NYLS correlations suggest low year-to-year stability during infancy and early childhood, with little evidence overall for increasing stability. The median correlations for the nine dimensions are .33 from 1 to 2 years, .35 from 2 to 3, .28 from 3 to 4, and .33 from 4 to 5. In terms of long-term continuity to young adulthood, none of the nine dimensions shows a consistent pattern of correlations from infancy or early childhood to adulthood. The median correlations for the nine dimensions predicting adult temperament are .03 at 1, .00 at 2, .11 at 3, .15 at 4, and .04 at 5 years.

Louisville Twin Study. During the past decade, the LTS has turned its attention to temperament, although data are as yet limited to the first two years of life (Wilson & Matheny, 1986). Using a parental rating questionnaire designed to assess the nine NYLS dimensions of temperament, the study revealed much higher correlations than did the NYLS, which employed unstructured interviews with parents; some of the difference in correlations between the two studies can be attributed to the use of 6-month intervals in the LTS and 12-month intervals in the NYLS. As indicated in Figure 5.12, the median correlations suggest an increase in stability during the second year of life: .34 from 6 to 12 months, .43 from 12 to 18 months, and .62 from 18 to 24 months for a sample of nearly 100 children. This trend toward increasing stability occurs for all but the Intensity and Persistence dimensions. The results for the individual dimensions do not correspond to the NYLS results from 1 to 2 years. For example, in contrast to the NYLS, which found negligible stability for Approach/Withdrawal during the first three years, the LTS correlations in-

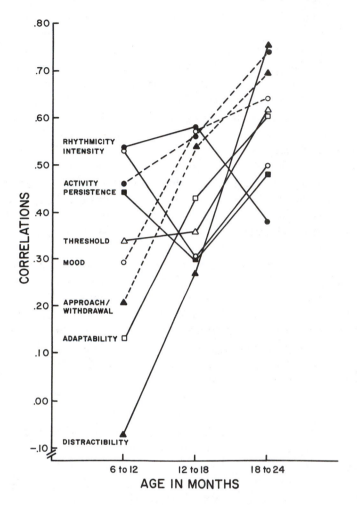

Figure 5.12. Six-month correlations for the New York Longitudinal Study dimensions of temperament in the Louisville Twin Study (Wilson & Matheny, 1986).

crease from .21 to .54 to .70 during the first two years. All three comparisons among the correlations for Adaptability are significantly different, suggesting a linear increase in age-to-age correlations for Approach/Withdrawal.

In addition to parental ratings, the LTS includes tester ratings on the IBR and IBR-like ratings based on videotaped observations of children in standardized situations in the laboratory. Scales to assess three IBR factors derived by Matheny (1980) were correlated across 6-month intervals for

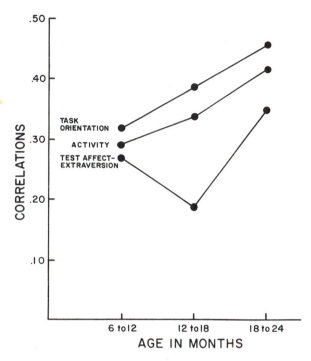

Figure 5.13. Six-month correlations for tester Infant Behavior Record ratings in the Louisville Twin Study (Matheny, 1983).

approximately 300 infants (Matheny, 1983). The correlations, shown in Figure 5.13, are substantially lower than the correlations for parental rating data; the greatest 6-month correlation is only .46. The stability correlations increase across the three age comparisons, although not as dramatically as they did for parental ratings; none of the increases are significant. The median correlations for the three 6-month comparisons are .29, .31, and .41, respectively.

Age-to-age correlations for ratings based on videotaped observations of more than 100 children in standardized laboratory situations are shown in Figure 5.14 (Matheny, Wilson, & Nuss, 1984; Wilson & Matheny, 1983, 1986). The stabilities for the videotape ratings are similar on average to those reported in Figure 5.13 for tester IBR ratings. The median correlations for the four ratings at the three ages are .38, .34, and .48. Unlike the tester IBR ratings, increases in stability occur only during the second half of the second year. However, the dimensions assessed are different for the tester IBR ratings and the videotape ratings.

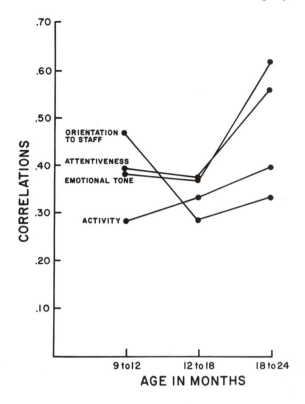

Figure 5.14. Six-month correlations for videotape Infant Behavior Record ratings of temperament in the Louisville Twin Study (Wilson & Matheny, 1986).

In summary, the LTS data suggest some increase in stability of temperament during the first two years for parental ratings and possibly for tester ratings on the IBR. The results also indicate that patterns of age-to-age correlations may differ for different dimensions.

Colorado Adoption Project. CAP year-to-year correlations from 1 to 4 years are depicted in Figure 5.15 for parental ratings on the CCTI and in Figure 5.16 for tester ratings on the IBR. As in the LTS, parental ratings yield year-to-year correlations that are substantially greater than stabilities for tester ratings. The CAP and LTS results are not directly comparable because the CAP results are based on 1-year intervals from 1 to 4, whereas the LTS data involve 6-month intervals, during years 1 and 2. Nonetheless, the LTS shows a consistent increase in stability during infancy; similarly, the CAP shows increases across all four CCTI dimensions from 1 to 2 years

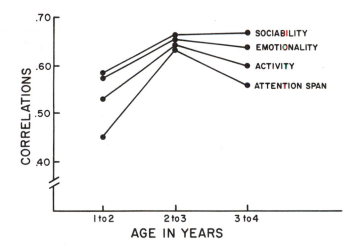

Figure 5.15. CAP year-to-year correlations for Colorado Childhood Temperament Inventory scales.

versus from 2 to 3 years. These differences in year-to-year correlations are significantly different for Attention Span given the sample size of 446 and 396 for the two comparisons. These increases in year-to-year stability, however, do not continue into early childhood; the correlations from 2 to 3 years are quite similar to those from 3 to 4. The median stabilities are .65 from 2 to 3 and .62 from 3 to 4.

As in the 6-month IBR correlations in the LTS, the CAP 12-month

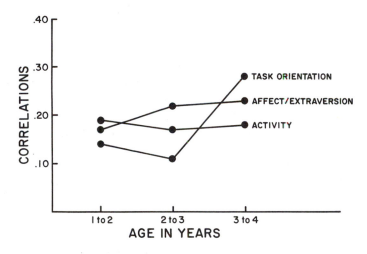

Figure 5.16. CAP year-to-year correlations for Infant Behavior Record scales.

correlations for the IBR are modest, about .20. Moreover, the CAP 1-year correlations do not change from 1 to 2 years versus 2 to 3 versus 3 to 4 with one reasonable exception: Stability increases significantly for Task Orientation from 2 to 3 years versus from 3 to 4.

In summary, year-to-year correlations for parental ratings of temperament are nearly as great as stability for cognitive development. Stabilities for tester ratings and videotape ratings are lower. In general, stability increases during infancy, although it appears that some traits show different patterns of developmental change. Long-term correlations to adulthood are negligible from infancy and early childhood in the NYLS, suggesting that change prevails over continuity in long-term comparisons between childhood and adulthood for temperament.

Behavior problems

A major goal of the NYLS (e.g., Chess & Thomas, 1984) was to relate temperament in infancy and childhood to adjustment later in life. Composite scores of difficult temperament were constructed for each of the first five years in which a high score represents a child who fusses frequently and who withdraws from and is slow to adapt to novel situations. Year-to-year correlations suggest modest stability, which appears to decrease, although none of the correlations are significantly different: .42 from 1 to 2 years, .37 from 2 to 3, and .29 from 3 to 4 (Thomas & Chess, 1986). Correlations with a difficult temperament score in adulthood suggest an increase in long-term stability after the second year, although again the correlations with adult temperament do not differ significantly for any of the years: .17 from 1 year, .09 from 2, .31 from 3, and .37 from 4. It is odd that the correlations from 3 to adulthood and from 4 to adulthood are greater than the correlation from 3 to 4.

Early adult adjustment (17 to 24 years) in diverse areas (including social functioning, school functioning, sexual adjustment, family relationships) was rated from interview transcripts. A composite adjustment score was related to difficult temperament in infancy and early childhood. Some evidence for a transition after the second year emerged, although again the differences in correlations were not statistically significant: The correlations with adult adjustment were .08 for difficult temperament in the first year, − .09 from the second year, − .21 from the third year, and − .32 from the fourth year.

Some relevant data are available from the CAP. In infancy, contextual problems of sleeping, eating, and diapering were assessed via parental report. However, these problems are so specific to infancy that little variance remains in early childhood. For this reason, these questions were not asked of parents when their children were 3 and 4 years old. This is a crude example of a transition – the behavior in question diminishes to such an extent that little variance remains.

The CAP dimension of Difficult Temperament has been assessed using a similar measure at each year from 1 to 4: an unrotated first principal component derived from parental ratings of the nine NYLS dimensions and a general rating of overall difficultness. Year-to-year correlations for difficult temperament are comparable to those reported in Figure 5.15 for other parental temperament ratings and do not increase during infancy and early childhood. In addition, similar results were obtained for two CCTI scales related to behavior problems included at all four years: Reaction to Foods and Soothability, with a significant increase in stability for Reaction to Foods from 1 to 2 years (.48) to 2 to 3 years (.67).

Conclusions

As discussed at the beginning of this chapter, little is known about developmental change from the perspective of individual differences. Change can occur for variances, covariances (factor structure), and age-to-age correlations. We examined these types of data for height and weight, cognitive development, personality/temperament, and behavior problems.

In general, when changes are found, they tend to indicate increases in all three facets of change. That is, variances increase, covariances increase, and age-to-age stability increases. The changes are not sudden or dramatic; the safest hypothesis is that, when they occur, changes are linear during infancy and early childhood.

Results differ across the domains of height and weight, cognitive development, and personality, and they are also likely to differ for dimensions within each domain. Height and weight are remarkably stable during infancy and early childhood and in their prediction of adult scores: Correlations from childhood to adulthood are about .75 for height and .45 for weight. In contrast, the most noticeable feature of cognitive development is an increase in stability. For example, correlations from 1 to 2 years are about .40, and correlations from 2 to 3 years are about .60. Similar results emerged from comparisons of long-term correlations from childhood to adulthood: .25 at 1, .40 at 2, .45 at 3, and .50 at 4 years. Temperament also shows some increases in stability, especially during infancy and especially for parental ratings, although the pattern of developmental change differs for the different dimensions. Some increase in stability is also suggested for behavior problems and adjustment.

Concerning developmental changes in factor structure, a major change occurs for cognition: Toward the end of the second year, language items come to dominate the unrotated first principal component for cognitive items, an index of general cognitive ability. In contrast, the factor structure of temperament remains unchanged during infancy and early childhood.

Another major approach to the study of developmental changes and transitions goes beyond description and prediction to consider etiological changes in development, the forte of developmental behavioral genetics. Even in the absence of developmental changes in phenotypic variance, within-age covariance, and between-age covariance, genetic and environmental provenances of variance and covariance can change. This is the topic of the next chapter.

6 Transitions and changes: genetic and environmental etiologies

> It must be borne in mind that the divergence of development, when it occurs, need not be ascribed to the effect of different nurtures, but it is quite possible that it may be due to the appearance of qualities inherited at birth, though dormant.
>
> Francis Galton (1875)

In addition to the descriptive and predictive changes discussed in the preceding chapter, developmental change can be seen in terms of etiology – changes in genetic as well as environmental influences. Changes in environmental influences can be explored without behavioral genetics; for example, the effects of prematurity on individual differences in social and mental development tend to diminish during infancy (Kopp, 1983). Behavioral genetics, however, provides a particularly powerful and general approach to the study of developmental changes in etiologies of individual differences.

From a behavioral genetics perspective, three kinds of etiological change can be considered; these mirror the phenotypic changes described in Chapter 5. The most basic phenotypic change that can occur is a change in variance, although changes in the magnitude of phenotypic variance are difficult to interpret because measures are not comparable across ages. The analogous genetic concept – change in heritability – is easier to interpret because it refers to a proportion of phenotypic variance due to genetic differences among individuals rather than to the absolute magnitude of variance. Similarly, developmental changes in environmental components of variance can be explored. A second descriptive type of developmental change involves phenotypic factor structures. The analogous etiological concept is a change in patterns of genetic correlations and environmental correlations among measures; this is the essence of multivariate behavioral genetics (DeFries & Fulker, 1986). Changes in heritability and changes in genetic and environmental factor structures involve cross-sectional analyses. The third issue is longitudinal: age-to-age genetic correlations and environmental correlations. Analogous to phenotypic age-to-age correlations are genetic and environmental contributions to age-to-age correlations within infancy and early childhood as well as long-term correlations from infancy and early childhood to middle childhood, adolescence, and adulthood; this is the essence of developmental behavioral genetics (Plomin, 1986a).

Answers to etiological questions concerning developmental change will not necessarily be the same as answers at the descriptive level. Although phenotypic changes in variances, in covariance structures, and in age-to-age predictions imply that the genetic and environmental sources of variance and covariance are changing, the nature of these etiological changes may be quite different from phenotypic changes because genetic and environmental factors can operate independently, even in opposite directions. In terms of variance changes, genetic variance could decrease while environmental variance increases, leaving the total phenotypic variance unaltered. Similarly, for developmental changes in covariance structures, genetic covariance could increase while environmental covariance decreases. For example, genetic influences on cognitive abilities might increasingly coalesce toward general cognitive ability, whereas environmental factors could push toward differentiation. In terms of prediction, increasing genetic continuity could be counterbalanced by environmental discontinuity. These counterbalancing influences would obscure changes in phenotypic variances and covariances. For this reason, etiological studies of developmental change are needed regardless of the message heralded by descriptive and predictive phenotypic studies.

It should be emphasized that the term "genetic change" in developmental behavioral genetics denotes changes in the effects of genes on behavioral differences among individuals, not molecular changes in the transcription of DNA. Although developmental behavioral genetics includes analysis at the molecular level, understanding the molecular basis of genetic change is difficult because development at the molecular level in eukaryotes is incredibly complex, with many regulatory mechanisms that seem to work in concert as rheostats rather than as simple on–off switches. Thus, the current focus of developmental behavioral genetics is on the genetic and environmental provenances of behavioral differences among individuals in a population, rather than on molecular mechanisms.

In this chapter, the concepts of etiological change are described and the data relevant to such change during infancy and early childhood, as found in the CAP and other studies, are reviewed. Data from adoptive and nonadoptive siblings in the CAP make it possible to explore changes in heritability, genetic and environmental relationships among measures, and year-to-year genetic and environmental correlations. The number of sibling pairs in which both members of the pair have been tested is 67 adoptive and 82 nonadoptive pairs at 1 year, 61 and 70 at 2 years, 50 and 54 at 3 years, and 42 and 43 at 4 years. This sample size is modest for quantitative genetic analyses. Even at 1 year, it yields 80% power to detect adoptive-sibling correlations, which provide direct estimates of shared environmental influence, only when the correlation is greater than .30. Detection of genetic influence, which involves the difference between nonadoptive- and adoptive-sibling correlations, attains 50% power only when the correlations differ by .30 or more. Even though the sample size permits the detection of only large effects, these data will be presented for two reasons. First, data of this type are critical for developmental analyses because they complement the parent–offspring CAP data with the contemporaneous relationship of siblings; second, data for young adoptive siblings have not previously been reported.

CAP parent–offspring comparisons also provide an interesting perspective on genetic etiologies of developmental change. Because the parents were tested as adults and their offspring were studied as infants and young children, parent–offspring data provide important evidence regarding the etiology of change and continuity from early in life to adulthood. In this chapter, we examine correlations between measures of biological mothers and their adopted-away offspring at 1, 2, 3, and 4 years, with an eye on changes in these correlations from infancy to early childhood. Comparisons between biological mothers and their adopted-away offspring provide powerful, direct estimates of genetic mediation of continuity from infancy and early childhood to adulthood.

The emphasis in this chapter is on the concepts of developmental change and on the use of basic correlational data from twin and adoption designs to discern developmental trends. Later chapters are more concerned with precise estimation of quantitative genetic parameters and testing explicit models relevant to some of the issues addressed in this chapter.

Changes in genetic and environmental components of variance

Heritability is a descriptive statistic referring to the portion of observed variability of a given trait that can be accounted for by genetic differences among individuals in a particular population at a particular time, as described in the next chapter. As a descriptive statistic, it will change as genetic and environmental factors change. Populations can change over time because of cohort effects that bring different environmental contingencies to bear or because of genetic changes due to migration or changes in mating patterns. The point of this section is that heritability may also change as a function of age among members of the same population if environmental or genetic influences change during development. For example, heritability will increase if the proportion of phenotypic variance due to genetic influence increases or if the proportion of environmental variance decreases. It is possible, however, that the relative amount of phenotypic variance due to genetic variance could remain unchanged, even if completely different sets of genes were transcribed at the two ages. Thus, similar heritabilities at two or more ages do not necessarily imply genetic stability. This issue of age-to-age change in genetic covariance is the topic of a later section of this chapter.

Consider the classical twin design, which assesses heritability by comparing the resemblance of identical twins (who are 100% similar genetically) to that of fraternal twins (who are roughly 50% similar genetically for segregating genes that affect the trait in an additive manner). For example, an increase in heritability as a function of age could be due to an increased difference between identical- and fraternal-twin correlations. Such an increased difference could arise either because the identical-twin correlation increases to a greater extent than the fraternal-twin correlation or because the fraternal-twin correlation decreases to a greater extent than the identical-twin correlation.

Correlations for adoptive and nonadoptive siblings can be employed in a similar manner to estimate developmental changes in heritability. Nonadoptive siblings, like other first-degree relatives, are 50% similar genetically for segregating genes. Hereditary similarity is zero for adoptive siblings in the absence of selective placement. Thus, if heredity influences a trait, the correlation for nonadoptive siblings will exceed the correlation for adoptive siblings. Correlations for nonadoptive and adoptive siblings in the CAP – the only extant data on adoptive siblings in infancy and early childhood – are presented in this chapter; Chapter 7 introduces a model-fitting approach to the analysis of nonadoptive- and adoptive-sibling resemblance.

Although the CAP siblings were tested within 2 weeks of their birthdays, age gaps within the pairs differ, and the age gap is larger for adoptive siblings (3.3 years) than for nonadoptive siblings (2.6 years). In addition, same-sex and opposite-sex pairs of siblings were included; 46% of the pairs were same sex. These family structure variables could affect sibling resemblance. For example, pairs with larger age gaps might be less similar than pairs close in age, and opposite-sex pairs might be less similar than same-sex pairs. The effects of age spacing and gender on sibling resemblance were examined using hierarchical multiple regression (HMR; Cohen &

Cohen, 1975). HMR can be employed to assess whether sibling resemblance differs as a function of age spacing by regression of the younger sibling's score on the older sibling's score, the siblings' age gap (number of days between the siblings' birthdays), and an interaction variable constructed as the product of the older sibling's score and the pair's age gap. After the "main effects" of the older sibling's score and age gap are removed, the significance of the interaction variable is tested to determine whether sibling resemblance differs as a function of age gap. The effects of gender were tested in a similar fashion; in this case, the interaction variable is a "dummy" variable in which same-sex pairs were coded as 1 and opposite-sex pairs were coded as -1. HMR analyses for the major CAP variables yielded no more significant interactions between sibling resemblance and spacing or gender than would be expected on the basis of chance alone. Furthermore, the few significant effects that emerged were not consistent across age or across variables, nor did they account for much variance. For these reasons, age spacing and gender will not be considered in sibling analyses in this book; if they were considered, however, these family structure variables would not noticeably change the reported results.

Although few developmentalists have considered the issue of developmental change in heritability, most would probably guess that, as children develop, they experience more diverse environments, and thus environmental variance will increasingly account for phenotypic variance. In other words, heritability will decrease during development. This is explicitly the view among Soviet developmentalists (e.g., Mangan, 1982). However, as indicated in the following review, when changes in heritability are found, they are most often in the opposite direction (Plomin, 1986a). In terms of transitions from infancy to early childhood, the issue is whether any marked change in heritability occurs during the first four years of life.

Height and weight

Figures 6.1 and 6.2 present twin correlations for height and weight, respectively, for about 400 pairs of twins from the Louisville Twin Study (Wilson, 1976). The results suggest sharply increasing heritability during the first year of life. For both height and weight, heritabilities are zero at birth; in fact, fraternal twins are more similar than identical twins at birth. This may be due to the fact that identical twins are subject to greater intrauterine competition: About 70% of identical twins are monochorionic, which produces some degree of vascular anastomosis and could result in twins receiving unequal nutrition (Bulmer, 1970).

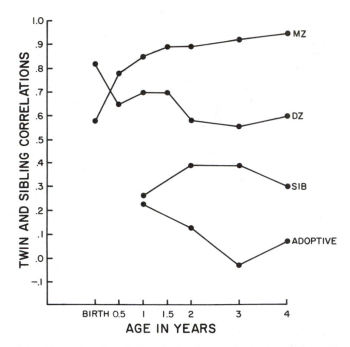

Figure 6.1. Correlations for height of twins in the Louisville Twin Study (adapted from Wilson, 1976) and of nonadoptive and adoptive siblings in the CAP.

During the first year, correlations for identical twins increase and correlations for fraternal twins decrease, with the result that heritabilities increase. For height, heritabilities are .26 at 6 months and .62 at 2 years; for weight, the heritabilities are .36 and .68, respectively. For height, the steepest increases in heritabilities occur between birth and 6 months and between 18 and 24 months; after 2 years, heritabilities do not change much. For weight, increases in heritability are marked from birth to 6 months and from 6 to 12 months, with little change after the first year. Despite the low heritabilities during the first year, the twin correlations are quite high, suggesting that most of the variance during the first year is due to environmental influences shared by the twins.

The CAP sibling correlations for height and weight, also shown in Figures 6.1 and 6.2, are consistent with the hypothesis that genetic influence increases from 1 to 2 years for height but not for weight. In addition, both the twin and adoption data suggest high heritabilities for height and weight in early childhood. The CAP data also support the hypothesis of special twin effects in that nonadoptive-sibling correlations are substantially lower than the fraternal-twin correlations. Because twins are frequently prema-

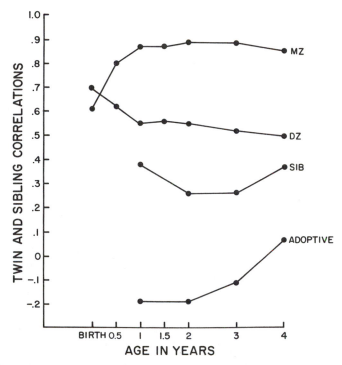

Figure 6.2. Correlations for weight of twins in the Louisville Twin Study (adapted from Wilson, 1976) and of nonadoptive and adoptive siblings in the CAP.

ture and have low birth weights, it is likely that perinatal factors exert a major influence during the first year in twins.

In summary, the data for height and weight suggest abrupt increases in heritability during infancy for height and weight and a leveling out of genetic influence at high levels by early childhood.

Cognitive development

Cognitive development might be expected to show results that are different from those for height and weight because scores on tests of mental development are more plastic than inches or pounds.

In the longitudinal Louisville Twin Study (LTS; Wilson, 1983), the Bayley Scales of Infant Development have been administered through 24 months of age, the Stanford–Binet is employed at 30 and 36 months, and the Wechsler Preschool and Primary Scale of Intelligence is utilized at 48 months. Figure 6.3 summarizes two decades of research involving approximately 200 pairs of twins.

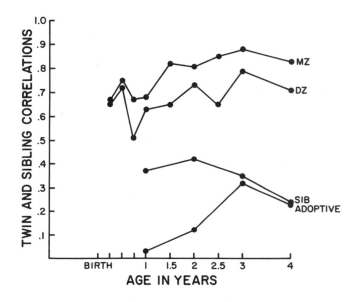

Figure 6.3. Correlations for IQ of twins in the Louisville Twin Study (adapted from Wilson, 1983) and of nonadoptive and adoptive siblings in the CAP.

Unlike the results for height and weight, heritabilities bounce up and down during the first three years, probably because the heritabilities are low and thus involve large standard errors of estimate. Nonetheless, some slight overall increase can be seen: Heritabilities increase approximately 5% per year, from 10% to 25%, from 1 to 4 years. By 4 years, heritability is still only half the magnitude of heritability for IQ scores in adolescence and adulthood.

As in the case of height and weight, twin correlations for mental tests are substantial; in fact, the twin correlations tend to exceed the age-to-age correlations discussed in Chapter 5. Because heritabilities are low, these results suggest that environmental factors shared by members of twin pairs are very influential. Also similar to the results for height and weight, shared environmental influence is greater for twins than for nontwin siblings. For 35 twin/sibling pairs tested at the same age in the LTS, the sibling correlation is about .30 lower than the fraternal-twin correlation.

What accounts for this large environmental effect? One possibility is situational. In the LTS, twins were tested on the same day, whereas the younger siblings were tested at least a year later. However, the fact that the twins were tested by different examiners in different rooms makes it less likely that artifacts of this type could be responsible for the high twin correlations.

As in the case of physical characteristics, a more likely explanation is perinatal problems. For singletons, the correlation between birth weight and 8-month Bayley scores is about .20 (Broman, Nichols, & Kennedy, 1975). In twins, however, the correlations are .50, .48, and .30 at 3, 6, and 12 months, respectively, and they continue to decline to .14 at 2 years and to .11 at 3 years (Wilson, 1977). Although twin correlations corrected for birth weight are not available, it is likely that twin correlations during the first year are substantially inflated by shared perinatal influences specific to twins.

The LTS results suggesting little genetic variance in Bayley scores during the first year of life are confirmed by a report of 8-month Bayley scores for more than 300 pairs of twins participating in the Collaborative Perinatal Project (Nichols & Broman, 1974). Although identical- and fraternal-twin correlations were .84 and .55, respectively, for the total sample, removing data from the 8% of the twins who had Bayley scores of less than 57 yielded twin correlations of .55 for both identical and fraternal twins. The Collaborative Perinatal Project also reported a sibling correlation of .22 for 4,347 pairs of nontwin siblings at 8 months, even lower than the LTS twin/sibling correlations during the first year. Similarly, the Fels longitudinal study yielded a correlation of .24 for 142 pairs of nontwin siblings in the first year (McCall, 1972).

Figure 6.3 also lists CAP correlations for nonadoptive and adoptive siblings for Bayley scores at 1 and 2 years and for Stanford–Binet scores at 3 and 4 years – the first report employing the sibling adoption design for mental development in infancy and early childhood. The results suggest a pattern of results quite different from the twin results in that heritability, assessed in terms of the difference between the nonadoptive- and adoptive-sibling correlations, is significant and substantial in infancy and decreases sharply in early childhood. At 1, the adoptive correlation is .03, suggesting that Bayley scores are not at all affected by shared environmental influence – in sharp contrast to the twin data, which suggest that more than half of the total variance is shared environmentally by twins. Shared environmental influence is also low at 2 years but increases at 3 and 4 to levels comparable to those reported for studies of older adopted children.

Taken at face value, the nonadoptive- and adoptive-sibling correlations suggest that genetic influence is considerable at 1 and 2 years and fades in importance at 3 and 4. In contrast, shared environmental influence is negligible during infancy and becomes moderately important in early childhood. These results may not be as incongruent with the twin results as they seem. The twin results suggest only modest heritability at 3 and 4 years; if heritability is about .20, the CAP sample size would provide only

Table 6.1. *Nonadoptive- and adoptive-sibling correlations for cognitive measures in the CAP*

Measure	Year	Nonadoptive		Adoptive	
		r	*N* (pairs)	*r*	*N* (pairs)
Bayley MDI	1	.37	82	.03	67
	2	.42	70	.12	61
Stanford–Binet	3	.35	54	.32	50
	4	.24	43	.23	43
CAP general factor	3	.44	52	.18	44
	4	.10	37	.20	39
Bayley Verbal	1	.22	82	.21	66
Bayley Lexical	2	.27	70	.03	68
Bayley Verbal	2	.31	70	.05	60
CAP Verbal	3	.11	55	−.05	50
	4	.42	43	.17	42
Bayley Means–End	1	.24	82	−.16	66
Bayley Spatial	2	.14	70	.06	60
CAP Spatial	3	.33	55	.24	51
	4	.12	43	.27	42
CAP Perceptual Speed	3	.18	55	.08	49
	4	.12	43	−.08	39
CAP Memory	3	.14	54	.19	51
	4	.05	41	.09	41
SICD	2	.29	69	.08	56
	3	.21	53	.10	50

12% power to detect concomitant differences between nonadoptive and adoptive sibling correlations. Moreover, the lack of twin evidence for genetic influence at 1 and 2 years may be due to the overwhelming influence of perinatal factors on twins during infancy. As usual, more research is needed to confirm these hypotheses; from the point of view of developmental change, however, it is interesting to consider the possibility that genetic influence is greater in infancy than the twin data have suggested and that shared environmental influence increases from infancy to early childhood as assessed directly by adoptive siblings.

Results of other cognitive tests also indicate only modest genetic influence in early childhood. The sibling correlations are summarized in Table 6.1. Although an unrotated first-principal-component score derived from the CAP battery of specific cognitive abilities suggested some (but nonsignificant) genetic influence at 3 years, no genetic influence was suggested for this independent measure of general cognitive ability at 4. In addition, as in the case of Stanford–Binet scores at 3 and 4, adoptive-sibling correlations suggest moderate influence of shared environment. Of the specific cognitive abilities, verbal ability appears to show the most genetic influence by the second year of life. The Bayley Verbal scale at 1 year shows no genetic influence and suggests that shared environment accounts for about 20% of the variance. In contrast, the two Bayley verbal scales at 2 years, which appear to assess production and comprehension, indicate substantial genetic influence. The CAP Verbal factor at 3 years suggests modest genetic influence, and the CAP Verbal factor at 4 years shows substantial genetic influence. In addition, the Sequenced Inventory of Communication Development (SICD) measure of communicative development suggests moderate genetic influence at 2 and 3 years. The possibility of some slight genetic influence emerges for the Spatial factor, except at 4 years; Perceptual Speed also yields nonadoptive-sibling correlations that are somewhat higher than adoptive-sibling correlations at 3 and 4. The CAP Memory factor suggests no genetic influence.

These results are not easily encapsulated. Although the CAP sibling data, especially for IQ, suggest that heritability decreases and shared environment increases, twin data suggest slight increases in genetic influence and slight decreases in shared environment. The strong effect of perinatal influences on the mental development of twins could obfuscate genetic analyses using infant twins; the small CAP sibling sample size, coupled with apparently modest heritabilities, hampers the sibling adoption analyses. Finally, as discussed later, CAP parent–offspring results, like the twin results, suggest slightly increasing genetic mediation of parent–offspring resemblance from infancy to early childhood. Although parent–offspring resemblance is complicated by genetic correlations between childhood and adulthood, the parent–offspring results for IQ imply that the sibling adoption design may have underestimated heritability at 3 and 4 years.

Analyses of specific cognitive abilities using Bayley scales, CAP factors, and the SICD yielded the clearest evidence of genetic influence on verbal ability. Because no genetic influence emerged at 1 year, these results suggest increasing genetic influence on verbal ability during infancy. Results for spatial and perceptual speed abilities were also consistent with the possibility of genetic influence, although developmental trends could not be discerned. Memory showed no genetic influence, as measured in early childhood.

The safest conclusion, of course, is that much more must be learned about changes in the relative magnitude of genetic and environmental influences in the cognitive realm during infancy and early childhood.

Motor development

Although motor development was the focus of much research in the 1920s and 1930s (see review by Dewey, 1935), it has received little attention in recent years. Twin results for the Bayley Motor Scale yield results quite similar to those for the Bayley Mental Scale: On average at 6, 9, 12, and 18 months, identical- and fraternal-twin correlations are .79 and .69, respectively (Wilson & Harpring, 1972).

As in the case of the Bayley Mental Scale, CAP sibling data suggest greater genetic influence in infancy on the Bayley Motor Scale than do the twin data: Nonadoptive- and adoptive-sibling correlations are, respectively, .43 and .03 at 1 year, .17 and − .09 at 2 years, and .33 and − .09 at 3 years for fine motor development. A scale of gross motor development at 3, however, showed no genetic influence and suggested substantial shared environmental influence; the sibling correlations were .27 and .37, respectively. The twin results are consistent with the hypothesis of an increase in genetic influence during infancy, although results from the CAP sibling adoption design do not show clear developmental trends.

Temperament

It is difficult to compare heritabilities for temperament across ages because, unlike IQ, dozens of traits have been studied and no standard measures exist. One measure, which has the dual advantages of being objective and of rating children in similar, and somewhat stressful, structured situations, is the Infant Behavior Record (IBR), and it has been employed in both the LTS and CAP.

Infant Behavior Record. Again, the most informative study by far is the LTS, although most of the reports from that study are as yet limited to the first two years of life. Figures 6.4, 6.5, and 6.6 describe the LTS twin results for three major factors derived from tester ratings on the IBR for approximately 85 identical twin pairs and 50 fraternal twin pairs (Matheny, 1980).

As seen by the differences between the identical- and fraternal-twin correlations, heritabilities on average are substantial for the three dimensions. As noted earlier, standard errors of estimate for heritability are large, and perhaps for this reason and the relatively small sample size, the heritabilities jounce considerably. Although Task Orientation and Test Affect-Extraversion show no consistent developmental trends, Activity suggests a pattern of increasing heritability during the second year.

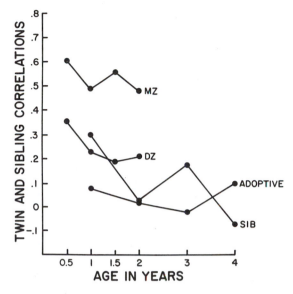

Figure 6.4. Correlations for IBR Task Orientation in the Louisville Twin Study (adapted from Matheny, 1980) and for nonadoptive and adoptive siblings in the CAP.

A persistent problem with twin studies of temperament is that heritability estimates often exceed identical-twin correlations, a situation indicative of a violation of the twin model because identical twins covary perfectly on all sources of genetic variance. The problem may be due to the fact that in doubling the difference between identical- and fraternal-twin correlations one assumes that nonadditive genetic variance is unimportant. In terms of additive genetic values (sum of the average effects of all genes that influence a character and that thus "breed true"), identical twins are identical, whereas fraternal twins, like other first-degree relatives, resemble each other 50% on average in terms of segregating genes. Thus, the covariance of identical twins contains all of the additive genetic variance, but the covariance of first-degree relatives contains only half of the additive genetic variance. With regard to nonadditive genetic variance, siblings share only a quarter of genetic variance due to dominance and relatively little genetic variance due to epistasis; in contrast, identical twins share all nonadditive genetic effects. Thus, if nonadditive genetic variance is important for a trait, the expected correlation for fraternal twins is less than half the correlation for identical twins. Lykken (1982) has argued that nonadditive genetic variance is especially important in the realm of personality. If nonadditive genetic variance is important, designs based on

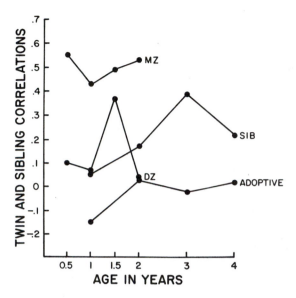

Figure 6.5. Correlations for IBR Test Affect-Extraversion in the Louisville Twin Study (adapted from Matheny, 1980) and for nonadoptive and adoptive siblings in the CAP.

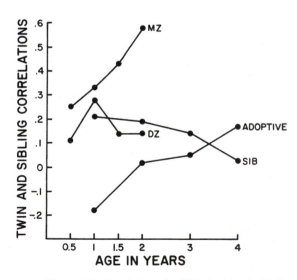

Figure 6.6. Correlations for IBR Activity in the Louisville Twin Study (adapted from Matheny, 1980) and for nonadoptive and adoptive siblings in the CAP.

first-degree relatives such as parent–offspring and sibling designs will not uncover as much evidence for genetic influence as will twin studies.

This appears to be the case for the CAP nonadoptive- and adoptive-sibling correlations. The CAP includes IBR ratings scored in the same manner as in the LTS; CAP results for nonadoptive and adoptive siblings are also included in Figures 6.4, 6.5, and 6.6. Unlike cognitive measures, the IBR factors yield correlations for CAP nonadoptive siblings that are similar to the correlations for fraternal twins at 1 and 2 years. This suggests that the perinatal factors that so strongly affect the mental development scores of twins are less important in the realm of temperament. Genetic influence is suggested because the adoptive sibling correlations are generally lower than the correlations for nonadoptive siblings, although no consistent developmental trends in heritability are apparent and heritabilities from the sibling adoption data are, on average, lower than heritabilities estimated from twin data. Similar to the twin results, heritability is suggested for Activity at 2 years; however, the sibling data suggest little genetic influence at 3 and 4 years for Activity, at least as rated by a tester during the administration of standardized tests. The evidence suggesting genetic influence is particularly impressive because older siblings were rated by a tester on average 3 years earlier than younger siblings.

It is noteworthy that this first report of young adoptive siblings indicates little effect of shared environment on temperament.

Parental ratings. Both the LTS and CAP include IBR-like ratings from videotaped observations. However, the LTS sample – about 30 pairs of each type – is not yet large enough to warrant discussion of these results (Wilson & Matheny, 1986). In the CAP, videotape ratings have not been fully analyzed.

Another approach to temperament – and by far the mostly widely used method in infancy and early childhood – involves parental ratings. The LTS has not, until recently, employed parental rating questionnaires to assess temperament. However, personality ratings were extracted from parental interviews at 6, 24, and 36 months for approximately 70 pairs of identical twins and 40 pairs of fraternal twins (Wilson, Brown, & Matheny, 1971). The results were presented in terms of percentage of twin pairs concordant for such items as crying, activity, and accepting people – items that may be related, respectively, to emotionality, activity, and sociability. In each comparison, the concordance for identical twins exceeded the concordance for fraternal twins. The differences in concordances were lower at 6 months than at 24 or 36 months. Other twin studies using parental information about twins' temperament for cross-sectional samples spanning

Table 6.2. *Nonadoptive- and adoptive-sibling correlations for parental ratings of temperament in the CAP*

Measure	Year	Nonadoptive		Adoptive	
		r	N (pairs)	r	N (pairs)
CCTI Emotionality	1	.23	77	.01	60
	2	.03	66	.20	58
	3	−.04	48	.20	46
	4	−.10	44	.32	39
CCTI Activity	1	.20	76	.05	60
	2	−.01	66	−.03	58
	3	.16	48	−.10	46
	4	−.11	44	−.18	39
CCTI Sociability	1	.10	76	.15	60
	2	.11	66	−.07	58
	3	.12	48	.17	46
	4	−.10	44	−.09	39
CCTI Attention Span	1	.23	77	.14	60
	2	.16	66	−.21	58
	3	.01	48	.18	46
	4	.19	43	.01	39

infancy and early childhood also generally suggest genetic influence, although the developmental trends are difficult to discern (Plomin, 1986a).

In the CAP, the Colorado Childhood Temperament Inventory (CCTI; Rowe & Plomin, 1977) was rated by both the mother and father at each year to assess Emotionality, Activity, Sociability, and Attention Span. Nonadoptive and adoptive sibling correlations at 1, 2, 3, and 4 years are listed in Table 6.2; midparent ratings – that is, the average rating of the mother and father – were used in an attempt to improve the reliability of these ratings.

In contrast to the twin results, little evidence of genetic influence is found for parental ratings; across the four years and four traits, the average nonadoptive and adoptive sibling correlations are .07 and .05, respectively. No consistent developmental changes are suggested for heritability or shared environment. By comparison with other data, however, increased genetic influence later in childhood is implied in that studies of older children tend to find correlations of about .20 for first-degree relatives and .05 for adoptive relatives (Plomin, 1986a). Shared environment appears to be unimportant throughout development; one possible exception is Emotionality, which shows increasing shared environmental influence for adoptive siblings, although this does not replicate for nonadoptive siblings. The small sibling sample for parental ratings of children's total behavioral problems on the Child Behavior Checklist at 4 years yielded extremely high correlations for both nonadoptive and adoptive siblings (.68 and .65, respectively), although this could be due to differences among parents in their willingness to report problems.

A scale of Difficult Temperament was created at all four years from parental ratings; it also yielded results similar to those for CCTI parental ratings of temperament: no evidence of genetic influence or of developmental changes in heritability or shared environment. The average nonadoptive- and adoptive-sibling correlations across the four years were .06 and −.03, respectively.

Summary. In the domain of temperament, twin and adoption data converge on the conclusion that shared environment is of little importance for either tester ratings or parental ratings. For tester ratings on the IBR, both twin and the CAP sibling data suggest genetic influence; for parental ratings, twin studies generally reveal evidence of genetic influence, whereas the CAP sibling data do not. More to the point of the chapter, however, is the issue of developmental change in genetic and environmental components of variance. A circumspect conclusion concerning temperament is that no marked, consistent changes are discernible in heritability or in shared environment during infancy and early childhood.

Television viewing

Children begin to watch television in early childhood. Surprisingly, CAP data suggest that heredity is a factor in the amount of television watched at both 3 and 4 years. At 3, nonadoptive- and adoptive-sibling correlations are .51 and .26, respectively, and at 4, the sibling correlations are .52 and .34. Moreover, these correlations are not a function of IQ as measured by the Stanford–Binet test at 3 or 4; the correlation between television viewing and IQ is −.01 at 3 and −.10 at 4. The results hint at the possibility that heritability declines from 3 to 4 years, although the relatively small sample sizes suggest that a safer conclusion is that heritability is similar at 3 and 4 years.

Summary

An attempt to summarize the results for height and weight, mental and motor development, temperament, and television viewing would be hazardous given the limited resolving power of the methods and sample sizes that have been brought to bear on the issue of developmental change in the magnitude of genetic and environmental components of variance early in life. Nonetheless, the three domains of development – physical, cognitive, and personality – suggest three different patterns of results. For height and weight, abrupt increases in heritability are seen in infancy; this may also be the case for motor development. Twin studies suggest that shared environment declines markedly during infancy and early childhood; CAP sibling data, however, suggest that this may be a special twin effect – perinatal problems of twins may be responsible.

For IQ, the sibling adoption data suggest that genetic influence declines and the influence of shared environment increases from infancy to early childhood, although the twin data are not in agreement. For verbal ability, an increase in genetic influence is suggested from 1 to 2 years; genetic influence is in evidence at 3 and 4 years as well. For temperament and television viewing, no marked developmental changes are apparent for heritability or for shared environment.

Tentative though these hypotheses must be, they at least signify the possibility of developmental changes in genetic and environmental components of variance.

Cross-sectional changes in genetic covariance among measures

In Chapter 5, changes in phenotypic intercorrelations among measures were discussed as a second category of developmental change. An analogous type of etiological change involves genetic and environmental contributions to the covariance among measures. Although no research has as yet compared the results of such analyses of the covariance among measures throughout infancy and early childhood, we shall describe this multivariate approach because of its potential importance in developmental analyses, as well as its relevance to the following discussion of age-to-age genetic correlations. A model-fitting approach to multivariate analysis that emphasizes model testing and parameter estimation is presented in Chapter 10.

Multivariate behavioral genetic analysis (DeFries & Fulker, 1986) disentangles genetic and environmental sources of covariance among traits rather than analyzing the variance of each trait considered individually. As shown in Figure 6.7, the essence of multivariate analysis is the decomposition of phenotypic covariance between two traits measured on the same individuals into genetic and environmental sources of covariance. The phenotypic correlation between the two traits – a phenotypically standardized covariance – is the sum of a genetic component ($h_x h_y r_G$) and an environmental component ($e_x e_y r_E$), both of which are also phenotypically

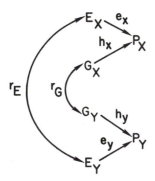

Figure 6.7. Decomposition of the phenotypic correlation between traits X and Y within an age. (Adapted from Plomin & DeFries, 1979.)

standardized covariances (Plomin & DeFries, 1979). The genetic component of the phenotypic correlation between the two traits is the genetic correlation r_G weighted by the product of the square roots of the heritabilities $h_x h_y$ of each of the traits. The genetic correlation is the correlation between genetic deviations that affect one trait and genetic deviations that affect another trait regardless of the heritabilities of the traits.

Any behavioral genetic design that can estimate genetic and environmental components of the variance of a single trait can also be used to estimate genetic and environmental components of the covariance between two traits. Using the sibling adoption design as an example, instead of correlating one sibling's score with the cosibling's score on the same variable, sibling cross-correlations can be analyzed. A cross-correlation is the correlation between one sibling's score on X and the other sibling's score on Y. In all respects, quantitative genetic analysis of the covariance between traits is parallel to analysis of the variance of a single trait. For example, in univariate analysis, genetic variance and environmental variance sum to the phenotypic variance; in bivariate analysis, genetic covariance and environmental covariance sum to the phenotypic covariance. In univariate analysis, doubling the difference between nonadoptive and adoptive sibling correlations estimates heritability, the proportion of phenotypic variance that can be accounted for by genetic variance. In bivariate analysis, doubling the difference between nonadoptive and adoptive sibling cross-correlations estimates the genetic contribution to the phenotypic correlation. The ratio of the genetic covariance and the phenotypic covariance is bivariate heritability (Plomin & DeFries, 1979). Dividing the phenotypically standardized genetic component of covariance $h_x h_y r_G$ by the product of the square roots of the two traits' heritabilities $h_x h_y$ yields the genetic correlation r_G. The genetic correlation of a variable with itself, of course, is 1.0; thus, the phenotypically standardized genetic covariance $h_x h_y r_G$ reduces to $h_x h_x$, that is, h^2, or heritability, in the univariate case.

The phenotypically standardized genetic covariance $h_x h_y r_G$ and the genetic correlation r_G have different, but equally interesting interpretations. Because $h_x h_y r_G$ is the genetic correlation weighted by the square roots of the heritabilities of each of the traits, it expresses the extent to which the phenotypic correlation between two traits is mediated genetically. The genetic correlation refers to the correlation between genetic deviations that affect one trait and genetic deviations that affect another trait regardless of the heritability of the traits. Developmental change in either term is noteworthy.

The CAP parent–offspring design is not very useful for estimating genetic correlations among measures in infancy and early childhood, because the parents were tested as adults and their offspring are infants and young children. As discussed in the following section, parent–offspring correlations are complicated by the fact that we do not know the extent to which genetic effects in infancy and early childhood are correlated with genetic effects in adulthood. Parent–offspring cross-correlations among measures are further complicated because it cannot be assumed that the genetic correlation between two traits in childhood is the same as the genetic correlation between the traits in adulthood. Nonetheless, we have attempted multivariate model-fitting analyses using parent–offspring data, and these are presented in Chapter 10.

The CAP sibling data are useful for multivariate analyses, as are twin data; however, as mentioned earlier, the relatively small sample size restricts the power of CAP sibling analyses. Although members of sibling pairs are not the same age, adoptive and nonadoptive siblings in CAP have been tested at the same age. As noted earlier, genetic mediation of the phenotypic correlation between two traits is surmised when cross-correlations for nonadoptive siblings exceed those for adoptive siblings. In terms of developmental changes during infancy and early childhood, we wish to compare the genetic contribution to phenotypic covariance among measures across the first few years of life. Although the CAP sibling sample is small, the data will exemplify the concept of multivariate analysis and will provide a preliminary exploration of changes in genetic covariance during infancy and early childhood. In the preceding section, we noted that heritability estimates at 1 and 2 years fluctuate considerably for the CAP sibling data and for available analyses of twin data as well. For this reason, we shall emphasize the genetic component of covariance $h_x h_y r_G$, obtained by doubling the difference between nonadoptive and adoptive sibling cross-correlations rather than attempt to estimate genetic correlations, which would require that we divide the genetic component of covariance $h_x h_y r_G$ by the product of the square roots of the traits' heritabilities $h_x h_y$.

Height and weight

The most well conditioned data for such analyses are physical data. Phenotypic correlations between height and weight are .65, .65, .71, and .65, respectively, at 1, 2, 3, and 4 years. The substantial heritabilities of the two traits, described in the previous section, might lead to the expectation that the phenotypic correlation between height and weight is mediated primarily by genetic factors. However, the genetic component of covariance depends not only on the heritabilities of the two traits but also on the genetic correlation between them. In other words, the genetic component of covariance between two traits $(h_x h_y r_G)$ will be low even when heritabilities of both traits are high if the genetic correlation is low, that is, if the genetic deviations that affect one trait overlap only slightly with the genetic deviations that affect the other trait. If the genetic component of covariance between height and weight were low, it would follow that the phenotypic correlation between the two traits must be mediated environmentally.

We averaged the two cross-correlations – the younger sibling's height versus the older sibling's weight and vice versa. For nonadoptive siblings, the cross-correlations are .33, .35, .37, and .46, respectively, at 1, 2, 3, and 4 years. The fact that these correlations are about half the phenotypic correlations between height and weight is consistent with the hypothesis that the phenotypic correlation is mediated genetically. However, the sibling cross-correlations could be mediated by shared family environment because nonadoptive siblings share family environment as well as heredity. Cross-correlations for adoptive siblings put this hypothesis to the test because, in the absence of selective placement, cross-correlations for adoptive siblings can be mediated only by family environment, not heredity. For the CAP adoptive siblings, the cross-correlations between height and weight are .00, .04, $-.10$, and .14, indicating that shared environment is not an important source of covariance between height and weight. Comparing the nonadoptive- and adoptive-sibling cross-correlations suggests that the phenotypic correlation between height and weight is mediated genetically.

Doubling the difference between the nonadoptive and adoptive correlations suggests the following estimates of $h_x h_y r_G$ at the four ages: .66, .62,

.54 (treating the adoptive sibling cross-correlation at 3 years as zero), and
.64. These results suggest that the phenotypic relationship between height
and weight is largely genetic in origin and that genetic mediation of the
relationship is stable during infancy and early childhood. Parenthetically,
the sibling cross-correlations of .33 and .00 at 12 months cast doubt on the
CAP finding of little heritability for height at that age; $h_x h_y r_G$ cannot be
substantial unless the heritability of X and Y and their genetic correlation
are substantial. However, if the heritability of height were lower in infancy
than in early childhood, as seems to be the case, and if $h_x h_y r_G$ remains
stable, decreasing genetic correlation between height and weight is implied.
In other words, as genetic effects on height increase, those genetic effects
correlate to a lesser extent with genetic effects on weight.

Thus, although genetic mediation of the relationship between height and
weight remains stable during infancy and early childhood, it is possible
that the genetic correlation between height and weight decreases during
infancy.

Temperament and cognition

It is not surprising that the phenotypic correlation between height and
weight is primarily mediated genetically or that the magnitude of genetic
mediation changes little early in life. What about behavioral traits? One
problem in selecting traits for genetic analyses of covariance is that it is
difficult to detect genetic covariance when the phenotypic correlation is
low. Unless a substantial phenotypic correlation exists between two traits,
huge samples are required to detect sibling cross-correlations and, especially, *differences* in cross-correlations for nonadoptive and adoptive siblings. Although the genetic correlation itself can be substantial when the
phenotypic correlation is low – for example, when the heritability of either
trait is low so that the product $h_x h_y r_G$ does not contribute much covariance
even when r_G is substantial – the error of estimation of the genetic correlation under this condition is considerable because the small component
of genetic covariance $(h_x h_y r_G)$ must be divided by the small component
$h_x h_y$, and both components entail large errors of estimate.

Another aspect of this issue is that the genetic component of phenotypic
covariance will be difficult to detect if the heritability of either trait is low,
regardless of the magnitude of the phenotypic correlation. That is, even
if the phenotypic correlation is substantial, the genetic component of covariance $h_x h_y r_G$ will be low if h_x, h_y, or r_G is low.

Nonetheless, these cases in which phenotypic correlations or heritabilities are low yield important information: They imply that the genetic

component of covariance is unimportant. That is, in the case of low phenotypic correlations, to the extent that the traits are heritable, genetic factors that affect one trait are largely independent of genetic factors that affect the other – in other words, the genetic correlation between the traits is low.

The relationship between temperament and cognitive development provides an example. Analyses of CAP data indicate that phenotypic correlations between parental ratings of temperament and Bayley Mental Development Index (MDI) scores are low in infancy (Plomin & DeFries, 1985a); sibling cross-correlations are correspondingly low for both nonadoptive and adoptive siblings. Thus, to the extent that heredity affects these two measures, these genetic effects do not overlap significantly. Furthermore, this nonrelationship shows no sign of change during infancy and early childhood.

One exception to the rule of low phenotypic correlations between temperament and cognitive development occurs for tester ratings on the IBR. At 2 and 3 years, IBR ratings of Affect-Extraversion and of Task Orientation correlate moderately with Bayley MDI scores (at 2), Stanford–Binet IQ scores (at 3), and SICD scores (at 2 and 3). The average phenotypic correlation between the two IBR scales and the cognitive measures is .36. However, at 2 years, the cross-correlations are near zero for both nonadoptive and adoptive siblings, indicating that the phenotypic temperament–cognition association is not mediated genetically, nor is it mediated by shared environmental influence. One possibility is that tester ratings on these two IBR scales are influenced by children's cognitive competence: Children who do well on the cognitive measures are likely to seem happier and more task oriented. At 3, the phenotypic temperament–cognition correlations show evidence of mediation by shared environmental factors. For example, the phenotypic correlation between IBR Affect-Extraversion and Stanford–Binet IQ is .34 and the correlation between IBR Task Orientation and SICD total scores is .48; the nonadoptive- and adoptive-sibling cross-correlations are .24 and .27, respectively, for the association between IBR Affect-Extraversion and Stanford–Binet IQ, and the cross-correlations for IBR Task Orientation and IQ are .32 and .24. Shared environmental influence could emerge if, for example, mothers influence their children's happiness and outgoingness and these traits then affect performance on the IQ test. The cross-correlations of .32 and .24 hint at the possibility of genetic mediation in the relationship between Task Orientation and IQ. The results for the relationship between Task Orientation and SICD are even more suggestive of genetic influence because the nonadoptive-sibling cross-correlation is .22 and the adoptive-sibling cross-correlation is $-.11$. These results do not tell a simple story; they do suggest, however, that the etiologies of temperament–cognition covariance change from 2 to 3 years.

Difficult temperament and emotionality

The case of low heritability is also informative. For example, one of the highest bivariate correlations in the CAP infancy data is between Difficult Temperament and CCTI Emotionality. The correlation is .60 at 12 months and .55 at 24 months. However, the sibling adoption design suggests little heritability for either of these traits. As expected, the sibling cross-correlations are low for both nonadoptive and adoptive siblings, suggesting that the phenotypic correlation between difficult temperament and emotionality is not mediated genetically. As mentioned earlier, although the genetic correlation r_G could be substantial when the genetic component of covariance $h_x h_y r_G$ is low, the genetic correlation cannot be estimated reliably when $h_x h_y r_G$ is low, because the genetic correlation is estimated by dividing $h_x h_y r_G$ by the product $h_x h_y$.

Mental and motor development

The comparison between mental and motor development is one for which the phenotypic correlation and heritabilities are moderate. Scores on the Bayley MDI and the Bayley Psychomotor Development Index (PDI) correlate .42 at 1 and .18 at 2 years. To what extent is this relationship mediated genetically, and is there evidence for developmental change? At 12 months, the nonadoptive-sibling cross-correlation is .23 and the adoptive-sibling cross-correlation is $-.01$, suggesting substantial genetic mediation of the relationship between mental and motor development. At 2 years, however, the phenotypic correlation is low, and the cross-correlations for nonadoptive and adoptive siblings also indicate that $h_x h_y r_G$ is low. The cross-correlations are .01 for nonadoptive siblings and .18 for adoptive siblings. Thus, the data are compatible with a hypothesis of genetic differentiation of mental and motor development during infancy.

Cognitive and communicative development

Another example of bivariate analysis involves the relationship between cognitive and communicative development, as measured by the Bayley MDI and the SICD, respectively. They correlate highly, .67 at 2 years and

.63 at 3 years, and both appear to be influenced by heredity. Cross-correlations are .32 and .04 for nonadoptive and adoptive siblings, respectively, at 2 years, and .36 and .16 at 3 years. Thus, these results suggest substantial and stable genetic mediation of the relationship between cognitive and communicative development. The increasing adoptive-sibling cross-correlation suggests a possible increase in mediation due to shared environment as well.

Expressive and receptive communicative skills

A related example concerns the relationship between expressive and receptive communicative skills as assessed by the SICD at 2 and 3 years. The phenotypic correlations are .51 at 2 and .52 at 3; the nonadoptive- and adoptive-sibling cross-correlations are .25 and −.02 at 2 and .12 and .11 at 3. Thus, at 2 years, the phenotypic relationship between the two variables is substantially mediated by genetic factors; however, the genetic relationship between expressive and receptive communicative skills appears to diminish at 3 years, with increased mediation of shared environment.

Summary

These bivariate analyses are merely illustrative of cross-sectional changes in genetic covariance between measures. Nonetheless, the results point to different but reasonable developmental patterns. Although the magnitude of genetic mediation of the correlation between height and weight does not change, it is likely that the genetic correlation between height and weight decreases during infancy; similar results emerged for the relationship between communicative and cognitive development. For mental and motor development, genetic mediation of the phenotypic relationship decreases from 1 to 2 years, suggesting genetic differentiation; similar results were observed for the relationship between expressive and receptive communicative skills. For both comparisons involving communication, shared environmental mediation – as evidenced by cross-correlations for adoptive siblings – appears to increase from 2 to 3 years. When phenotypic correlations are low, as in the relationship between temperament and cognition, genetic covariance is also low, which indicates nonoverlapping genetic effects on the two variables. When heritabilities are low but phenotypic correlations are high, as in the relationship between difficult temperament and

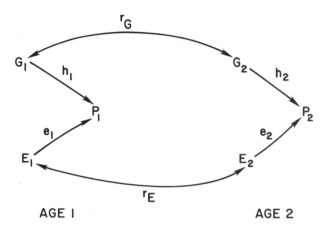

AGE 1   AGE 2

Figure 6.8. Decomposition of phenotypic stability for Trait X from Age 1 to Age 2. (Adapted from Plomin & DeFries, 1981.)

emotionality, environmental mediation of the relationship is implied. The latter relationships do not appear to change developmentally.

At the minimum, these analyses, with their diverse but reasonable results, exemplify an important direction for research on the topic of developmental change.

Age-to-age genetic covariance

Developmental changes in heritability and changes in genetic covariance among variables are cross-sectional concepts. The third concept of genetic change is the most important: age-to-age genetic covariance. The concept of age-to-age genetic covariance follows from the simple extension of multivariate analysis to longitudinal data (Plomin, 1986b; Plomin & DeFries, 1981). In longitudinal analysis, genetic and environmental contributions to phenotypic stability are especially interesting because they refer to the etiology of age-to-age change and continuity, the core issue of developmental transitions.

In the case of longitudinal data, the phenotypic correlation refers to phenotypic stability between a trait measured at one age and a trait (not necessarily the "same" trait) measured at another age in the same individuals. As indicated in Figure 6.8, phenotypic stability can be decomposed into genetic and environmental components of stability. The genetic contribution to stability $h_1 h_2 r_G$ is the age-to-age genetic correlation r_G weighted by the product of the square roots of heritabilities at each age. When divided by the phenotypic stability, this is analogous to bivariate heritability, as described above. The age-to-age genetic correlation indicates the extent to which genetic effects at one age correlate with those at another age regardless of the heritability at each age. That is, genetic deviations at Age 1 could correlate perfectly with genetic deviations at Age 2 even though the genetic deviations at each age make only a small contribution to phenotypic variance. If phenotypic stability is zero between two ages, both genetic and environmental mediation must be zero (except in the unlikely event that a positive genetic covariance is offset by a negative environmental covariance).

In terms of developmental change, the important point is that, to the extent that genetic variance at two ages does not covary between the ages, genetic change is implicated. In this way, low age-to-age genetic correlations can serve as important markers of developmental change during infancy and early childhood. Because phenotypic stability correlations are often only modest in magnitude, whereas heritabilities are often moderate and sometimes substantial, it is likely that genetics is a potent source of developmental change.

As discussed earlier in a more general context, genetic correlations do not address molecular mechanisms. For example, the same genes need not be transcribed at the two ages even if the genetic correlation is 1.0: The relevant genes at Age 2 might no longer be actively transcribed, but their structural legacy (e.g., differences in neural networks) could produce a genetic correlation between Age 1 and Age 2. Conversely, if a genetic correlation between two points in development is zero, actively transcribed genes that affect the trait at Age 1 could continue to be actively transcribed at Age 2 if their gene products no longer have the same effect at that time. In other words, genetic correlation refers to covariance between the genetic deviations that affect two traits rather than to the transcription and translation of the same genes.

Although analyses of age-to-age genetic and environmental correlations will undoubtedly become a hallmark of developmental behavioral genetic analyses in the future, they require longitudinal data, and few longitudinal behavioral genetic studies have been conducted. In fact, in addition to the classic Skodak and Skeels (1949) adoption study of IQ, only two long-term longitudinal behavioral genetic studies have been reported: the Louisville Twin Study (Wilson, 1983) and the CAP. The studies complement each other in design because the twin design provides estimates of genetic parameters for children of comparable ages, as does the CAP sibling adoption design. In contrast, the parent–offspring adoption design, from a genetic perspective, is like an "instant" longitudinal study from childhood to adulthood. Thus, twin and sibling designs are useful for assessing genetic correlations within childhood. When twin and sibling data are combined with CAP parent–offspring data, genetic stability from childhood to adulthood can be estimated.

The LTS data have not been analyzed in terms of age-to-age genetic correlations. Analyses of the longitudinal twin data from this study have employed twin trend correlations based on age-to-age profiles. Trend correlations are complex functions of heritabilities at each age and genetic and phenotypic correlations among the ages. In addition, it is difficult to use trend correlations to study transitions, because trend correlations assess the similarity of twins for patterns of spurts and lags across several longitudinal data points. In the LTS, the results of analysis of twin trend correlations for longitudinal profiles are generally similar to the average twin results for scores at each age, perhaps because trend correlations include twin similarity both for overall level and for age-to-age changes (Wilson, 1986).

CAP sibling analysis of age-to-age genetic covariance

Adoptive and nonadoptive sibling data can be used to assess age-to-age genetic covariance during infancy and childhood. The purpose of this section is to present CAP data on age-to-age sibling cross-correlations for nonadoptive and adoptive siblings and to consider their implications for developmental change during infancy and early childhood.

When phenotypic age-to-age covariance is less than the reliable variance of the measure, developmental change has occurred, change that could be genetic or environmental in origin. If phenotypic stability is lower than the geometric mean of the heritabilities at each age, the genetic correlation between ages must be less than unity. For example, in the LTS, the 6-month stability for tester ratings on the IBR is about .40 during infancy (Figure 5.13), whereas heritabilities average .50 or greater (Figures 6.4 to 6.6). If the phenotypic stability were mediated entirely genetically, the genetic correlation would be .80, which implies some slight genetic change. However, in the more likely scenario in which some phenotypic stability is mediated environmentally, the genetic correlation could be much lower. For example, if half of the phenotypic stability is mediated environmentally, the age-to-age genetic correlation would be .40, suggesting substantial genetic change across ages.

In the previous section on multivariate analysis, we noted that developmental changes in genetic covariance among variables are difficult to detect unless phenotypic correlations and heritabilities are substantial. Without these conditions, nonadoptive- and adoptive-sibling cross-correlations are low and thus statistical power becomes a problem in detecting differences between nonadoptive- and adoptive-sibling cross-correlations and especially in comparing such correlational differences across ages. Similarly in longitudinal analysis, genetic mediation of phenotypic stability is difficult to detect if phenotypic stability is low. The case with the greatest power to detect age-to-age genetic change is one in which heritabilities are substantial at both ages. At the extreme, if heritabilities are high and phenotypic stability is low, the age-to-age genetic correlation can be safely assumed to be negligible and we can conclude that genetic change is important.

Height and weight. Physical characteristics provide a useful benchmark for developmental analyses. Table 6.3 lists CAP phenotypic correlations and nonadoptive and adoptive sibling cross-correlations for longitudinal comparisons across infancy and early childhood. The phenotypic correlations differ slightly from those in Chapter 5 because correlations in Table 6.3 are based on children in the sibling sample rather than on all children in the CAP sample. The cross-correlations are averaged for younger sibling at age 1 versus older sibling at age 2 and vice versa.

For height, phenotypic stability from year to year is mediated nearly entirely by genetic factors. Doubling the difference between the nonadoptive and adoptive sibling cross-correlations estimates $h_1 h_2 r_G$; in each case, these estimates are close to the phenotypic stability from year to year, suggesting that stability is genetic in origin. Dividing these estimates of $h_1 h_2 r_G$ by $h_1 h_2$ (heritabilities were presented earlier in this chapter) suggests that year-to-year genetic correlations are, on average, unity for height.

The picture for weight is somewhat different. Considering the negative adoptive sibling cross-correlations as zero, $h_1 h_2 r_G$ estimates are about .20 less than each year-to-year phenotypic correlation, suggesting that environmental factors are responsible for about 30% of the substantial phenotypic stability for weight. As in the case of height, however, estimates of year-to-year genetic correlations are unity, implying that genetic effects on weight at one age are isomorphic with genetic effects on weight at other ages.

In summary, and not surprisingly, CAP sibling data for height and weight suggest that year-to-year genetic change is negligible.

Behavioral development. Behavioral development would seem more likely than height or weight to evidence genetic change. Table 6.3 includes age-to-age sibling cross-correlations for cognitive and personality variables.

Table 6.3. *CAP sibling adoption analysis of age-to-age covariance*

| | Phenotypic correlations | | | Sibling cross-correlations | | | | | |
| | | | | Nonadoptive | | | Adoptive | | |
Measure	1–2 years	2–3 years	3–4 years	1–2 years	2–3 years	3–4 years	1–2 years	2–3 years	3–4 years
Height	.63	.68	.72	.34	.43	.37	.09	.05	.03
Weight	.77	.89	.84	.27	.31	.34	−.13	−.07	−.03
IQ	.36	.48	.59	.15	.25	.37	.14	.06	.22
Verbal[a]	.28	.31	.48	.02	.18	.34	.09	−.03	.13
Spatial[b]	.20	.27	.39	.21	.18	.20	−.11	−.03	.20
CCTI Emotionality	.57	.58	.68	.11	.02	−.14	.13	.03	.24
CCTI Activity	.58	.68	.58	.18	.18	.11	.09	−.11	−.19
CCTI Sociability	.59	.62	.63	.16	.12	.11	.05	.04	−.07
CCTI Attention Span	.42	.66	.60	.09	.14	.09	.09	−.02	−.04
Difficult Temperament	.54	.61	.54	.09	−.04	−.21	.04	−.16	−.21

[a]Bayley scales of Verbal at 1 year, Verbal-Symbolic at 2, and CAP Verbal at 3 and 4 years.
[b]Bayley scales of Means–End at 1 year, Spatial at 2 years, and CAP Spatial at 3 and 4 years.

As noted earlier, age-to-age genetic change cannot be important if genetic variance does not affect a characteristic. As discussed earlier, parental ratings of temperament show little evidence of genetic influence during infancy and early childhood. Table 6.3 indicates that, as expected on the basis of low heritability, genetic mediation of the substantial year-to-year stability for parental CCTI ratings is negligible: The average nonadoptive-sibling cross-correlation for the four CCTI traits is .10 for nonadoptive siblings and .03 for adoptive siblings. No trends are apparent across ages or across traits. Because $h_1 h_2 r_G$ is low, the substantial stability of parental ratings must be mediated environmentally; one possibility is that this finding represents an artifact of parental ratings – the stability is in the minds of parents.

Because $h_1 h_2 r_G$ is negligible, as are h_1 and h_2, it is risky to assess r_G, the genetic correlation. Nonetheless, it should be noted that, if heritability is very low at each age, a high genetic correlation could occur even when $h_1 h_2 r_G$ is low; this appears to be the case for parental ratings of temperament. In other words, even though genetic variance has only a slight effect on parental ratings of temperament, genetic deviations that affect a trait at one age correlate highly with genetic deviations that affect the trait at another age.

Parental ratings of Difficult Temperament yielded results similar to those for the CCTI scales – high phenotypic stability but low genetic mediation. Not listed in Table 6.3 are Bayley IBR results for tester ratings of temperament because the IBR is applicable only at 1 and 2 years; although we attempted to construct IBR analogs at 3 and 4 years, the factor structure at 3 and 4 differs, which vitiates longitudinal comparisons. However, the results at 1 and 2 are relevant. Only one of the three IBR scales – Affect-Extraversion – displayed genetic influence at both 1 and 2 years, and this scale is the only one to suggest genetic mediation of phenotypic stability from years 1 to 2. However, IBR stability is low from 1 to 2 for Affect-Extraversion, which implies that all of the phenotypic stability is mediated genetically.

IQ shows some genetic influence, and it also yields modest and increasing phenotypic stability throughout infancy and early childhood. As indicated in Table 6.3, sibling cross-correlations indicate no genetic mediation of stability from 1 to 2 years but considerable genetic mediation from 2 to 3 and from 3 to 4. The results for CAP Verbal are similar to those for IQ; CAP Spatial results, however, suggest genetic mediation of stability from 1 to 2 and from 2 to 3, but not from 3 to 4. In general, $h_1 h_2 r_G$ (doubling the difference between the nonadoptive and adoptive sibling cross-correlations) is similar to the phenotypic stability from year to year, suggesting that genetic mediation can account for phenotypic stability for cognitive development after infancy.

It is interesting if, as suggested by the CAP sibling data, age-to-age genetic continuity is negligible for IQ and verbal ability from 1 to 2 years and then increases from 2 to 3 and from 3 to 4. Because the CAP sibling data indicate substantial heritability at 1 and 2, the negligible estimate of $h_1 h_2 r_G$ from age 1 to 2 suggests considerable genetic change from 1 to 2 – that is, the genetic correlation between 1 and 2 years is negligible. Because the CAP sibling data indicate low heritability at 3 and 4 years, the substantial estimates of $h_1 h_2 r_G$ from 2 to 3 and from 3 to 4 imply that genetic correlations are unity. In fact, these estimates of genetic correlations are greatly in excess of unity, suggesting the more likely possibility that CAP sibling estimates of heritability at 3 and 4 are too low. They are lower than twin estimates and, as we shall see in the next section, they are lower than estimates based on CAP parent–offspring comparisons.

Summary. The small sample size and attendant large errors of estimation urge caution in relying on these results. However, the results suggest some exciting possibilities in considering age-to-age genetic change and continuity. As expected, results for height indicate that phenotypic stability is entirely mediated genetically; for weight, both genetic and environmental factors affect stability. For both height and weight, genetic correlations are near unity – that is, little or no genetic change occurs during infancy and early childhood. In contrast, parental ratings of temperament, although displaying substantial phenotypic stability from year to year, show negligible genetic influence at each year and thus negligible genetic mediation. One question for future research concerns the environmental source of the substantial phenotypic stability: Does it reside in the minds of parents? Tester ratings on the IBR indicate genetic influence for one dimension, and it is that dimension that shows genetically-mediated continuity. In terms of cognitive development, it is an intriguing possibility that, as indicated by CAP sibling data (but not by twin data), heritability is considerable for Bayley scores at 1 and 2 years but that genetic mediation of stability from 1 to 2 is low, suggesting substantial genetic change from 1 to 2. Genetic correlations for IQ in early childhood appear to be substantial, even though the CAP sibling data suggest low heritability. The finding of increasing age-to-age genetic correlations for IQ correspond to results for parent–offspring analyses, which are discussed in the next section.

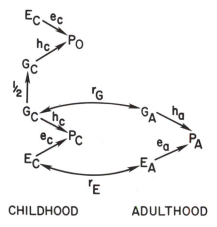

CHILDHOOD   ADULTHOOD

Figure 6.9. Path model illustrating correlations between biological parents tested as children (P_C) and as adults (P_A) and their adopted-away offspring tested as children (P_O). (Adapted from Plomin & DeFries, 1985b.)

CAP analyses of genetic correlations from childhood to adulthood

In this section, we outline the role of genetic correlation in parent–offspring resemblance, present biological-mother/adoptee correlations from the point of view of genetic correlations, and foreshadow Chapter 10's model-fitting analyses of genetic continuity from childhood to adulthood in terms of developmental changes in genetic correlations. A schematic path diagram illustrating the genetic relationship between biological mothers and their adopted-away children is presented in Figure 6.9. Although the diagram looks complicated, it merely combines the information on genetic correlation from Figure 6.8 with the usual genetic relationship between parents and offspring. The left side of Figure 6.9 depicts the traditional genetic expectation for the relationship between parents and their offspring, $0.5h^2$. However, this traditional approach assumes that developmental genetic change is unimportant. Heritabilities for parents and offspring are assumed to be the same, and the genetic correlation between adulthood (i.e., parents) and childhood (i.e., offspring) is assumed to be 1.0. In Figure 6.9, these assumptions are appropriate because the left side of the path diagram depicts expected parent–offspring similarity with the parent as a child of the same age as the adopted-away child. Of course, biological mothers in the CAP cannot be studied as children; this is the reason for the right side of Figure 6.9. This part of the path diagram merely indicates, as in Figure 6.8, that genetic resemblance from childhood to adulthood is a function of the genetic correlation and that heritabilities in childhood and adulthood can differ. From Figure 6.9, the expectation for the correlation between biological mothers and their adopted-away children is $0.5h_ah_cr_G$. If the genetic correlation between childhood and adulthood is 1.0 and if heritabilities are the same in childhood and adulthood, this reduces to the familiar $0.5h^2$.

In summary, resemblance between biological mothers and their adopted-away offspring involves not only heritability of the measure in childhood and in adulthood, but also the genetic correlation between childhood and adulthood. Thus, changes in correlations between biological mothers and their adopted-away children at 1, 2, 3, and 4 years could be brought about because of changes in heritability at those ages or by changes in genetic correlations between those ages and adulthood. In this sense, the CAP parent–offspring design is not powerful for detecting heritability in childhood. Parent–offspring resemblance also requires genetic continuity between childhood and adulthood as well as heritability at each age – but this is the design's strength as well: Finding significant parent–offspring resemblance implies not only significant heritability in childhood and in adulthood but also significant genetic continuity between childhood and adulthood.

Statistical power represents a serious problem in these analyses. Because the expected genetic resemblance between biological parents and their adopted-away children is the usual 50% resemblance weighted by the products of the square roots of heritability in childhood, heritability in adulthood, and the genetic correlation between childhood and adulthood, parent–offspring resemblance will be modest at most. In fact, it would be difficult to detect parent–offspring resemblance unless all three factors are substantial, because they are multiplied to produce the parent–offspring expectation. For example, if a trait is 50% heritable in childhood and in adulthood and the genetic correlation for the trait is .50 between childhood and adulthood, the expected parent–offspring correlation is .125. A correlation of this magnitude would require a sample of more than 600 biological mothers and their adopted-away infants to detect the correlation with 80% power ($p < .05$, one-tailed; Cohen, 1977). The CAP sample size provides about 50% power to detect such correlations, which means that significant genetic influence of this magnitude will go undetected half of the time. This problem is exacerbated if correlations for biological mothers and their adopted-away offspring are compared across 1, 2, 3, and 4 years of age. For example, the IQ correlation between biological mothers and their adopted-away children in infancy is about .10 (Plomin & DeFries,

1985a). Even if the genetic contribution doubles during the transition to early childhood, a sample size of well over a thousand pairs would be needed to detect the difference between the correlations of .10 and .20 with 80% power. If the genetic contribution tripled – too much to expect – more than 300 pairs would be needed to attain 80% power to detect a significant difference between the correlations of .10 and .30.

The CAP sample size yields only 20% power to detect differences in biological-mother/adoptee correlations such as .10 versus .20 and only 50% power to detect differences between correlations of .10 versus .30. Moreover, biological-mother/adoptee correlations are unlikely to be detected if, during childhood, the age-to-age genetic correlation is low. That is, if genetic influences at year 1 are not substantially correlated with genetic influences at year 2, it is unlikely that genetic effects in infancy will correlate with genetic effects in adulthood. The preceding section indicated that height, weight, and mental development yielded substantial genetic correlations from year to year in infancy and early childhood; genetic correlations were low for temperament measures. Thus, there is some chance of finding biological-mother/adoptee correlations for the former variables, but not the latter.

In the following subsections, correlations between biological mothers and their adopted-away offspring are emphasized because their resemblance directly estimates $0.5h_ah_cr_G$. Although resemblance between non-adoptive parents and their children also includes $0.5h_ah_cr_G$, it is complicated by environmental factors. Nonetheless, it is possible to incorporate all of the CAP data – including biological, adoptive, and nonadoptive mothers and fathers – in these analyses; model-fitting analyses of this type are described in Chapter 8. The present discussion is concerned to a greater extent with concepts of developmental change and simple analyses pertinent to the exploration of these concepts rather than with parameter estimation or model testing.

Height and weight. With these caveats in mind, the correlations for major variables between biological mothers and their adopted-away offspring can be compared during infancy and early childhood. As depicted in Figure 6.10, CAP parent–offspring results for height are similar to the childhood-to-adulthood longitudinal data shown in Figure 5.6 in the sense that they show at most a slight increase from 1 to 4 years. The magnitude of the parent–offspring correlations is approximately half that of the child–adult longitudinal correlations in Figure 5.6, which is to be expected, because parents and children are only half as similar as children are with themselves as adults.

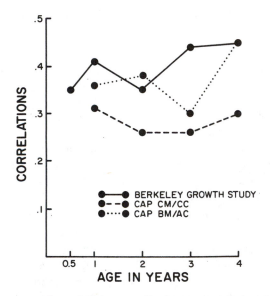

Figure 6.10. Parent–offspring correlations for height during infancy and early child-hood for CAP biological mothers and adopted-away children (BM/AC) and control (nonadoptive) mothers and children (CM/CC) and for control mothers and children in the Berkeley Growth Study.

Correlations between biological mothers' height and the height of their adopted-away offspring at 1, 2, 3, and 4 years are .36, .38, .30, and .45. Both biological-mother and control-mother correlations are similar to the average weighted correlation of .31 from 20 parent–offspring studies of height for children from 5 to 13 (Mueller, 1976). Parent–offspring corre-lations for 50 families in the Berkeley Growth Study, also included in Figure 6.10, are somewhat higher than these average correlations.

Parent–offspring correlations for weight, presented in Figure 6.11, sug-gest roughly the same conclusion: slight increases in child-to-adult genetic continuity from 1 to 4 years. In the CAP, correlations between biological mothers and their adopted-away offspring are similar to those of nona-doptive parents, with the exception of the 12-month correlation. Figure 6.11 also indicates that biological-mother/adoptee correlations are similar to correlations for nonadoptive-parent/adoptee comparisons in the CAP and in the Berekely Growth Study. In a review of nine parent–offspring studies of children from 5 to 13, the average weighted correlation was .26 (Mueller, 1976), which is similar to the average correlation in Figure 6.11.

Thus, these data, which can be seen as an "instant" longitudinal study from childhood to adulthood, suggest that phenotypic stability from child-

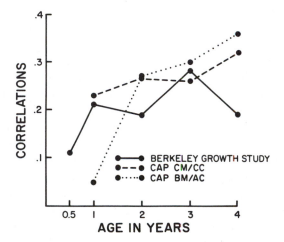

Figure 6.11. Parent–offspring correlations for weight during infancy and early child-hood for CAP biological mothers and adopted-away children (BM/AC) and control (nonadoptive) mothers and children (CM/CC) and for control mothers and children in the Berkeley Growth Study.

hood to adulthood for height and weight is mediated largely by genetic factors and that genetic continuity from childhood to adulthood increases slightly from 1 to 4 years.

Cognitive development. In the preceding chapter, Figure 5.10 presented longitudinal correlations for IQ from childhood to adulthood, correlations that were generally significant but of moderate size. If these longitudinal correlations are due entirely to genetic influence, the expected correlations between parents and their children are only half those in Figure 5.10. At these low magnitudes of correlation, statistical power is a critical issue, especially in the attempt to detect differences in parent–offspring correlations from one age to the next.

Few studies other than the CAP are directly relevant to these issues. The famous study by Skodak and Skeels (1949) did not begin until after infancy; the average age of the children at their first testing was 26 months, and the ages varied from 6 months to 6 years. The reported biological-mother/adoptee IQ correlation for 63 pairs was .00 at the average age of 26 months and .28 at the average age of 51 months. However, the wide age range within these average months led us to compute biological-mother/adoptee correlations for a narrow age band using the raw data provided by Skodak and Skeels. For 39 mother–child pairs in which infants were tested between 12 and 24 months, the correlation is −.01; between

24 and 36 months, the correlation is .20 for 24 pairs; and between 36 and 48 months, the correlation is .18 for 27 pairs. Although $h_a h_c r_G$ apparently increases from the second to the third year, the small sample sizes do not permit any confidence in these age comparisons.

Data of this type from two other adoption studies are not useful because of technical problems. A cross-sectional study of the relationship between biological mothers' IQ and Kuhlman test scores of their adopted-away children between the ages of 1 and 5 years was reported by Snygg (1938). Unfortunately, there is no doubt that the biological mothers were a biased sample because "girls who had passed high school entrance examinations were seldom asked to take psychological tests" (Snygg, 1938, p. 403); their average IQ was only 78, and the range was probably restricted, although no information concerning variance was provided in the brief report. In a third study (Casler, 1976), in which the Gesell test was administered five times from 2 to 27 months, selective placement was intentionally practiced and results were presented only in terms of Gesell subtest scores for the infants.

Although it is not especially surprising that there are few adoption studies in infancy, it is astonishing that there appears to be only one small study of IQ of nonadoptive parents and their infant offspring (Eichorn, 1969). The only other relevant data of which we are aware is a study reporting correlations between nonadoptive mothers' WAIS Vocabulary and Block Design scores and Bayley MDI scores of their offspring at 12 and 24 months (Gottfried & Gottfried, 1984). For Vocabulary, the mother–offspring correlations were −.01 and .18 at 12 and 24 months, respectively; for Block Design, the correlations were −.03 and .03.

Figure 6.12 presents CAP IQ correlations between biological mothers and their adopted-away offspring, which suggest some genetic continuity from infancy to adulthood. Correlations for nonadoptive mothers and their children are similar. On average, the mother–child correlations increase somewhat, from about .10 at 1 to about .20 at 4 years.

As indicated in the discussion of Figure 6.9, the phenotypic correlation between biological mothers and their adopted-away offspring represents $0.5 h_a h_c r_G$. Thus, we can estimate the genetic contribution to phenotypic stability between childhood and adulthood, $h_a h_c r_G$, by doubling the biological-mother/child correlations in Figure 6.12. These estimates are similar to the average child-to-adult IQ correlations from the Berkeley Growth Study and the Guidance Study shown in Figure 5.6, suggesting that nearly all of the phenotypic covariance from infancy and childhood to adulthood is mediated genetically.

Age-to-age genetic correlations can be roughly estimated by dividing

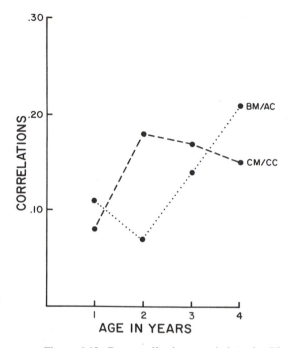

Figure 6.12. Parent–offspring correlations for IQ during infancy (Bayley MDI scores) and early childhood (Stanford–Binet IQ scores) for CAP biological mothers and adopted-away children (BM/AC) and control (nonadoptive) mothers and children (CM/CC).

$h_a h_c r_G$ by $h_a h_c$, the product of the square roots of heritabilities in childhood and in adulthood. As noted earlier, heritabilities from the LTS twin correlations and the CAP sibling adoption correlations are quite different. Using heritability estimates from the twin sample from Figure 6.3 (.10, .16, .18, and .24, at 1, 2, 3, and 4, years, respectively), .50 for adult heritability of IQ (Plomin & DeFries, 1980), and the correlation between biological mothers and their adopted-away offspring as an estimate of $0.5 h_a h_c r_G$, genetic correlations to adulthood are approximately 1.0 from 1, 2, 3, and 4 years. Thus, although these estimates may be inflated by heritability estimates that are too low or by assortative mating, the results suggest surprisingly high genetic correlations from childhood to adulthood. Moreover, the magnitude of the genetic correlations does not appear to change substantially during infancy and early childhood. Chapter 8 describes a path model that uses these data as well as the other data from the CAP to assess genetic stability more rigorously; these model-fitting analyses also suggest significant and substantial genetic stability from childhood to adulthood, although genetic correlations are estimated to be considerably less than 1.0, which leaves room for genetic change as well as continuity.

The CAP sibling adoption design suggests higher heritability in infancy and lower heritability in childhood than do the twin data. Thus, using these estimates of heritability results in lower genetic correlations from infancy to adulthood (.38 from 1 year and .26 from 2 years). Genetic correlations in early childhood, however, are impossibly high (much greater than 1.0), suggesting again that the CAP sibling adoption data have underestimated heritability at 3 and 4 years.

In summary, the CAP parent–offspring data for IQ imply that nearly all of the phenotypic covariance from childhood to adulthood is mediated genetically. Genetic correlations from childhood to adulthood are very high.

Tables 6.4 and 6.5 present biological-, adoptive-, and nonadoptive-parent/offspring correlations for the major CAP measures. Biological-mother/adoptee correlations for specific cognitive abilities are lower than for IQ; however, correlations for nonadoptive mothers and their children are consistent with the possibility of some genetic mediation from childhood to adulthood, although less than for IQ. Using the biological-mother/adoptee correlations, for example, suggests that the genetic contribution to phenotypic resemblance between childhood and adulthood is only about .15 for Verbal and about .10 for Spatial. As discussed earlier, heritability of specific cognitive abilities is probably lower than for IQ: Even if genetic correlations from childhood to adulthood were substantial, genetic stability from childhood to adulthood would be lower as a result. The SICD at 2 and 3 years yields results similar to Verbal.

Temperament and adjustment. It is unlikely that any parent–offspring resemblance will be observed for measures of temperament in the CAP because of the negligible phenotypic stabilities between childhood and adulthood in the New York Longitudinal Study and because age-to-age genetic correlations during childhood appear to be low. Furthermore, even for much older children, parent–offspring correlations for control families are only about .15 (Plomin, 1986a). The expectation of low correlations is borne out in Table 6.5, which presents parent–offspring correlations for temperament measures. The IBR correlations are based on tester ratings, and the CCTI ratings are derived from the average of adoptive mothers' and fathers' ratings of the children's temperament. Parent–offspring correlations for biological mothers and their adopted-away offspring are particularly interesting for two reasons: Parent–offspring resemblance can be

Table 6.4. *CAP parent–offspring correlations for height, weight, and cognitive abilities*

Measure	Age	Biological		Adoptive		Nonadoptive	
		Mother	Father	Mother	Father	Mother	Father
Height	1	.36	.05	.15	.05	.31	.35
	2	.38	.26	.17	−.01	.26	.29
	3	.30	.22	.07	.04	.26	.35
	4	.45	.03	.13	.01	.32	.30
Weight	1	.05	.02	.05	.01	.23	.25
	2	.27	.03	.02	.01	.27	.19
	3	.30	.06	.05	.01	.26	.24
	4	.36	.04	.05	.00	.32	.28
IQ	1	.11	.29	.10	.06	.08	.08
	2	.07	.30	.08	.05	.18	.15
	3	.14	.18	.15	.21	.17	.14
	4	.21	.44	.21	.15	.15	.12
Verbal[a]	1	.03	.07	−.04	.07	.09	−.01
	2	.07	.27	.02	.03	.09	.09
	3	.08	.07	.08	.06	.15	.25
	4	.08	.06	.11	.13	.19	.10
Spatial[b]	1	.10	.02	−.02	.10	.02	−.01
	2	.10	.08	−.04	.00	.22	.09
	3	.02	.13	−.01	.13	.20	.15
	4	.05	−.01	−.04	.03	.11	.22
SICD[c]	2	.05	.36	.14	.20	.11	.05
	3	.09	.08	.09	.07	.18	.15
Perceptual Speed	3	.09	−.10	−.03	.08	.17	.08
	4	−.03	.22	−.03	.02	.15	.09
Memory	3	.14	.32	.10	−.12	−.03	−.10
	4	−.03	−.08	.14	−.05	.03	−.06

[a]Bayley scales of Verbal at 1 year, Verbal-Symbolic at 2 years, and CAP Verbal at 3 and 4 years as correlated with parental verbal ability.
[b]Bayley scales of Means–End at 1 year, Spatial at 2 years, and CAP Spatial at 3 and 4 years as correlated with parental spatial ability.
[c]Total score for the SICD measure of communicative development as correlated with parental verbal ability.

due only to heredity, and the adoptees and biological mothers are rated by different individuals.

The parent–offspring correlations are low, especially for the IBR ratings. Some suggestion of genetic influence for Sociability-Shyness can be seen. No consistent pattern of changing genetic influence emerged. Emotionality,

Table 6.5. *CAP parent–offspring correlations for IBR, CCTI, and Difficult Temperament*

Child measure	Age (years)	Parent measure	Biological		Adoptive		Nonadoptive	
			Mother	Father	Mother	Father	Mother	Father
IBR Affect-Extraversion	1	EAS Emotionality-Fear	.02	−.01	.02	.03	.03	.10
	2		−.07	.26	.00	.01	−.07	−.08
	3		.02	.22	−.03	−.05	−.05	−.06
	4		−.04	.13	−.07	−.03	.17	−.01
IBR Affect-Extraversion	1	EAS Sociability	.03	.30	.00	.08	.07	.09
	2		.04	.02	−.03	.00	.14	−.06
	3		.04	−.11	.01	−.06	−.03	−.02
	4		.09	.20	−.07	.11	−.01	.05
IBR Activity	1	EAS Activity	.09	−.04	.07	.17	−.05	.06
	2		−.08	−.25	−.01	.13	.01	.05
	3		−.03	.10	.02	.02	.00	.12
	4		−.06	.23	−.01	−.07	−.05	.06
IBR Task Orientation	1	EAS Impulsivity	.06	−.06	−.07	.11	.05	.08
	2		.07	.07	.04	−.06	−.04	−.07
	3		.03	.24	.01	−.01	.09	.01
	4		.07	.18	−.08	−.04	.02	.11
CCTI Emotionality	1	EAS Emotionality	.04	−.11	.13	.10	.04	.16
	2		.01	−.02	.17	.05	.05	.09
	3		−.03	.10	.18	.04	.07	.09
	4		−.05	.03	.17	−.04	.04	.05

		EAS Activity		EAS Sociability		EAS Impulsivity	16PF Neuroticism
CCTI Activity	1	.03	-.19	.03	.04	.03	.15
	2	.05	.15	.05	.02	-.01	.04
	3	-.03	.28	.03	.15	-.08	.04
	4	-.01	.08	-.06	.02	-.05	.07
CCTI Sociability	1	.07	-.15	.12	.16	.27	.10
	2	.09	-.02	.11	.19	.19	.12
	3	.13	.09	.12	.15	.10	.03
	4	.08	-.14	.11	.07	.01	-.03
CCTI Attention Span	1	-.01	.15	-.05	-.19	.13	.03
	2	.00	-.16	-.03	-.20	.00	-.04
	3	-.02	-.21	-.11	-.07	-.01	-.08
	4	.08	-.35	-.06	-.05	.00	-.07
Difficult Temperament	1	.04	-.19	.03	.08	.13	.11
	2	.01	-.10	.09	.03	.13	.08
	3	.10	-.17	.08	.15	.04	.09
	4	.02	-.07	.10	.04	.03	-.04

Sociability, and Impulsivity also suggest some shared environmental influence at all ages, although the possibility exists that this is a bias due to the use of parental self-reports and parental ratings of their children's temperament. Many other combinations of variables yielded results similar to those reported in Table 6.5, such as comparisons between mothers' Extraversion and children's Sociability and between mothers' Neuroticism and children's Emotionality.

Although adjustment per se was not assessed for CAP parents, we were able to explore parent–offspring resemblance using Neuroticism as assessed by Cattell's 16PF and Difficult Temperament in children. Neither in infancy nor in early childhood did Difficult Temperament of adoptees correlate significantly with Neuroticism of biological mothers.

Doubling the biological-mother/adoptee correlations for temperament and adjustment in order to estimate $h_a h_c r_G$ suggests little genetic contribution to phenotypic stability from infancy and childhood to adulthood. If heritability is moderate in infancy and childhood, as it appears to be in adulthood, genetic covariances are likely to be low for these domains. This would imply that genetic change rather than continuity dominates for temperament and adjustment, both within infancy and childhood and from infancy and childhood to adulthood.

Summary

Exploration of genetic and environmental etiologies of developmental change is too new to yield clear conclusions. A summary of this chapter, however, may help the reader integrate its numerous concepts and results. In Chapter 5, three major descriptive types of developmental changes in variance and covariance were discussed. The present chapter considered etiological analogs: developmental change in heritability and environmentality, patterns of genetic and environmental correlations among measures, and age-to-age genetic and environmental correlations. Early in the chapter we noted that descriptive and etiological changes in development need not produce the same results. The most notable demonstration of this principle is that low phenotypic stability can mask substantial age-to-age genetic correlations. For example, individual differences in cognitive development show modest year-to-year phenotypic correlations in infancy and early childhood, and phenotypic correlations from infancy and early childhood to adulthood are also moderate. However, genetic correlations within infancy and childhood and, most surprisingly, from childhood to adulthood are substantial. This important result suggests that genetic factors that affect individual differences in cognitive scores at one age overlap substantially with genetic effects at even much later ages.

The first type of etiological analysis – developmental change in heritability – suggests an interesting hypothesis: When heritability changes during development, it increases. Part of the importance of this hypothesis lies in its counterintuitive nature. As discussed earlier, most developmentalists would guess that environmental variance, not genetic variance, increasingly explains phenotypic variance as children grow up and experience more and more diverse environmental influences. For height and weight, heritability increases during infancy, reaching high levels by early childhood. For cognitive development, the picture is not as clear. Twin data suggest that heritability increases about 5% per year, from 10% to 25% from 1 to 4 years, whereas CAP sibling adoption data suggest greater heritability in infancy. Even at 4 years, the twin data indicate that heritability of IQ scores is only half that of later childhood, adolescence, and adulthood. For measures of temperament and television viewing, extant research is not yet adequate to posit developmental trends in heritability. On the basis of current evidence, heritability of temperament does not appear to change much during infancy and early childhood.

The second type of etiological change in development focuses on the etiology of covariance among measures rather than the variance of each measure considered individually. From a genetic perspective, the issue is whether genetic covariance among measures changes during development. For example, height and weight correlate substantially, and this phenotypic correlation is mediated almost completely by genetic covariance; the extent of genetic mediation does not appear to change during infancy and early childhood. That is, the genes that affect individual differences in height are also responsible for individual differences in weight. The results for the relationship between communicative and cognitive development are similar to those for height and weight.

When relationships involve low phenotypic correlations (e.g., between temperament and cognitive abilities), genetic mediation is difficult to detect. Such cases are informative because they imply that genetic factors that affect one trait are largely independent of genetic factors that affect the other trait given that both traits are heritable. The case of low heritability, which is relevant to the high phenotypic correlation between Difficult Temperament and Emotionality, is also informative in suggesting that genetic factors are not significantly involved in the association between the two measures.

Another example of etiological change in development is the association between mental and motor development, in which the phenotypic correlation diminishes from 1 to 2 years. This change in phenotypic resemblance between mental and motor development during infancy reflects a reduction in their genetic correlation, which suggests possible genetic differentiation. Similar results were obtained for the relationship between expressive and receptive communicative skills.

We know least about the most important type of etiological change in development – changes in age-to-age genetic correlations – because these analyses require longitudinal data. In this chapter, we examined data for year-to-year change and continuity during infancy and early childhood and for long-term comparisons from childhood to adulthood using the parent–offspring design as an instant longitudinal study from childhood to adulthood. As mentioned earlier, the surprise is that genetic correlations during infancy and early childhood – and even from infancy and early childhood to adulthood – may be quite substantial for mental development as well as for height and weight. In other words, genetic influences at one age appear to correlate substantially with genetic influences at another age. As explained earlier, genetic correlations can be substantial even when phenotypic stability correlations are modest, as is the case for cognitive development. Nearly all of this modest phenotypic stability appears to be mediated genetically. Height, weight, and IQ also show slight increases in genetic continuity from infancy and early childhood to adulthood.

Less genetic continuity is found for other variables. Specific cognitive abilities yield some evidence of year-to-year genetic mediation, and similar to the results for IQ, verbal ability shows increasing genetic continuity during infancy and early childhood. Genetic continuity from childhood to adulthood is lower for specific cognitive abilities than for IQ. Both year-to-year and child-to-adult genetic continuity is low for temperament and adjustment, even though year-to-year phenotypic stability is greater than for IQ. To the extent that these variables are heritable, these results suggest that genetic change is more important than continuity.

The goal of the present chapter has been to present these new concepts of etiological changes in development at an expository, intuitive level. However, model-fitting approaches are needed to provide more formal tests of these hypotheses and to utilize all of the data simultaneously. In the case of the CAP data, the analyses include adoptive and nonadoptive parents as well as biological parents; the present chapter focused only on the latter data.

Model fitting is the topic of the next two chapters. Chapter 7 presents a didactic overview of model fitting; Chapter 8 applies parent–offspring and sibling models to the CAP data, extends the models to analyze stability from childhood to adulthood, and describes multivariate model fitting.

7 Introduction to model fitting

The full adoption design allows us to investigate the etiology of individual differences in behavior in a direct and straightforward manner. The design is both simple and powerful, and the summary statistics it yields provide a broad description of this etiology, as we have seen in the preceding chapter. The correlation between the behavior of the adopted child and that of its adoptive parents provides direct evidence of the importance of shared environment independent of inherited, or genetic, influences. The correlation between the behavior of the adopted child and that of the biological parents from whom the child has been separated since birth provides direct evidence of the importance of genetic influences independent of the home environment. In nonadoptive families these two influences are always confounded and there is no direct way to evaluate their relative importance.

Simple correlations estimated from adoption data provide a very broad description that, for many purposes, may be quite sufficient for an understanding of the etiology of individual differences. Alternatively, a model of transmission may be assumed that facilitates estimates of genetic and environmental transmission parameters. The adoptive-parent/adopted-child correlation provides an estimate of the proportion of variance due to shared environmental influences (c^2), whereas the biological-parent/adopted-child correlation estimates one-half of heritability (h^2). This simple model implies that expected parent–child correlations in nonadoptive families, which are due to both heredity and shared environmental influences, contain c^2 and $0.5h^2$. Thus, the three correlations are functions of only two parameters. To estimate these parameters, model-fitting methods can be employed that evaluate the three statistics simultaneously and thereby utilize all of the available information. Such an approach was developed by Jinks and Fulker (1970) to fit biometrical models to a variety of familial correlations.

With data such as those that have been collected in the CAP, it is possible

157

to move beyond such simple models and pose more complex questions concerning the dynamics of familial influences. For example, because non-adoptive parents provide both genetic and environmental influences on their child, these influences may well be correlated for several aspects of behavior. We might expect a positive relationship in the case of intellectual development, although, as in the example of compensatory education, a negative correlation is also possible. In the case of personality development, a negative relationship has sometimes been suggested (Cattell, 1982); for example, a parent aware of the likelihood of an inherited, "undesirable" influence may try to provide a counteracting environment for the child. With regard to genotype–environment (GE) correlation, as this phenomenon is called (see Chapter 10), a number of interesting questions arise: What is its magnitude relative to the independent effects of genes and environment? How does it alter the simple interpretation of our summary statistics? What would we expect to happen to this GE correlation during successive generations of family life? Questions such as these are difficult to answer without examining our assumptions and the underlying logic of the adoption design in more detail.

Another complexity arises when we consider the fact that people choose spouses who resemble themselves to some extent: that is, they assortatively marry. What implication does this have for the interpretation of adoption data? For example, how does assortative mating affect an evaluation of the relative importance of genetic and environmental influences? How does it affect our evaluation of GE correlation? Does it induce correlations between genotype and environment?

In addition to these technical issues, there is the practical matter of possible selective placement to consider. Although selective placement has been found to be minimal in the CAP (see Chapter 4), it will be important to assess how the presence of selective placement could affect our evaluation of adoption data.

In order to explore these more complex issues, several models will be formulated and then fitted to adoption data to estimate various genetic and environmental transmission parameters. We shall employ the methodology of path analysis, which specifies the model assumptions explicitly and facilitates the derivation of expected correlations that are functions of the transmission parameters. An excellent introduction to path analysis and model fitting has recently been published (Loehlin, 1987). The primary objectives of the present chapter are threefold: (1) to provide a more formal development of the methodology of model fitting, (2) to illustrate its application to the analysis of both sibling and parent–offspring data, and (3) to demonstrate the utility of the model-fitting approach in estimating pa-

Figure 7.1. Path diagram of basic quantitative genetic model, where G is the genotypic value, E the environmental deviation, and P the observed phenotypic value.

rameters and testing alternative hypotheses using optimal statistical methods.

Quantitative genetic model

The basic linear model of quantitative genetics (see Falconer, 1981) assumes that an individual's observed phenotypic value P is caused by a latent genotypic value G plus an environmental deviation E, that is,

$$P = G + E. \tag{7.1}$$

The value G for a character that is conferred on an individual by its genotype is the expected P for that genotype assessed over a random sample of environments. Of course, E can be defined in an analogous manner, that is, the average effect of an individual's environment in combination with a random sample of genotypes.

From Equation (7.1), it follows that the observed phenotypic variance σ_P^2 is a simple function of the genotypic variance σ_G^2 and the environmental variance σ_E^2,

$$\sigma_P^2 = \sigma_G^2 + \sigma_E^2, \tag{7.2}$$

when G and E are uncorrelated. By dividing both sides of Equation (7.2) by σ_P^2, it can be seen that

$$1 = \sigma_G^2/\sigma_P^2 + \sigma_E^2/\sigma_P^2 = h^2 + e^2, \tag{7.3}$$

where h^2 and e^2 are heritability and environmentality, respectively. As indicated in Equation (7.3), h^2 and e^2 are proportions of variance in P due to variation in G and E, respectively; thus, $h^2 = r_{GP}^2$ and $e^2 = r_{EP}^2$, when G and E are uncorrelated.

Wright (1921) first expressed familial correlations as a function of h^2 more than 60 years ago using his method of path analysis. He defined a path coefficient as the proportion of the standard deviation of a dependent variable caused by variation in an independent variable. Thus, h and e are path coefficients (see Figure 7.1). These path coefficients are equivalent

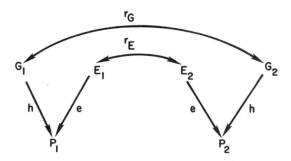

Figure 7.2. Path diagram of the resemblance between siblings, where r_G is the additive genetic correlation and r_E the environmental correlation.

to correlations, that is, $h = r_{GP}$ and $e = r_{EP}$, when G and E are independent.

Application to sibling data

By extending the simple path diagram depicted in Figure 7.1, familial relationships of various kinds can be represented. For example, the resemblance of pairs of individuals reared together as siblings is shown in Figure 7.2. Employing Wright's tracing rules, it can be seen that the expected correlation between the phenotypic values of pairs of siblings is $hr_G h + er_E e = h^2 r_G + e^2 r_E$, where r_G is the genotypic correlation of siblings and r_E is a corresponding correlation between their environmental deviations. For simplicity of exposition, we assume an additive genetic model, ignoring possible complexities due to nonlinear gene interactions. (See Crow, 1986, for a recent discussion of the validity of this assumption regarding quantitative characters.) From genetic theory, $r_G = .5$ for full siblings when mating is at random and zero for adoptive sibling pairs. In contrast, r_E can only be estimated empirically, except in the special case of separated siblings reared in uncorrelated environments, in which case $r_E = 0$.

An alternative path model of sibling resemblance partitions the environmental deviations into shared (E_c) and nonshared (E_w) parts. As shown in Figure 7.3, the expected correlation between siblings can then be more simply expressed as $h^2 r_G + c^2$, where c^2 is the proportion of the phenotypic variance due to variation in environmental influences shared by siblings. Because E_{w1} and E_{w2} are uncorrelated, they do not contribute to sibling resemblance. Thus, the expected phenotypic correlations of nonadoptive and adoptive sibling pairs are functions of h^2 and c^2 as follows:

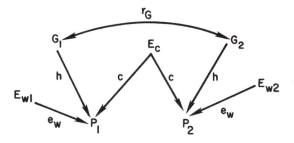

Figure 7.3. Alternative representation of the phenotypic resemblance of siblings, where E_c is that part of the environmental deviation that is shared and E_{w1} and E_{w2} are independent.

$$\text{nonadoptive } r_P = 0.5h^2 + c^2, \tag{7.4}$$

$$\text{adoptive } r_P = c^2. \tag{7.5}$$

This very simple model of sibling resemblance can readily be fit to real data. For example, the correlations for height at 2 years of age are .39 ± .13 for 45 CAP nonadoptive sibling pairs and .13 ± .14 for 49 adoptive pairs. From the above expectations it can be seen that c^2 is estimated directly from the adoptive-pair correlation, that is, $c^2 = .13 ± .14$, whereas h^2 is estimated from twice the difference between the nonadoptive- and adoptive-sibling correlations, that is, $h^2 = 2(.39 - .13) = .52 ± .38$. Because of the direct manner in which c^2 is estimated, its standard error is equivalent to that for the adoptive-sibling-pair correlation. The standard error for h^2 is twice the square root of the sum of the variances of the adoptive- and nonadoptive-sibling correlations [i.e., $2(.13^2 + .14^2)^{1/2} = .38$].

One highly desirable feature of model fitting is the opportunity to test hypotheses by fitting alternative models to the data. For example, given the nonsignificant c^2 estimate for height at 2 years of age, c^2 can be dropped from the model. Thus, a reduced model (Model 1) can be hypothesized in which it is assumed that the observed nonadoptive-sibling correlation is solely due to $0.5h^2$ and that $c^2 = 0$. The discrepancy of the adoptive correlation from zero provides a test of the adequacy of this model. Because this correlation is clearly not significantly different from zero, Model 1 is adequate to explain the observed correlations and yields an estimate of $h^2 = 2(.39 ± .13) = .78 ± .26$. Conversely, we could test an alternative reduced model (Model 2) in which h^2 is hypothesized to be zero. In that case, c^2 would be estimated as the average of the adoptive and nonadoptive correlations. However, given that the nonadoptive correlation is signifi-

Table 7.1. *Model fit to CAP sibling correlations for height at 2 years of age*

Siblings	r	Model 1	Model 2	Weight (W)	$E(r)$ 1	2	$r - E(r)$ 1	2	$W[r - E(r)]^2$ 1	2
Nonadoptive	.39	$0.5h^2$	c^2	59.76	.39	.26	.00	.13	0.00	1.01
Adoptive	.13	0	c^2	48.52	.00	.26	.13	$-.13$	0.82	0.82
$\chi^2_{(1)}$									0.82	1.83
p									0.36	0.18

Note: $\chi^2 = \Sigma W[r - E(r)]^2$, where $W = 1/\sigma_r^2 = (N - 2)/(1 - r^2)^2$.

cantly different from zero, whereas the adoptive correlation is not, Model 2 appears to be less plausible than Model 1.

The adequacy of these alternative reduced models can be explored further by a comparison of their relative fits to the observed correlations, as shown in Table 7.1. The expected nonadoptive- and adoptive-sibling correlations are indicated for the two models, as are the deviations of the observed from the expected correlations. In order to compute chi-square (χ^2) values, these deviations are weighted by the inverse of the sample variance of the observed correlations. Individual contributions to chi-square goodness of fit are shown in addition to the total χ^2 and associated p values with one degree of freedom. As expected, neither model can be rejected given the rather small sample size. However, Model 1 appears to fit the data somewhat better than does Model 2.

Although this example of fitting alternative models to CAP sibling correlations is very simple, it illustrates several principles involved in more realistic model-fitting applications: (1) It yields appropriate parameter estimates given the assumptions of each model; (2) it provides standard errors for these parameter estimates; and (3) it provides a goodness-of-fit test to aid in the evaluation of alternative models. The application of these model-fitting methods to the estimation of parameters and testing of alternative hypotheses is even more relevant to the analysis of CAP parent–offspring data.

Application to parent–offspring data

Intergeneration transmission of genetic and environmental influences can be depicted by a path diagram similar to that used for sibling resemblance. As shown in Figure 7.4, the path between the additive genetic values of

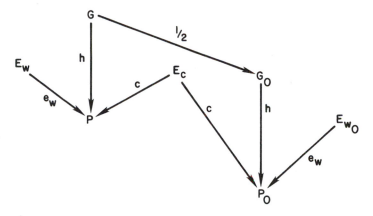

Figure 7.4. Path diagram of single-parent/child resemblance.

biological parents and children is again .5. For both nonadoptive and adoptive families, common environmental influences may also contribute to observed parent–child similarity. However, because parents and their children are less contemporaneous than sibling pairs, estimates of c^2 for the two relationships may differ. Of course, c^2 is expected to be zero for biological-parent/adopted-child relationships, and genetic resemblance should not contribute to adoptive relationships. Thus, each of the three parent–offspring relationships generated by the CAP adoption design can be expressed as a function of h^2 and c^2: $0.5h^2$ for biological parent/adopted child, c^2 for adoptive parent/adopted child, and $0.5h^2 + c^2$ for nonadoptive parents and children.

To illustrate a method for estimating parameters from data sets with more relationships than parameters, this simple model was fit to mother–child IQ correlations (first-principal-component scores of mothers and Stanford–Binet IQ at 3 years of age for children), as shown in Table 7.2. The data consist of three observed mother–child correlations, but only two parameters are to be estimated; thus, an estimation procedure that fits the model to the three correlations simultaneously is required. The approach employed in Table 7.2 is weighted least squares, in which the correlations are regressed onto the coefficients of the model parameters. As in the previous example, discrepancies between the expected and observed correlations are weighted by the inverse of the sampling variance of the observed correlations. This weighted-least-squares procedure yields a minimum chi-square fit for evaluation of the model and standard errors for the resulting parameter estimates.

The calculations required to estimate the parameters employ matrix

	r	N	Weight (W)	Model h²	c²	E(r)	r − E(r)	W[r − E(r)]²
Biological mother/adopted child	.14	202	208.07	.5	0	.10	.04	0.333
Adoptive mother/adopted child	.15	201	208.27	0	1	.11	.04	0.333
Nonadoptive mother/child	.17	189	198.30	.5	1	.21	−.04	0.317

$$W = (N - 2)/(1 - r^2)^2$$

$$\chi^2_{(1)} = \Sigma W[r - E(r)]^2 = .983$$

$$p > .3$$

Model matrix

$$\mathbf{X} = \begin{bmatrix} 0.5 & 0 \\ 0 & 1 \\ 0.5 & 1 \end{bmatrix}$$

Weight matrix

$$\mathbf{W} = \begin{bmatrix} 208.07 & 0 & 0 \\ 0 & 208.27 & 0 \\ 0 & 0 & 198.30 \end{bmatrix}$$

Correlation matrix

$$\mathbf{Y} = \begin{bmatrix} .14 \\ .15 \\ .17 \end{bmatrix}$$

Parameter matrix

$$\boldsymbol{\beta} = \begin{bmatrix} h^2 \\ c^2 \end{bmatrix}$$

Then $\boldsymbol{\beta} = (\mathbf{X'WX})^{-1}\mathbf{X'WY}$

$$\mathbf{X'WX} = \begin{bmatrix} 0.5 & 0 & 0.5 \\ 0 & 1 & 1 \end{bmatrix} \begin{bmatrix} 208.07 & 0 & 0 \\ 0 & 208.27 & 0 \\ 0 & 0 & 198.30 \end{bmatrix} \begin{bmatrix} .5 & 0 \\ 0 & 1 \\ .5 & 1 \end{bmatrix} = \begin{bmatrix} 101.59 & 99.15 \\ 99.15 & 406.54 \end{bmatrix}$$

$$(\mathbf{X'WX})^{-1} = 1/[(101.59 \times 406.57) - (99.15^2)] \begin{bmatrix} 406.54 & -99.15 \\ -99.15 & 101.59 \end{bmatrix} = \begin{bmatrix} .012918 & -.003150 \\ -.003150 & .003228 \end{bmatrix}$$

$$\mathbf{X'WY} = \begin{bmatrix} 0.5 & 0 & 0.5 \\ 0 & 1 & 1 \end{bmatrix} \begin{bmatrix} 208.07 & 0 & 0 \\ 0 & 208.27 & 0 \\ 0 & 0 & 198.30 \end{bmatrix} \begin{bmatrix} .14 \\ .15 \\ .17 \end{bmatrix} = \begin{bmatrix} 31.42 \\ 64.95 \end{bmatrix}$$

$$\hat{\boldsymbol{\beta}} = (\mathbf{X'WX})^{-1}\mathbf{X'WY} = \begin{bmatrix} .012918 & -.003150 \\ -.003150 & .003228 \end{bmatrix} \begin{bmatrix} 31.42 \\ 64.95 \end{bmatrix} = \begin{bmatrix} .20 \\ .11 \end{bmatrix}$$

$$\mathbf{SE}(\boldsymbol{\beta}) = \begin{bmatrix} .012918 \\ .003228 \end{bmatrix}^{1/2} = \begin{bmatrix} .11 \\ .06 \end{bmatrix} \qquad \mathbf{z}_{\hat{\beta}} = \begin{bmatrix} 1.82 \\ 1.83 \end{bmatrix} \qquad \mathbf{p} = \begin{bmatrix} .04 \\ .03 \end{bmatrix} \text{ one-tailed}$$

multiplication and inversion, as outlined in Table 7.2. The equations follow from standard regression theory in which parameters are chosen to minimize the χ^2 function shown in the table. This Procrustean approach yields estimates of $h^2 = .20 \pm .11$ and $c^2 = .11 \pm .06$. Since these parameters are variance ratios and, thus, can take only positive values, a one-tailed test of statistical significance is appropriate. Consequently, p values for both parameter estimates are less than .05. The two parameters have been estimated from three observed correlations; thus, as shown in Table 7.2, the model can be tested for its goodness of fit to the observed correlations. Estimates of the expected correlations are obtained by substituting estimates of h^2 and c^2 into the corresponding model expectation. For example, the expected biological-mother/adopted-child correlation is $(.5)(h^2) + (0)(c^2) = (.5)(.20) + (0)(.11) = .10$. Squared deviations of observed from expected correlations are weighted to compute individual contributions to χ^2. The obtained chi-square value of .98 has one degree of freedom and a corresponding p value greater than .3, indicating that this very simple h^2 and c^2 model adequately fits the data.

One simplifying assumption that has been made in the above analysis is that the three observed correlations are independent. However, the adoptive-mother/adopted-child and biological-mother/adopted-child correlations are clearly not independent since both correlations are based on data from the same children. Because selective placement is minimal in the CAP, this independence problem may not be serious for the present application. However, when the full data set that includes measures for both fathers and mothers is analyzed, an estimation procedure that accommodates the multivariate nature of the data should be employed. This added complexity will be discussed later in this chapter when a more comprehensive CAP model of genetic and environmental transmission is outlined.

Environmental transmission

In the preceding sections on sibling and parent–child resemblance, a very general model of shared environmental influence has been employed; that is, no specific mode of environmental transmission has been assumed. Obviously, a variety of mechanisms could be envisioned that cause family members to share environmental influences. For example, both members of sibling pairs experience many general features of the home environment provided by their parents as well as broader aspects of their social environment. One plausible cause of shared environmental influence between parents and children is the direct impact of parental phenotype on the children's environment. This model was first employed by Wright (1931)

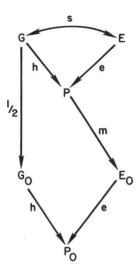

Figure 7.5. Path diagram of parent–child resemblance with environmental transmission via parental phenotype.

in a reanalysis of data from Burks's (1928) classic adoption study of mental development. Jencks (1972) subsequently elaborated Wright's model, and, with minor modifications, this model has been adopted for the analysis of CAP cognitive data (e.g., Fulker & DeFries, 1983).

A path model of single-parent/child resemblance that incorporates environmental transmission for a character is depicted in Figure 7.5. The effect of parental phenotype on child's environment is represented by the path coefficient m. The addition of parental phenotypic transmission to the model has several important implications. First, this model implies the existence of GE correlation s. Following Wright's tracing rules, $r_{G_O E_O} = .5hm + .5sem = .5m(h + se) = s$, when s has reached equilibrium across generations. Second, the standardized phenotypic variance now also includes a component due to GE covariance. In Equations (7.2) and (7.3), it was assumed that G and E are uncorrelated; if G and E are correlated, Equation (7.2) becomes

$$\sigma_P^2 = \sigma_G^2 + \sigma_E^2 + 2\,\text{cov}(GE), \tag{7.6}$$

and Equation (7.3) will include a component due to GE correlation:

$$1 = h^2 + e^2 + 2her_{GE} = h^2 + e^2 + 2hse. \tag{7.7}$$

Third, the expected phenotypic correlation between parent and child also becomes a function of s as follows:

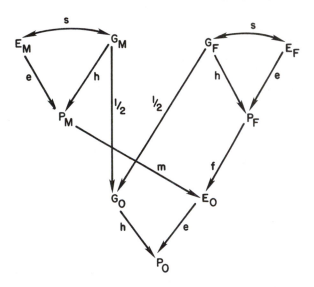

Figure 7.6. Path diagram of parent–child resemblance in which the phenotypes of both father (F) and mother (M) causally influence the child's environment.

$$r_{PP_O} = .5h^2 + .5hse + em$$
$$= .5h(h + se) + em. \tag{7.8}$$

When the phenotypes of both father and mother causally influence the child's environment, an additional source of GE correlation results. As can be seen from Figure 7.6,

$$s = .5m(h + se) + .5f(h + se)$$
$$= .5(h + se)(m + f), \tag{7.9}$$

where m and f are the maternal and paternal environmental transmission parameters. The expectation for the phenotypic variance is again $h^2 + e^2 + 2hse$, but with s as redefined above, and the expected mother–child and father–child correlations are $.5h(h + se) + em$ and $.5h(h + se) + ef$, respectively.

In the case of adoptive families (see Figure 7.7), the expected biological-mother/adopted-child correlation is $.5h'(h + se)$, whereas that for adoptive-mother/adopted-child pairs is $e'm$, where

$$h' = \sigma_G \sigma_{P_{AO}} = \sigma_G \sigma_{P_O}/\sigma_{P_O} \sigma_{P_{AO}} = h\sigma_{P_O}/\sigma_{P_{AO}} \tag{7.10}$$

and

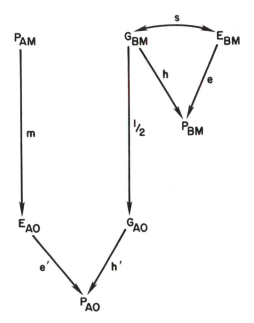

Figure 7.7. Path diagram of biological-mother/adopted-child and adoptive-mother/adopted-child resemblance.

$$e' = e\sigma_{P_O}/\sigma_{P_{AO}}. \tag{7.11}$$

These distinctions between h and h' and between e and e' are necessary because the standardized phenotypic variance for nonadopted children ($\sigma^2_{P_O}$) is $h^2 + e^2 + 2hse = 1$, whereas that for adopted children ($\sigma^2_{P_{AO}}$) is $h^2 + e^2 = 1 - 2hse$ because adopted children do not experience passive GE correlation.

It might seem odd that resemblance between biological mothers and their adopted-away offspring is increased by GE correlation, even though biological mothers transmit genes alone to their offspring. The correlation between the additive genetic values of biological mothers and adoptees remains .50; however, the correlation between biological mothers' *phenotype* and their offspring's genotype is a function of s: In Figure 7.7, if G_{BM} causally influences variance in G_{AO} and if E_{BM} and G_{BM} are correlated, then E_{BM} and G_{AO} are also correlated, resulting in increased resemblance between P_{BM} and P_{AO}.

Thus, the expected parent–child correlations in adoptive families can be expressed in terms of h and e as follows:

$$r_{P_{BM}P_{AO}} = .5h(h + se)\sigma_{P_O}/\sigma_{P_{AO}} \tag{7.12}$$

and

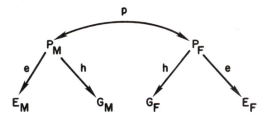

Figure 7.8. Reverse path diagram used to derive the expected genotypic and environmental correlations between mates, where p is the observed mate correlation.

$$r_{P_{AM}P_{AO}} = em\sigma_{P_O}/\sigma_{P_{AO}}. \tag{7.13}$$

The corresponding covariances are $.5h(h + se)\sigma_P\sigma_{P_O}$ and $em\sigma_P\sigma_{P_O}$, which sum to yield the expected nonadoptive-parent/child correlation when the phenotypic standard deviation for members of nonadoptive families is 1. As will be noted in a later section, the full CAP model is fitted to covariances rather than to correlations.

Assortative mating

For the sake of simplicity, random mating was assumed in our previous models of familial resemblance. However, nonzero correlations between spouses are frequently noted, implying that marriage has not been entirely random. The process of marital assortment has implications for models of genetic and environmental transmission, depending on the manner in which it occurs. For example, if spouses assort on the basis of their phenotypes, correlations are induced between their genotypic values and environmental deviations. As illustrated in the reverse path diagram (see Wright, 1978) shown in Figure 7.8,

$$r_{G_MG_F} = h^2p, \tag{7.14}$$

$$r_{E_ME_F} = e^2p, \tag{7.15}$$

and

$$r_{G_ME_F} = r_{E_MG_F} = hep, \tag{7.16}$$

where p is the phenotypic spouse correlation. Thus, phenotypic assortative mating induces correlations among the causes of the spouses' phenotypic values and has implications for both genetic and environmental transmission.

As can be seen in Figure 7.9, phenotypic assortative mating increases the genetic resemblance between parents and their children as follows:

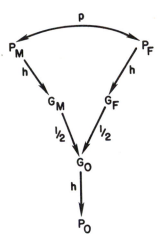

Figure 7.9. Path diagram of genetic resemblance between parents and children in the presence of phenotypic assortative mating.

$$r_{P_M P_O} = .5h^2 + .5h^2p = .5h^2(1 + p). \qquad (7.17)$$

As illustrated in Figure 7.10, a corresponding increase in environmental resemblance also occurs, that is,

$$r_{P_M P_O} = em + efp = e(m + fp). \qquad (7.18)$$

Including both genetic and environmental transmission in the same model adds the further complication of introducing GE correlation s, in which case the reverse path from parental phenotype to parental genotype becomes $h + se$ (see Fulker & DeFries, 1983), as shown in the full CAP model described in the following section.

Full CAP Model

The full model of genetic and environmental transmission in the presence of assortative mating is represented for nonadoptive families in Figure 7.11. Expected correlations were derived following the tracing rules of path analysis and are presented as covariances in the top portion of Table 7.3. Correlations are in brackets and are multiplied by standard deviations of the variables because the model is fitted to unstandardized variances and covariances.

Although selective placement has been found to be minimal in the CAP, for the sake of completeness its effects are modeled in the path diagram of genetic and environmental transmission in adoptive families shown in

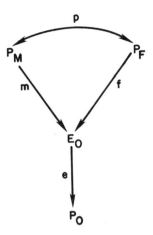

Figure 7.10. Path diagram of environmental resemblance between parents and children in the presence of phenotypic assortative mating.

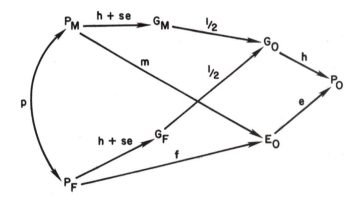

Figure 7.11. Path diagram of genetic and environmental transmission in nonadoptive families.

Figure 7.12. By comparing Figures 7.11 and 7.12, it can be seen that spouse resemblance for adoptive and nonadoptive parents is assumed to be similar. However, assortative mating may differ for biological (unwed) parents of adopted children. Because of this possibility, a different assortative mating parameter for biological parents of adopted children (q) is included in the full model. Expected covariances derived from Figure 7.12 are presented in the lower portion of Table 7.3. For those relationships involving adopted children, the expectations inside the brackets are covariances standardized

Table 7.3. *Expectations of variances and covariances derived from path diagrams*

Variable	Expectation
Nonadoptive families	
$P_M P_F$	$[p]\sigma_P^2$
$P_M P_O$	$[.5h(h + se)(1 + p) + e(m + pf)]\sigma_P\sigma_{P_O}$
$P_F P_O$	$[.5h(h + se)(1 + p) + e(f + pm)]\sigma_P\sigma_{P_O}$
P_M	$[h^2 + e^2 + 2hse]\sigma_P^2$
P_F	$[h^2 + e^2 + 2hse]\sigma_P^2$
P_O	$[h^2 + e^2 + 2hse]\sigma_{P_O}^2$
$r_{G_O E_O}$	$.5(h + se)(f + m)(1 + p)$
Adoptive families	
$P_{BM}P_{BF}$	$[q]\sigma_P^2$
$P_{BM}P_{AM}$	$[x_2]\sigma_P^2$
$P_{BM}P_{AF}$	$[x_1]\sigma_P^2$
$P_{BM}P_{AO}$	$[.5h(h + se)(1 + q) + e(fx_1 + mx_2)]\sigma_P\sigma_{P_O}$
$P_{BF}P_{AM}$	$[x_4]\sigma_P^2$
$P_{BF}P_{AF}$	$[x_3]\sigma_P^2$
$P_{BF}P_{AO}$	$[.5h(h + se)(1 + q) + e(fx_3 + mx_4)]\sigma_P\sigma_{P_O}$
$P_{AM}P_{AF}$	$[p]\sigma_P^2$
$P_{AM}P_{AO}$	$[.5h(h + se)(x_2 + x_4) + e(m + pf)]\sigma_P\sigma_{P_O}$
$P_{AF}P_{AO}$	$[.5h(h + se)(x_1 + x_3) + (f + pm)]\sigma_P\sigma_{P_O}$
P_{BM}	$[h^2 + e^2 + 2hse]\sigma_P^2$
P_{BF}	$[h^2 + e^2 + 2hse]\sigma_P^2$
P_{AM}	$[h^2 + e^2 + 2hse]\sigma_P^2$
P_{AF}	$[h^2 + e^2 + 2hse]\sigma_P^2$
P_{AO}	$[h^2 + e^2 + he(h + se)(mx_4 + fx_3 + mx_2 + fx_1)]\sigma_{P_O}^2$
$r_{G_{AO} E_{AO}}$	$.5(h + se)(mx_4 + fx_3 + mx_2 + fx_1)$

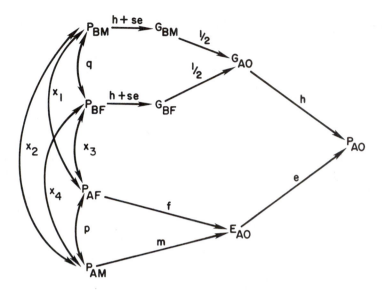

Figure 7.12. Path diagram of genetic and environmental transmission in adoptive families.

on the basis of the phenotypic standard deviations of nonadoptive family members.

Because family data are inherently multivariate, the full model was fitted to CAP data using an estimation procedure that accommodates the lack of statistical independence among the various covariance estimates. For example, when data from nonadoptive families each containing a father, a mother, and a child are analyzed, the two parent–child covariances are based on data from the same children. Thus, rather than summarizing the data using only two correlations, a 3×3 covariance matrix provides a more complete description of the interrelationships among the three measures. In a corresponding manner, data from adoptive families generate a 5×5 covariance matrix involving scores of adoptive fathers, adoptive mothers, biological fathers, biological mothers, and adopted children. For those adoptive families for which data from biological fathers are not available, a corresponding 4×4 covariance matrix results.

In order to fit the full model to the three covariance matrices simultaneously, an estimation procedure was employed that accounts for the sampling distribution of covariance matrices. The simple method previously outlined employing weighted least squares can be generalized to the multivariate case, where

$$\chi^2 = \sum \frac{N}{2} \{[S - E(S)]S^{-1}\}^2 \tag{7.19}$$

and is summed over the three matrices. The term $S - E(S)$ is the observed covariance minus the expected, and S^{-1} provides a weight for the discrepancy. However, this method is strictly appropriate only for very large samples. Thus, we employed a more general maximum-likelihood estimation procedure similar to that used by Jöreskog and Sörbom (1976) for the analysis of structural equation models. We assume that the observations have a multivariate normal distribution so that the observed covariance matrices are distributed according to the Wishart. Thus, the following function is minimized:

$$F = \sum_{k=1}^{m} N_k \{\ln|E(S_k)| - \ln|S_k| + tr[S_k E(S_k)^{-1}] - p_k\}, \tag{7.20}$$

where N_k is the degree of freedom of the kth matrix and p_k is the order of the matrix. In our analysis, p_k varies from 3 to 5 and we sum over three matrices.

Because the expected covariances derived from the full model are nonlinear, linear regression methods cannot be used to minimize this function. Instead, numerical methods such as Newton–Raphson are required. Although these methods involve lengthy iterative estimation procedures, numerous optimization computer packages are available to implement these procedures. A convenient package that we have used extensively for this purpose is MINUIT, developed by CERN (1977), the European Organization for Nuclear Research (see Fulker & DeFries, 1983, for a brief description of the MINUIT optimization error analysis routines).

To illustrate the fitting of the full model to CAP data, adult height of parents was compared with the height of their children at 3 years of age. The basic data to which the model was fit are the three covariance matrices: a 3×3 matrix based on data from 163 nonadoptive families (mother, father, child), a 5×5 matrix based on data from 40 adoptive families with complete data, and a 4×4 matrix based on data from 143 adoptive families in which data are not available from biological fathers. These three observed matrices are presented in Table 7.4, with correlations included above the diagonal, variances on the diagonal, and covariances below the diagonal.

The full model was fit to the three observed covariance matrices simultaneously, with the result shown in the first column of Table 7.5. Eleven free parameters (including two variances) were estimated, and two (e and f) were computed because they are functions of the estimated parameters. As can be seen in Table 7.5, $\chi^2 = 26.52$, d.f. $= 20$, $.2 > p > .1$, indicating that

Table 7.4. *Observed correlations (above diagonal), variances, and covariances (below diagonal) among family members for height of parents as adults and their children at 3 years of age*

| | Nonadoptive families (N = 163) | | |
	M	F	O
Mothers (M)	5.88	0.27	0.25
Fathers (F)	1.69	6.62	0.35
Offspring (O)	1.04	1.54	2.96

| | Adoptive families, complete data (N = 40) | | | | |
	BM	BF	AM	AF	AO
Biological mothers (BM)	8.10	0.06	0.13	0.04	0.37
Biological fathers (BF)	0.46	6.82	0.17	0.16	0.21
Adoptive mothers (AM)	1.22	1.47	10.86	0.44	0.23
Adoptive fathers (AF)	0.23	0.87	3.10	4.62	0.38
Adopted offspring (AO)	1.55	0.79	1.11	1.21	2.15

| | Adoptive families, no data on biological fathers (N = 143) | | | |
	BM	AM	AF	AO
Biological mothers (BM)	6.90	0.14	0.08	0.36
Adoptive mothers (AM)	0.96	6.96	0.20	0.02
Adoptive fathers (AF)	0.55	1.38	6.71	−0.09
Adopted offspring (AO)	1.53	0.09	−0.38	2.68

the full model provides an adequate fit to the data. The degrees of freedom for this χ^2 goodness-of-fit test are computed as the difference between the number of elements in the three covariance matrices and the number of parameters estimated from the model, that is, $6 + 15 + 10 - 11 = 20$.

By inspection of the parameter estimates and their associated standard errors, it can be seen that only h and p are statistically significant. In contrast, the four selective placement parameters (x_1, x_2, x_3, and x_4) are small, inconsistent, and nonsignificant. Maternal and paternal environmental transmission parameter estimates (m and f) are near zero, as expected for height, as is s, which is a function of the environmental transmission parameters. As explained by Fulker and DeFries (1983), f is calculated by assuming that $r_{G_OE_O}$ in Table 7.3 is equivalent to s (which is the case if equilibrium has been reached after many generations of such environmental and genetic transmission) and then solving for f using the other parameter estimates. Substitution of the estimates for h and s into the expression $h^2 + 2hse + e^2 = 1$ resulted in the estimate of $e = .68$. Although p was significant whereas q was not, q was estimated from a relatively small sample of biological parents (40 pairs).

Table 7.5. *Maximum-likelihood parameter estimates ± SE obtained from CAP height data*

Parameter	Model 1 (full model)	Model 2 ($p = q$)	Model 3 ($p = q$, $x_1 = x_2 = x_3 = x_4 = 0$)	Model 4 ($p = q$, $x_1 = x_2 = x_3 = x_4 = 0$, $s = m = 0$)	Model 5 ($p = q$, $x_1 = x_2 = x_3 = x_4 = 0$, $s = m = 0$, $h = 0$)
h	$.74 \pm .07$	$.73 \pm .07$	$.73 \pm .07$	$.72 \pm .04$	.00
s	$-.02 \pm .05$	$-.02 \pm .05$	$-.01 \pm .05$	.00	.00
m	$-.05 \pm .09$	$-.05 \pm .09$	$-.02 \pm .08$	.00	.00
p	$.26 \pm .05$	$.24 \pm .05$	$.24 \pm .05$	$.24 \pm .05$	$.24 \pm .05$
q	$.13 \pm .13$	$.24 \pm .05$	$.24 \pm .05$	$.24 \pm .05$	$.24 \pm .05$
x_1	$.07 \pm .07$	$.07 \pm .07$	.00	.00	.00
x_2	$.13 \pm .07$	$.13 \pm .07$	.00	.00	.00
x_3	$-.02 \pm .17$	$.02 \pm .17$	.00	.00	.00
x_4	$.13 \pm .12$	$.14 \pm .11$	.00	.00	.00
σ_P^2	6.76	6.76	6.77	6.77	6.77
σ_C^2	2.74	2.74	2.75	2.76	2.75
e	.68	.69	.69	.70	1.00
f	.01	.01	.01	.00	.00
χ^2	26.52	27.53	32.09	32.19	82.30
d.f.	20	21	25	27	28
p	$.2 > p > .1$	$.2 > p > .1$	$.2 > p > .1$	$.2 > p > .1$	$<.001$
Difference χ^2	—	1.01	4.56	0.10	50.11
d.f.	—	1	4	2	1
p	—	$>.3$	$>.3$	$>.9$	$<.001$

Thus, p and q do not differ significantly and may be equated in more parsimonious alternative models.

Four alternative reduced models were subsequently fit to the data to test various hypotheses regarding assortative mating, selective placement, and cultural and genetic transmission: Model 2 equates p and q; Model 3 constrains the selective placement parameters to be zero, as well as equating p and q; Model 4 drops both selective placement and cultural transmission from the model and equates p and q; and Model 5 additionally constrains h to be zero. The results of fitting these four reduced models to the data are also presented in Table 7.5, and it can be seen that the fits for Models 2, 3, and 4 are adequate ($.2 > p > .1$ in each case). The difference in χ^2 between any two models tests the significance of the parameters equated or dropped from the more parsimonious model. When Model 2 is compared with Model 1, for example, the difference $\chi^2 = 1.01$, d.f. $= 1$, $p > .3$. Thus, constraining p and q to be equal appears to be fully justified. When Model 3 is compared with Model 2, the change in $\chi^2 = 4.56$, d.f. $= 4$, $p > .3$, confirming the absence of selective placement. Comparing Models 4 and 3, the difference in $\chi^2 = 0.10$, d.f. $= 2$, $p > .9$, clearly indicating the absence of environmental transmission. However, when h is constrained to be zero, the change in $\chi^2 = 50.11$, d.f. $= 1$, $p < .001$; thus, h cannot be dropped from the model without a significant loss of goodness of fit. It is of interest that the estimates for h and p are highly consistent across the various models, suggesting the robustness of the obtained results. The significance of h and p for a character such as height, as well as the lack of significance for selective placement and environmental transmission, is highly plausible and suggests that the model and estimation procedure employed in this analysis should be adequate for the analysis of other CAP data as well.

Conclusion

In summary, the model-fitting methods illustrated in this chapter facilitate a rigorous and thorough evaluation of the CAP data. The approach has been illustrated employing a range of models and estimation procedures from the very simple analysis of sibling data to more complex analyses of parent–offspring data from the full adoption design. In each case, a specific model is formulated, the model is fitted to observed data, parameters and their associated standard errors are estimated, and alternative hypotheses are tested. The purpose of this methodology is to evaluate the data thoroughly and extract as much information as possible using a hypothesis-testing approach. These methods were employed to analyze other CAP data reported in the following chapters.

8 Fitting sibling and parent–offspring models in the Colorado Adoption Project

In this chapter we report results from model-fitting analyses of data from the Colorado Adoption Project using the simple sibling and parent–offspring models developed in the preceding chapter as well as extending the model to include age-to-age genetic correlations and to consider the multivariate case. As discussed in Chapter 7, model fitting has several advantages over less sophisticated approaches to the interpretation of behavioral genetic data: It yields appropriate parameter estimates given the assumptions of a model; it provides standard errors for these parameter estimates; and it provides goodness-of-fit tests to aid in the evaluation of alternative models.

Sibling model

A simple model can be used to represent the sibling adoption design because the essence of this design lies in the comparison between two correlations: the correlations for adoptive and nonadoptive siblings. The sibling model, illustrated in the path diagram of Figure 7.3, was applied to the adoptive- and nonadoptive-sibling correlations presented in Chapter 6. The model involves only three parameters: heritability and shared and nonshared environment. As specified in Equations (7.4) and (7.5), the model assumes that the observed nonadoptive-sibling correlation is a function of half the heritability of the trait and of shared environmental influence; the adoptive-sibling correlation arises only from shared environmental influence – in the absence of selective placement, heredity does not contribute to the resemblance of adoptive siblings. In Chapter 7, the model was applied to sibling data for height at 2 years and yielded an estimate of .52 ± .38 for heritability and .13 ± .14 for shared environment. Two reduced models were also evaluated: In Model 1 the observed nonadoptive sibling correlation is due solely to heredity – that is, shared environment is hypothesized to be zero; in Model 2, heritability is hypothesized to be zero. In the analysis of 2-year-old height data, neither reduced model could

179

be rejected, although Model 1 appeared to fit the data somewhat better than Model 2.

In Table 8.1, estimates of heritability and shared environment and their standard errors are listed for the full model as applied to sibling data for the major CAP measures. The parameter estimates are the same as those discussed in Chapter 6 because heritability and shared environment are estimated in the same manner. Heritability is estimated as twice the difference between the correlations for nonadoptive and adoptive siblings, and the correlation for adoptive siblings is used to estimate the shared-environment parameter. The standard errors of estimate emphasize the need for large samples; the ratio of the estimate to its standard error must be about 2 or greater to be significant ($p < .05$) using a two-tailed test. As can be seen in Table 8.1, the current CAP sibling sample size cannot yield significant estimates of heritability unless heritability is very large. Nonetheless, significant heritability emerges for a few traits – height, weight, IQ, motor development, and two of the Infant Behavior Record (IBR) measures. As indicated in Chapter 6, significant genetic influence is rarely found for specific cognitive abilities or for temperament, given the current sample size. For example, the average heritability for the four specific cognitive ability measures at 3 and 4 years is .14; if the true effect size is of this magnitude, more than a thousand pairs of each type of sibling would be needed to detect statistically significant heritability. With 60 pairs of each type – the average size of the CAP sample across the four years – only 50% statistical power can be brought to bear on the detection of heritabilities of .50.

The longitudinal design of the CAP attenuates this problem slightly because it provides an opportunity to compare results across the years. For example, although the heritability of height is statistically significant only at year 3, the heritability estimates at 2 and 4 years are also substantial. Furthermore, it is noteworthy that some traits show moderate heritability at several ages: height at 2, 3, and 4; weight at all four years; IQ at 1 and 2; SICD at 2 and 3; CAP Verbal at 3 and 4; CAP Perceptual Speed at 3 and 4; Psychomotor Development Index (PDI) Motor Development at 1 and 2; IBR Affect-Extraversion at all four years; and IBR Activity at 1 and 2. This is a two-edged sword: When genetic influence emerges at just one age – as is the case for Colorado Childhood Temperament Inventory (CCTI) Attention Span – the results may be suspect. However, as discussed in Chapter 6, it is possible that genetic influence is sufficiently fine grained to yield change during the period of a year. For example, the second year of life may provide a window on individual differences in attention span that highlights genetic differences among children.

Table 8.1. *Model-fitting results from the CAP sibling adoption design*

Measure	Age	Full model $h^2 \pm SE$	Full model $c^2 \pm SE$	Model 2 (heritability is zero, $h^2 = 0$) h^2	c^2	χ^2	p	Model 3 (shared environment is zero, $c^2 = 0$) h^2	c^2	χ^2	p
Height	1	.06 ± .37	.23 ± .14	.00	.25	0.0	>.80	.52	.00	2.7	>.05
	2	.52 ± .38	.13 ± .14	.00	.26	1.8	>.10	.78	.00	0.8	>.30
	3	1.00 ± .46	−.11 ± .18	.00	.14	5.0	<.05	.78	.00	0.4	>.50
	4	.46 ± .51	.07 ± .20	.00	.19	0.8	>.30	.60	.00	0.1	>.70
Weight	1	1.14 ± .36	−.19 ± .14	.00	.10	11.1	<.01	.76	.00	1.8	>.20
	2	.90 ± .38	−.19 ± .13	.00	.04	5.0	<.02	.52	.00	1.8	>.20
	3	.58 ± .44	−.03' ± .17	.00	.12	1.8	>.10	.52	.00	0.0	>.90
	4	.60 ± .50	.07 ± .20	.00	.22	1.2	>.20	.74	.00	0.1	>.70
IQ	1	.68 ± .31	.03 ± .12	.00	.20	5.0	<.05	.74	.00	0.1	>.80
	2	.60 ± .33	.12 ± .13	.00	.27	3.6	>.05	.84	.00	0.9	>.30
	3	.06 ± .35	.32 ± .13	.00	.34	0.0	>.80	.70	.00	6.1	<.02
	4	.02 ± .42	.23 ± .15	.00	.24	0.0	>.90	.48	.00	2.4	>.10
SICD	2	.42 ± .34	.08 ± .13	.00	.19	1.5	>.20	.58	.00	0.4	>.50
	3	.22 ± .38	.10 ± .14	.00	.16	0.3	>.50	.42	.00	0.5	>.30
CAP IQ[a]	3	.52 ± .37	.18 ± .15	.00	.31	2.1	>.10	.88	.00	1.5	>.20
	4	−.20 ± .47	.20 ± .16	.00	.15	1.1	>.20	.20	.00	1.6	>.20
CAP Verbal	3	.32 ± .38	−.05 ± .14	.00	.03	0.6	>.30	.22	.00	0.1	>.70
	4	.50 ± .40	.17 ± .15	.00	.30	1.6	>.20	.84	.00	1.2	>.20
CAP Spatial	3	.18 ± .35	.24 ± .13	.00	.29	0.2	>.70	.66	.00	3.2	>.05
	4	−.30 ± .41	.27 ± .14	.00	.20	0.5	>.50	.24	.00	3.4	>.05

Table 8.1. (*continued*)

Measure	Age	Full model		Model 2 (heritability is zero, $h^2 = 0$)				Model 3 (shared environment is zero, $c^2 = 0$)			
		$h^2 \pm$ SE	$c^2 \pm$ SE	h^2	c^2	χ^2	p	h^2	c^2	χ^2	p
CAP Perceptual Speed	3	.20 ± .38	.08 ± .14	.00	.13	0.3	>.70	.36	.00	0.3	>.50
	4	.40 ± .44	−.08 ± .16	.00	.02	0.8	>.50	.24	.00	0.2	>.50
CAP Memory	3	−.10 ± .38	.19 ± .14	.00	.17	0.1	>.70	.28	.00	1.9	>.10
	4	−.08 ± .45	.09 ± .16	.00	.07	0.0	>.80	.10	.00	0.3	>.50
PDI Motor Development	1	.80 ± .30	.03 ± .12	.00	.23	7.4	<.01	.86	.00	0.1	>.80
	2	.52 ± .38	−.09 ± .14	.00	.04	2.0	<.05	.34	.00	0.4	>.50
CAP^b Fine	3	.84 ± .38	−.08 ± .14	.00	.30	0.5	>.30	.66	.00	7.4	<.01
Gross	3	−.28 ± .38	.37 ± .13	.00	.12	4.8	<.05	.46	.00	0.4	>.50
IBR Task Orientation	1	.44 ± .31	.08 ± .12	.00	.19	1.9	>.10	.60	.00	0.4	>.50
	2	.00 ± .35	.03 ± .13	.00	.03	0.0	>.99	.06	.00	0.1	>.80
	3	.40 ± .41	−.02 ± .16	.00	.08	1.0	>.30	.36	.00	0.0	>.80
	4	−.34 ± .42	.10 ± .15	.00	.02	0.6	>.30	−.14	.00	0.4	>.50
IBR Affect/Extraversion	1	.40 ± .33	−.15 ± .12	.00	−.05	1.5	>.20	.10	.00	1.6	>.20
	2	.28 ± .35	.03 ± .13	.00	.10	0.6	>.30	.34	.00	0.1	>.80
	3	.82 ± .38	−.02 ± .15	.00	.11	4.8	<.05	.78	.00	0.0	>.90
	4	.40 ± .44	.02 ± .16	.00	.12	0.8	>.30	.44	.00	0.0	>.90
IBR Activity	1	.78 ± .33	−.18 ± .12	.00	.02	6.1	<.02	.42	.00	2.2	>.10
	2	.34 ± .35	.02 ± .13	.00	.11	0.9	>.30	.38	.00	0.0	>.80
	3	.18 ± .40	.05 ± .15	.00	.10	0.2	>.50	.28	.00	0.1	>.70
	4	−.28 ± .42	.17 ± .15	.00	.10	0.4	>.50	.06	.00	1.2	>.20

CCTI Emotionality	1	.44 ± .34	.01 ± .13	.00	.12	1.7	>.10	.46	.00	0.0	>.90
	2	-.34 ± .35	.20 ± .13	.00	.12	0.9	>.30	.06	.00	2.4	>.10
	3	-.48 ± .41	.20 ± .14	.00	.08	1.4	>.20	-.08	.00	1.9	>.10
	4	-.84 ± .42	.32 ± .15	.00	.11	3.9	<.05	-.20	.00	4.7	<.05
CCTI Activity	1	.30 ± .34	.05 ± .13	.00	.13	0.8	>.30	.40	.00	0.2	>.70
	2	.04 ± .35	-.03 ± .35	.00	-.02	0.0	>.90	-.02	.00	0.1	>.80
	3	.52 ± .41	-.10 ± .15	.00	.03	1.0	>.30	.32	.00	0.5	>.50
	4	.14 ± .44	-.18 ± .16	.00	-.15	0.2	>.50	-.22	.00	1.3	>.20
CCTI Sociability	1	-.10 ± .34	.15 ± .13	.00	.13	0.1	>.70	.20	.00	1.4	>.20
	2	.36 ± .35	-.07 ± .13	.00	.02	1.0	>.30	.22	.00	0.3	>.50
	3	-.10 ± .40	.17 ± .14	.00	.15	0.1	>.80	.24	.00	1.4	>.20
	4	-.02 ± .44	-.09 ± .16	.00	-.10	1.4	>.20	-.20	.00	0.3	>.50
CCTI Attention Span	1	.18 ± .34	.14 ± .13	.00	.19	0.3	>.50	.46	.00	1.2	>.20
	2	.74 ± .35	-.21 ± .13	.00	.03	3.8	<.05	.32	.00	2.7	>.10
	3	-.34 ± .41	.18 ± .14	.00	.10	0.7	>.30	.02	.00	1.5	>.20
	4	.36 ± .44	.01 ± .16	.00	.10	0.7	>.30	.38	.00	0.0	>.95
Difficult Temperament	1	.10 ± .34	.18 ± .13	.00	.21	0.1	>.70	.46	.00	2.0	>.10
	2	.22 ± .35	-.10 ± .13	.00	.05	1.4	>.20	.02	.00	0.6	>.30
	3	.38 ± .42	-.12 ± .15	.00	.03	1.0	>.50	.14	.00	0.6	>.30
	4	.04 ± .44	-.09 ± .16	.00	-.08	0.0	>.90	-.14	.00	0.3	>.30
CBC[c]	4	.06 ± .38	.65 ± .13	.00	.67	0.0	>.80	1.36	.00	24.1	<.01

[a] Unrotated first-principal-component score derived from the CAP battery of specific cognitive abilities.

[b] CAP motor battery scores for fine and gross motor development.

[c] The sibling sample size for the Child Behavior Checklist is much smaller (21 adoptive and 16 nonadoptive pairs) than for other variables because the CBC was left with the parents to be completed following the home visit; especially for the younger siblings at 4 years, this procedure created a delay in the availability of CBC data at 4 years for the present analyses.

Greater power accrues to the detection of the shared-environment parameter – standard errors are half the magnitude of those for heritability – because this parameter is estimated directly from the adoptive-sibling correlation rather than from a difference in correlations. The standard errors of .12 to .15 in Table 8.1 indicate that parameter estimates of shared environment that account for about 25 to 30% of the variance are statistically significant; 50% statistical power is available to detect such effects. However, the number of significant estimates of shared environment scarcely exceeds chance: Only 4 of the 61 comparisons reach statistical significance.

Longitudinal comparisons suggest that shared environment for IQ increases from infancy to early childhood; the parameter estimates increase from .03 and .12 at 1 and 2 years to .32 and .23 at 3 and 4 years. The unrotated first-principal-component score from the CAP cognitive battery at 3 and 4 yields estimates of .18 and .20, which are consistent with the hypothesis that shared environment accounts for a substantial amount of IQ variance in early childhood. Similar results emerge from parental ratings of children's emotionality; however, the negative heritability estimates for this measure cast doubt on this result. The only other measure to show substantial shared environmental influence involves parental ratings of the children's behavioral problems as assessed by the Child Behavior Checklist; as mentioned in Chapter 6, the sample is quite small for this variable, and the result could derive from differences in parents' willingness to report problems.

As explained in the preceding chapter, model fitting is particularly valuable for comparing alternative models. In the case of the CAP sibling data, two reduced models were considered. In Model 2, the genetic parameter was constrained to be zero in order to test the significance of genetic influence, and in Model 3 the shared-environment parameter was set to zero in order to test the significance of shared environmental influence. Table 8.1 indicates chi-square goodness of fit and associated *p* values with one degree of freedom for the two reduced models. The results correspond closely to what would be expected based on the standard errors of estimates from the full model.

Although the sibling model is simple because it involves only two groups and two parameters, it illustrates the estimation of parameters and their standard errors from a model, the derivation of goodness-of-fit indices, and the comparison of alternative models. Interpretation of such results becomes more dependent on model fitting as designs become more complex in terms of the number of parameters estimated and the number of groups involved – as in the CAP parent–offspring design.

Parent–offspring model

The CAP parent–offspring design is more complex than the sibling design in that it involves three relationships – biological, adoptive, and nonadoptive parents and children – and additional parameters beyond heritability and shared environmental influence – selective placement, assortative mating, genotype–environment correlation, and direct environmental transmission from parental phenotype to offspring. The full model is depicted in a path diagram in Figure 7.11 for nonadoptive families and in Figure 7.12 for adoptive families.

Height

In Chapter 7, the full parent–offspring model was fit to three observed covariance matrices for height at 3 years: a 3×3 matrix based on data from nonadoptive families, a 5×5 matrix based on complete data from adoptive families, and a 4×4 matrix based on data from adoptive families in which data are not available for biological fathers. Eleven free parameters (including two variances) were estimated; two parameters were computed because they are functions of the estimated parameters. Expectations for the variances and covariances derived from the path diagram are listed in Table 7.3. Maximum-likelihood model-fitting analyses indicated that only heritability and assortative mating were statistically significant for height at 3 years. Selective placement and phenotypic parental environment transmission were negligible.

Four reduced models were also fit to test hypotheses regarding assortative mating, selective placement, and environmental and genetic transmission. Testing more parsimonious models is particularly important in maximum-likelihood analyses because the standard errors of parameter estimates are only approximate due to the numerical methods by which they are calculated. Model 2 equates assortative mating for biological parents with assortative mating for adoptive and nonadoptive parents ($p = q$); Model 3 constrains selective placement to be zero in addition to equating p and q; Model 4 drops selective placement and genotype–environment correlation in addition to the constraints of Model 3; and Model 5 additionally constrains heritability to be zero. The results of these analyses for 3-year height, shown in Table 7.5, indicated that Models 2, 3, and 4 cannot be rejected. Comparing the chi-square differences between the models indicated that p and q can be equated, that selective placement can be ignored, and that environmental transmission from the parental phenotype is of negligible importance. Model 5, dropping the

Table 8.2. *Maximum-likelihood parameter estimates for the full parent–offspring model obtained from CAP height data*

Parameter	Year 1	Year 2	Year 3	Year 4
h	.72 ± .07	.81 ± .08	.74 ± .07	.74 ± .07
s	.00 ± .05	−.07 ± .07	−.02 ± .06	.02 ± .06
m	.00 ± .08	−.02 ± .10	−.05 ± .09	.06 ± .09
p	.28 ± .05	.24 ± .05	.26 ± .05	.26 ± .05
q	.06 ± .11	.07 ± .12	.13 ± .13	.16 ± .12
x_1	.13 ± .06	.13 ± .07	.07 ± .07	.05 ± .08
x_2	.16 ± .06	.12 ± .07	.13 ± .07	.11 ± .07
x_3	.07 ± .16	.03 ± .18	−.02 ± .17	−.09 ± .16
x_4	.19 ± .12	.21 ± .12	.13 ± .12	.14 ± .12
V_p	6.66 ± .30	6.90 ± .32	6.76 ± .33	6.67 ± .34
V_c	2.02 ± .15	2.29 ± .18	2.74 ± .22	3.69 ± .32
e	.70	.64	.68	.66
f	.01	−.12	.01	−.01
χ^2, 20 d.f.	24.13	26.53	26.52	39.15
p	>.20	>.10	>.10	<.05

genetic parameter, can be rejected, however, thus implying significant genetic influence.

For height at 1, 2, 3, and 4 years, parameter estimates for the full model are presented in Table 8.2, and the results of the reduced models are summarized in Table 8.3. The chi-squares for the full model at 1, 2, and 3 years indicate a reasonable fit of the model to the data. The parameter estimates and their standard errors indicate that passive genotype–environment correlation, selective placement, and maternal and paternal environmental transmission are negligible. Similar to the analyses at 3 years, the results at the other years indicate substantial genetic resemblance between parents and their children. The only other significant parameter is assortative mating, which appears to be greater for adoptive and non-adoptive parents (parameter p) than for biological parents (parameter q).

The reduced models at all 4 years yield similar results to those discussed in Chapter 7 for 3-year-olds. At all four years, Model 4 is reasonable; parental effects and genotype–environment correlation are of negligible importance. However, Model 3 yields a marginally significant chi-square difference ($p < .10$) at 2 years and a significant effect at 1 year ($p < .05$). This suggests that selective placement may be of some importance for height, although it is difficult to understand how selective placement can be of diminishing importance during development. The highly significant

Table 8.3. *Reduced models for height*

	Model 2 $(p = q)$	Model 3 $(p = q, x = 0)$	Model 4 $(p = q, x = 0,$ $m = f = 0,$ $s = 0)$	Model 5 $(p = q, x = 0,$ $m = f = 0,$ $s = 0, h = 0)$
Year 1				
χ^2	27.50	38.02	38.34	98.42
d.f.	21	25	27	28
p	>.10	<.05	>.05	<.001
Difference χ^2	3.37	10.52	0.32	60.08
d.f.	1	4	2	1
p	>.05	<.05	>.80	<.001
Year 2				
χ^2	28.25	36.30	38.14	95.87
d.f.	21	25	27	28
p	>.10	>.05	>.05	<.001
Difference χ^2	1.72	8.05	1.84	57.73
d.f.	1	4	2	1
p	>.10	>.05	>.30	<.001
Year 3				
χ^2	27.53	32.09	32.19	82.30
d.f.	21	25	27	28
p	>.10	>.10	>.10	<.001
Difference χ^2	1.01	4.56	0.10	50.11
d.f.	1	4	2	1
p	>.30	>.30	>.90	<.001
Year 4				
χ^2	39.78	43.51	44.47	103.26
d.f.	21	25	27	28
p	<.01	<.02	<.02	<.001
Difference χ^2	0.63	3.73	0.96	58.79
d.f.	1	4	2	1
p	>.30	>.30	>.50	<.001

Note: Model 2 is tested against the full model (Table 8.2), and each subsequent model is tested against the previous model.

chi-square difference for Model 5 at each year indicates significant genetic influence.

IQ

A similar model was fit to IQ data at each year. Parameter estimates for the full model are listed in Table 8.4, and the tests of the reduced models

Table 8.4. *Maximum-likelihood parameter estimates for the full parent–offspring model obtained from CAP IQ data*

Parameter	Year 1	Year 2	Year 3	Year 4
h	.29 ± .13	.40 ± .10	.35 ± .09	.47 ± .09
m	.02 ± .05	.07 ± .05	.10 ± .06	.12 ± .06
f	.04 ± .05	.02 ± .05	.11 ± .05	.06 ± .05
p	.27 ± .04	.25 ± .04	.26 ± .05	.23 ± .05
q	.28 ± .13	.22 ± .14	.27 ± .13	.35 ± .15
x_1	.01	.00	−.01	.07
x_2	.00	.02	.02	.12
x_3	.04	.02	.05	.03
x_4	.06	.03	.08	.10
s	.01	.02	.05	.06
e	.95	.91	.92	.86
χ^2, 20 d.f.	30.94	32.55	27.58	24.49
p	>.05	<.05	>.10	>.20

are presented in Table 8.5. The chi-squares for the full model indicate that it provides a reasonable fit to the data at 3 and 4 year. At 1 year, the model provides a marginally adequate fit to the data ($p > .05$), but not at 2 years. As indicated in the next section, the model fits considerably better when it takes into account the possibility of different heritabilities in childhood and adulthood and when the genetic correlation between childhood and adulthood is considered.

As in the case of height, selective placement is near zero and environmental transmission from the phenotype of the parent is less than .10 on average. Assortative mating is significant and similar for the biological parents and for the adoptive and nonadoptive parents. Heritability (the square of the h parameter) is significant at each year, with an increase from .08 at 1 to .22 at 4 years. Most of the variance, however, is environmental; e^2 is .90 at 1 and .74 at 4 years.

The reduced models in Table 8.5 test the significance of these parameters. The assortative mating parameters p and q can be equated (Model 2) and selective placement can be set to zero (Model 3) at all four years. Environmental transmission from the parental phenotype and passive genotype–environment correlation can be set to zero (Model 4) at years 1 and 2; however, as suggested by the parameter estimates in Table 8.4, setting m and f to zero at year 3 results in a significantly worse fit. Similarly, when the genetic parameter is set to zero, the fit is marginally worse at years 1 and 3 and significantly worse at years 2 and 4, suggesting significant genetic influence.

Table 8.5. *Reduced models for IQ*

	Model 2 $(p = q)$	Model 3 $(p = q, x = 0)$	Model 4 $(p = q, x = m = f = s = 0)$	Model 5 $(p = q, x = m = f = s = 0, h = 0)$
Year 1				
χ^2	30.94	31.12	32.13	35.86
d.f.	21	25	27	28
p	>.05	>.10	>.20	>.10
Difference χ^2	.00	.18	1.01	3.73
d.f.	1	4	2	1
p	1.0	>.99	>.50	>.10
Year 2				
χ^2	32.60	32.80	34.68	44.30
d.f.	21	25	27	28
p	>.05	>.10	>.10	<.05
Difference χ^2	.05	.20	1.88	9.62
d.f.	1	4	2	1
p	>.80	>.99	>.30	<.01
Year 3				
χ^2	27.58	28.03	35.67	31.09
d.f.	21	25	27	27
p	>.10	>.30	>.10	>.20
Difference χ^2	.00	.45	7.64	3.05
d.f.	1	4	2	1
p	1.0	>.98	<.05	>.05
Year 4				
χ^2	25.14	27.96	32.54	35.93
d.f.	21	25	27	27
p	>.20	>.30	>.20	>.10
Difference χ^2	.65	2.82	4.58	7.56
d.f.	1	4	2	1
p	>.40	>.50	>.05	<.01

Note: Model 2 is tested against the full model (Table 8.4), and each subsequent model is tested against the previous model.

Specific cognitive abilities

The CAP specific cognitive ability measures at 3 and 4 years were also subjected to model fitting. The parameter estimates for Verbal and Spatial (Table 8.6) indicate significant genetic influence at 3 years for Verbal and at 3 and 4 for Spatial. Assortative mating is substantial for Verbal for

Table 8.6. *Maximum-likelihood parameter estimates for the full parent–offspring model obtained from CAP Verbal and Spatial data*

	Verbal		Spatial	
Parameter	Year 3	Year 4	Year 3	Year 4
h	.42 ± .11	.24 ± .18	.35 ± .16	.44 ± .12
s	.03 ± .02	.04 ± .02	.02 ± .02	.01 ± .02
m	.03 ± .06	.16 ± .06	.03 ± .07	−.05 ± .07
p	.34 ± .04	.26 ± .05	.09 ± .05	.06 ± .05
q	.00 ± .30	.00 ± .29	.00 ± .07	.00 ± .25
x_1	.05 ± .07	.07 ± .07	−.04 ± .07	−.01 ± .07
x_2	.03 ± .07	.02 ± .07	.09 ± .07	.15 ± .07
x_3	.21 ± .14	.25 ± .13	−.11 ± .25	−.32 ± .18
x_4	−.02 ± .14	.09 ± .14	.29 ± .16	.20 ± .16
f	.08	.04	.09	.10
e	.89	.96	.93	.89
χ^2, 20 d.f.	16.06	23.51	29.98	22.55
p	>.70	>.25	>.05	>.30

adoptive and nonadoptive parents (p) but not for biological parents (q); little assortative mating occurs for Spatial. The environmental transmission parameters m and f are generally weak; the only significant estimate is for m at 4 years for Verbal. The reduced models (Table 8.7) indicate a significant difference in p and q for Verbal at 3 years (Model 2); otherwise, p and q can be equated. Selective placement can be set to zero (Model 3), as can parental environmental transmission and passive genotype–environment correlation (Model 4), with the exception of Verbal at 4 years. Finally, significant genetic influence is implied by the significant chi-square changes that emerge when genetic influence is set to zero (Model 5) for Verbal and Spatial at both 3 and 4 years.

Model-fitting results also indicate genetic influence for Perceptual Speed at 3 and 4 years, but not for Memory. Table 8.8 indicates marginally significant genetic influence for Perceptual Speed at 3, and h is significant at 4. Assortative mating is modest for both Perceptual Speed and Memory; selective placement is negligible. The reduced models reported in Table 8.9 indicate that, for Perceptual Speed, p can be set equal to q (Model 2), and selective placement (Model 3) as well as parental environmental transmission and passive genotype–environment correlation (Model 4) can be set to zero; the fit of the model is worsened, however, when genetic influence is set to zero (Model 5). Memory yields different results: Although the chi-square differences are not significant, the fit between the model and the data is perturbed when p is set equal to q (note in Table 8.8 that

Table 8.7. *Reduced models for Verbal and Spatial ± data*

	Model 2 $(p = q)$	Model 3 $(p = q, x = 0)$	Model 4 $(p = q, x = m = f = s = 0)$	Model 5 $(p = q, x = m = f = s = 0, h = 0)$
Verbal, year 3				
χ^2	22.47	18.60	21.00	33.56
d.f.	21	25	27	28
p	>.40	>.70	>.70	>.10
Difference χ^2	6.41	2.54	2.40	12.56
d.f.	1	4	2	1
p	<.05	>.60	>.20	<.01
Verbal, year 4				
χ^2	27.29	20.53	39.10	43.53
d.f.	21	25	27	28
p	>.10	>.10	>.05	<.05
Difference χ^2	3.78	3.24	8.57	4.43
d.f.	1	4	2	1
p	>.05	>.20	<.05	<.05
Spatial, year 3				
χ^2	32.10	35.88	37.88	45.52
d.f.	21	25	27	28
p	>.05	>.05	>.05	<.05
Difference χ^2	2.12	3.78	2.00	7.64
d.f.	1	4	2	1
p	>.10	>.40	>.30	<.05
Spatial, year 4				
χ^2	23.13	28.90	31.13	37.76
d.f.	21	25	27	28
p	>.20	>.20	>.20	>.05
Difference χ^2	.58	5.77	2.23	6.53
d.f.	1	4	2	1
p	>.40	>.20	>.30	<.05

Note: Model 2 is tested against the full model (Table 8.6), and each subsequent model is tested against the previous model.

p is less than q), when selective placement is set equal to zero (note in Table 8.8 that there is some negative selective placement for x_3 and positive selective placement for x_4), and when parental environmental transmission and passive genotype–environment correlation are set to zero. There is no effect, however, when genetic influence is set to zero, indicating that heredity does not mediate parent–offspring resemblance for memory.

Table 8.8. *Maximum-likelihood parameter estimates for the full parent–offspring model obtained from CAP Perceptual Speed and Memory data*

Parameter	Perceptual Speed		Memory	
	Year 3	Year 4	Year 3	Year 4
h	.27 ± .16	.31 ± .14	.15 ± .70	.01 ± .02
s	.02 ± .01	.01 ± .01	−.01 ± .01	.00 ± .01
m	.04 ± .06	.00 ± .06	.03 ± .06	.01 ± .06
p	.16 ± .05	.19 ± .05	.11 ± .05	.11 ± .05
q	.18 ± .13	.18 ± .13	.16 ± .13	.26 ± .12
x_1	−.02 ± .07	.01 ± .08	−.07 ± .07	−.03 ± .08
x_2	.00 ± .08	−.03 ± .09	−.09 ± .07	−.05 ± .07
x_3	−.16 ± .12	−.17 ± .12	−.18 ± .14	−.27 ± .14
x_4	−.01 ± .15	−.02 ± .15	.22 ± .15	.14 ± .15
f	.09	.02	−.12	−.07
e	.96	.95	.99	.99
χ^2, 20 d.f.	21.85	21.97	28.02	26.76
p	>.30	>.30	>.05	>.10

Shyness

Shyness has been suggested to be one of the most heritable personality dimensions in infancy, childhood, and adulthood (Plomin & Daniels, 1986). Model-fitting analyses were conducted for parental ratings of CCTI Sociability (which primarily assesses shyness) and parental self-report ratings of the second-order 16PF factor Extraversion. The reason for comparing CCTI Sociability with 16PF Extraversion rather than with EAS Sociability is that the latter scale assesses gregariousness rather than shyness. However, 16PF Extraversion is not an ideal measure of parental shyness because it includes facets of personality other than shyness.

Parameter estimates are listed in Table 8.10 and the results of fitting reduced models are described in Table 8.11. The genetic influence parameter h increases from .00 at 1 year to .18 at 2 and to .24 and .22 at 3 and 4; however, the standard errors indicate that h is not statistically significant. Fitting reduced Model 5 yields a marginally significant effect at 2 and 3 years, suggesting the possibility of genetic influence.

The parameter estimates in Table 8.10 implicate some parental environmental transmission at 1 and 2 years and an odd pattern of *negative* selective placement, especially involving the small sample of biological fathers as related to adoptive fathers. The assortative mating coefficient for wed couples is somewhat greater than that for the biological parents, but the difference is not significant. The reduced models in Table 8.11

Table 8.9. *Reduced models for Perceptual Speed and Memory data*

	Model 2 $(p = q)$	Model 3 $(p = q, x = 0)$	Model 4 $(p = q,$ $x = m = f$ $= s = 0)$	Model 5 $(p = q,$ $x = m = f$ $= s = 0,$ $h = 0)$
Speed, year 3				
χ^2	22.35	23.50	23.53	27.50
d.f.	21	25	27	28
p	>.30	>.50	>.60	>.40
Difference χ^2	.50	1.15	.03	3.97
d.f.	1	4	2	1
p	>.40	>.80	>.95	<.05
Speed, year 4				
χ^2	21.98	24.12	24.34	27.26
d.f.	21	25	27	28
p	>.30	>.40	>.50	>.40
Difference χ^2	.01	2.14	.22	2.92
d.f.	1	4	2	1
p	>.90	>.60	>.80	<.08
Memory, year 3				
χ^2	28.14	34.12	39.63	39.84
d.f.	21	25	27	28
p	>.05	>.05	>.05	>.05
Difference χ^2	.12	6.14	5.35	.21
d.f.	1	4	2	1
p	>.60	>.05	>.05	>.50
Memory, year 4				
χ^2	29.77	32.36	36.43	36.43
d.f.	21	25	27	28
p	>.10	>.10	>.05	>.20
Difference χ^2	1.01	4.59	4.07	.00
d.f.	1	4	2	1
p	>.20	>.20	>.10	>.99

Note: Model 2 is tested against the full model (Table 8.8), and each subsequent model is tested against the previous model.

confirm these interpretations. Model 2 ($p=q$) fits, and the chi-square difference is modest. Setting selective placement to zero (Model 3) significantly worsens the fit at 1 year and yields a marginally worse fit at the other years. Some evidence for parental environmental transmission is seen from the fit of Model 4 in that the chi-square is significant at 1 year and marginally significant at 2.

Table 8.10. *Maximum-likelihood parameter estimates for the full parent–offspring model for CCTI Sociability (Shyness) and 16PF Extraversion*

Parameter	Year 1	Year 2	Year 3	Year 4
h	.00 ± .80	.18 ± .19	.24 ± .16	.22 ± .18
m	.14 ± .04	.05 ± .04	.03 ± .05	− .03 ± .06
f	.02 ± .05	.12 ± .05	.06 ± .05	− .02 ± .06
p	.22 ± .04	.21 ± .04	.24 ± .04	.20 ± .06
q	.00 ± .14	.03 ± .25	.01 ± .24	.01 ± .24
x_1	.02	− .01	.03	.02
x_2	− .11	− .11	− .05	− .08
x_3	− .54	− .53	− .55	− .54
x_4	− .05	− .05	− .06	− .04
s	.00	.02	.01	− .01
e	1.00	.98	.97	.98
χ^2, 20 d.f.	31.54	33.51	25.24	26.75
p	<.05	<.05	>.10	>.10

Although the parent–offspring model is considerably more complex than the sibling model, it is only a first step toward modeling the complexity of familial resemblance. It is most important in the present context that genetic change during development be considered, as discussed in Chapter 6. Rather than assuming, as in the present parent–offspring model, that genetic influences in childhood are the same as genetic influences in adulthood, genetic change and continuity during childhood and from childhood to adulthood can be modeled explicitly. These extensions of model fitting to longitudinal data are considered in the following section, which also combines sibling and parent–offspring models.

Modeling genetic change and continuity

The most important question in developmental behavioral genetics concerns the extent to which genetic factors underlie age-to-age change and continuity. Because genetics is often implicitly associated with stability, the most novel aspect of this question is the extent to which genetics underlies the changes that are pandemic during development. Phenotypic stability correlations for behavioral development are often modest in magnitude, whereas heritabilities are often moderate and sometimes substantial; thus, it is reasonable to expect that genetics is a potent source of developmental change.

Answers to this question require longitudinal data. As discussed in Chapter 6, few longitudinal behavioral genetic studies have been conducted; for

Table 8.11. *Reduced models for Shyness data*

	Model 2 $(p = q)$	Model 3 $(p = q, x = 0)$	Model 4 $(p = q,$ $x = m = f$ $= s = 0)$	Model 5 $(p = q,$ $x = m = f$ $= s = 0,$ $h = 0)$
Year 1				
χ^2	32.29	41.82	44.08	44.08
d.f.	21	25	27	28
p	>.05	<.05	<.05	>.05
Difference χ^2	.75	9.53	6.52	.00
d.f.	1	4	2	1
p	>.30	<.05	<.05	>.99
Year 2				
χ^2	33.98	43.01	47.54	51.16
d.f.	21	25	27	28
p	<.05	<.05	<.01	<.01
Difference χ^2	.47	9.03	4.53	3.62
d.f.	1	4	2	1
p	>.40	>.05	>.10	>.05
Year 3				
χ^2	26.07	32.91	33.66	36.66
d.f.	21	25	27	28
p	>.20	>.10	>.10	>.10
Difference χ^2	.83	6.84	.75	3.0
d.f.	1	4	2	1
p	>.30	>.10	>.50	>.05
Year 4				
χ^2	27.32	34.99	35.49	35.58
d.f.	21	25	27	28
p	>.10	>.50	>.10	>.10
Difference χ^2	.57	7.67	.50	.09
d.f.	1	4	2	1
p	>.40	>.05	>.40	>.70

Note: Model 2 is tested against the full model (Table 8.10), and each subsequent model is tested against the previous model.

this reason, only a glimmer of future answers to this question can as yet be seen. In Chapter 6 the concepts of genetic change and continuity were illustrated with the basic data of correlations and cross-correlations for the CAP sibling design and the parent–offspring design. The longitudinal sibling or twin design is particularly useful for assessing genetic and environmental change and continuity from year to year during childhood because of the similarity of age of siblings and twins as compared with that of parents and offspring. In contrast, the parent–offspring adoption design can be viewed as an instant longitudinal study from childhood to adulthood, and its data can be analyzed to provide information about genetic and environmental sources of long-term developmental change and continuity.

The present chapter extends the parent–offspring model described in Chapters 6 and 7, to consider longitudinal analyses of change and continuity. Specifically, the parent–offspring model is elaborated to make explicit the fact that, in the CAP, parents are assessed as adults and their offspring are assessed as children. The longitudinal parent–offspring model is applied to CAP data on IQ, the only behavioral trait for which information is as yet available to satisfy the requirements of the model of longitudinal continuity and change from childhood to adulthood.

Longitudinal model fitting using the sibling adoption design

Although the CAP sibling sample size is not yet adequate for conducting longitudinal model fitting of year-to-year correlations, it should be noted that longitudinal twin models have been proposed and these are equally applicable to the sibling adoption design. These models begin with the basic concept of an age-to-age genetic correlation (Plomin & DeFries, 1981). One approach aims to assess the extent to which genes that affect a phenotype are general across age or specific to each age (Eaves, Long, & Heath, 1986; McArdle, 1986); the latter approach is noteworthy in its attempt to analyze growth curves and to incorporate multivariate analysis. However, these twin models do not use longitudinal twin data; instead, they rely on the age-to-age phenotypic correlations and use heritabilities at each age in an attempt to solve for genetic correlations across age. The reason for this is that these approaches rely on Louisville Twin Study reports of cross-sectional twin data: "More refined analyses, however, require additional statistics, including the cross-twin correlations over time, so that the developmental effects of genes and environment may be distinguished more effectively" (Eaves et al., 1986, p. 159). The use of longitudinal twin data in model fitting has been incorporated in another model that has been applied to computer-generated twin data (Boomsma & Molenaar, 1987).

The CAP sibling model illustrated in Figure 7.3 can easily be extended to the longitudinal case. As specified in Equations (7.4) and (7.5), the sibling model refers to a single trait measured for each sibling at the same age; the equations can be rewritten to emphasize this point:

$$\text{nonadoptive } r_{P_x P_x} = 0.5 h_x h_x + c_x c_x,$$

$$\text{adoptive } r_{P_x P_x} = \qquad c_x c_x.$$

Combining this model with the longitudinal path model illustrated in Figure 6.8 leads to a longitudinal path model of the sibling adoption design that is merely the repetition of Figure 7.3 at two ages; the only additions are the genetic and environmental correlations between the ages. Rather than using sibling correlations for the same trait at the same age, the longitudinal model focuses on sibling "cross-correlations," which, as explained in Chapter 6, refer to correlations between one sibling's score at one age and the other sibling's score at another age. The expectations for age-to-age cross-correlations are analogous to those for within-age correlations, with the addition of genetic and environmental correlations:

$$\text{nonadoptive } r_{P_1 P_2} = 0.5 h_1 h_2 r_G + c_1 c_2 r_{E_c},$$

$$\text{adoptive } r_{P_1 P_2} = \qquad c_1 c_2 r_{E_c}.$$

As discussed in Chapter 6, the genetic contribution to phenotypic stability is the age-to-age genetic correlation r_G weighted by the square roots of heritabilities at each age. The age-to-age genetic correlation indicates the extent to which genetic effects at one age correlate with those at another age regardless of heritability at each age. Age-to-age genetic correlations of less than 1.0 indicate genetic change during development if heritability at each age is nonzero.

Longitudinal model fitting using the parent–offspring adoption design

Because parents and their offspring are so different in age, it is important to extend the parent–offspring model to consider the possibility of genetic change between childhood and adulthood. That is, genetic similarity between parents studied as adults and their offspring assessed as children depends on the extent of genetic change from childhood to adulthood. This genetic change is indexed by the genetic correlation; in the case of parents and offspring, the genetic correlation refers to the long-term correlation between genetic effects on a phenotype in childhood and the genetic effects on a phenotype in adulthood, not the short-term year-to-year genetic correlations considered in the preceding section. In the simple parent–offspring model, the genetic correlation between adulthood and childhood is assumed to be 1.0 and heritabilities in adulthood and childhood are assumed to be the same. The goal of this extension of the parent–offspring model is to develop a model free of these assumptions.

Previous attempts to develop longitudinal parent–offspring models have focused on year-to-year stability within infancy and childhood rather than long-term stability from childhood to adulthood (Baker, DeFries, & Fulker, 1983; LaBuda, DeFries, Plomin & Fulker, 1986); these analyses revealed that year-to-year stability is not attributable to genetic and environmental influences predicted by parental phenotype. The present section describes a new approach to longitudinal change and continuity from childhood to adulthood using the parent–offspring model and incorporating genetic correlations from childhood to adulthood (DeFries, Plomin, & LaBuda, 1987).

Figure 7.4 presents a path diagram of parent–offspring resemblance analogous to the sibling model in that resemblance can be expressed as $0.5h^2$ for biological parent–adopted child, c^2 for adoptive parent–adopted child, and $0.5h^2 + c^2$ for nonadoptive parents and their children. This model can be extended by adding genetic and environmental correlations between childhood and adulthood, as illustrated in the path diagram of Figure 6.9. The left side of the path diagram depicts expected parent–offspring similarity with the parent as a child of the same age as the child. The rest of the path diagram indicates that genetic resemblance from childhood to adulthood is a function of the genetic correlation between childhood and adulthood and that heritabilities in childhood and adulthood can differ. Thus, resemblance between biological parent and adopted-away child is represented as $0.5h_c h_a r_G$. If the genetic correlation between childhood and adulthood is 1.0 and if heritabilities are the same in childhood and adulthood, this reduces to $0.5h^2$.

The important point of this extension of the parent–offspring model is that significant resemblance between biological parents and their adopted-away children has three requirements: The characteristic must be heritable in childhood, it must be heritable in adulthood, and the genetic correlation between infancy and adulthood for the characteristic must be positive. As discussed in Chapter 6, it would be difficult to detect parent–offspring resemblance unless all three elements were substantial because, in effect, parent–offspring resemblance depends on their product. When significant parent–child resemblance is found, we know that the three requirements have been met to some extent: Heritabilities in childhood and in adulthood are significant (and likely to be substantial), and the genetic correlation between childhood and adulthood is significant (and probably substantial). In other words, the CAP parent–offspring model-fitting analyses in Chapter 7 that revealed evidence for significant genetic influence implicitly gave evidence for substantial genetic correlations from childhood to adulthood.

This simple parent–offspring model was extended in Chapter 7 to con-

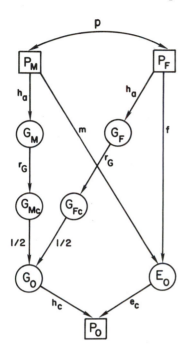

Figure 8.1. Path diagram representing genetic and environmental transmission in nonadoptive families. (From DeFries, Plomin, & LaBuda, 1987.)

sider environmental transmission of parental phenotype on child's environment, passive genotype–environment correlation, assortative mating, and selective placement. A further extension to incorporate the concept of genetic correlation between childhood and adulthood and differing heritabilities in childhood and adulthood is presented in Figure 8.1 for nonadoptive families and in Figure 8.2 for adoptive families (DeFries et al., 1987). The advantage of this model as compared with the examination of biological-mother/adoptee correlations in Chapter 6 is that it simultaneously analyzes data from all three family types, explicitly testing the significance of the longitudinal genetic correlation, and models the effects of phenotypic assortative mating and selective placement. For example, as seen in Chapter 7, moderate assortative mating for cognitive abilities occurs in the CAP; ignoring assortative mating leads to overestimates of the longitudinal genetic correlation. The model does not include genotype–environment correlation because model-fitting analyses described in Chapter 7 indicate that it is of little importance and solution of the model requires limits on the number of estimated parameters. As indicated in Figure 8.1, a correlation between genetic and environmental influences on the child

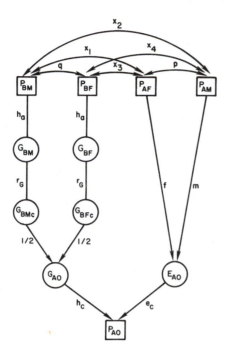

Figure 8.2. Path diagram representing genetic and environmental transmission in adoptive families. (From DeFries, Plomin, & LaBuda, 1987.)

will be induced if both genetic and environmental transmission occur; thus, the validity of the assumption of no genotype–environment correlation is supported if either genetic or environmental transmission is not significant. Because genotype–environment correlation is assumed to be zero, it is possible to standardize G, E, and P to zero mean and unit variance for both adopted and nonadopted children and their parents.

Table 8.12 contains the three expected correlations among the three manifest variables for nonadoptive families and the 10 expected correlations among the five manifest variables in adoptive families. These are the same as the expectations for the simple parent–offspring model presented in Table 7.3, except that the expectations are not weighted by phenotypic variance, there is no genotype–environment correlation, and the genetic component of resemblance has been weighted by the genetic correlation from childhood to adulthood.

Resolution of the model requires independent heritability estimates in childhood and in adulthood. Childhood estimates of heritability can be obtained from the CAP sibling adoption design; however, no comparable estimates of adult heritability are available. For this reason and because

Table 8.12. *Expected parent–offspring correlations in a longitudinal model*

Variable	Expected correlation
Nonadoptive families	
P_M, P_F	p
P_M, P_O	$0.5h_a h_c r_G (1 + p) + e_c(m + pf)$
P_F, P_O	$0.5h_a h_c r_G (1 + p) + e_c(m + pf)$
Adoptive families	
P_{BM}, P_{BF}	q
P_{AM}, P_{AF}	p
P_{BM}, P_{AF}	x_1
P_{BM}, P_{AM}	x_2
P_{BF}, P_{AF}	x_3
P_{BF}, P_{AM}	x_4
P_{BM}, P_{AO}	$0.5h_a h_c r_G (1 + q) + e_c(x_1 f + x_2 m)$
P_{BF}, P_{AO}	$0.5h_a h_c r_G (1 + q) + e_c(x_3 f + x_4 m)$
P_{AF}, P_{AO}	$e_c(f + pm) + 0.5h_a h_c r_G (x_1 + x_3)$
P_{AM}, P_{AO}	$e_c(m + pf) + 0.5h_a h_c r_G (x_2 + x_4)$

Source: DeFries, Plomin, and LaBuda (1987).

the CAP sibling adoption sample is still small, twin data were employed for this purpose. Figures 8.3 and 8.4 describe path models of parent–offspring resemblance for twins tested as adults or children, respectively. The former path diagram adds the genetic correlation from childhood to adulthood as in Figures 8.1 and 8.2. A latent variable E_t with path coefficient t has been added to account for any unique resemblance between members of twin pairs that is not due to parent–child transmission (e.g., special shared environmental influences due to twin contemporaneity). Especially for cognitive abilities, twins have been found to share environmental influences to a greater extent than do other family members, such as nontwin siblings (Plomin, 1986a).

Data from parents of twins were not included in the application of this model because such data are not available. For this reason, it is assumed that assortative mating of parents of twins is similar to that of adoptive and nonadoptive parents of singletons. It is also assumed that environmental transmission is similar in families of twins and singletons. As indicated in Table 8.13, these assumptions make it possible to express expected identical- and fraternal-twin correlations in terms of t and the parent–child model parameters. It should be mentioned that a combined parent–offspring and sibling model for CAP has been developed to address

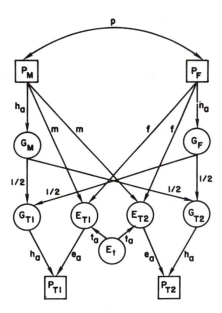

Figure 8.3. Path diagram of genetic and shared family environmental transmission in families of twins tested as adults (T1, twin; T2, co-twin; a, adult). (From DeFries, Plomin, & LaBuda, 1987.)

the issue of longitudinal genetic influence from childhood to adulthood; analyses employing this model will be especially interesting as the longitudinal sample size of adoptive siblings increases (Corley, 1987).

Results of fitting the longitudinal parent–offspring model to IQ data in CAP

The parent–offspring/twin model was applied to IQ data at 1, 2, 3, and 4 years of age using CAP data for parents and offspring, the Louisville Twin Study correlations for identical- and fraternal-twin pairs at 1, 2, 3, and 4 years of age (Wilson, 1983), and, for older twins, the correlations reported by Loehlin and Nichols (1976). Although the latter twin correlations are based on young adults and scholastic ability tests, the sample is large (1,300 identical- and 864 fraternal-twin pairs), and the obtained correlations are typical of other twin studies of IQ (Bouchard & McGue, 1981). As discussed in Chapter 7, the CAP data provide a 3 × 3 variance–covariance matrix for nonadoptive families; a 5 × 5 matrix for adoptive families with complete data on biological mothers, biological fathers, adoptive mothers, adoptive fathers, and adopted children; and a 4 × 4 matrix for adoptive

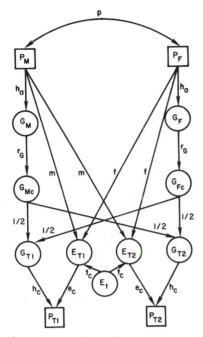

Figure 8.4. Path diagram of genetic and shared family environmental transmission in families of twins tested as children (T1, twin; T2, co-twin; a, adult; c, child). (From DeFries, Plomin, & LaBuda, 1987.)

Table 8.13. *Expected twin correlations in a longitudinal model of parent–offspring resemblance*

Variable	Expected correlation
Adult twins	
P_{T1}, P_{T2} (identical)	$h_a^2 + e_a^2 (m^2 + f^2 + 2mfp + t_a^2)$
P_{T1}, P_{T2} (fraternal)	$0.5h_a^2 (1 + h_a^2 p) + e_a^2 (m^2 + f^2 + 2mfp + t_a^2)$
Child twins	
P_{T1}, P_{T2} (identical)	$h_c^2 + e_c^2 (m^2 + f^2 + 2mfp + t_c^2)$
P_{T1}, P_{T2} (fraternal)	$0.5h_c^2 (1 + h_a^2 r_G p) + e_c^2 (m^2 + f^2 + 2mfp + t_c^2)$

Source: DeFries, Plomin, and LaBuda (1987).

families lacking information from biological fathers. In the case of twins, 2 × 2 correlation matrices (identical- and fraternal-twin correlations for children tested at each age and for adults) were analyzed.

Parameter estimates and standard errors resulting from the fit of the full

Table 8.14. *IQ parameter estimates ($\pm SE$) for the full longitudinal parent–offspring/twin model for children*

Parameter	Year 1	Year 2	Year 3	Year 4
p	.22 ± .05	.20 ± .05	.22 ± .05	.23 ± .06
q	.32 ± .13	.26 ± .15	.34 ± .13	.34 ± .13
x_1	− .01 ± .07	− .02 ± .07	− .03 ± .07	.06 ± .08
x_2	.03 ± .07	.08 ± .07	.09 ± .08	.15 ± .08
x_3	− .08 ± .14	− .10 ± .15	− .05 ± .14	− .02 ± .15
x_4	− .07 ± .16	.04 ± .15	.10 ± .16	.17 ± .16
f	.06 ± .06	.07 ± .06	.07 ± .06	− .01 ± .07
m	.06 ± .07	.07 ± .07	.10 ± .06	.11 ± .08
t_a	.83 ± .02	.83 ± .02	.82 ± .03	.82 ± .03
t_c	.80 ± .03	.87 ± .02	.91 ± .01	.87 ± .02
h_a	.74 ± .04	.73 ± .04	.74 ± .04	.74 ± .04
h_c	.32 ± .25	.41 ± .11	.43 ± .07	.51 ± .09
r_G	.42 ± .50	.61 ± .33	.56 ± .28	.75 ± .27
χ^2	19.45	20.35	18.79	19.73
d.f.	20	20	20	20
p	>.50	>.30	>.50	>.50

Source: DeFries, Plomin, and LaBuda (1987).

model to the data are presented in Table 8.14. The chi-square goodness-of-fit index implies that the full model adequately represents the data at each age. The assortative mating parameters (p and q), selective placement (x_1 through x_4), environmental transmission (f and m), twin shared environment (t_a and t_c), and the square root of heritability for adults (h_a) are stable across the four ages despite differences in sample size. Assortative mating is moderate both for biological parents (q) and for adoptive and nonadoptive parents (p); selective placement parameters (x_1 through x_4) are near zero; and shared environmental transmission from the parental phenotype (f and m) is low. The finding that shared environmental influence between parents and children is low is not unusual. For example, in a study of 94 adoptive families, the IQ correlation between adoptive mothers and their adopted children at 4 years of age was .07 (Fisch, Bilek, Deinard, & Chang, 1976).

In contrast, estimates of the square root of heritability for adults (h_a) and twin shared environment (t_a and t_c) are large. As expected on the basis of the discussion in Chapter 6, the heritability of IQ in infancy and in childhood increases: .10, .17, .18, and .26 at 1, 2, 3, and 4 years, respectively. The twin shared-environment parameter is remarkably high and stable across ages.

Of greatest interest in the present context is the childhood-to-adulthood genetic stability parameter r_G estimated at each age. As indicated in Table 8.14, this parameter is moderate at 1 year of age (.42) but increases to .75 by 4 years. Despite the large standard error attached to these estimates, the genetic correlation is significant at 3 and 4 years. The estimates are lower than those previously reported (LaBuda et al., 1987; Plomin & DeFries, 1985b), primarily because assortative mating is considered in the present model. Nonetheless, the estimates of genetic correlations suggest that genetic effects on IQ scores in early childhood are substantially correlated with genetic effects on IQ scores in adulthood. However, the genetic correlations are not unity, which means that genetic change also plays a role in the development of cognitive ability.

As mentioned in previous chapters, the standard errors of the parameter estimates are only approximate because of the numerical methods employed to compute them; comparing the goodness of fit of alternative models using chi-square provides significance tests that are more robust. A series of models were fit, as shown in Table 8.15. Models 2, 3, 5, and 6 are the same as the reduced models examined in Chapter 7, except that Models 5 and 6 test the significance of heritability in childhood and in adulthood, respectively. In addition, Model 4 tests the fit of a model in which assortative mating is zero for all three types of parents and the x parameters are also zero. Model 7 tests the significance of the genetic correlation at each age.

As shown in Table 8.15, the chi-square difference for Model 2 indicates the acceptability at each age of dropping selective placement and setting assortative mating for biological parents equal to assortative mating for adoptive and nonadoptive parents, a finding that also emerged from the simple model-fitting analyses presented earlier in this chapter. Model 3 retains the constraints of Model 2 but also assumes the absence of environmental effects of parental IQ on children's IQ; the changes in chi-square indicate that this model is also acceptable at each age. As discussed earlier, finding no effect for environmental transmission supports the decision to drop the genotype–environment parameter from the longitudinal model.

Model 3 is the most parsimonious of the models for which adequate fits to the data were obtained. Parameter estimates obtained from the fit of Model 3 are similar to those estimated from the full model (Table 8.14) with one exception: The r_G parameter of genetic stability is about .25 greater at each age, because in this reduced model all parent–child resemblance is assumed to be due to genetic influences. Although the parent–offspring environmental transmission parameters are not significant, all but one are positive and are thus read by the model as contributing to the genetic correlation between adult parents and their children.

Model 4 retains the constraints of Model 2 as well as assumes that

Table 8.15. *Fit of reduced models for the longitudinal parent–offspring/twin model for IQ*

Model	Age	Model statistics χ^2	Model statistics d.f.	Change statistics χ^2	Change statistics d.f.	Change statistics $p <$
2 ($p = q, x = 0$)	1	20.67	25	1.22	5	.95
	2	22.27	25	1.92	5	.90
	3	21.44	25	2.65	5	.80
	4	24.62	25	4.89	5	.50
3 ($p = q, x = 0, m = f = 0$)	1	22.54	27	1.87	2	.50
	2	24.30	27	2.03	2	.50
	3	25.12	27	3.68	2	.20
	4	27.15	27	2.53	2	.30
4 ($p = q = 0, x = 0$)	1	41.83	26	21.16	1	.001
	2	38.40	26	16.13	1	.001
	3	41.34	26	19.90	1	.001
	4	43.46	26	18.84	1	.001
5 ($p = q, x = 0, h_a = 0$)	1	292.37	26	271.70	1	.001
	2	296.93	26	274.66	1	.001
	3	295.59	26	274.15	1	.001
	4	303.59	26	278.97	1	.001
6 ($p = q, x = 0, h_c = 0$)	1	22.55	26	1.88	1	.20
	2	29.66	26	7.39	1	.01
	3	34.23	26	12.79	1	.001
	4	41.14	26	16.52	1	.001
7 ($p = q, x = 0, r_G = 0$)	1	22.05	26	1.38	1	.30
	2	26.62	26	4.35	1	.05
	3	25.61	26	4.17	1	.05
	4	33.28	26	8.66	1	.01

Note: Model 2 is tested against Model 1 (Table 8.14), whereas all others are tested against Model 2.
Source: DeFries, Plomin, and LaBuda (1987).

assortative mating is absent; this hypothesis can be rejected with considerable confidence. The large chi-square change for Model 5 indicates that adult heritability is highly significant. Correspondingly, Model 6 tests the hypothesis that IQ heritability is zero during infancy and childhood. Although this hypothesis cannot be rejected for 1-year-olds, there is evidence for significant heritability at 2, 3, and 4 years of age.

Of special interest is Model 7, which constrains the longitudinal genetic correlation to be zero. As indicated in Table 8.15, this hypothesis cannot be rejected for 1-year-olds; however, the longitudinal genetic correlations are significantly different from zero at the later ages. These results provide the strongest available evidence of significant genetic stability for IQ from early childhood to adulthood.

One question that arises from the finding of substantial genetic stability is the following. How can genetic stability be so high when genetic variance increases so dramatically – from about .10 in infancy to .20 in early childhood to .50 in adulthood? For example, if the genetic correlation were 1.0, any increase in heritability from childhood to adulthood would present a paradox. Although the magnitude of the genetic correlations for IQ is not necessarily discrepant with the increase in heritability, it is interesting heuristically to consider the possibility that the effects of genes that cause individual differences early in life become amplified during development. In other words, although genetic variation accounts for a smaller proportion of the observed variance of cognitive ability in infancy and early childhood than in adulthood, the effects of many of the same genes may be manifested increasingly as development proceeds (DeFries et al., 1987).

Another implication of these results is that they predict some phenotypic stability for IQ from early childhood to adulthood. As discussed earlier, the genetic contribution to phenotypic stability is a function of the longitudinal genetic correlation between the two ages and the square roots of the heritabilities at each age. If either of the heritabilities is low, the genetic contribution to phenotypic stability (i.e., $h_a h_c r_G$) will also be low. The results in Table 8.14 suggest that the genetic contribution to phenotypic stability is .10 from 1 year to adulthood, .18 from 2 years, .18 from 3 years, and .28 from 4 years. As discussed in Chapter 5, phenotypic stability from 1, 2, 3, and 4 years of age to adulthood is about .25, .40, .45, and .50, respectively. Thus, the present results suggest that the proportion of phenotypic stability between childhood and adulthood that is mediated genetically is .40, .46, .40, and .57 at 1, 2, 3, and 4 years, respectively.

Although a surprising amount of genetic variance that affects IQ scores in childhood covaries with genetic influences on adult IQ, genetic change is also apparent in these results. Across the four years, the average genetic correlation is .58, which means that about half of the genetic variance in childhood does not covary between childhood and adulthood. Thus, phenotypic change during development is also brought about in part by genetic change.

This analysis focuses on IQ because it is the only behavioral trait for which heritability estimates are available in childhood and in adulthood. Even though change exceeds continuity for IQ, it is one of the most stable behavioral traits. The vast majority of other behavioral traits show little stability from childhood to adulthood; in CAP analyses, parent–offspring resemblance is slight, which implies that genetics underlies phenotypic instability to the extent that these traits are heritable. Thus, change, including genetic change, is the predominant force for most of behavioral development, and for this reason developmental behavioral genetics must maintain its focus on genetic change as well as continuity.

Multivariate model fitting

As discussed in Chapter 6, one of the three forms of genetic change during development involves changes in patterns of genetic correlations and environmental correlations among measures, which is the essence of multivariate quantitative genetic analysis (DeFries & Fulker, 1986). Rather than considering genetic and environmental sources of covariance across age as in the preceding chapter on longitudinal analysis, multivariate analysis focuses on genetic and environmental covariance among measures at a particular age. The concept of age-to-age genetic correlations was in fact derived from multivariate analysis (Plomin, 1986b; Plomin & DeFries, 1981). Developmental interest in multivariate analysis per se lies in comparisons of genetic and environmental correlations and covariance structures across ages to determine, for example, whether genetic reorganization occurs during development. In Chapter 6, cross-correlations for adoptive and nonadoptive siblings in the CAP were presented for this purpose. These analyses suggested interesting results, such as the following. The phenotypic relationship between height and weight appears to be largely genetic in origin and this genetic mediation ($h_x h_y r_G$) is stable during infancy and early childhood; there was some suggestion that the genetic correlation r_G between height and weight decreases during this period of development. For mental and motor development, the analysis of sibling cross-correlations was compatible with the hypothesis of genetic differentiation of mental and motor development during infancy – that is, the genetic correlation between the two traits decreases. Other relationships that were examined from this perspective included the relationship between cognitive (Bayley Mental Development Index, MDI) and communicative (Sequenced Inventory of Communication Development, SICD) development and between expressive and receptive communicative skills as assessed by the SICD. For these two comparisons, genetic correlations appear to remain stable developmentally.

The present chapter considers multivariate extensions of the sibling and the parent–offspring models presented in Chapter 7. The sibling multivariate model is applied to the relationship between temperament and cognition, and the parent–offspring multivariate model is applied to the relationship among specific cognitive abilities.

The history of multivariate behavioral genetics began with Darwin (1859/1958), who wrote about "correlated variation" and stated that "the whole organisation is so tied together during its growth and development, that when slight variations in any one part occur, and are accumulated through natural selection, other parts become modified" (p. 139). A recent special issue of the journal *Behavior Genetics* (edited by DeFries & Fulker, 1986) describes the considerable advances in multivariate behavioral genetics that have been made in recent years. Most multivariate research has involved twin analyses of matrices of cross-covariances (e.g., Eaves & Gale, 1974; Fulker, Baker, & Bock, 1983). In the present chapter, this approach is applied to data from the sibling adoption design. Bivariate parent–offspring models have also been formulated (e.g., McGue, 1983; Neale & Fulker, 1984; Vogler & DeFries, 1985). Until recently, it has been difficult to derive expectations for path-analytic models that go beyond the bivariate case, especially for models that incorporate assortative mating and cross-assortative mating. This problem has been remedied by Vogler's (1985) extension of path analysis to the general multivariate case using matrix notation, an approach employed in the parent–offspring model described later.

Multivariate sibling model

The basic concepts of multivariate analysis using cross-correlations for adoptive and nonadoptive siblings in the CAP were discussed in Chapter 6. The twin design and the sibling adoption design are particularly useful for this purpose, because twins – and siblings in the CAP – are studied at the same age. The multivariate sibling model described in this section is based on a multivariate twin model (Fulker et al., 1983; LaBuda, DeFries, & Fulker, 1987) that has been adapted to the sibling adoption design and applied to the analysis of the relationship among cognitive and temperament measures at 2 years of age (Thompson, Fulker, DeFries, & Plomin, 1988).

The sibling model employs a components-of-covariance approach, in which a mean cross-products matrix is formed between and within adoptive and nonadoptive pairs using MANOVA; the diagonals of these matrices are the mean squares between and within pairs. The expectation for each element in the matrices is the same as that described in terms of the basic sibling model (Chapter 7), except that mean squares and cross-products are used rather than correlations. In the univariate case, the expected mean squares between and within sibling pairs (standarized) are as follows,

$$\text{nonadoptive between} = 1.5h^2 + 2c^2 + w,$$

Table 8.16. *Phenotypic correlations among cognitive and temperament measures at 2 years*

	IBR Af–Ex	IBR TO	Difficult Temperament	SICD	Bayley MDI
IBR Af–Ex	—				
IBR TO	.56	—			
Difficult Temperament	−.36	−.38	—		
SICD	.30	.23	−.14	—	
Bayley MDI	.55	.56	−.27	.43	—

Abbreviations: Af–Ex, Affect-Extraversion; TO, Task Orientation.
Source: Thompson, Fulker, DeFries, and Plomin (1988).

$$\text{nonadoptive within} = 0.5h^2 \qquad + w,$$
$$\text{adoptive between} = \quad h^2 + 2c^2 + w,$$
$$\text{adoptive within} = \quad h^2 + \qquad w,$$

where w refers to environmental variance not shared by members of a sibling pair. Intraclass correlations can be derived from mean squares between (MSB) and within (MSW) as follows: $(MSB - MSW) / (MSB + MSW)$. The expectations for these correlations are the familiar $0.5h^2 + c^2$ for nonadoptive sibling pairs and c^2 for adoptive sibling pairs. Using matrix notation, the same expectations are applicable to multivariate matrices of genetic and shared and nonshared environment.

Fitting this model to observed matrices of mean squares and cross-products for nonadoptive and adoptive siblings yields univariate estimates of heritability and shared and nonshared environment as well as genetic and environmental components of covariance among the traits. The model was applied to CAP data for two cognitive measures and three temperament measures at 2 years of age: the MDI, the SICD, Bayley's IBR Affect-Extraversion, IBR Task Orientation, and the CAP measure of Difficult Temperament. The phenotypic correlations among the measures at 2 years of age are listed in Table 8.16. The measures are moderately intercorrelated, with the exception of the correlation between SICD and Difficult Temperament. The negative correlations between Difficult Temperament and the other measures are in the expected direction, with more difficult children obtaining lower scores on the other measures.

Mean-square and cross-product matrices for nonadoptive and adoptive sibling pairs are listed in Table 8.17. As noted earlier, these mean squares can be converted to correlations and cross-correlations for the two types

Table 8.17. *Mean-square and cross-product matrices for 2-year-old nonadoptive and adoptive siblings in the CAP*

	IBR Af–Ex	IBR TO	Difficult Temperament	SICD	Bayley MDI
Nonadoptive					
Between:					
IBR Af–Ex	64.41				
IBR TO	9.40	10.32			
Difficult Temperament	−0.74	−0.35	0.89		
SICD	34.13	11.58	−2.54	99.03	
Bayley MDI	5.29	16.14	−4.92	135.33	368.96
Within:					
IBR Af–Ex	45.17				
IBR TO	8.36	9.91			
Difficult Temperament	−0.34	−0.40	0.87		
SICD	24.65	7.89	−0.65	55.19	
Bayley MDI	27.53	10.21	0.63	52.68	149.79
Adoptive					
Between:					
IBR Af–Ex	38.56				
IBR TO	1.18	8.79			
Difficult Temperament	0.27	0.02	0.72		
SICD	18.85	1.21	.00	67.83	
Bayley MDI	19.09	8.78	.62	69.91	227.45
Within:					
IBR Af–Ex	38.26				
IBR TO	6.93	9.70			
Difficult Temperament	−0.48	−0.06	.84		
SICD	10.53	1.25	−1.15	59.85	
Bayley MDI	17.88	4.44	−2.71	66.11	183.08

Abbreviations: Af–Ex, Affect-Extraversion; TO, Task Orientation.
Source: Thompson, Fulker, DeFries, and Plomin (1988).

of siblings. For example, the sibling correlations for nonadoptive and adoptive siblings, respectively, are .42 and .11 for the MDI and .28 and .06 for the SICD. Sibling cross-correlations between the MDI and SICD are .44 and .03 for nonadoptive and adoptive siblings, respectively. These correlations and cross-correlations are similar to those presented in Chapter 6. As discussed in Chapter 6, doubling the difference between the cross-correlations for nonadoptive and adoptive siblings suggests a genetic contribution $h_x h_y r_G$ to the phenotypic correlation that is too high, .82, much higher than the phenotypic correlation. However, the substantial error of estimation that surrounds this estimate suggests that the result be inter-

Table 8.18. *Nonshared-environment correlation matrix for 2-year-old nonadoptive and adoptive siblings in the CAP*

	IBR Af–Ex	IBR TO	Difficult Temperament	SICD	Bayley MDI
IBR Af–Ex	.87				
IBR TO	.35	.98			
Difficult Temperament	−.10	−.05	.98		
SICD	.57	.28	−.08	.51	
Bayley MDI	.52	.25	−.07	.41	.33

Abbreviations: Af–Ex, Affect-Extraversion; TO, Task Orientation.
Source: Thompson, Fulker, DeFries, and Plomin (1988).

preted simply to indicate substantial genetic covariance between the two measures.

Chapter 6 also discussed environmental mediation $e_x e_y r_E$ and the environmental correlation r_E; in the present example, because $h_x h_y r_G$ is so much greater than the phenotypic correlation, $e_x e_y r_E$ is substantially negative, −.39. The multivariate sibling model distinguishes environmental sources of covariance that are due to shared and nonshared environment. The adoptive-sibling cross-correlation directly estimates the contribution of shared environment to the phenotypic correlations; in the case of the MDI and SICD at 2 years, shared environment is of little importance. The environmental contribution to the phenotypic correlation is due nearly exclusively to nonshared environmental factors.

Matrices of genetic and environmental covariance parameter estimates (e.g., $h_x h_y r_G$) were obtained by the simultaneous fit of the matrices of expectations to the observed matrices using LISREL. The diagonals of these matrices are the estimates of heritability and shared and nonshared environmental influence, respectively. Table 8.18 presents the nonshared environmental matrix; matrices of genetic and shared environmental covariances were not informative. As indicated earlier, the CAP sibling adoption design at 2 years suggests substantial genetic influence on the cognitive measures (MDI and SICD) but not on the temperament measures; shared environmental influence is minimal, and most of the variance is due to nonshared environment. Off-diagonals of the matrices are of greatest interest to the present multivariate discussion. As noted earlier, MDI and SICD are highly correlated genetically, suggesting that many of the same genes affect the two measures; in contrast, as shown in Table 8.18, environmental correlations in the nonshared-environment matrix are similar to the phenotype matrix in that intercorrelations emerged among IBR

Affect-Extraversion, IBR Task Orientation, and the two cognitive measures. Difficult Temperament, however, is only slightly related to these other measures. This suggests that the phenotypic structure observed among these cognitive and temperament variables may be due primarily to nonshared environmental influences. One possibility, suggested by Thompson et al. (1988), is that events idiosyncratic to the test session influence children's test performance on each of the test-related measures. For instance, if an event affects a child's mood state on the morning of the test session, it could affect the child's performance on the MDI and SICD, as well as tester ratings on the IBR Affect-Extraversion and Task Orientation scales, but not the parents' trait ratings of Difficult Temperament.

Although estimates of genetic and environmental components of covariance can be obtained without using multivariate model fitting, a major advantage of model fitting is its capacity to test a model and, especially, alternative models. Several factor models were fit to the data, as explained by Thompson et al. (1988). The first analysis tested a two-factor model in which one factor represents the two cognitive measures and another factor represents the temperament measures. The fit of this model departed significantly from the observed data; in other words, the hypothesis that independent sets of genetic and environmental influences affect the two domains can be rejected.

A full model with one general factor and five specifics for each of the genetic and environmental components fit the data well (χ^2, 20 d.f. = 27.8, p = .58). To test the significance of the covariances and variances, two reduced models were compared with the full model. The first reduced model set the genetic matrix equal to zero; the resulting change in chi-square was significant, indicating that the genetic variance–covariance matrix is nonzero (change in χ^2, 10 d.f. = 26.6, $p < .01$). The second reduced model set the shared-environment matrix to zero. The resulting χ^2 did not differ significantly from the full model, suggesting that shared environment is not an important source of variation or covariation among these variables.

The best model appears to be one in which genetic covariance occurs only between the two cognitive measures, shared environment is unimportant, and nonshared environment yields a general factor as well as unique influences on each variable. This model was tested by allowing only the MDI and SICD to load on the general genetic factor, setting the shared-environment matrix to zero, and allowing one general factor and five specific factors for the nonshared-environment matrix. This model fit well with a χ^2 of 45.2 (d.f. = 43, $p > .20$).

Multivariate parent–offspring model

The multivariate parent–offspring model is a direct extension of the univariate parent–offspring model presented in Chapter 7, with the major
exception that each parameter now represents a matrix rather than a single
parameter. This model was first described by Rice, Fulker, and DeFries
(1986); the present section is based on that article (see also Rice, Carey,
DeFries, & Fulker, in press). By means of the methods of multivariate
path analysis (Vogler, 1985), the etiologies of variation and covariation
among traits and their genetic and environmental correlational structures
can be assessed. As in the univariate parent–offspring model in Chapter
7, heritabilities are assumed to be the same in childhood and adulthood,
and the genetic correlation between childhood and adulthood is assumed
to be unity; in addition, in the multivariate model, genetic correlations
among traits are assumed to be the same in childhood and adulthood.
These assumptions must be made in order to reduce free parameters to a
manageable number.

Specifically, multivariate model fitting involves the substitution of column vectors of standardized deviations from the mean for the latent and
observed variables; matrices of correlations are substituted for the correlations indicated by double-headed arrows in the univariate path model,
and matrices of path coefficients are substituted for individual path coefficients. By using the standard rules of path analysis, as well as a few
additional rules formulated by Vogler (1985), multivariate expectations
can be derived. The elegance of this approach lies in its use of a path
diagram that is no more complex than that appropriate for the univariate
path diagram.

Multivariate path diagrams of genetic and environmental transmission
in nonadoptive and adoptive families are depicted in Figures 8.5 and 8.6,
respectively. The corresponding matrix symbols are defined in Table 8.19.
One difference between these path diagrams and the univariate path diagrams in Chapter 7 (Figures 7.11 and 7.12) is that the effects of selective
placement have been omitted from the multivariate path diagrams in order
to simplify the model, given that selective placement is negligible in the
CAP. It should be noted that matrices **h, e, 1/2,** Γ and Φ employed in
the multivariate path diagrams are diagonal, whereas **M, m, f,** and **s** are
full nonsymmetric matrices because they accommodate possible cross-
relationships among variables in the model.

The expected covariance matrix among variables for nonadoptive mothers, nonadoptive fathers, and their children is presented in partitioned
form in the top portion of Table 8.20. The product of each pair of vectors

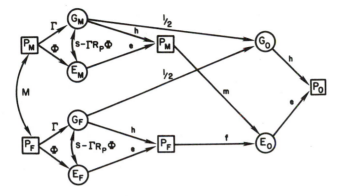

Figure 8.5. Path diagram representing multivariate parent–offspring transmission in nonadoptive families. (From Rice, Fulker, & DeFries, 1986.)

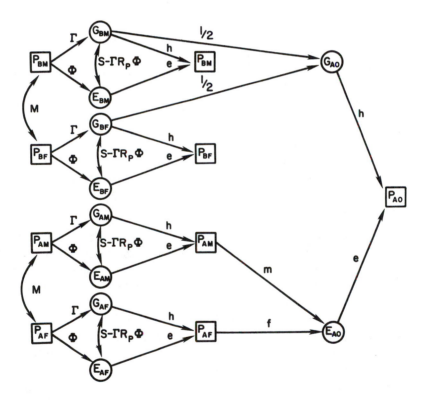

Figure 8.6. Path diagram representing multivariate parent–offspring transmission in adoptive families. (From Rice, Fulker, & DeFries, 1986.)

Table 8.19. *Variables, path coefficients, and correlations used in the multivariate parent–offspring model*

Symbol	Description
P_M, P_F, P_O, P_{BM}, P_{BF}, P_{AM}, P_{AF}, P_{AO}	Column vector of phenotypes of nonadoptive mothers (M), nonadoptive fathers (F), and offspring (O); biological mothers (BM) and fathers (BF); adoptive mothers (AM) and fathers (AF) and adopted offspring (AO)
h	Diagonal matrix of the square root of heritabilities
e	Diagonal matrix of the square root of the environmentalities
s	Nonsymmetric matrix of genotype–environment correlations among the measures
Γ	Diagonal matrix (**h** and **se**) made up of only the univariate elements of **h**, **s**, and **e** for the measures
Φ	Diagonal matrix (**e** + **sh**) made up of only the univariate elements of **h**, **s**, and **e** for the measures
R_P	Symmetric matrix of phenotypic correlations among the measures
R_G	Symmetric matrix of genetic correlations among the measures
R_E	Symmetric matrix of the nontransmissible environmental correlations among the measures
m	Nonsymmetric matrix of the transmissible maternal environmental influences on the measures
f	Nonsymmetrix matrix of the transmissible paternal environmental influences on the measures
M	Nonsymmetric matrix of mate phenotypic correlations among the measures
$V_P^{1/2}$	Diagonal matrix of phenotypic standard deviations for adult measures
$V_O^{1/2}$	Diagonal matrix of phenotypic standard deviations for offspring measures

Source: Rice, Fulker, and DeFries (1986).

in the first column yields a 4 × 4 expected covariance matrix. These expected covariances are expressed in terms of the matrix symbols defined in Table 8.19 and their transposes (indicated by a prime). The expected covariance matrix among the cognitive variables for biological parents, adoptive parents, and adopted children is presented in partitioned form in the bottom portion of Table 8.20. Except for those expectations involving adopted children, the expected covariance matrices in Table 8.20 are expressed as correlation matrices inside brackets and are scaled by diagonal matrices of phenotypic standard deviations outside the brackets. Expressions inside brackets that involve adopted children are standardized covariances. As can be seen by comparing the diagonal elements of the expected covariance matrices for nonadopted and adopted children, the

Table 8.20. *Expected nonadoptive, adoptive, and biological parent–offspring covariances derived from path diagrams of the multivariate model using matrix notation*

Variables	Expected covariance
Nonadoptive	
P_M, P'_F	$V_P^{1/2}[M]V_P^{1/2}$
P_O, P'_M	$V_O^{1/2}[\frac{1}{2}h(\,(R_G h' + se') + \Gamma M') + e(mR_P + fM')]V_P^{1/2}$
P_O, P'_F	$V_O^{1/2}[\frac{1}{2}h(\,(R_G h' + se') + \Gamma M) + e(fR_P + mM)]V_P^{1/2}$
P_M, $P'_M = P_F$, P'_F	$V_P^{1/2}[R_P]V_P^{1/2}$
P_O, P'_O	$V_O^{1/2}[R_P]V_O^{1/2}$
Adoptive	
P_{BM}, P'_{BF} $= P_{AM}$, P'_{AF}	$V_P^{1/2}[M]V_P^{1/2}$
P_{AO}, P'_{BM}	$V_O^{1/2}[\frac{1}{2}h(\,(R_G h' + se') + \Gamma M')]V_P^{1/2}$
P_{AO}, P'_{BF}	$V_O^{1/2}[\frac{1}{2}h(\,(R_G h' + se') + \Gamma M)]V_P^{1/2}$
P_{AO}, P'_{AM}	$V_O^{1/2}[e(mR_P + fM')]V_P^{1/2}$
P_{AO}, P'_{AF}	$V_O^{1/2}[e(fR_P + mM)]V_P^{1/2}$
P_{BM}, P'_{BM} $= P_{BF}$, P'_{BF} $= P_{AM}$, P'_{AM} $= P_{AF}$, P'_{AF}	$V_P^{1/2}[R_P]V_P^{1/2}$
P_{AO}, P'_{AO}	$V_O^{1/2}[hR_G h' + eR_E e']V_O^{1/2}$

Constraints

$$R_P = hR_G h' + hse' + es'h' + eR_E e'$$
$$r_{G(O)E(O)} = s = \frac{1}{2}\{[R_G h' + se') + \Gamma M']m'$$
$$+ [(R_G h' + se') + \Gamma M]f'\}$$

Source: Rice, Fulker, and DeFries (1986).

expected standardized phenotypic variances for the latter group are less than unity in the presence of positive genotype–environment correlations.

The multivariate parent–offspring model has been applied to CAP data on specific cognitive abilities at 4 years (Rice, Fulker, & DeFries, 1986). The results of a confirmatory factor analysis of data from 4-year-old children were consistent with the existence of four correlated factors and simple structure (Rice, Corley, Fulker, & Plomin, 1986); as described in Chapter 4, these factors at 4 appear to be similar to the adult factors Verbal, Spatial,

Perceptual Speed, and Memory. For the 4-year-olds, test scores were standardized and summed to construct the four scale scores; this method of constructing composite scores was employed to provide measures of the four dimensions of specific cognitive abilities indicated by factor analysis while retaining covariation among them for multivariate genetic analysis.

The multivariate path model was fit to variances and covariances calculated separately for adoptive and nonadoptive families. These form a 12 × 12 matrix when based on the four measures of specific cognitive abilities of nonadoptive mothers, nonadoptive fathers, and their children. For adoptive families in which complete data are available for biological fathers, biological mothers, adoptive fathers, adoptive mothers, and adopted children, these statistics comprise a 20 × 20 covariance matrix. For those families in which data from biological fathers are not available, a 16 × 16 covariance matrix was calculated. These variance–covariance matrices are included in the article by Rice, Fulker, and DeFries (1986).

As in other model fitting, the path models were fit to these observed covariance matrices by means of a maximum-likelihood estimation procedure described in Chapter 7. In addition to the omission of selective placement from the model, assortative mating parameters were fixed at observed values in order to reduce the number of free parameters to be estimated in the model. The full model was fit to the three observed covariance matrices subject to the constraints listed at the bottom of Table 8.20. The constraint pertaining to the phenotypic correlation matrix ensures that its diagonal elements are unity for all nonadopted individuals and leads to estimates of **e** as residual parameters. The constraint pertaining to genotype–environment correlation, **s**, assumes that maternal environmental transmission and paternal environmental transmission are responsible for the correlations and that equilibrium exists between generations. Thus, **s** and **m** are estimated as free parameters in the model, whereas **f** is derived from the constraint.

The multivariate parameters obtained by fitting the full model to the data are listed in Table 8.21. The matrix of assortative mating and cross-assortative mating correlations, **M**, is nonsymmetric, with rows corresponding to specific cognitive abilities of mothers and columns to those of fathers. In general, assortative mating tends to be positive; however, except for verbal ability, it is not substantial. Cross-trait assortative mating is somewhat lower than that for isomorphic characters. The average diagonal correlation is .19, whereas the average off-diagonal correlation is .10. Although there is no obvious pattern of cross-trait assortative mating, some asymmetry is apparent, with the verbal ability of women being more strongly identified with the four abilities in men than the converse.

Table 8.21. *Parameter estimates for the multivariate parent–offspring model for 4-year-old specific cognitive abilities in the CAP*

Parameter	Verbal	Spatial	Perceptual Speed	Memory
Assortative mating				
Verbal	.36	.19	.30	.18
Spatial	.06	.07	.06	.10
Perceptual Speed	.17	.11	.20	.11
Memory	− .05	.06	− .05	.13
Maternal environment				
Verbal	.06	− .07	− .09	.08
Spatial	.01	.04	.01	.00
Perceptual Speed	− .04	.03	.01	.15
Memory	− .01	.05	.05	.09
Paternal environment				
Verbal	.09	− .01	− .03	− .01
Spatial	.02	.13	.03	− .06
Perceptual Speed	.06	− .02	.12	− .04
Memory	.05	.04	− .02	− .15
Genotype–environment correlation				
Verbal	.01	.04	.04	.03
Spatial	.00	.05	.04	.03
Perceptual Speed	− .01	.04	.05	.03
Memory	.00	.03	.04	.01
Genetic correlation				
Verbal	1.00	.86	.56	.57
Spatial		1.00	.89	.69
Perceptual Speed			1.00	.79
Memory				1.00
Environmental correlation				
Verbal	1.00	.29	.39	.21
Spatial		1.00	.31	.18
Perceptual Speed			1.00	.12
Memory				1.00

Source: Rice, Fulker, and DeFries (1986).

In this multivariate system, heritabilities – assumed to be the same in childhood and adulthood – indicate some genetic influence and some evidence for differential heritability: .15 for Verbal, .17 for Spatial, .10 for Perceptual Speed, and .04 for Memory. The **m** and **f** matrices include measures of environmental transmission from mothers' and fathers' phenotypes and appear to be weak. No obvious pattern of differences within or

Table 8.22. *Summary of reduced models for the multivariate parent–offspring analysis of 4-year-old specific cognitive abilities in the Colorado Adoption Project*

Model	Likelihood (L)	χ^2	d.f.	p
1 (Full)	− 1478.03	—	—	—
2 ($\mathbf{m} = \mathbf{s} = 0$)	− 1490.44	$2(L_1 - L_2) = 24.82$	32	.80
3 ($\mathbf{m} = \mathbf{s} = 0$, $\mathbf{R}_G$ equal)	− 1492.69	$2(L_2 - L_3) = 4.50$	4	.30
4 ($\mathbf{m} = \mathbf{s} = 0$, $\mathbf{R}_G = 1$)	− 1492.80	$2(L_3 - L_4) = 0.22$	1	.60
5 ($\mathbf{m} = \mathbf{s} = 0$, $\mathbf{R}_G = 0$)	− 1495.63	$2(L_2 - L_5) = 10.38$	5	.06
6 ($\mathbf{m} = \mathbf{s} = \mathbf{R}_G = \mathbf{h} = 0$)	− 1499.14	$2(L_2 - L_6) = 17.40$	9	.04

Source: Rice, Fulker, and DeFries (1986).

between the matrices of maternal and paternal influences is apparent; however, their net effect is to cause small, but generally positive genotype–environment correlations (**s**).

As indicated in Table 8.21, in the genetic correlation matrix – which is assumed to be the same for parents and children – the elements of $\mathbf{R}_G$ are consistently higher than those of $\mathbf{R}_E$. Estimates of $\mathbf{R}_G$ and $\mathbf{R}_E$ from reduced models (see below) also yielded substantial genetic correlations and modest environmental correlations. The generally high values of $\mathbf{R}_G$ indicate that the four specific cognitive abilities are influenced by many of the same genes and imply that genetic transmission involves general intelligence, at least in the context of this multivariate system with adult parents and 4-year-old children.

As mentioned earlier, the numerical methods used to derive standard errors are inaccurate, especially when many parameters are estimated simultaneously; comparing the relative fits of different models using chi-square is a more appropriate and robust procedure. Differences in log-likelihoods, the function minimized in maximum-likelihood estimation, were used to compare models; with large samples, twice the difference between two log-likelihoods is distributed as chi-square. With a complex multivariate model, many hypotheses can be tested. Because the environmental transmission parameters were small, they were dropped from the model first, that is, **m** and **s** were constrained to be zero in Model 2. As shown in Table 8.22, dropping these 32 parameters from the model yields a χ^2 of 24.82 ($p = .80$), suggesting that environmental transmission from the parental phenotype – within and across abilities – is nonsignificant.

Models 3, 4, and 5 retain the $\mathbf{m} = \mathbf{s} = 0$ constraint and test alternative hypotheses regarding $\mathbf{R}_G$. As shown in Table 8.22, the genetic correlations in R_G cannot be shown to differ from each other (Model 3) nor from unity (Model 4). However, the poor fit of Model 5 suggests that the genetic correlations are greater than zero. Finally, dropping both h and R_G in Model 6 demonstrates significant genetic variance–covariance in parent–offspring transmission of specific cognitive abilities.

In summary, at 4 years of age, the multivariate parent–offspring model indicates significant and highly intercorrelated genetic influences and the absence of environmental transmission based on parental phenotype for verbal, spatial, perceptual speed, and memory abilities. The average genetic correlation is .74, implying that 74% of the heritable variation is general and 26% is specific. In contrast, only 23% of the environmental variation is general and 77% is specific. Two recent twin studies lend support to these conclusions, especially to the surprising finding that specific cognitive abilities are highly correlated genetically. One study of 40 identical and 40 fraternal pairs of adult twins concluded that the major source of covariance among the subtests of the Wechsler Adult Intelligence Scale (WAIS) is common genetic covariance, although genetic correlations among the subtests were not reported (Tambs, Sundet, & Magnus, 1986). Environmental results from this study are also concordant: Most of the environmental covariation among the WAIS subtests was specific to each test; also, little influence of shared environment emerged. Evidence of substantial genetic correlations also emerged from a twin study of subtests of the Wechsler Intelligence Scale for Children – Revised (LaBuda et al., 1987). However, in this study, correlations due to within-pair environmental influences were small, whereas those due to shared environmental influences were intermediate; this finding does not necessarily contradict the CAP finding of negligible shared environmental influence because the CAP results are based on parent–offspring comparisons rather than twins.

As indicated at the beginning of this section, the major developmental implication of multivariate research lies in comparisons across ages. For example, it is reasonable to hypothesize that specific cognitive abilities become increasingly differentiated during childhood. Although assessment of specific cognitive abilities is a problem in infancy, analyses of CAP infancy data led to the conclusion that "genes that differentially affect specific cognitive abilities are not expressed until after infancy" (Plomin & DeFries, 1985a, p. 335). Factors based on Bayley items, the Bayley items themselves, and various language measures revealed significant parent–offspring resemblance for parental IQ but not for parental specific verbal, spatial, perceptual speed, and memory abilities. For example, variability in rates of language acquisition by infants was related to IQ of biological and nonadoptive parents, not to parental verbal ability or other specific cognitive abilities. These results suggest that the nature of infant intelligence as it relates genetically to adult cognition involves g, general cognitive ability. The results at 4 years indicate that genetic effects on specific cognitive abilities continue to be quite general – that is, the genes that affect one specific cognitive ability affect the others to a substantial degree. Nonetheless, some genetic differentiation is observed in that about 25% of the heritable variation is unique to each of the specific cognitive abilities.

Summary

In this section, the univariate sibling and parent–offspring models presented in Chapter 7 were extended to the multivariate case. The multivariate sibling model was applied to the interrelationship among temperament and cognitive measures at 2 years of age. The results indicate genetic independence of temperament and cognition, although cognitive (Bayley MDI) and communicative (SICD) development are highly correlated genetically. The best-fitting model involves genetic covariance only between the MDI and SICD, no shared environment, and nonshared environment. Nonshared environment affects the temperament and cognitive measures in two ways: as a general factor affecting all measures and as a source of unique variance for each measure.

The multivariate parent–offspring model was applied to specific cognitive abilities at 4 years. Substantial genetic correlations emerged among verbal, spatial, perceptual speed, and memory abilities, indicating that, from the vantage point of this multivariate parent–offspring model, the genes that affect one specific cognitive ability affect the others to a substantial degree – 75% of the heritable variation may be general in its effect.

This chapter ends a two-chapter series describing model fitting, the most important advance in quantitative genetic analysis in recent years. Chapter 7 introduced model fitting and described univariate sibling and parent–offspring models. In the present chapter, these models were applied to the major CAP measure at 1, 2, 3, and 4 years of age, extended to consider age-to-age genetic change and continuity, and generalized to the multivariate case. Subsequent chapters, especially Chapters 10 and 11, also include results of model-fitting analysis.

Although all of the chapters in this book represent environmental as well as genetic concepts, methods, and results, the following three chapters focus on topics at the interface between nature and nurture: genotype–

environment interaction, genotype–environment correlation, and genetic influence on measures of the family environment. A final chapter summarizes what we know as well as what we need to learn about the origins of individual differences during infancy and early childhood.

9   Interactions

It is reasonable to expect that descriptive and explanatory relationships in development involve complex interactions rather than simple main effects. For example, an easy temperament might buffer a child against a difficult environment; conversely, stress may have a disproportionate effect on vulnerable children (Garmezy & Rutter, 1983). Organismic specificity in reaction to environments is one of the major hypotheses that emerges from a thorough review of early experience and human development:

> Both from basic and applied data it has become increasingly clear that the relationship of early experience to development will be mediated by the nature of the organism on which the experience impinges. Unfortunately, virtually nothing is known about the specific organismic characteristics which mediate differential reactivity to the early environment. (Wachs & Gruen, 1982, p. 247)

In this chapter, we explore interactions using the CAP data in early childhood. The word "interaction" has many connotations, and it is important to be clear about its use. We limit our search for interactions to statistical interactions, the type of interaction typically derived in analysis of variance that involves the sum of squares remaining after main effects and within-cell variation is removed: "The phenomenon is well named. Interaction variations are those attributable not to either of two influences acting alone but to joint effects of the two acting together" (Guilford & Fruchter, 1973, p. 249). In other words, interactions represent conditional relationships in which the relationship between X and Y depends on another variable. There are other ways to construe coaction of independent variables; Rutter (1983), for example, describes 10 types of interactions as they affect outcomes or processes, only some of which would be detected by analyses of statistical interactions. Although these other concepts are interesting, consideration of statistical interactions alone is a complicated task, as this chapter attests.

A major reason for the complexity of interactional analysis is that no theory exists to guide the selection of types of interaction analyses or the variables to be included in these analyses. Any combination of three variables can be explored for evidence of interactions. For example, the major domains of the CAP consist of assessments of children, of parents, and of family environments. Relationships between any two domains can be examined as a function of the third. Developmentalists would be likely to treat the child variables as the predicted variable and the parental and environmental variables as predictors. Parent–offspring resemblance, for example, can be examined as a function of family environment. Perhaps offspring resemble their parents to a greater extent in certain types of families – cohesive, expressive families, for instance. Similarly, relationships between measures of the family environment and measures of children's development might interact with characteristics of the parents that are not isomorphic to the predicted child variable, as in the previous example of environmental interactions that affect parent–offspring resemblance. For example, the HOME might be more strongly related to children's IQ for less educated parents. When several measures of parents, environments, and children are available, possibilities for such analyses escalate sharply.

In addition, interactions can be considered within as well as across domains of child, parental, and environmental measures. For example, parent–offspring resemblance for cognitive ability might interact with parental personality or children's personality. Possible interactions also abound within a single domain: The relationship between any two variables for a child can be examined as a function of a third variable. The number of possible interactions quickly becomes overwhelming. In the CAP, the major measures number about 50 for parents, about 30 for children at each year, and about 20 for environmental assessments at each year, which makes possible nearly a half-million two-way interactions. Moreover, longitudinal analyses mean that the relationship between any two measures, each at any year, can be examined as a function of any third measure at any year; the four years of assessment in CAP bring the possibilities for interaction analyses to the millions. Finally, the possibilities become nearly limitless when we consider higher-order interactions among variables.

In analyses of the CAP data in early childhood, genotype–environment interaction has been highlighted because adoption data alone permit exploration of this type of interaction. In addition, three other types of interactions have been explored: interactions involving parent–offspring resemblance, interactions involving longitudinal changes in IQ, and temperament–environment interactions. In these analyses, we sampled broadly among our measures of the family environment and of the personality, cognition, and adjustment of children and their parents. Before the CAP results are presented, however, an approach in developmental psychology with interaction at its core, the interactional paradigm, is considered.

The interactional paradigm

The dual goals of the interactional paradigm are to emphasize that the person and the environment are enmeshed and that, within the individual, behavior is the result of the interplay among complex psychological and biological subsystems (Magnusson, 1985). In the extreme, the interactional paradigm would imply that empirical research on the person, the environment, or genetics makes no sense because each of these is lost in the swirl of ongoing bidirectional interactions. However, few interactionists would argue that we cannot assess the interactions in sufficient detail to obtain at least a glimpse, for example, of the child's productive vocabulary or the linguistic environment provided by parents. The fact that high test–retest reliabilities can be obtained for measures of children's development and their environment speaks against the extreme view. The usual interactional position is more moderate – permitting assessments of persons and of environments, but emphasizing interactions between them: "Thus, this view leads to the conclusion that models for individual functioning should focus simultaneously on person factors, environment factors, and the interaction between them" (Magnusson & Allen, 1983, p. 7).

In addition to interaction, the interactional paradigm emphasizes the reciprocal character of person–environment interactions:

Reciprocity implies that the individual is influenced by his environment at each stage of development, and at the same time that he influences the environment. Thus, the individual is not a passive receiver of external stimulation from the outer world; rather, he is an active and intentional actor who interprets the information about environmental conditions and events and acts upon the environment in the frame of reference of his own mediating system and with his own plans, motives, goals, and so forth. He seeks some environments and avoids others, and he can change his environment by acting directly upon it. (Magnusson & Allen, 1983, p. 7)

In our view, this description of reciprocity involves correlation rather than interaction: Personal characteristics are said to correlate with characteristics of the environment. Although interactionists do not distinguish between correlations of this sort and interactions, the distinction has been emphasized in quantitative genetic theory. Genotype–environment interaction, described in the following section, indicates that the effect of environment depends on individuals' genetic propensities. Genotype–environment correlation, described in the next chapter, denotes the correlation between environmental influences and genetic propensities. One of the three types of genotype–environment correlation is called "active," and it refers to correlations brought about by individuals seeking or creating environments correlated with their genetic propensities, as exemplified in the preceding quotation.

How does the interactional paradigm affect research? There is considerably more writing than research in the area; as Rutter (1983) notes, "such research is necessary if we are to test in rigorous fashion the assumptions that underlie transactional models of development (an essential step if such models are to be more than a trendy posture or position" (p. 306). In the same article, Rutter suggests:

The interactionist perspective should give rise to quite specific hypotheses on the particular types of interactions that are hypothesized to be operating. Unless such hypotheses can be formulated and translated into testable operationalized predictions, the interactionist perspective will not lead to a better understanding of developmental processes. (p. 315)

For the most part, the impact of the interactional paradigm on empirical research appears to be general – encouraging the use of multivariate and longitudinal research strategies in order to capture the changing interactions between children and their environments as well as among subsystems within children – rather than leading to specific testable hypotheses. For example, a proponent of the interactional paradigm conducted a longitudinal study of delinquency and social adjustment among individuals from 10 to 28 years of age (Magnusson, 1988). Data collection included biological (e.g., onset of puberty), psychological (e.g., personality questionnaires), and environmental (e.g., parents' education and income) measures. The analyses were longitudinal and often crossed domains. For example, age at onset of puberty was correlated with the amount of alcohol consumed as an adult. Analyses tended to emphasize interactions; for example, the relationship between age at onset of puberty and alcohol use was found to differ as a function of age, in that early maturers drink more early in adolescence but not later in adolescence or in adulthood. The emphases of the interactional paradigm on multivariate, longitudinal analyses of interaction are certainly meritorious; however, interactions were not hypothesized a priori and it is not clear how many of the scores of possible interactions were examined before these significant interactions were found.

In general, it has not been easy to document interactions. For example, personality is one area in which a considerable amount of research has addressed the issue of interaction. Three examples of interaction research programs in this area have had disappointing results. Although personality researchers have focused on personality–situation interaction (Endler &

Magnusson, 1976; Magnusson & Endler, 1977), it remains unclear how much of the variance outside the laboratory is due to persons, environments, and their interaction. Developmentalists have also looked for personality interactions without success. For example, the Lerners' programmatic research on the goodness-of-fit model of temperament is an exemplar of research on one hypothesized type of interaction (Lerner et al., 1986). However, few interactions have been found. For example, in a recent study of adolescents, 86 hierarchical multiple regression (HMR) analyses (explained later in this chapter) were conducted involving the prediction of various outcome measures by temperament, environmental demand, and their interaction. Of the 86 HMR analyses, 38 yielded a significant overall R^2; of these, only five significant temperament–environment interactions were observed (Windle et al., 1986).

As another example, Maccoby and Jacklin (1983) studied temperament–environment interactions of several varieties and came to the following conclusion:

In our current longitudinal work, we have assessed several aspects of children's "temperaments" (e.g., activity level, "difficultness"). We have searched for instances in which children of different temperaments have been affected differently by a given parental behavior. So far we have not found such interactions. . . . On the whole, however, there is a notable absence in the research literature of demonstrations that a given environmental input has a different effect on infants and young children of varying temperaments, and it may be that the phenomenon is not very powerful. (p. 77)

In a more general vein, Rutter (1983) concludes that "interactions are known to occur, but they are far from invariable occurrences. Under many, if not most, circumstances, effects are additive and, moreover, people tend to show broadly similar responses to the same environmental stimuli" (p. 296).

In summary, the interactional paradigm has contributed at a conceptual level to our understanding of developmental processes by its insistence on the complexity and reciprocity of person–environment transactions. As yet, however, the paradigm has led to few testable hypotheses concerning interactions, few interactions have been identified empirically, and the amount of variance accounted for by interactions is not impressive.

Our less than optimistic view of interactions has its origins in our analyses of the CAP infancy data (Plomin & DeFries, 1985a). We explored genotype–environment interactions, interactions between temperament and environment in their effect on behavioral problems, stability of infant measures from 12 to 24 months as it interacts with environmental variables, environmental stability as it interacts with parental characteristics, and various relationships as they interact with gender. We reached the conclusion that "when individual differences among CAP infants have been found to be related to genetic or environmental factors, the relationship is additive; nonadditive interactions rarely account for a significant portion of variance" (Plomin & DeFries, 1985a, p. 341). In the present chapter, we examine these and other interactions to determine whether this conclusion based on infancy data generalizes to early childhood.

Genotype–environment interaction

As indicated earlier, genotype–environment interaction denotes an interaction in the statistical, analysis-of-variance sense of a conditional relationship: The effect of environmental factors depends on genotype. This is decidedly different from the frequently cited statement that "the organism is a product of its genes and its past environment" (Anastasi, 1958, p. 197) or, more recently, that "there can be no behavior without an organism and there can be no organism without genes" (Gottlieb, 1983, p. 5). As explained in Chapter 3, quantitative genetics does not apply to an organism or the organism; its focus is on variance, differences among individual organisms in a population.

Hypothetical genotype–environment interactions are illustrated in Figure 9.1 in a 2 × 2 framework in which children with genetic propensities toward low or high scores on a particular trait are reared in environments low or high for a particular attribute. How we determine the genotypic contribution will be described later. The point of Figure 9.1 is that main effects and interactions are independent. Main effects can occur without interaction, as in the top example, and interactions can occur without main effects, as in the bottom example of a disordinal interaction. The most likely type of interaction, however, is an ordinal interaction, as exemplified in the middle graph of the figure: An environmental factor has an effect on children of a certain genotype. For example, emotional and unemotional children might not differ in adjustment when reared in a stable environment (E_1); however, in an unstable environment (E_2), behavioral problems might erupt for emotional children but not for those who are less emotional.

If behavioral differences among children are to some extent due to nonadditive interactions between their genetic propensities and their experiences, genotype–environment interaction will add to the phenotypic variance created by genetic and environmental main effects. It is difficult, however, to determine the overall contribution of genotype–environment interaction to phenotypic variance or the extent to which variance due to genotype–environment interaction is read as genetic variance or environmental variance in behavioral genetic analyses. One of the major advan-

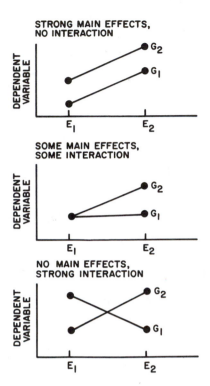

Figure 9.1. Genotype–environment interactions are independent of main effects of genotype (G_1 and G_2) and of environments (E_1 and E_2).

tages of the adoption design is that it is less affected by genotype–environment interaction than is the twin design (Plomin, 1986a). Genotype–environment interaction does not contribute to resemblance between genetically related individuals in uncorrelated environments, nor does it contribute to resemblance between genetically unrelated individuals in the same adoptive family.

Although it is difficult to estimate the overall contribution of genotype–environment interaction to phenotypic variance, quantitative genetic methods are particularly valuable for isolating specific genotype–environment interactions. Most of this research has been conducted with nonhuman animals, although human data from adoption studies are also relevant. Rearing various inbred strains of mice in various environments permits direct tests to be made of genetic effects, environmental effects, and genotype–environment interaction. For example, in a series of studies involving thousands of mice, Henderson (1967, 1970, 1972) systematically explored genotype–environment interaction. Few significant and consistent interactions were found (see review by Fuller & Thompson, 1978).

In research with humans, it is not possible to select genotypes as different as inbred strains of mice, nor is it possible to subject them to environments as extreme as those used in laboratory research on nonhuman animals. Human behavioral genetic researchers have the mixed blessing of working with naturally occurring genetic and environmental variation. The cost is a loss of experimental control; the benefit is an increased likelihood that the results of the research will generalize. A method for isolating specific genotype–environment interactions using the adoption design has been proposed (Plomin, DeFries, & Loehlin, 1977). The test is analogous to the method used in the strain-by-treatment mouse studies. As illustrated in Figure 9.1, genotype–environment interaction can be conceptualized within a 2 × 2 factorial arrangement in which one variable is the genotype and the other is the environment. For any dependent variable, the design can be used to investigate the effect of genotype independent of the environment, the effect of the environment independent of genotype, and genotype–environment interaction.

Adoption studies permit the use of this design for human data. The *genotype* of adopted children can be estimated from measures of their biological parents. The environment of adopted children can be estimated using any measure of their adoptive home environment or any characteristic of their adoptive parents. For example, one cell would contain scores on a dependent variable for adopted children who receive both genotypes and environments likely to lead to low scores on the dependent variable. Reanalysis of data from the classic adoption study by Skodak and Skeels (1949) using educational levels of the biological and adoptive parents as measures of genotype and environment, respectively, and IQ of the adopted children as the dependent variable indicated that the genetic main effect is highly significant and that the environmental main effect and genotype–environment interaction are not statistically significant (Plomin et al., 1977).

A more powerful use of the data entails analysis of the same variables in a continuous rather than dichotomous manner using HMR (Cohen & Cohen, 1975), which removes main effects of genotype and environment and then assesses their interaction. The interaction term is a "dummy" variable created by the product of the main variables of "genotype" and "environment," although other models of interaction such as threshold effects could also be employed. The results of an HMR analysis of the Skodak and Skeels data are consistent with those of the 2 × 2 analysis of variance.

The use of adoptive parents' education provides a limited vision of the environment, just as biological parents' education is a weak index of genotype. Plomin et al. (1977) concluded:

We feel that the use of adoption data to screen for genotype-environment interaction is an unusually promising tool for the more refined analysis of environmental effects in psychology. . . . We reiterate the need for detailed studies of the biological and adoptive parents, the adopted children, and extensive environmental assessments. This would permit an interesting variety of analyses. For example, one could analyze the effects of adopted children's genotypes, childrearing practices of adoptive parents, and the interaction between the two, using some relevant aspect of the adopted children's behavior as a dependent variable. Any aspect of the genotype and of the environment can in this way be screened for genotype–environment interaction with respect to any trait in the children, provided only that all three are measurable. (p. 317)

CAP analyses in infancy

Providing these recommended data is a goal of the CAP. HMR analyses were applied to the CAP infancy data at 12 and 24 months in order to assess genotype–environment interaction (Plomin & DeFries, 1985a). For mental development, 15 analyses of genotype–environment interaction were conducted using biological mothers' IQ as an estimate of genotype and several indices of environmental influence in the adoptive homes: adoptive mothers' and fathers' IQ, the Home Observation for Measurement of the Environment (HOME) general factor, and two second-order factors from the Family Environment Scale (FES). The dependent measures were the 12- and 24-month Bayley Mental Development Index (MDI) scores and the average of the 12- and 24-month Bayley scores. None of the interactions was significant. Thus, systematic, nonlinear effects of genetic and environmental influences on infant mental development are not apparent from the CAP data.

The same conclusion was drawn from analyses of genotype–environment interaction in other domains of infant development. For behavioral problems, 30 genotype–environment analyses produced only four significant interactions. In the domain of infant temperament, 80 genotype–environment interaction analyses were conducted and only two significant interactions were found, fewer than expected on the basis of chance alone when $p < .05$. It has been noted, however, that tests of interactions are conservative (Cronbach, 1987); moreover, the novelty of this approach warrants mention of the significant interactions. In one case, the environmental measure was a HOME factor, Restriction-Punishment, and it interacted significantly with biological mothers' activity to predict 12-month-old activity (R^2 change $= .027, p < .05$). Even though there was no main effect of biological mothers' activity level on their adopted-away infants' activity, activity scores of adoptees were high when their biological mothers were highly active if the adoptees were reared in restrictive adoptive homes. One possible interpretation of this interaction is that parental restrictiveness exacerbates genetic predispositions toward high activity.

The other significant interaction is especially interesting. Adopted infants' activity at 24 months of age was significantly predicted by the interaction between biological mothers' activity and FES Traditional Organization (R^2 change $= .031, p < .05$). In families low on the FES Traditional Organization factor, genetic differences in activity level were revealed. This suggests that genetic differences among children emerge more clearly in less constrained environments – a hypothesis that has been proposed on the basis of genotype–environment interaction research within mice (Henderson, 1970).

Two other genotype–environment interaction analyses of the CAP infancy data support this hypothesis, even though the interactions attained probability values of only .10. The two interactions appear to be other than chance phenomena, for two reasons: The interaction in both cases explains more than the usual amount of variance at both 12 and 24 months, and the interactions at both 12 and 24 months support the hypothesis that genetic differences among children emerge more clearly in less constrained environments. Both interactions involve infants' emotionality as predicted by biological and adoptive mothers' Emotionality-Anger, and the interactions are similar at 12 and 24 months: Genetic differences in infants' emotionality appear only when adoptive mothers are low in emotionality. When adoptive mothers are above average in emotionality, adopted infants are emotional regardless of their genetic predisposition.

These tenuous findings should not obscure the main point that these first analyses of genotype–environment interaction revealed so few significant interactions. However, these analyses were limited to infancy, and it is possible that genotype–environment interactions are more apparent later in childhood.

CAP analyses in early childhood

The 3- and 4-year-old data in CAP were analyzed in a similar manner in order to explore the generalizability of the infancy results. For mental development, Stanford–Binet IQ was employed as the dependent variable for adopted children at 3 and 4 years. The environmental measure was the

HOME general factor in the adoptive families, and the "genetic" variable was biological mothers' IQ. At neither 3 nor 4 years was genotype–environment interaction significant; the R^2 change for the HMR interaction term was only .001 at both 3 and 4 years. The three rotated HOME factors at 3, two rotated HOME factors at 4, two second-order FES factors, and adoptive mothers' and fathers' IQ were employed as environmental measures in 11 additional HMR analyses; none of the analyses yielded a significant interaction with biological mothers' IQ in predicting the IQ of adopted children at 3 or 4 years. The average R^2 change for the interaction term in these analyses was .003, ranging from .000 to .009.

Similar analyses were conducted for 3-year-old scores on the Sequenced Inventory of Communication Development (SICD). Although no significant genotype–environment interactions were detected using biological mothers' IQ as the genetic variable and HOME factors and two second-order FES factors as environmental variables, two marginally significant interaction effects emerged from these six analyses. The relationship between adoptee IQ and biological-mother IQ differed as a function of HOME Encouraging Developmental Advance factor (R^2 change = .016, $p = .07$) and FES Personal Growth (R^2 change = .012, $p = .07$). In order to interpret these interactions, biological-mother IQ and the environmental measures were divided at their mean and 2×2 ANOVA analyses were conducted with adoptee IQ as the dependent variable.

Despite the loss of information that comes from dichotomizing the variables, the 2×2 ANOVA results indicate a nearly significant genotype–environment interaction effect ($p = .08$), in addition to significant main effects for biological-mother IQ and for HOME Encouraging Development Advance. The results for the interaction between biological-mother IQ and the HOME factor as they relate to SICD scores at 3 are depicted in Figure 9.2. The interaction indicates that greater genetic differences among the children are observed when mothers are more involved (HOME Maternal Involvement). An alternative phrasing of this interaction is that differences on the HOME factor relate to children's IQ only when the biological mothers of the children are above average in IQ.

The second marginally significant interaction involves biological-mother IQ and FES Personal Growth as they predict adoptees' 3-year SICD scores (Figure 9.3). Unlike the preceding interaction, this interaction shows no main effects of genotype or environment; however, the interaction indicates that a family environment high on the Personal Growth factor has a positive effect on SICD scores of adoptees whose biological mothers are lower than average in IQ. In other words, cohesiveness and expressiveness of families

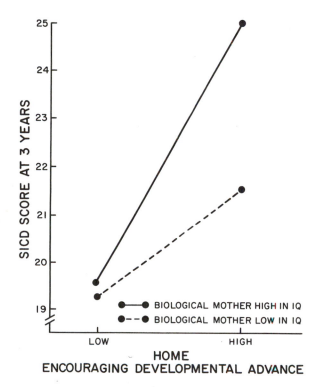

Figure 9.2. Genotype–environment interaction. Biological mothers' IQ interacts with HOME Encouraging Developmental Advance to predict communicative development (SICD) at 3 years.

have little effect on the communicative development of inherently bright children, but they have a large effect on less bright children.

Although these results may be useful heuristically, it should be emphasized that neither interaction is statistically significant, and each accounted for only about 1% of the variance of IQ. The R^2 change was .01 on average for the interaction term in these six HMR analyses, with a range from .001 to .016.

Behavioral problems as perceived by the parents were assessed by the Child Behavior Checklist (CBC) total score at 4 years of age. Hundreds of genotype–environment interaction analyses could be conducted using combinations of biological mothers' behavioral problems and personality traits with adoptive parents' behavioral problems, personality, and home environment measures as they predict adoptees' behavioral problems at 4 years.

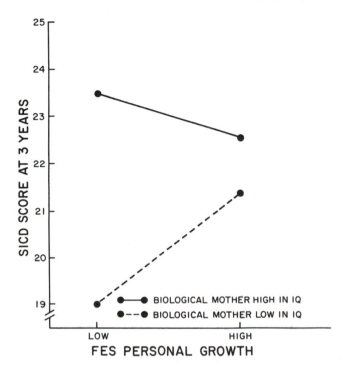

Figure 9.3. Genotype–environment interaction: Biological mothers' IQ interacts with FES Personal Growth to predict communicative development (SICD) at 3 years.

In one set of analyses, the environmental measures were the adoptive mothers' scores for the same variables (neuroticism and extraversion) used for the biological mothers. Adoptive mothers' 16PF Neuroticism was used in interaction with biological mothers' Neuroticism to predict adoptees' behavioral problems as assessed by the CBC. This interaction yielded an R^2 change of .018, which was not significant. Again, although weak, the interaction is interesting (Figure 9.4). Adoptees showed behavioral problems regardless of their adoptive mothers' neuroticism when their biological mother was neurotic; adoptees whose biological mothers were low in neuroticism showed behavioral problems only when their adoptive mother was neurotic. A similar analysis involving extraversion of biological mothers and adoptive mothers suggested no interaction (R^2 change = .000).

In a second set of analyses, the "genetic" variables were biological mothers' scores on the five EAS scales, and the environmental measures employed were the two second-order FES factor scores obtained from the adoptive families when the child was 3 years old. None of these 10 HMR

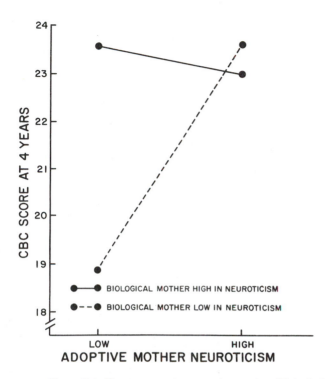

Figure 9.4. Genotype–environment interaction. Biological mothers' 16PF Neuroticism interacts with adoptive mothers' Neuroticism in predicting behavioral problems (CBC) at 4 years.

analyses yielded a significant interaction term; the average R^2 change was .002 and the range was .000 to .012. The largest R^2 change involved biological mothers' Emotionality-Anger as it interacts with FES Traditional Orientation in adoptive homes to affect adoptees' CBC behavioral problem scores. Like the other interactions, the environmental measure had little effect on behavioral problems of adoptees whose biological mothers were high on the Emotionality-Anger scale. In contrast, behavioral problems were strongly related to the FES factor when biological mothers were low on the Emotionality-Anger scale; for these children, controlling environments reduced behavioral problems.

HMR analyses of temperament were also conducted. Dependent variables at 3 and 4 years included the Colorado Childhood Temperament Inventory (CCTI) scales of Emotionality, Activity, Sociability, and Attention Span. In the first set of HMR analyses, these four measures at each age were predicted by a comparable personality measure of the biological mother and by the two FES second-order factors. For example, biological mothers' 16PF Neuroticism was used in interaction with one of the two second-order FES dimensions to predict CCTI Emotionality. In addition to these 16 HMR analyses, we also used biological mothers' Emotionality-Anger to predict CCTI Emotionality, because this comparison yielded some evidence for genotype–environment interaction in infancy – which brings the total of HMR analyses of this type to 20. The other pairings were mothers' Activity and children's CCTI Activity, Sociability and CCTI Sociability, and Impulsivity and CCTI Attention Span.

The 20 HMR analyses yielded no significant genotype–environment interactions, although the average R^2 change was greater than usual (mean R^2 change = .009; range = .000 to .025). The interaction between biological-mother Activity and FES Traditional Organization, which was significant at 2 years, was not replicated at 3 or 4. These results suggest that the earlier findings were specific to infancy or that they were due to chance. One marginally significant interaction (R^2 change = .025, $p < .06$) emerged for FES Personal Growth, which interacted with biological-mother Emotionality-Anger in predicting CCTI Emotionality at 4 years. As illustrated in Figure 9.5, this interaction was reasonable; FES Personal Growth slightly increased the emotionality of children whose biological mothers were high on the Emotionality-Anger factor, but it decreased the emotionality of children whose biological mothers were low in Emotionality-Anger; however, it is odd that, in families low in FES Personal Growth, a reversal of the expected genetic effect emerged. Moreover, this interaction did not occur at 3 years.

We conducted 10 additional HMR analyses for the CCTI, employing adoptive mothers' personality as the environment measure and using the same measures for both the adoptive and biological mothers (i.e., at each year, 16PF Neuroticism vs. CCTI Emotionality, Emotionality-Anger vs. CCTI Emotionality, Activity vs. CCTI Activity, Sociability vs. CCTI Sociability, and Impulsivity vs. CCTI Attention Span). Once again, we observed no significant interactions for these 10 analyses (mean R^2 change = .005; range = .002 to .009). In the infancy data at 1 and 2 years, there was a hint of interaction involving infants' emotionality as predicted by biological and adoptive mothers' Emotionality-Anger. Analyses at 3 and 4 did not support this finding.

We also examined interactions of the latter variety using CAP's IBR-like tester ratings at 3 and 4 years, matching IBR Affect-Extraversion with maternal 16PF Extraversion, IBR Activity with Activity, and IBR Task Orientation with Impulsivity. IBR Affect-Extraversion at 3 years yielded a marginally significant interaction (R^2change = .03, $p = .09$). Adoptive mothers' extraversion made little difference to the extraversion of adoptees

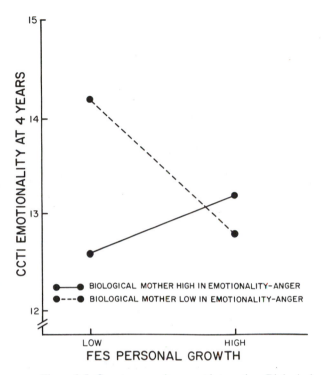

Figure 9.5. Genotype–environment interaction. Biological mothers' Emotionality-Anger interacts with FES Personal Growth to predict CCTI Emotionality at 4 years.

genetically predisposed toward extraversion (i.e., whose biological mothers were high on the Extraversion factor); however, adoptive mothers' extraversion substantially increased the extraversion of adoptees whose biological mothers were low on the Extraversion factor. This appears to be another example in which environmental influences primarily affect children without strong genetic predispositions. However, this interaction could not be replicated at 4 years (R^2 change = .002, p = .65). These six HMR analyses yielded an average R^2 change of .01.

In summary, the results of our genotype–environment interaction analyses in early childhood confirm the basic finding of few interactions in infancy. In fact, of the 67 HMR interactions mentioned, not one was statistically significant ($p < .05$); finding fewer interactions than expected by chance suggests that HMR criteria for significance are too conservative, and for this reason, we examined the few marginally significant interactions that emerged from these analyses. The results indicate that, for the SICD, encouraging developmental advance has a positive effect only for bright children; in contrast, warmth of a home has an effect on the SICD only for children who are less bright. Interactions with behavioral problems and temperament suggest interactions of the latter type: The environment has an effect on children without a strong genetic propensity. For example, when their biological mothers are high on the Neuroticism factor, adopted children have more behavioral problems regardless of the neuroticism of their adoptive mothers; however, adoptive mothers' neuroticism leads to increased behavioral problems for children whose biological mothers are low on the Neuroticism factor.

General limitations of CAP analyses of interaction are discussed toward the end of this chapter. However, one limitation specific to analyses of genotype–environment interaction is that phenotypic scores of biological mothers provide a relatively weak estimate of adopted children's genetic propensities. At most, biological mothers' phenotype will correlate only .50 with adopted-away children's phenotype. Moreover, as explained in Chapter 6, the correlation of .50 presumes heritabilities of 1.0 for the child and adult measures as well as a genetic correlation of 1.0 between childhood and adulthood. If heritabilities or the child-to-adult genetic correlation are less than 1.0, mothers' phenotype will correlate less than .50 with the child's phenotype. The use of biological midparent scores could improve the genotypic estimate; however, too few biological fathers have been tested to permit analyses of biological midparents in CAP. Although it would be useful to have a better genotypic estimate such as identical twins adopted apart, it should be noted that the biological mothers' phenotype provides sufficient power to produce significant main effects for genotype; however, few genotype–environment interactions emerge from these analyses. Thus, as they stand, these results support the conclusion that genetic and environmental influences on individual differences in development in infancy and early childhood coact primarily in an additive manner.

Interactions involving parent–offspring resemblance

A related type of interaction of special relevance to behavioral genetics is the interaction of factors that affect parent–offspring resemblance. Genotype–environment interaction can be phrased in this way: Resemblance between biological mothers and their adopted-away children differs as a function of a particular environment. In the case of genotype–environment interaction, however, we tend to focus on the differential impact of the environment on children as a function of heredity estimated from biological parents' scores; in this section, we consider mediators of parent–offspring resemblance that involve characteristics of children as well as those of parents and environments. Although some thought has been given to the possibility that parent–offspring resemblance differs as a function of social class and other demographic characteristics, more fine grained analyses of interactions have not been considered. One exception is an analysis of parent–offspring personality resemblance in the Texas Adoption Project as a function of the consistency of children's personality ratings (Loehlin, Horn, & Willerman, 1981). Consistency was defined as an absolute standard score difference less than 1.0 between parental ratings and children's self-report. Parent–offspring resemblance was considerably greater for children with consistent personality ratings. However, CAP infancy analyses of this type – selecting families in which infants were rated similarly by parents and by testers – did not yield higher parent–offspring correlations (Plomin & DeFries, 1985a).

Parent–offspring resemblance can be studied as a function of any characteristic of the parents, children, or family environments. For example, parent–offspring resemblance for IQ can be studied as it interacts with parental personality, child personality, and environment. One could hypothesize that parent–offspring IQ resemblance will be greater when parents are more sociable, when children are less emotional, or when the family environment is cohesive and expressive.

We explored factors that might interact with parent–offspring resemblance for IQ using the 3- and 4-year data from CAP. Although we were particularly interested in interactions involving environmental measures, we began with parental and child personality. We examined midparent–offspring IQ resemblance as a function of midparent scores on Extraversion, Neuroticism, and Depression and as a function of children's Difficult Temperament, CCTI Emotionality, CCTI Activity, CCTI Sociability, IBR Affect-Extraversion, IBR Task Orientation, and IBR Activity. Adoptive and nonadoptive families were combined for these analyses for three reasons: Our focus is more general than genotype–environment interaction – considering factors that mediate parent–offspring resemblance due to environmental as well as genetic factors; second, combining the families gives greater power to detect interactions; and third, by adding a contrast code for adoptive versus nonadoptive status, three-way interactions can be examined to determine whether the two-way interactions differ as a function of adoptive status. For example, finding a stronger interaction in nonadoptive families signals genetic involvement in the interaction; however, few of the three-way interactions with adoptive status were significant. The 10 HMR analyses involving parental and child personality were conducted separately at 3 and at 4 years; only one of the 20 HMR analyses yielded a significant interaction; the mean R^2 change for the interaction terms was

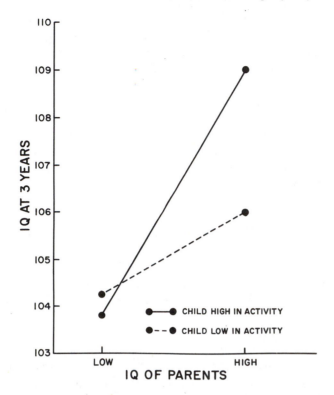

Figure 9.6. Interaction involving parent–offspring resemblance. Parent–offspring IQ resemblance differs as a function of children's CCTI Activity at 3 years.

.003 and the range was .000 to .01. The first significant interaction that has emerged so far from our interaction analyses involves IBR Activity, which interacts with midparent IQ in its effect on IQ at 3 (R^2 change = .01). However, this interaction disappeared when a 2 × 2 ANOVA was conducted to interpret the interaction, which suggests that the interaction is complex; moreover, this interaction could not be replicated at 4 years (R^2 change = .000).

Another marginally significant interaction on parent–offspring resemblance for IQ also involves activity at 3 years: CCTI Activity at 3 interacts with parent–offspring IQ resemblance (R^2 change = .009, p = .06). As indicated in Figure 9.6, parent–offspring IQ resemblance depends on the activity level of the offspring. The interaction could be interpreted to indicate that the effect of parental IQ on children's IQ is greater when children are high in activity level.

HMR analyses of the interaction between environmental variables and parent–offspring IQ resemblance employed fathers' occupational status, mothers' and fathers' education, HOME general and rotated factors at 3 and 4 years, and the two second-order FES factors at 3 years (mean R^2 change = .002; range = .000 to .005). One of the 13 HMRs showed a significant interaction: HOME Toys factor at 3 years interacted with parent–offspring IQ resemblance ($p < .04$); this interaction was also marginally significant at 4 years ($p < .10$). ANOVA analyses suggests that the positive relationship between the Toys factor and children's IQ is stronger when parents have higher IQs. We also explored six other interactions using three FES primary scales that seemed particularly relevant – Cohesion, Achievement Orientation, and Intellectual-Cultural Orientation – but to no avail (mean R^2 change = .001; range = .00 to .001).

In summary, these analyses suggest that parent–offspring resemblance for IQ is not affected by interactions with parental personality, children's personality, or measures of the family environment. In order to determine whether this finding generalizes to other domains, we examined selected parent–offspring comparisons for personality as a function of the same set of environmental measures. At 3 and 4 years, interactions between the HOME and FES environmental variables and parent–offspring resemblance were explored for three parent–offspring personality comparisons: parental 16PF Extraversion and offspring CCTI Sociability, parental 16PF Neuroticism and offspring CCTI Emotionality, and parental EAS Activity and CCTI Activity. The 33 HMR analyses yielded only two significant interactions, a number expected on the basis of chance alone. Although the HOME general factor and the rotated Maternal Involvement factor interacted significantly with parent–offspring resemblance for Sociability at 3 years, these interactions did not emerge at 4 years. The mean R^2 change was .004 and the range was .000 to .02. Thus, it appears that the interaction of parent–offspring resemblance for personality as well as for IQ with standard measures of the environment is not important.

Interactions involving longitudinal change in IQ

Attempts to predict age-to-age changes can be viewed as analyses of interaction: The relationship between behaviors at two ages differs as a function of characteristics of the individual or of environments. For example, Jessor's (1983) work demonstrates differential psychosocial change from adolescence to early adulthood as a function of attitudes toward conventionality. Another example is Dunn and Kendrick's (1982) research in which mothers' behavior toward their firstborn children was shown to change following the birth of a second child.

The prediction of longitudinal change in IQ scores has long interested developmentalists (McCall, Appelbaum, & Hogarty, 1973). For example, Caldwell and Bradley (1978) divided their sample of infants and toddlers into those who, from 6 to 36 months, increased 20 IQ points or more, those who decreased 20 IQ points or more, and those who changed by less than 20 IQ points. They concluded on the basis of discriminant analyses that "the HOME appears to provide a rather sensitive index of change in relative mental test performance from the first year of life to age three" (p. 47). However, the results of such analyses of change scores are questionable because such changes can be highly correlated with IQ scores at either age, and the HOME is correlated with IQ. The issue is whether the HOME is related to IQ changes independently of its direct relationship to IQ.

Another approach to the analysis of IQ change rephrases the question in interaction terms and uses HMR, asking whether the relationship between IQ scores at 3 and 4 years, for example, differs as a function of HOME scores. The main effects of 3-year IQ scores and HOME scores as they predict 4-year IQ are removed in the first step of the HMR, and then the interaction between 3-year IQ and the HOME is tested in the second step. A significant interaction indicates a conditional relationship between stability from 3 to 4 years and the HOME. In this vein, Coates and Lewis (1984) have reported that early cognitive status interacts with maternal behavior in predicting later cognitive performance.

HMR analyses of this type for stability between Bayley MDI scores at 12 and 24 months indicated no significant interaction with the HOME general factor in previous analyses of CAP data (Plomin & DeFries, 1985a). HMR analyses of 3- and 4-year Stanford–Binet IQ scores were conducted using the 3-year HOME rotated factors and the general factor. IQ scores clearly change from 3 to 4 years: The correlation from 3 to 4 is .56, and the average absolute IQ change from 3 to 4 is 10 IQ points; changes of 15 IQ points or more occurred for 23% of the children. However, the HOME variables did not interact significantly with IQ stability from 3 to 4. The HOME general factor at 3 years yielded an R^2 change of .001, and the three primary factors at 3 yielded R^2 changes of .003, .000, and .001, respectively. Analyses employing the two second-order FES factors at 3 years yielded similar results; R^2 change was .000 and .001.

Interactions with IQ stability need not be limited to analyses of environmental measures. For example, personality characteristics of the parents and of the children can be examined for their involvement in IQ stability. Neurotic parents, for instance, might have an increasingly adverse effect on children's mental development. Similarly, IQ scores of children who are "difficult" might decline relative to their less difficult agemates. As in the analyses of factors interacting with parent–offspring resemblance, we examined IQ stability from 3 to 4 years as a function of midparent scores on Extraversion, Neuroticism, and Depression; and as a function of children's Difficult Temperament, CCTI Emotionality, CCTI Activity, CCTI Sociability, IBR Affect-Extraversion, IBR Task Orientation, and IBR Activity at 3 years of age, combining adoptive and nonadoptive families. None of the 10 HMR analyses was significant (mean $R^2 = .001$; range = .000 to .003).

We suspect that genetic factors are involved in age-to-age IQ changes, as suggested by the marked similarity of age-to-age profiles of spurts and lags for identical twins (Wilson, 1983) and by CAP longitudinal analyses described in Chapters 6 and 9. Although the CAP parent–offspring design is less than ideal for analyses of age-to-age change in childhood, it is nonetheless interesting to ask if any characteristics of biological mothers predict IQ changes from 3 to 4 years. For example, one might hypothesize that biological mothers' personality characteristics interact with developmental changes in adoptees' mental development, an interaction that could be called genotype–stability interaction. We examined interactions between Extraversion, Neuroticism, and Depression of biological mothers and IQ stability from 3 to 4 years for adoptees. Although none of these three interactions was significant (R^2 change = .001, .013, and .000, respectively), the interaction with biological mothers' 16PF Neuroticism was marginally significant ($p < .07$) and interesting: IQ stability was greater from 3 to 4 years for adoptees whose biological mothers were lower in Neuroticism (Figure 9.7).

In summary, no significant interactions emerged from our analyses of interactions between IQ changes from 3 to 4 years and measures of family environment, parental personality, and children's personality. This finding implies that, with the exception of identical twins, we are not as yet able to predict changes in IQ from 3 to 4 years.

Temperament–environment interactions as they predict IQ and behavioral problems at 4 years

In this final section on interaction, we report HMR analyses that focus on the interaction between temperament and environment in predicting IQ and behavioral problems at 4 years of age. This topic has interested environmentalists and temperament researchers because temperament is thought to be an important organismic characteristic that mediates the effect of environmental influences on developmental outcomes (Plomin &

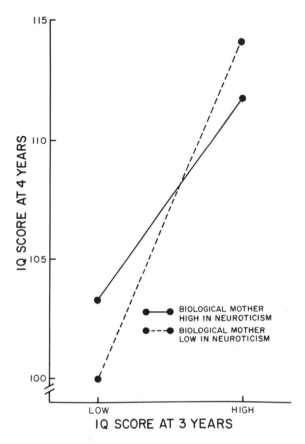

Figure 9.7. Genotype–stability interaction. IQ stability from 3 to 4 years differs as a function of biological mothers' 16PF Neuroticism.

Dunn, 1986; Wachs & Gruen, 1982). Wachs and Gandour (1983) have found, for example, that infants classified as "easy" are more sensitive to environmental influences than are "difficult" infants. Difficult temperament has also been shown to interact with mothers' social support: Mothers' support systems have a greater effect when their children are difficult (Crockenberg, 1981). The goodness-of-fit model of Thomas and Chess (e.g., 1977) hypothesizes that interactions between temperament and environment, especially mismatches, have an important role in the etiology of adjustment. A systematic program of research to assess the effects of such interactions has been conducted by the Lerners and their colleagues (e.g., Lerner et al., 1986). Some support for the model has been provided by studies of school-aged children, although, as mentioned earlier, relatively few interactions have been found (Windle et al., 1986). Another systematic approach to temperament–environment interactions also yielded few significant interactions (Maccoby & Jacklin, 1983). One hopeful sign is that, although Cronbach and Snow (1975) found few Aptitude × Treatment interactions in education, Personality × Treatment interactions frequently occurred. In a meta-analysis of Personality × Educational treatment interactions in six studies, significant interactions were found; for example, open classrooms do not work well for children who have problems of self-control (Barclay, 1983).

In the CAP infancy data, we explored interactions between temperament and environment as they predict behavioral problems (Plomin & DeFries, 1985a). Of 48 HMR analyses, seven statistically significant interactions were found; none of the interactions was systematic across ages or measures, and their interpretations were obscure. However, behavioral problems in infancy consist primarily of sleeping and eating and usually disappear by early childhood. For this reason, we were interested in conducting similar interaction analyses using 4-year-old outcome measures for IQ (Stanford–Binet) and behavioral problems (total score on the CBC). We conducted HMR analyses to predict 4-year-old IQ and behavioral problems using measures of the children's temperament (four CCTI scales and three IBR scales) as they interact with measures of the environment (HOME general factor and two FES second-order factors). Thus, 42 HMR analyses were conducted (seven temperament measures × three environmental measures for IQ and the same number of CBC scores). We began the search for interactions using contemporaneous assessments of temperament and environment, reasoning that these should be more likely to yield significant interactions with 4-year outcomes than would analyses of data from infancy.

Only one significant interaction was observed in analyses of IQ and behavioral problems. The average R^2 change due to temperament–environment interaction was .004 for IQ (range = .000 to .031) and .003 for behavioral problems (range = .000 to .012). The significant interaction for IQ involved the HOME general factor as it interacts with CCTI Emotionality in predicting IQ at 4 years (R^2 change = .031, p = .002).

As Figure 9.8 suggests, the HOME has little effect on IQ scores of children rated low in Emotionality; however, IQ scores of children high in Emotionality are related to the HOME. At 4 years (bottom of Figure 9.8), the significance of the interaction is due to its disordinal nature; the crossover does not occur for the 3-year analysis, which is also of marginal significance (R^2 change = .006, p = .10) with independent assessments of IQ, Emotionality, and the HOME. Both interactions indicate that the

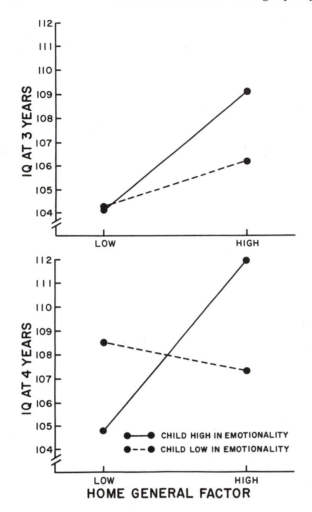

Figure 9.8. Temperament–environment interaction. At 3 years (top) and at 4 years (bottom), CCTI Emotionality interacts with the HOME general factor in predicting IQ.

HOME especially affects children high in Emotionality. One hypothesis to account for this interaction is that emotional children are more reactive and perhaps more responsive to parental behavior assessed by the HOME, which leads to higher IQ scores. Alternatively, children with higher IQs may be perceived to be more emotional by responsive parents who score high on the HOME.

For behavioral problems as assessed by the CBC, one interaction was

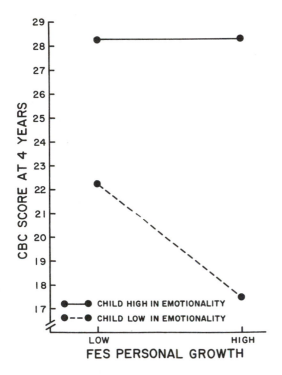

Figure 9.9. Temperament–environment interaction. CCTI Emotionality interacts with FES Personal Growth in predicting behavioral problems (CBC) at 4 years.

significant: Emotionality as it interacts with FES Personal Growth in predicting behavioral problems. As illustrated in Figure 9.9, highly emotional children are at risk for behavioral problems regardless of the cohesiveness of their family; children of low emotionality, however, have fewer behavioral problems in a supportive family environment. None of the other 20 interactions with the CBC was nearly significant. Despite these possible exceptions to the rule, it appears that children's temperament and family environment do not often interact in their prediction of IQ and adjustment at 4 years of age.

Conclusions

Although few systematic interactions have been found, they are perhaps sufficiently interesting to motivate further research in this difficult area. The results are so meager that they do not suggest hypotheses as to the form or substance of interactions. Using genotype–environment interaction as an example, the hypothesis that genetic differences among children emerge more clearly in less constrained environments fits in some cases (e.g., genetic differences among adoptees in CBC behavioral problems are large when adoptive mothers are low in neuroticism) but not in others (e.g., genetic differences emerge more clearly for SICD communicative development scores when mothers encourage developmental advance). Nor do the data correspond well to another hypothesis that the environment should be especially effective for children without strong genetic propensities. It is likely that different forms of interaction will apply to different combinations of environmental and developmental variables (Bergeman & Plomin, in press).

Despite the few interactions that have emerged from these analyses – and there are fewer significant interactions than expected on the basis of chance alone – the general conclusion still stands that, when individual differences among children are related to environmental or to genetic factors, the associations are primarily additive. Nonadditive interactions rarely account for a significant portion of variance: In the 198 interaction analyses reported in this chapter for the CAP early childhood data, only five significant interactions were found, and even these accounted for no more than 3% of the variance.

We do not doubt that some variance in behavioral development is caused by interactions. For example, a rare event might occur at a time when a child is particularly vulnerable. Seemingly insignificant interactions might affect development substantially. Indeed, such stochastic possibilities seem so multitudinous that it makes findings of main effects all the more remarkable. However, the results presented in this chapter indicate that systematic interactions are difficult to isolate.

Limitations on the capacity of the CAP sample to detect interactions should be mentioned. As always, our results are bounded by sample size, for instance. The probability of detecting significant interactions will increase as the number of subjects increases, as the number of variables decreases, and as the amount of variance explained by the interaction increases in proportion to the total variance explained by the multiple regression (Cohen & Cohen, 1975). Given the CAP sample size and R^2 of 10 to 20%, our analyses had approximately 80% power to detect interactions that account for 5% of the total variance. However, if interaction effects account for as little as 1% of the variance, one would need a sample size of more than 600 to detect a significant interaction with 80% power given an R^2 of 10 to 20%. One could argue that interactions that account for less than 1% of the variance are not very important.

A second type of limitation involves the normal range of environments sampled in the CAP. As discussed in Chapter 4, the CAP sample is reasonably representative of white middle-class families; nonetheless, the extremes of the population are not sampled. It is possible, for example, that environmental effects on behavioral development are more pronounced in markedly disadvantaged circumstances, which is the conclusion of a review of family and school influences on cognitive development (Rutter, 1985). A related suggestion is that interactions may emerge more readily in response to specific environmental interventions; as mentioned earlier, personality has been shown to interact with educational interventions to affect outcome (Barclay, 1983).

Another limitation is that our interaction analyses have been confined to infancy and early childhood. It is possible that interaction cannot be detected until middle childhood or later, a possibility that can be explored in the future using CAP data at 7, 9, 10, and 11 years.

Finally, it is possible that other combinations of parental measures, environmental measures, and measures of children's development would yield more evidence of interaction. Perhaps measures of behavior and of environment are not yet sophisticated enough to detect relationships other than additive ones. It is also possible that interactions are so specific in terms of individuals and environments that they are essentially idiosyncratic and will thus remain in the category of unexplained variance.

These possibilities emerged from a symposium at the 1985 meeting of the Society for Research in Child Development on the topic of organism–environment interaction (Wachs, 1985). Researchers from diverse fields in child development convened to discuss problems they had experienced in finding interactions and to suggest future directions for such research. However, despite their suggestions for new ways of approaching the problem, the symposiasts conveyed little optimism that interactions would soon be found.

We must keep our minds open to the possibility that additivity accounts for much more variance than does interaction. In terms of genetics, this does not seem implausible. Genetic variation evolved because of its direct effects on phenotypes – interactions with environments cannot be transmitted hereditarily. Despite the physiological complexity with which DNA-coded polypeptides indirectly affect behavior, any genetically induced variations that affect behavior even slightly can summate to produce considerable behavioral variation among individuals, variations that will be shared by genetically related individuals. Quantitative genetic designs permit us to assess the polygenic variation that arises from many small genetic effects. The same may be true for environmental influence, although, unlike the situation in genetics, we have no way to assess the sum of all environmental variations that affect the phenotype other than as the residual variance left after genetic variance has been estimated.

Among behavioral scientists, educational researchers have put the most effort into finding interactions, specifically interactions involving aptitude and treatment. However, after two decades of research, Cronbach and Snow (1975), in their definitive review on the topic of Aptitude × Treatment interactions, reached the following conclusion:

We have reviewed findings on the hunches of a decade or more ago. No Aptitude × Treatment interactions are so well confirmed that they can be used directly as guides to instruction. . . . While results in Aptitude × Treatment interaction studies have often been negative, this does not deny the hypotheses. Most studies used samples so small that a predominance of "chance results" was rendered inevitable. What the results deny is the hope that a few years of research on a limited scale will produce both a solid theory and a set of practically useful generalizations about instruction. Learner × Treatment interaction is an essentially new scientific problem, and reaching consolidated understanding in such matters often requires decades. (pp. 492–4)

Although developmentalists are only beginning to explore interactions systematically, so far the results are much the same as in Aptitude × Treatment interaction research: Few interactions are found for genotype–environment interaction, interactions involving parent–offspring resemblance, longitudinal interactions, and temperament–environment interactions as they affect IQ and adjustment. Continuing this research is certainly worthwhile; the few interactions that emerged from these analyses indicate how interesting it would be to discover systematic interactions.

The next chapter considers a topic that is often confused with genotype–environment interactions but that is conceptually quite different and has yielded to research more readily than has interaction.

10   Genotype–environment correlation

Genotype–environment interaction, the topic of the preceding chapter, denotes an interaction in the statistical, analysis-of-variance sense of a conditional relationship: The effect of environmental factors depends on genotype. In contrast, genotype–environment correlation literally refers to a correlation between genetic deviations and environmental deviations as they affect a particular trait. In terms of a 2 × 2 table depicting low versus high genotypes reared in low versus high environments, evidence for genotype–environment interaction is obtained from a comparison of cell means (e.g., cells 1 and 4 vs. cells 2 and 3). In contrast, genotype–environment correlation is indicated by the frequency of individuals in the cells (e.g., more children of "high genotype" are likely to experience the "high environment"). In other words, genotype–environment correlation describes the extent to which children are exposed to environments on the basis of their genetic propensities. For example, if shyness is heritable, children genetically predisposed toward shyness will have shy parents on the average who are likely to provide a "shy" environment for their children – that is, modeling shy behavior and providing relatively few opportunities for interactions with strangers. Such proclivities can be reinforced in interactions with nonfamily members: Reactions of unfamiliar children and adults to a shy child are unlikely to be rewarding or successful for the child, thus enhancing the child's tendencies toward shyness. In addition to these passive and reactive forms of genotype–environment correlation, children can actively select or create their own environments by avoiding strangers or by being a wallflower in situations with strangers.

In this chapter, we discuss these three types of genotype–environment correlation – passive, reactive, and active – and research that assesses their importance and isolates specific effects. Genotype–environment correlation has been of interest to behavioral geneticists because it represents variance that is neither solely genetic nor solely environmental, but both. It is also an important concept for developmental psychology: It is what develop-

253

mentalists frequently mean when they write about genotype–environment "interaction." For example, as discussed later, reactive genotype–environment correlation represents a detectable form of child-to-parent direction of effects in the sense that parents respond to gene-based characteristics of their child. A recent specific example of the potential importance of genotype–environment correlation for developmentalists can be seen in the shift of developmental research on "goodness-of-fit" (matching of temperament and context) interactions to a conceptualization based on genotype–environment correlation:

> Thus, the literature on genotype–environment correlations . . . allows us to suggest the person–context relational processes that may be involved in children's fits between temperaments and contexts. . . . In short, the creation of correlations with their contexts may be the most potent way in which individuals are producers of their own development. (Windle & Lerner, 1986, p. 115)

In more general terms, genotype–environment correlation is important for developmentalists because the concept suggests new ways of thinking about developmental transactions between nature and nurture. A notable example is a theory of development based on genotype–environment correlation that hypothesizes that the influence of the passive kind of genotype–environment correlation declines from infancy to adolescence, whereas that of the active kind increases (Scarr & McCartney, 1983).

Three types of genotype–environment correlation

The three examples of ways in which shy children might be exposed to "shy" environments are examples of three categories of genotype–environment correlation that should be distinguished (Plomin, DeFries, & Loehlin, 1977). *Passive* genotype–environment correlation is most often considered in behavioral genetics. By virtue of sharing genes as well as family environment with their parents, nonadopted children are passively exposed to environments correlated with their genetic propensities. For example, both heredity and environment conspire to foster verbal ability in children of highly verbal parents. The passive form of genotype–environment correlation is often considered in quantitative genetic analyses such as the parent–offspring model presented in Chapter 7, in which genotype–environment correlation was represented as s, the correlation between G and E. However, this interesting and reasonable form of double-barreled influence of parents on children has not been considered by developmentalists.

Much less frequently studied, but probably much more important, are reactive and active forms of genotype–environment correlations. *Reactive* or evocative genotype–environment correlation refers to experiences of the child that derive from reactions of other people to the child's genetic propensities. It relates to one type of child-to-parent direction of effects in which parents respond to gene-based characteristics of their child. For example, verbally fluent children may be reinforced for their verbal performance in their successful verbal encounters not only with family members but also with peers and teachers. At the other end of the distribution, children with poor verbal skills can evoke feedback from their environments that further diminishes their fluency.

Active genotype–environment correlation occurs when children actively select or create environments that are correlated with their genetic proclivities – dubbed niche picking or niche building by Scarr and McCartney (1983), who suggest that it is likely to be a crucial process by which genotype plays out its role in development. Children who enjoy wordplay can find it in repartee with peers and adults. Budding wordsmiths can ply their trade with like-minded people or, in their stead, with authors of the ages through the pages of their books. Children without such proclivities are likely to do other things with their spare time.

Passive genotype–environment correlation requires interactions between genetically related individuals. Reactive genotype–environment correlation can be induced by anyone who reacts to children on the basis of their genetically conditioned dispositions. Active genotype–environment correlation can be brought about not just by anybody but by anything that results in a correlation between genetic and environmental deviations. It should be mentioned that genotype–environment correlation can be negative, even though examples of positive correlations come to mind more readily. For example, children slow to acquire language may be given special attention to accelerate their learning. It has been suggested that negative genotype–environment correlation may be common for personality (Cattell, 1973). Using dominance as an example, "society likes to 'cut down' individuals naturally too dominant and to help the humble inherit the earth" (Cattell, 1973, p. 145).

Cattell refers to such examples of negative reactive genotype–environment correlation as "coercion to the biosocial norm." Passive and active genotype–environment correlations can also be negative. Easily angered parents may have children with a proclivity toward quick temper, and yet expressions of anger in their children are likely to cause such parents to lose their temper and apply strong doses of negative reinforcement. Although it is difficult to imagine examples of negative passive genotype–environment correlation in the realm of abilities, it is not too far-fetched to speculate that parents with high verbal ability take a laissez-faire attitude toward their children's verbal development because of a feeling that the ability comes naturally. In contrast, some parents whose verbal skills are poor might recognize their disability and work harder to foster their children's development of such skills. Negative genotype–environment correlation of the active type sounds pathological because individuals would not be expected to seek environments that rub against the grain of their propensities. However, it is possible, for example, that emotionally unstable children might seek calm environments and stable friends to steady their psyches, thus producing negative genotype–environment correlations of the active type. In terms of abilities, children at the lower end of the distribution might try harder, practice more, and seek help in order to maximize their potential, whereas children at the other end of the distribution might take their talent for granted. Cattell (1982) has described other ways in which negative genotype–environment correlation might emerge.

Two major issues should be addressed in terms of these three categories of genotype–environment correlation. First, how important is genotype–environment correlation – that is, how much of the variance does it explain for various domains of development? Second, can specific genotype–environment correlations be isolated when environmental factors are assessed directly? The remainder of the chapter addresses these two issues.

Genotype–environment correlation: components of variance

In this section, we examine genotype–environment correlation using only phenotypic resemblance among relatives – that is, without directly assessing the environment – to estimate the genotype–environment correlation component of variance of the quantitative genetic model. As described in Chapter 7, the fundamental tenet of quantitative genetic theory is that phenotypic deviations are attributable to genetic deviations and to environmental deviations, $P = G + E$. This axiom should not be read as "an individual's phenotype is due to the genotype and the environment." It refers to an individual's phenotypic deviation from the mean of the population, not to the phenotype of an individual.

This distinction is important, because it addresses a common source of confusion about the axiom $P = G + E$, especially as it relates to genotype–environment correlation: How is it possible to separate genetic and environmental influences on a phenotype when there can be no phenotype unless an individual has both a genotype and an environment? How can behavior occur without both an organism and an environment? The answer to these rhetorical questions is, of course, that there can be no behavior without an organism to behave and an environment in which to behave.

However, this truism misses the point: Quantitative genetics applies to differences among individuals in a population, not to a single individual. Phenotypic differences among individuals can indeed be due solely to genetic differences when environmental differences are held constant; similarly, environmental differences can be solely responsible for phenotypic differences when genetic differences are held constant.

A component of variance due to genotype–environment correlation enters the quantitative genetic model when G and E, expressed as deviations from the population mean, are squared and summed in order to express them as components of variance, as indicated in Chapter 7:

$$
\begin{aligned}
P &= G + E, \\
\sigma_P^2 &= \Sigma \, P^2/N = \Sigma \, (G+E)^2/N \\
&= (\Sigma \, G^2 + \Sigma \, E^2 + 2 \, \Sigma \, GE)/N \\
&= \sigma_G^2 + \sigma_E^2 + 2\sigma_{GE}
\end{aligned}
$$

i.e., $\quad V_p = V_G + V_E + 2 \operatorname{cov}(GE).$

In other words, when G and E are correlated positively, twice the covariance between genotype and environment is added to the phenotypic variance. If genotype–environment correlation is negative, it will decrease, rather than increase, phenotypic variance. This component of variance is neither genetic nor environmental – it is both. Even when G and E are perfectly correlated, V_G and V_E continue to make their contribution to phenotypic variance. In fact, correlations between genetic and environmental deviations will contribute substantially to phenotypic variance only when both genetic variance and environmental variance are substantial. Moreover, variance due to genotype–environment correlation cannot exceed the sum of genetic and environmental variances (Jensen, 1976).

How much of the phenotypic variance is due to the genotype–environment correlation component of variance? Most work has been devoted to assessing passive genotype–environment correlation, as discussed in the following section.

Passive genotype–environment correlation: variance comparisons

Two major methods have been used to assess passive genotype–environment correlations: comparing variances of adopted and nonadopted individuals, and using path models of parent–offspring resemblance that incorporate passive genotype–environment correlation. Variance of adopted children should be less than the variance of nonadopted children if passive genotype–environment correlation is influential, because adoptive parents do not contribute both genes and environment to the environment of their adopted children; thus, the phenotypic variance of adopted children has one less component of variance than that of non-adopted children. The variance difference between nonadoptive and adoptive families divided by the variance in nonadoptive families is an estimate of the proportion of phenotypic variance due to passive genotype–environment correlation.

Three problems are associated with this approach. One is that selective placement could increase the variance of adopted children and thus reduce the estimate of passive genotype–environment correlation. The second problem is that restriction of range for biological parents or for adoptive parents could lower variance for adopted children. However, if data are available for parents, these become empirical issues. The third problem is that large samples are needed because the standard error of a difference in variances is large, as discussed by Loehlin and DeFries (1987). They indicate, for example, that a sample of 150 adopted and 150 nonadopted children yields a standard error of about 1.2 IQ points for the difference in IQ standard deviations, and they show that differences of this magnitude create sizable differences in estimates of passive genotype–environment correlation. Their review of IQ data from five adoption studies indicates that the range of IQ standard deviation differences between adopted and nonadopted children is 0 to 3 IQ points, which yields estimates of the proportion of variance due to genotype–environment correlation that range from − .04 to .69. The median estimate is .20, which suggests that a substantial amount of IQ variance may be due to passive genotype–environment correlation.

CAP data add to this literature in four ways. First, variances for a large sample of adopted and nonadopted children can be compared across many measures, not just IQ. Second, variances for adoptive and biological parents of the adoptees can be compared in order to assess the possibility of either genetic or environmental restriction of range. Third, selective placement can be assessed because data are available for adoptive and biological parents. Fourth, because the CAP children are studied longitudinally, CAP data can address developmental changes in the magnitude of genotype–environment correlation, such as the childhood decline in the influence of passive genotype–environment correlation posited by Scarr and McCartney (1983).

Do variances differ for adopted and nonadopted children? In Chapter 4, standard deviations are presented for adopted and nonadopted children in the CAP. Although few variances differed significantly for adopted and nonadopted children, variances for nonadopted children tend to be greater on average than variances for adopted children, suggesting the presence of some passive genotype–environment correlation. In the remainder of this section, variances for adopted and nonadopted children in the CAP are contrasted for diverse measures for the purpose of assessing passive genotype–environment correlation.

Height and weight. Passive genotype–environment correlation seems unlikely for height because parents would not seem able to provide an environment correlated with the genes they bequeath to their children. For weight, it is reasonable to think that heavier parents might provide both the genes and the food needed to produce chubby babies. However, CAP results suggest a slightly different picture. There is no shared environmental effect for weight. Correlations between weight of adoptive parents and weight of their adopted children from 1 to 4 years center around .02. In contrast, some slight correlation between height of adoptive parents and their adopted children is observed in CAP: Parent–offspring correlations for height, averaged for adoptive mothers and fathers, are .10 at 1, .08 at 2, .06 at 3, and .08 at 4 years. These adoptive parent–offspring correlations are apparently due to selective placement; height is the only variable in the CAP that shows selective placement. Selective placement correlations for height are .15 between biological mothers and adoptive fathers and .14 between biological mothers and adoptive mothers.

For weight, variances for nonadopted and adopted children are similar at each age, suggesting that passive genotype–environment correlation is unimportant. In fact, variances are slightly lower at each age for nonadopted children than for adopted children. For height, variances for nonadopted children tend to be greater (13% on average across the four years) than for adopted children, despite the presence of selective placement for height, which will increase the variance of adopted children. It is difficult to imagine any shared environmental influence relevant to height that parents can transmit to their offspring in the form of passive genotype–environment correlation; for this reason, the result may best be ascribed to chance. However, a highly speculative possibility concerns the relationship between height and IQ. As indicated earlier, IQ appears to show passive genotype–environment correlation. In several studies, height correlates about .25 with IQ (Jensen, 1980); height may show passive genotype–environment correlation because of its correlation with IQ. Nutritional factors, for example, could account for passive genotype–environment correlation for height as well as for the correlation between height and IQ.

Cognitive development. Differences between variances for adopted and

Table 10.1. *Passive genotype–environment correlation for IQ: variances of adopted and nonadopted children in the CAP*

| Measure | Age | IQ variances | | Variance due to passive genotype–environment correlation (%)[a] |
		Adopted	Nonadopted	
Bayley MDI	1	134.6	151.3	11.0
Bayley MDI	2	216.1	256.0	15.6
Stanford–Binet IQ	3	196.0	201.6	2.8
Stanford–Binet IQ	4	139.2	141.6	1.7

[a]Computed as the variance for nonadopted children minus the variance for adopted children divided by the variance for nonadopted children.

nonadopted children occurred most consistently for Bayley Mental Developmental Index (MDI) scores in infancy. As shown in Table 10.1, variances for the Bayley MDI are more than 10% greater for nonadoptive than for adoptive children. This result is not due to greater variance for nonadoptive parents as compared with biological or with adoptive parents: As indicated in Table 4.3, variances for the 13 cognitive test scores for the three types of parents are quite similar. Selective placement correlations for IQ are negligible: IQ of biological mothers correlates .00 with IQ of adoptive fathers and adoptive mothers.

The amount of variance explained by passive genotype–environment correlation appears to decline in early childhood, as suggested by Scarr and McCartney (1983). For Stanford–Binet IQ at 3 and 4 years, passive genotype–environment correlation accounts for less than 3% of the variance. However, an unrotated first-principal-component score (standardized for all CAP children) yielded greater evidence for passive genotype–environment correlation than the Stanford–Binet (9% at 3 years and 8% at 4).

Is passive genotype–environment correlation also observed for specific cognitive abilities? In Chapter 4, standard deviations were presented for scales derived from Bayley items at 1 and 2 years (Table 4.8) and for the CAP battery of specific cognitive abilities at 3 and 4 years (Table 4.9). In general, adopted–nonadopted differences in variance are less for specific cognitive abilities than for IQ. In infancy, the two greatest variance differences involved the Imitation scale at 1 year (22%) and at 2 years (13%). The other two scales at 1 year yielded the same variance for adopted and nonadopted children. The only other scale to implicate passive genotype–environment correlation is the Verbal scale at 3 (11%). For the Bayley scales at 1 and 2 years, the average percent variance due to passive genotype–environment correlation is 7%. For the 3-year scales of specific cognitive abilities, variances for nonadopted children are 9% greater on average than variances for adopted children. At 4 years, however, there is no evidence for passive genotype–environment correlation: Variances for adopted children are slightly greater on average than variances for nonadopted children.

The suggestion of passive genotype–environment correlation for verbal development at 2 years but not at 3 is supported by Sequenced Inventory of Communication Development (SICD) results. The SICD Receptive, Expressive, and total scores at 2 years were greater for nonadopted children than for adopted children: 29, 10, and 19%, respectively. At 3, variances for adopted children were slightly greater than variances for nonadopted children for the SICD.

In summary, these cognitive results based on variance comparisons for adopted and nonadopted children suggest three hypotheses: Passive genotype–environment correlation affects general cognitive ability; it affects general cognitive ability to a greater extent than specific cognitive abilities; and its importance declines during early childhood. We shall see that the other approach to estimating passive genotype–environment correlation, parent–offspring model fitting, supports the first two hypotheses but not the third.

Personality. In Table 4.10, standard deviations were listed for the ratings by home testers on the Infant Behavior Record (IBR) at 1 and 2 years and on analogs of the IBR at 3 and 4. Passive genotype–environment correlation does not appear to be important in that, in about half of the comparisons, variances for adopted children are greater than variances for nonadopted children. However, one variance difference is large: For the Affect-Extraversion scale at 1, the variance for nonadopted infants exceeds the variance for adopted infants by 34%. At 2, the difference in variances for Affect-Extraversion accounts for 3% of the variance of the nonadopted children; at 3, the difference accounts for 8% of the variance; at 4, however the variance of the adoptees exceeds the variance for the nonadopted children. If passive genotype–environment correlation occurs for Affect-Extraversion, it is unlikely to be due to restricted personality variance of biological or adoptive parents (see Tables 4.4 and 4.5).

Passive genotype–environment correlation is not apparent for parental ratings on the Colorado Childhood Temperament Inventory (CCTI) at any of the four ages (Table 4.11). The variances for adopted and nonadopted children are similar, and in the majority of the comparisons, variances are in fact greater for adopted than for nonadopted children. The only slight evidence for passive genotype–environment correlations comes from the Emotionality scale at 1 and 2 years: The variances of nonadopted children exceed those of adopted children by 17% at 1 and by 12% at 2. At 3 years the variances are the same for Activity, and at 4 years the adoptee variance exceeds that of nonadopted children.

If there is passive genotype–environment correlation for IBR Affect-Extraversion or for CCTI Emotionality, it exists only in infancy. In both cases, variances for nonadopted children are greater than variances of adopted children only at 1 and 2 years of age. Thus, these findings provide additional support for Scarr and McCartney's (1983) hypothesis that the influence of passive genotype–environment correlation declines during childhood.

Behavioral problems. Variances for nonadopted and adopted children are similar for parental ratings of Difficult Temperament at years 1, 2, and 3; at year 4, however, the variance of nonadopted children is 10% greater than the variance of adopted children.

The Child Behavior Checklist (CBC) total problems score at 4 years also showed greater variance (6%) for nonadopted than for adopted children. When Internalizing and Externalizing second-order scales for boys and girls are contrasted (see Table 4.12), variances of adopted children exceed those of nonadopted children with one exception: For the Internalizing scale for girls, the variance for nonadopted girls is 25% greater than that for adopted girls.

Motor development. Passive genotype–environment correlation is not apparent for motor development scores in CAP at 1, 2, and 3 years. At 1 and 3, variances for adopted children exceed those for nonadopted children.

Summary. Comparisons between variances of adopted and nonadopted children reveal some evidence of passive genotype–environment correlation in the cognitive realm. Although in need of replication, these results are particularly interesting because they support Scarr and McCartney's (1983) theory that passive genotype–environment correlation declines in importance during childhood. However, we shall see that this hypothesis is not supported by model-fitting analyses, as discussed in the following section.

Outside the cognitive domain, no more passive genotype–environment correlation was found than would be expected on the basis of chance. It is possible that noncognitive aspects of development do not show evidence of passive genotype–environment correlation because neither shared environment nor heredity has much influence as assessed by means of the parent–offspring design of CAP. As discussed earlier, passive genotype–environment correlation can occur only in the presence of both genetic and environmental influence.

In the following section, these results are compared with those of a second method for assessing passive genotype–environment correlation that relies on parent–offspring model fitting.

Passive genotype–environment correlation: parent–offspring path models

Path models of parent–offspring similarity in adoptive and nonadoptive families provide a second source of information about passive genotype–environment correlation. As discussed in Chapters 7 and 8, the univariate parent–offspring model in CAP includes a parameter *s* to assess passive genotype–environment correlation. Estimation of this parameter derives from resemblance between nonadoptive parents and their offspring that is in excess of direct hereditary transmission, environmental transmission, assortative mating, and selective placement; the parameter estimate of *s* also includes variance differences between adopted and nonadopted children. As indicated in Equation (7.7), the genotype–environment correlation component of standardized phenotypic variance is 2 *hse*; the genotype–environment correlation is weighted by twice the product of the square roots of heritability and environmentality.

As previously noted, variance comparisons for height suggest the possibility of some passive genotype–environment correlation. Application of the CAP parent–offspring model to height, however, shows no evidence of passive genotype–environment correlation (see Table 8.3). Genotype–environment correlations *s* for height are $.00, -.07, -.02,$ and $.02$, respectively, at 1, 2, 3, and 4 years of age. It is not surprising that the two approaches yield different results, even though the model incorporates information concerning variance differences: Although the approach of comparing variances is more direct, the standard errors of differences between variances are large. Because the path model estimates *s* in the context of a model and provides maximum-likelihood estimates using all of the data, its results are likely to be more reliable.

Cognitive data. Earlier model-fitting analyses of IQ using data from samples of widely varying ages yielded different results concerning passive genotype–environment correlation for IQ. In three early approaches to model fitting of IQ data (Jencks, 1972; Jinks & Eaves, 1974; Rao, Morton, & Yee, 1976), genotype–environment correlation was found to be substantial, negligible, and moderate, respectively. Comparison of these models using a common data set of samples of widely varying ages indicates that the differences in the results are due primarily to differences in assumptions, and when passive genotype–environment correlation is adequately incorporated in a model, its estimates are positive, from .07 to .19 (Loehlin, 1978).

As discussed in the preceding section, comparisons of variances for adopted and nonadopted children yielded little evidence of passive genotype–environment correlation. Cognitive measures provided the only systematic evidence of passive genotype–environment correlation. Univariate parent–offspring model-fitting analyses presented in Chapter 8 also revealed some evidence of passive genotype–environment correlation s for Bayley MDI at 1 and 2 and for Stanford–Binet at 3 and 4 years: .01, .02, .05, .06, respectively. The estimates for Stanford–Binet are statistically significant. The contributions of passive genotype–environment correlation to the phenotypic variance ($2hse$) are .02, .03, .04, and .04, respectively. Although the model-fitting results agree with the variance results concerning the presence of passive genotype–environment correlation, the model-fitting estimates are lower and do not suggest a decline in passive genotype–environment correlation from infancy to early childhood. The reasons for this discrepancy are likely to be the same as those just described for height.

Model-fitting analyses were also applied to the CAP battery of specific cognitive abilities at 3 and 4 years. In accord with the variance results discussed in the preceding section, genotype–environment correlation s was lower for specific cognitive abilities than for IQ and was nonsignificant (see Tables 8.7 and 8.9). The proportions of phenotypic variance due to passive genotype–environment correlation ($2hse$) for Verbal, Spatial, Perceptual Speed, and Memory are, respectively, .02, .01, .01, and .00 at 3 years and .02, .01, .01, and .00 at 4 years. For SICD scores at 2 and 3, $2hse$ estimates are .01 and .04, respectively.

Temperament. The CAP parent–offspring model was also applied to CCTI Sociability-Shyness at all four years. Passive genotype–environment correlation was modest in these analyses; $2hse$ is .00, .01, .00, and .00 at 1 through 4 years.

Summary. One caveat must be considered. As mentioned earlier, finding passive genotype–environment correlation using parent–offspring model fitting depends on resemblance between nonadoptive parents and their children that exceeds resemblance due to direct hereditary and environmental transmission, assortative mating, and selective placement. However, in the CAP, parent–offspring correlations in nonadoptive families are rarely greater than those in adoptive families, as indicated in Chapter 6. In fact, evidence for hereditary influence in CAP is based largely on correlations between biological parents and their adopted-away offspring, not on comparisons between nonadoptive and adoptive families. Other adoption studies, most of which rely solely on parent–offspring comparisons between adoptive and nonadoptive families, find greater IQ resemblance in nonadoptive families than in adoptive families and also find on average greater evidence for passive genotype–environment correlation.

A reasonable hypothesis at this early stage of research is that there is some passive genotype–environment correlation for cognitive abilities, perhaps more for IQ than for specific cognitive abilities. If passive genotype–environment correlation influences other domains of development, its effects are minimal.

Reactive and active genotype–environment correlation

It seems reasonable to suppose that reactive and active genotype–environment correlations are more important than the passive variety, and perhaps increasingly important throughout development, as predicted by Scarr and McCartney's (1983) theory. Indeed, the plausibility of active genotype–environment correlation sometimes lures developmentalists into thinking that it accounts for all phenotypic variance. For this reason, we emphasize a point mentioned earlier: Variance due to genotype–environment correlation cannot exceed variance due to genes and variance due to environment, and it is substantial only when genetic and environmental variances are substantial, because the proportion of variance due to genotype–environment covariance is $2 \operatorname{cov}(GE)$. Consider individual differences in weight, which are highly heritable in infancy and childhood and in adulthood, as indicated in Chapter 6. If a measure of caloric intake were developed to assess children's nutritional environment, it would surely correlate with genetic differences among children in their propensity to gain weight. However, there can be no correlation unless there is variation in the propensity to gain weight as well as variation in caloric intake. If there were no genetic variation, the relationship between caloric intake and weight would be a purely environmental effect; if there were no variation in caloric intake, the relationship would be purely genetic. The essence of the issue, as mentioned earlier, is that, although genotype–environment correlation adds to the phenotypic variance, it does not subsume genetic and environmental variation.

At the same time, one might argue that the reactive and active types of genotype–environment correlation cannot be of much importance, for the following reason. If, in parent–offspring models, an environmental measure is substituted for the parental phenotype, a path can be added from the children's phenotype to this environmental index in order to depict genotype–environment correlation of the reactive type. (Active genotype environment correlation could be assessed, for example, if the environmental measure assessed the child's niche building or niche seeking.) This path would be included in models for adoptive families as well as for nonadoptive families, because parents and others respond to adopted children's hereditary differences just as they do to such differences among nonadopted children. In this way, for both adopted and nonadopted children, genotype–environment correlation adds to the correlation between the measure of the children's environment and measures of children's development. However, genotype–environment correlation can be no greater than the environment–development correlation in adoptive families, which, as discussed in the next chapter, tends to be low. Thus, this argument leads to the conclusion that reactive genotype–environment correlation does not account for much of the variance. However, this argument is limited to specific measures of the environment and does not refer to estimation of the overall contribution of reactive and active genotype–environment correlations to phenotypic variance.

In fact, no approach has as yet been devised to determine the extent to which estimates of heritability include variance due to genotype–environment covariance. All we can say is that $2 \, cov(GE)$ cannot exceed the sum of genetic and environmental variance. In the extreme case in which $2 \, cov(GE)$ is equal to the sum $V_G + V_E$, the proportion of variance due to genotype–environment covariance could be as great as .50. If $2 \, cov(GE)$ is included in the estimate of heritability, the heritability estimate would be .75 instead of .25. It is unlikely that reality corresponds to this extreme case; nonetheless, it is reasonable to expect that reactive and active genotype–environment correlation is an important source of phenotypic variance. Although we cannot estimate the proportion of phenotypic variance due to genotype–environment correlation of the reactive and active varieties, it is possible to identify specific reactive and active genotype–environment correlations when environmental measures are incorporated in adoption designs. This is the topic of the following section.

Isolating specific genotype–environment correlations

Even if reactive and active genotype–environment correlations do not account for much variance overall, specific genotype–environment correlations could be important. The previous section focused on estimating variance due to genotype–environment correlation without assessing the environment directly; in the present section, we attempt to use measures of the environment to isolate specific genotype–environment correlations.

The adoption design can be used to isolate specific genotype–environment correlations in human development (Plomin et al., 1977). The genotype of adopted children can be indexed by scores of their biological parents, and the environment of adopted children can be estimated using any measure of the adoptive home environment or characteristics of the adoptive parents. If adoptive parents react to their adopted children on the basis of genetic differences among the children, correlations between the scores of the biological parents and environmental measures should be observed. For example, if parents' responsiveness to their children depends on genetic differences in their children's sociability, a measure of adoptive parents' responsiveness would be expected to correlate with the sociability of the adopted children's biological mothers (which is a "genotypic" estimate of the adoptees' sociability). In the absence of selective placement, this test will detect genotype–environment correlation when there is a heritable relationship between the phenotype of the biological mother and the adopted child and when there is a relationship between the environmental measure and the adopted child's phenotype. Although these appear to be quite restrictive limitations, they actually define genotype–environment correlation: Genetic differences among children are correlated with differences among their environments.

Previous adoption studies do not permit the use of this test because no study obtained data on biological parents and adoptive home environments. For example, Skodak and Skeels (1949) obtained information only on the educational levels and socioeconomic status of adoptive parents, and these environmental measures cannot be expected to change in reaction to (reactive genotype–environment correlation) or be changed by (active genotype–environment correlation) the genetic predispositions of adopted children.

The CAP provides relevant comparisons because it included environmental measures such as Caldwell and Bradley's (1978) Home Observation for Measurement of the Environment (HOME) and Moos and Moos's (1981) Family Environment Scales (FES), which are described in Chapter

4. These measures can be used to explore the extent to which parents respond to genetic differences among their children, an example of reactive genotype–environment correlation. It should be noted that the genotypic estimate for the adopted children in the CAP is limited to biological mothers' scores. For a completely heritable trait that does not change genetically from childhood to adulthood, biological mothers' scores will correlate only .50 with scores of their adopted-away children. Can specific reactive genotype–environment correlations be identified using the complete CAP sample in infancy and extending the analyses to early childhood when, according to Scarr and McCartney's (1983) theory, reactive genotype–environment correlation is likely to increase?

No reactive genotype–environment correlation emerged for IQ–HOME comparisons. Biological mothers' IQ correlated −.02 with scores on the HOME in adoptive families at 12 months and .01 at 24 months. The data for early childhood also suggest little effect, although the correlations increase slightly: .05 at 3 years and .07 at 4 years. One might expect that, of the specific cognitive abilities, an adoptee's propensity toward verbal ability might elicit greater responsiveness in the adoptive family; however, correlations between biological mothers' verbal ability and HOME scores were also low at the four years – .01, .04, .06, and .00 – as were genotype–environment correlations for the other specific cognitive abilities.

Overall, only slightly more than a chance number of significant genotype–environment correlations emerged; however, the novelty of these data leads us to present the results briefly. Of 20 genotype–environment correlations between biological mothers' personality and HOME scores at the four years, two were significant. Both of these significant correlations were at 4 years. Adoptive mothers obtained higher HOME scores when the biological mothers of their adopted children were high on the Activity and Impulsivity scales (correlations of .16 and .17, respectively). Although it is not surprising that more lively children elicit greater responsiveness, the correlations at previous years are negligible: −.04, −.03, and .09, respectively, at 1, 2, and 3 years for Activity and −.05, −.03, and −.02 for Impulsivity. Nonetheless, in light of Scarr and McCartney's (1983) theory, it is interesting that significant correlations emerged at year 4 rather than at earlier years.

An interesting genotype–environment correlation also emerged at 4 years for biological mothers' self-reported depression. Adoptive mothers displayed less responsiveness as indexed by the HOME when biological mothers of their adopted child reported depression (correlation of −.19). Again, however, correlations at earlier years were negligible: .06, .04, and .01.

The FES yielded only a chance number of significant correlations with biological mothers' IQ although the FES would appear to be less sensitive to change in response to a child's characteristics than is the HOME because the FES assesses the general atmosphere of the family environment. Only a chance number of significant correlations were observed as well for biological mothers' personality; however, there were some noteworthy consistencies at 1 and 3 years when the FES was administered. The second-order FES factor Traditional Organization at 1 and 3 years correlated, respectively, .13 and .07 with biological mothers' 16PF Extraversion, suggesting that a genetic propensity toward extraversion in children elicits greater parental control. The second-order FES factor Personal Growth at 1 and 3 years correlated $-.12$ and $-.08$ with biological mothers' Neuroticism; perhaps a genetic tendency toward neuroticism in children leads parents to be less warm and expressive.

Personality scales also yielded a chance number of significant genotype–environment correlations. Sociability, which is related to 16PF Extraversion, yields a pattern of results similar to Extraversion: Correlations between biological mothers' Sociability and FES Traditional Organization were .13 at 1 year and .09 at 3 years. The only other consistent pattern of results emerged for Emotionality-Fearfulness: Correlations between biological mothers' Emotionality-Fearfulness and FES Traditional Organization were $-.15$ ($p < .05$) at 1 year and $-.12$ at 3 years, suggesting that parents exercise less control when their children are prone to being fearful. Finally, biological mothers' self-reported depression correlated $-.07$ and $-.11$ at 1 with FES Traditional Organization.

Summary. Stepping back from these possible examples of reactive genotype–environment correlation, we find in general few significant genotype–environment correlations, at least for this method and these measures. As mentioned earlier, these analyses of reactive genotype–environment correlation are quite limited in that biological mothers' scores provide a weak genotypic estimate of children's phenotype; also, the environmental measures, although widely used, yield few strong relationships with children's phenotypes. Genotype–environment correlation will not be detected unless there is a heritable relationship between the phenotype of the biological mother and her adopted-away child as well as a relationship between the environmental measure and the adopted child's phenotype.

Conclusions

Genotype–environment correlation represents a promising area for future developmental research. Research reviewed in this chapter suggests that the three types of genotype–environment correlation – passive, reactive, and active – may account for substantial variance, at least for IQ. Two strategies have been employed in an attempt to estimate the component of variance due to passive genotype–environment correlation. One is the comparison of variances for adopted and nonadopted children; when applied to the CAP data, this approach supports the hypothesis that passive genotype–environment correlation is an important source of variance for infant mental development and that its influence wanes in childhood. The influence of passive genotype–environment correlation as assessed by variance comparisons appears to be slight for other domains of development. A second method, parent–offspring model fitting, also yields evidence of passive genotype–environment correlation based on analyses of summary IQ data. CAP data confirm this conclusion, although passive genotype–environment correlation appears to be modest in infancy and early childhood. As in the comparison of variances for nonadopted and adopted children, passive genotype–environment correlation in model-fitting analyses is negligible in domains other than cognitive development.

Reactive and active genotype–environment correlation seem likely to be important sources of variance. Scarr and McCartney's (1983) developmental theory of genotype–environment correlation should serve to spur on this research because the theory posits that reactive and active forms of genotype–environment correlation become increasingly important during development.

The last part of the chapter attempts to identify specific sources of reactive genotype–environment correlation. Correlations between environmental measures in adoptive homes and IQ of biological mothers indicate little reactive genotype–environment correlation. Some hints of reactive genotype–environment correlation emerged for temperament, and significant effects were more likely to occur at 4 years of age than at earlier years, as suggested by Scarr and McCartney's theory.

Genotype–environment interaction and correlation are two examples of the usefulness of behavioral genetic concepts and methods for exploring the interface between nature and nurture. In the next chapter, we explore the effect of heredity on measures of environment and on the relationship between environmental measures and measures of development.

11   Genetics and measures of the family environment: the nature of nurture

Everything psychologists measure in the family environment is at least indirectly a measure of parental behavior. This is obvious for the two "superfactors" parental warmth and control, but it is just as true for physical aspects of the home environment such as number of books in the home. Consider, for example, the most widely used measure of the family environment, Caldwell and Bradley's (1978) Home Observation for Measurement of the Environment (HOME). Each of the 45 items clearly involves parental behavior; for example, the first item is "mother spontaneously vocalizes to child at least twice during visit." The six scales of the HOME also indicate the behavioral nature of the HOME: emotional and verbal responsivity of the mother, avoidance of restriction and punishment, organization of the physical and temporal environment, provision of appropriate play materials, maternal involvement with child, and opportunities for variety in daily stimulation.

If measures of the home environment are viewed as indirectly assessing parental behavior, variations in such parenting measures can be studied from a quantitative genetic perspective. This perspective leads us to investigate the etiology of differences in childrearing behavior among parents and to consider genetic as well as environmental components of variance. Genetic variance can lead to variability on a measure of parenting for two reasons. First, genetically influenced characteristics of the parents, such as cognitive abilities and personality, can affect the way they rear their children. In addition, parents might respond to genetically influenced characteristics of their children. Since 1968, when Richard Bell raised the issue of the direction of effects in socialization, developmentalists have explicitly considered the possibility that measures of the family environment might reflect rather than affect children's development. Reactive genotype–environment correlation, discussed in the preceding chapter, represents one kind of child-to-parent effect in which parents respond to gene-based propensities of their offspring.

271

This chapter explores environmental measures and their relationship to measures of children's development from the perspective of quantitative genetics. Two issues are of special interest: the contribution of genetics to the variance of environmental measures and the contribution of genetics to the covariation between environmental measures and measures of children's development.

Genetic variance and environmental measures

Genetic influence on measures of the home environment can be assessed by means of behavioral genetic methods such as twin and adoption designs.

The classical twin design

The classical twin design, comparing the resemblance of identical and fraternal twins, can be used to explore the etiology of variance on parenting measures in two ways: studying adult twins who are themselves parents and studying twin children and their parents.

Twins as parents. Although it is certainly reasonable to hypothesize that the way in which parents rear their children is influenced by the parents' own rearing as a child, it is also possible that heredity affects individual differences in parenting. If heredity is important, adult identical twins who are themselves parents will be more similar in their childrearing than will fraternal twins. For example, if twins who are parents were observed and interviewed on the HOME, the correlation of HOME scores for identical twins will be greater than the correlation for fraternal twins to the extent that heredity affects differences in parenting as assessed by the HOME. Despite the importance of understanding the etiology of individual differences in parenting styles, no research of this type has as yet been reported.

Studies of this type will find evidence of genetic influence to the extent that any characteristics of the parents are genetically related to the parenting measure. For example, sociability differences among parents might cause differences in their responsiveness to their children. In addition to genetic input from the parents themselves, twin studies of childrearing will yield evidence of genetic influence if parents respond to genetic differences among their children, a reactive genotype–environment correlation. That is, identical-twin parents will respond more similarly to their children than will fraternal twins because the children of a pair of identical twins are related to each other as half-siblings, whereas the children of a pair of fraternal twins are cousins.

In summary, if twin parents are observed and interviewed using the HOME instrument, identical twins will be more similar than fraternal twins, under two conditions: if any genetically influenced parental characteristics such as personality or cognitive abilities affect differences in parents' HOME scores, and if any heritable differences among their children affect parents' scores on the HOME.

Twins as children. In addition to the childrearing behavior of twin parents, the family environments of twin children reared in the same family can elucidate the nature of nurture. In the case of twin children, the environment of each child must be assessed independently; the analysis focuses on differences in the experiences of twins in the same family. Number of books in the home, for example, is not an appropriate item, because it can yield no reliable differences between members of a twin pair living in the same home. In this case, both identical- and fraternal-twin correlations will be 1.0, which appropriately indicates that all of the phenotypic variance is environmental in origin; more specifically, the environmental variation is of the shared variety.

In contrast, number of child's own books could be a useful item for detecting genetic variation. For example, number of child's own books could be assessed separately for each twin. Greater correlations for identical twins than for fraternal twins indicate genetic influence, suggesting that the number of books given to a child is related to heritable propensities – for example, the child's interest in reading. A study of twins as children assesses genetic influence that accrues because the environmental measure reflects heritable characteristics of the children. Less genetic influence is likely to be found for an environmental measure in a study of twins as children than in a study of twins as parents (discussed in the preceding subsection) because, in addition to assessing parents' responses to heritable characteristics of their children, the twins-as-parents design also assesses genetically influenced characteristics of parents that affect their childrearing.

A special case of the twins-as-children design involves ratings of the home environment by twin children. If children's perceptions accurately reflect their environment, the case is the same as the one just described: Genetic influence will be found when the environmental measure reflects gene-based differences among the children. However, if children's perceptions of their family environment are nonveridical, genetic effects can also stem from genetically influenced characteristics of the children that affect the way in which they view their experiences.

Pioneering research of this type was conducted by David Rowe (1981,

1983), who asked adolescent twins to rate their parents' behavior toward them. In two twin studies, Rowe found that adolescents' perceptions of parental warmth are substantially mediated by genetic factors, whereas analyses of perceptions of parental control show no genetic influence. This research was the first to find genetic influence on parenting, at least as viewed through the eyes of adolescents. Other behavioral genetic data, although not collected for the explicit purpose of assessing genetic influence on environmental measures, support the conclusions based on Rowe's research (reviewed by Plomin, 1986a).

Although subjective perceptions of experience may be as important as objective indices of the environment – for example, in predicting adjustment outcomes – it would be useful to compare results for more objective measures of the environment. If genetic influence were found only for subjective perceptions, this would suggest that genetic effects are limited to genetically influenced characteristics of children that affect their perceptions; that is, gene-based differences among children would not affect parenting. In addition, conclusions concerning genetic influence from twin designs are substantially buttressed by evidence from other behavioral genetic designs. Both of these issues are addressed in the following section.

Adoption designs

Adoption data are also pertinent to the issue of genetic influence on environmental measures. For example, resemblance on childrearing measures could be studied for siblings or twins reared apart in different families with uncorrelated environments. As in the case of the classical twin design, the subjects could be adult adopted-apart siblings rearing their own children or adopted-apart siblings in childhood and their parents. The environmental measure could be objective, as the HOME is, or it could be subjective in the sense that adopted-apart siblings would be queried about perceptions of their parenting. The preceding discussion of sources of genetic input for the twin design is equally applicable to the adoption design, although the demonstration of genetic influence is more direct in an adoption design involving adopted-apart relatives. For example, if the HOME, assessed in the different homes of adopted-apart siblings, yielded significant resemblance for the siblings, genetic influence would be implicated, suggesting that parents respond to genetically influenced characteristics of their children. The matching of adoptive families of adopted-apart siblings, selective placement, would inflate estimates of genetic influence using this design.

One study of adopted-apart twins in Sweden yielded results for perceptions of childhood family environment, viewed retrospectively some 50 years later, for a sample of 328 pairs of reared-apart twins and matched twins reared together whose average age at testing was 59 years (Plomin, McClearn, Pedersen, Nesselroade, & Bergeman, in press). Despite the differences between this study and Rowe's two studies, the results confirm Rowe's conclusions in that perceptions of warmth show significant genetic influence, whereas perceptions of control do not. For example, a warmth-related dimension labeled Cohesiveness yielded the highest correlation for identical twins reared apart (.41) for eight scales, and the lowest correlation (−.03) was observed for a scale called Control. Model-fitting analyses using the data for reared-apart and reared-together identical and fraternal twins confirm this conclusion and also indicate that the effects of selective placement are negligible.

Another sibling adoption design involves comparisons between the similarity of pairs of nonadoptive siblings reared together and the similarity of pairs of genetically unrelated children reared together, as in the CAP sibling adoption design. If genetic factors are important in the etiology of measured environmental differences, correlations for biological siblings will exceed those for genetically unrelated pairs reared together. Selective placement attenuates the clean separation of genetic and environmental influences in any adoption design. In the case of adoptive and nonadoptive siblings, however, the bias is a conservative one: If selective placement exists, it results in genetic similarity within pairs of adoptive siblings, decreasing the difference in correlations between biological and adoptive siblings and thus lowering estimates of genetic influence.

The same considerations apply concerning the origins of genetic influence depending on whether the environmental measure involves subjective perceptions or objective observations and whether the siblings are adults rearing their own families or young siblings living in the same family. As discussed in relation to the twin design, environmental measures that involve siblings' self-report can yield evidence for genetic influence, because parents respond to genetic differences among children and also because genetic characteristics of the siblings themselves affect the way they perceive their environments. One study of this type has been reported. By means of a self-report measure of nonshared family environment (i.e., siblings' perceptions of differences in their experiences), correlations for adolescent adoptive and nonadoptive siblings were compared (Daniels & Plomin, 1985). Genetic influence emerged, less for parental treatment than for the adolescents' perceptions of their siblings and peers – specifically, for perceptions of closeness of their siblings and for perceptions of differences in characteristics of the siblings' peer groups. If the adolescents'

Table 11.1. *Sources of genetic influence on family environmental measures*

Probands	Objective measures	Subjective measures
Parents	Genetically influenced characteristics of parents related to the environmental measure	Parental perceptions of the environment
	Parental responses to genetically influenced characteristics of offspring	Parental perceptions of their response to genetically influenced characteristics of offspring
Children	Parental responses to genetically influenced characteristics of children	Parental ratings: parental perceptions of their response to genetically influenced characteristics of children Children's ratings: (a) parental responses to genetically influenced characteristics of children; (b) effect of genetically influenced perceptions of children on their perceptions of parental behavior

perceptions are veridical, genetic influence evolves from differences in their actual treatment by parents, siblings, and peers. If their reports are non-veridical, genetic effects could be due to gene-based differences among the adolescents that affect perceptions of their experiences.

When, as in the CAP, objective measures of young siblings' family environments such as the HOME are employed, genetic influence can be gleaned from nonadoptive-sibling correlations that exceed those for adoptive siblings. Genetic influence will be observed if scores on the HOME are affected by genetic differences among children.

Before we turn to data from the CAP sibling adoption design that are relevant to the issue of genetic influence on environmental measures, it may be helpful to summarize this complicated discussion of sources of genetic influence on environmental measures. Table 11.1 reviews sources of genetic influence when the probands (twins or siblings) are themselves parents and when the probands are children; the table also distinguishes between objective measures and self-report measures. When probands are parents, genetically influenced characteristics of the parents as well as parental responses to genetically influenced characteristics of their children will be detected, regardless of whether the environmental measure is objective or subjective. However, objective and subjective measures could yield different results, because the parental and offspring correlates of these two types of measures could differ. If the probands are children, objective measures of their environment can detect genetic influence when the environmental measure reflects genetic differences in the children (i.e., passive or reactive genotype–environment correlation). This is also the case for parental perceptions of the environment; in addition, children's perceptions of their environment can also involve genetically influenced characteristics of the children that affect their perceptions.

This attempt to conceptualize sources of genetic influence on environmental measures for the major behavioral genetic designs is crude and in need of refinement, especially in terms of explicit path models. Nonetheless, it may be useful heuristically for thinking about the nature of nurture.

CAP sibling data

The CAP sibling design adds three special features to research on the topic of genetic influences on measures of family environment: The home environments of nonadoptive and adoptive siblings are assessed at younger ages than in previous studies; measures of environment do not rely on children's perceptions; and the assessments are longitudinal. The longitudinal nature of the CAP is important for two reasons. It permits the novel comparison of siblings' environment when siblings are the same age, and it provides developmental comparisons of the nature of nurture. In the CAP, HOME scores for adoptive and nonadoptive siblings were obtained separately for each child at 1, 2, 3, and 4 years of age.

Table 11.2 presents HOME correlations for adoptive and nonadoptive siblings at each age. Nonadoptive-sibling correlations for the HOME are substantial, about .50 on average during infancy and early childhood, even though the HOME assessments for the two children were obtained nearly 2 years apart on average. (These correlations are particularly impressive because 2-year stability on the CAP HOME measures is also about .50.) The sibling correlation at 3 years, however, is inexplicably lower than that at the other years. If genetic factors affect scores on the HOME, correlations for adoptive siblings will be lower than those for nonadoptive siblings. As indicated in Table 11.2, adoptive-sibling correlations are lower than nonadoptive-sibling correlations, again with the exception of scores at 3 years. Although the difference in correlations is statistically significant only at 4 years, these results suggest the possibility that HOME scores at least in part reflect genetic differences among children; moreover, the magnitude of the difference (with the exception of 3-year scores) suggests that genetic involvement may be substantial. Because the adoptive-sibling correlations are substantial, the results also indicate that environmental influences shared by siblings are also assessed by the HOME. Finding

Table 11.2. *HOME correlations for nonadopted and adopted siblings in the CAP*

| HOME measure | Year | Sibling correlations | |
		Nonadoptive	Adoptive
General factor	1	.50	.36
	2	.50	.32
	3	.29	.56
	4	.82	.65
Toys	1	.45	.38
	2	.54	.38
	3	.51	.67
	4	.80	.65
Maternal Involvement	1	.28	.30
	2	.18	.16
	3	.34	.18
	4	.32	.60
Encouraging Developmental Advance	1	.35	.21
	2	.47	.43
	3	.25	.27
Restriction-Punishment	1	.24	.04
	2	.13	−.06

shared environmental influence for the HOME is not surprising, because the same mother is interacting with each sibling.

Moreover, the HOME is not likely to be the best measure for detecting genetic influence in the family environment, because many of the items cannot be expected to reflect genetic differences among siblings in that the items are not specific to the child. For example, items such as those involving books and pets in the home seem unlikely to vary as a function of the child. Items of this type will not display genetic influence in the sibling adoption design; rather, they contribute to the shared-environment component of variance. As mentioned earlier in terms of twin analyses, items that are entirely the same for siblings will yield correlations of 1.0 for both adoptive and nonadoptive siblings, indicating that all of the phenotypic variance can be accounted for by the shared-environment component of variance.

In order to explore the possibility that some HOME item clusters show greater genetic influence than others, subscales of the HOME were analyzed. As described in Chapter 4, factor analyses of quantitative versions of the HOME items yielded four factors at 1 and 2 years (Toys, Maternal Involvement, Encouraging Developmental Advance, and Restriction-

Punishment); at 3 years, the factors were similar, except that the fourth factor did not emerge clearly; and at 4 years, only the first two factors were observed. As indicated in Table 11.2, this analysis suggests that genetic influence on the HOME is due primarily to the Toys factor; the results for the Toys factor were similar to those for the HOME general factor, suggesting genetic influence at 1, 2, and 4 years. Although the number of toys of different types might not appear to be sensitive to the particular child in that toys are handed down from older to younger siblings, it is possible that parents buy toys for each child that reflect the child's particular interests. The Maternal Involvement and Encouraging Developmental Advance factors showed little or no evidence of genetic influence. Correlations for nonadoptive and adoptive siblings averaged .28 and .31, respectively, for the Maternal Involvement factor and .36 and .30 for the Encouraging Developmental Advance factor. These results imply that mothers' involvement with and encouragement of their children are not affected by genetic differences among their children. The sibling correlations for the HOME factor of Restriction-Punishment are consistent with the possibility of genetic influence.

In summary, the results of the HOME analyses suggest three hypotheses: Parenting behavior as assessed by the HOME is influenced in part by genetic characteristics of children; parenting behavior that most reflects genetic differences among children involves the provision of toys; and maternal involvement and encouraging developmental advance do not appear to be a function of the genetic propensities of the child.

An interesting sidelight in the CAP is that the Family Environment Scale (FES) also displays some genetic influence. Because the FES is a measure of the social environment of the family, not of the environment specific to the child, it does not seem to be appropriate for these analyses. As mentioned previously, a completely nonspecific item such as books in the home would show correlations of 1.0 for both adoptive and nonadoptive siblings. However, in the CAP, the FES is completed by the parents as part of each child's assessment when the child is 1 and 3 years old. It is possible for this reason that parents' responses on the FES are somewhat influenced by characteristics of the child. For example, when completing the FES in the context of a test session that focuses on an "easy" child, parents' reports on the FES might indicate a less controlling family environment than would be the case if the test session were focused on a difficult child. Although this speculation seems far-fetched, it is interesting that the second-order FES factor Traditional Organization yields significantly greater nonadoptive-sibling correlations than adoptive-sibling correlations at both 1 and 3 years. At 1, the nonadoptive- and adoptive-sibling correlations are .83 and

.71, respectively, and at 2, the correlations are .89 and .72. The average correlation across the 10 FES primary scales is .73 for nonadoptive siblings and .64 for adoptive siblings at 1 year; at 3 years, the average correlations are .73 and .63. Thus, the sibling adoption design can detect genetic influence even on an apparently nonspecific environmental measure.

Research in collaboration with Judith Dunn on the CAP data adds another dimension to this area of research: videotaped observational data. Ratings were made of videotapes of mothers interacting with each of two siblings when each child was 12, 24, and 36 months old (Dunn & Plomin, 1986; Dunn, Plomin, & Daniels, 1986; Dunn, Plomin, & Nettles, 1985). One benefit of this approach is that environment (maternal behavior) specific to each child is assessed, unlike the situation with the HOME or FES. As with the HOME, these analyses indicate that mothers treat their successive children quite consistently when each child is studied at the same age. For two 12-month scales, maternal verbal responsiveness and maternal control, correlations for nonadoptive siblings and adoptive siblings were nearly identical. However, mothers' affection yielded correlations of .70 for nonadoptive siblings and .37 for adoptive siblings at 12 months (Dunn et al., 1985). Although the difference in correlations is not statistically significant given the small sample size for these videotape analyses, the finding is interesting because it is in the direction expected if mothers' behavior is influenced by genetic differences between their children and because it corresponds with Rowe's (1981, 1983) findings that measures of perceived parental affection show genetic influence, whereas measures of parental control do not.

The finding assumes greater significance because similar results were found in analysis of 24-month-olds and 36-month-olds. At 24 months, correlations for mothers' affection toward her two children were .60 for nonadoptive siblings and .31 for adoptive siblings. The item loading most highly on this scale of mothers' affection was maternal supportive presence, and the correlation for this item was .58 for nonadoptive siblings and −.04 for adoptive siblings. Even with the small sample size, this difference in correlations is statistically significant. At 36 months, the sibling correlation for the affection scale was .55 for nonadoptive siblings and −.05 for adoptive siblings. Thus, taken together, these observational results suggest that maternal affection, even though quite similar toward successive children of the same age, is affected by genetic differences between the children.

Implications

In summary, these first analyses of genetic mediation of environmental measures in infancy suggest that some of the variance on environmental measures such as the HOME and ratings based on videotaped observations of mother–child interaction may reflect differences among children that are genetic in origin. It should be noted that these analyses assess only a limited portion of possible genetic effects on environmental measures. As indicated earlier, a study of adult twins rearing their own families could assess in a straightforward manner the extent of genetic involvement in measures of the home environment. However, existing data are limited to behavioral genetic studies of children rather than parents. Studies of children assess primarily genetic influences brought about by parental responses to genetic differences among their children, and the results thus support the existence of reactive genotype–environment correlation, as described in Chapter 10. To the extent that parents do not respond to genetic differences among children, this approach will not uncover evidence for genetic influence on measures of the home environment even though a study of adult twins might reveal substantial genetic influence on the same environmental measures. This caveat holds for twin studies of children using parental reports or observations of the home environment as well as for children's perceptions of their environment if the children's perceptions accurately reflect their parents' behavior. If children's perceptions of their home environment are not at all veridical, twin studies using children's perceptions will reveal genetic influences mediated by characteristics of the children that affect their perceptions of home environment. Genetic influences of this type are likely to differ from those found in a study of home environments provided by adult twins rearing their own children.

The general implication of these findings is that labeling a measure environmental does not make it an environmental measure. Heredity can play a role in such measures via genetically influenced characteristics of the parents and children. One direction for research is to identify environmental measures most and least influenced genetically; this would advance our understanding of the nature of environmental influences in the family, and it might also help in planning interventions. A second direction for research is to identify parental and child characteristics that mediate genetic influence on environmental measures. Our analyses along these lines suggest that traditional measures of personality and cognition do not capture the genetically influenced concomitants of environmental measures in the intense, emotion-laden context of familial relationships (Plomin & DeFries, 1985a). For this reason, research on the mediators of genetic influence on environmental measures not only will extend our knowledge of environmental processes but may also lead to new ways of thinking about behavior of parents and children in the rich context of family interactions.

Genetic covariance in environment–development associations

Finding genetic variation in the underpinnings of environmental measures also raises the possibility that genetic influences mediate relationships between environmental measures and children's development. In other words, genetic effects on environmental measures such as the HOME might correlate with genetic effects on measures of development such as IQ, thus contributing to the phenotypic correlation between environmental measures and measures of development. This section addresses genetic and environmental etiologies of environment–development associations from the perspective of quantitative genetics. The discussion in the preceding section involved measurement of the environment alone, not measurement of children's development. In contrast, the present section focuses on the relationship between measures of the environment and measures of children's development. Genetic covariance can be found in environment–development associations only if there is genetic influence on the environmental measure as well as on the measure of development. Studies reviewed in the preceding section found some genetic influence on environmental measures; however, it should be noted that these studies assessed only a limited portion of possible genetic effects on such measures.

For developmentalists, the importance of this topic derives from the fact that relationships between environmental measures and measures of development have generally been assumed to be mediated causally via the environment. Relationships between environmental measures and children's behavior are interpreted in terms of X causing Y or Y causing X, the issue of the direction of effects in socialization (Bell, 1968). Both of these interpretations assume environmental mediation of the relationship: Children's development is altered by parents, or the behavior of parents is altered by their children. As in any correlation, however, in addition to X causing Y or Y causing X, the relationship between X and Y can be due to some third factor. The theme of this section is the possibility that heredity serves as a third factor of this type, mediating relationships between environmental measures and measures of behavioral development.

More than a century ago, Francis Galton (1875) considered this issue. In response to the assumption that parental correlates of children's development can be ascribed to environmental influence, he wrote:

I acknowledge the fact, but doubt the deduction. The child is usually taught by its parents, and their teachings are of an exceptional character, for the following reason. There is commonly a strong resemblance, owing to inheritance, between the dispositions of the child and its parents. They are able to understand the ways of one another more intimately than is possible to persons not of the same blood, and the child instinctively assimilates the habits and ways of thought of its parents.

Its disposition is "educated" by them, in the true sense of the word; that is to say, it is evoked earlier than it would otherwise have been. On these grounds, I ascribe the persistence of habits that date from the early periods of home education, to the peculiarities of the instructors, rather than to the period when the instruction was given. The marks left on the memory by the instructions of a foster-mother are soon spunged clean away. (p. 405)

The last sentence points to a method of assessing the extent to which heredity mediates relationships between environmental measures and measures of children's development: comparing environment–development relationships in nonadoptive families and adoptive families. This method and others are discussed in the following section.

Twin and sibling adoption designs

One approach to the detection of genetic influence on the covariance between environmental measures and measures of development involves multivariate analysis, which, as explained in Chapters 6 and 8, estimates genetic and environmental components of observed covariance between phenotypic measures, in contrast to the usual decomposition of the phenotypic variance of each measure considered separately. Rather than analyzing the phenotypic covariance between two behavioral measures, one can apply this approach to the analysis of the phenotypic covariance between an environmental measure and a behavioral measure if the environmental measure is viewed as a phenotype of the individual, as it can be for measures of perceived environment used in most of the research discussed earlier in this chapter.

For example, Rowe's studies suggest that parental affection, as perceived by adolescent twins, is genetically influenced. If measures of development – adjustment, for example – had been included in the same studies, twin cross-correlations could be used to determine the extent to which the relationship between perceived parental affection and adolescent adjustment is mediated genetically. If this particular environment–development relationship is mediated genetically, the cross-correlations between one twin's perceptions of parental affection and the other twin's adjustment will be greater for identical twins than for fraternal twins. That is, gene systems that affect perceptions of parental affection also affect adolescent adjustment. If the twin cross-correlations did not differ for the two types of twins, the results would suggest that the environment–development relationship is mediated by environmental factors. As in all such analyses of phenotypic covariance, if no phenotypic covariance exists between two particular measures, decomposition of phenotypic covariance into genetic and environmental components is thwarted.

As mentioned, this use of the twin method assumes that measures of perceived environment are phenotypes of the twins themselves, which is the case when perceptions of the environment are completely subjective. However, to the extent that these measures are veridical or when more objective measures of the environment are used, analyses of this type are not strictly applicable because the environmental measure cannot be viewed as a phenotype of the twin. More complicated models are needed; however, the crucial comparison for such models remains the cross-correlation between environmental measures and developmental measures for identical and fraternal twins. For example, if twin cross-correlations between the HOME, assessed separately for each child, and children's IQ are greater for identical twins than for fraternal twins, the relationship between the HOME and children's IQ must be influenced genetically to some extent. Such a finding would imply that genetically influenced IQ differences among children are related to genetically influenced differences in parental characteristics that are assessed indirectly by the HOME.

As in the use of twin children to study genetic influence on environmental measures, the twin cross-correlation approach to environment–development relationships can reveal evidence for genetic influence only to the extent that the environmental measure is sensitive to genetic differences between the children. If an environmental measure – for example, number of books in the home – does not differ for the two children, the identical-twin cross-correlation will be the same as the fraternal-twin cross-correlation. This result appropriately implies that the phenotypic environment–development correlation is mediated entirely by environmental influences shared by two children in the same family. Because the HOME includes some items that do not differ for two children, including the books in the home item, it guarantees that environment–development relationships will be found to be mediated at least in part by shared environmental influences. However, to the extent that the HOME–IQ relationship occurs because the HOME is sensitive to gene-based differences in IQ between members of a twin pair, the HOME–IQ cross-correlation for identical twins will exceed the cross-correlation for fraternal twins.

The same approach can be employed with adoptive and nonadoptive sibling pairs. In the case of twins, the coefficient of genetic relationship between twin children and their parents is .50, regardless of whether the twins are identical or fraternal. For this reason, a greater environment–development cross-correlation for identical twins than for fraternal twins indicates that the environmental measure reflects genetic differences between twins in a family. In contrast, adoptive and nonadoptive siblings differ not only in their coefficients of relationship with respect to each other but also with respect to their parents. Thus, differences in environment–development cross-correlations for adoptive and nonadoptive siblings could be due to parent-mediated genetic effects on the environment–development relationship as well as to parental responses to genetic differences between children in a family. In other words, genetic influence on the HOME–IQ relationship could occur because genetically influenced characteristics of the parents – for example, parental IQ – affect the HOME and the same gene-based characteristics of the parents also correlate with children's IQ. In addition, even if genetic differences among parents were not at all related to differences in their HOME scores, the relationship between the HOME and children's IQ could be mediated genetically if HOME scores assess parental responses to gene-based differences in children's IQ. Because the sibling adoption design includes these two sources of genetic mediation, it can yield results different from the twin design.

Despite this complication with the sibling adoption design, it remains the case that if environment–development cross-correlations are greater for nonadoptive siblings than for adoptive siblings, genetic factors must be implicated to some extent in the relationship between the environmental and developmental measures. We are aware of no twin or sibling adoption studies that compare cross-correlations for environmental and behavioral measures. However, CAP data for adoptive and nonadoptive siblings are useful in this regard, although caution is advised given the relatively small sample sizes for the CAP sibling analyses. As discussed in the preceding section, environmental measures in the CAP show some evidence of genetic influence in comparisons of adoptive- and nonadoptive-sibling correlations. To the extent that genetic effects on these environmental measures covary with genetic effects on specific behavioral measures, cross-correlations between the environmental and behavioral measures should be greater for nonadoptive siblings than for adoptive siblings. However, the major problem with these data is that environment–development relationships are generally weak, and as noted earlier, environment–development cross-correlations for siblings will be even lower, which means that the detection of differences in adoptive and nonadoptive sibling cross-correlations is difficult. Nonetheless, the novelty of this approach warrants a brief presentation of some of the CAP results.

CAP sibling data

Table 11.3 presents data from the sibling adoption design for the relationship between the HOME general factor and IQ (Bayley Mental Development Index at 1 and 2 years and Stanford–Binet IQ at 3 and 4). These

Table 11.3. *HOME–IQ phenotypic correlations for nonadopted children and cross-correlations for nonadoptive and adoptive siblings in the CAP*

IQ correlated with	Age	Phenotypic correlation	Nonadoptive cross-correlation	Adoptive cross-correlation
General factor	1	.05	.10	.11
	2	.42	.38	.09
	3	.15	.14	.28
	4	.16	.10	.15
Toys	1	.07	.18	.01
	2	.19	.21	.06
	3	.10	.05	.17
	4	.15	.06	.12
Maternal Involvement	1	.07	.05	.13
	2	.20	.20	.12
	3	.14	.34	.22
	4	.11	.13	.16
Encouraging Developmental Advance	1	−.01	−.04	.17
	2	.41	.40	.11
	3	.17	.18	.14
Restriction-Punishment	1	−.08	.02	.16
	2	.02	.01	−.13

relationships were selected because of their intrinsic interest and because they are among the few environment–development relationships that yield significant phenotypic correlations.

Although we selected HOME–IQ comparisons because they yielded some significant phenotypic correlations, the phenotypic relationships are nonetheless weak. As mentioned previously, if the magnitude of phenotypic environment – development correlations is low when environmental and developmental measures are correlated for the same individuals, cross-correlations between an environmental measure for one child and a developmental measure for the sibling are likely to be even lower, and the detection of genetic mediation in the comparison between nonadoptive- and adoptive-sibling cross-correlations is difficult. For example, a study with 50 pairs each of nonadoptive and adoptive siblings would have only 25% power ($p < .05$, one-tailed) to reject the null hypothesis when nonadoptive- and adoptive-sibling cross-correlations are .30 and .10, respectively.

Nonetheless, the results depicted in Table 11.3 provide hints of genetic mediation of environment–development relationships. The results for the HOME general factor at 2 years suggest genetic influence. The phenotypic correlation is .42, and the nonadoptive and adoptive sibling cross-correlations are significantly different, .38 and .09, respectively. At the other years, the results suggest little genetic involvement, although the phenotypic HOME–IQ correlations are so modest that it makes it unlikely that we could detect genetic mediation of the relationship.

HOME–IQ relationships were also examined for rotated HOME scores in addition to the HOME general factor; these are also presented in Table 11.3. The results for the HOME factor Encouraging Developmental Advance are similar to those for the HOME general factor. At 2 years, the correlation for nonadoptive siblings (.40) is significantly greater than the correlation for adoptive siblings (.11); the phenotypic correlation is .41. As indicated in Chapter 4, this HOME factor was defined by such items as mother consciously encourages developmental advance, mother provides structured learning experiences, and mother provides interesting activities for the child during the interview. It seems reasonable to expect that this scale might reflect genetically influenced propensities of children (reactive genotype–environment correlation) or passive genotype–environment correlation and thus show greater cross-correlations with IQ for nonadoptive than for adoptive siblings.

In addition, the HOME general factor at 2 years yields similar evidence of genetic influence on the Sequenced Inventory of Communication Development (SICD) measure of communicative competence. The phenotypic correlation for nonadoptive children is .35, and the nonadoptive- and adoptive-sibling cross-correlations are .33 and −.02, respectively. Also similar to the results for IQ, the HOME Encouraging Developmental Advance rotated factor shows genetic influence on the SICD at 2. The phenotypic correlation is .31, and the nonadoptive and adoptive sibling cross-correlations are .36 and −.03, significantly different. At 3, the three correlations are .23 (phenotypic), .23 (nonadoptive), and .23 (adoptive), suggesting no evidence of genetic influence. As with the HOME–IQ results, the other rotated HOME factors yielded no evidence of genetic influence.

Genetic mediation of the relationship between HOME Encouraging Developmental Advance and IQ at 2 years and communicative development at 2 is an interesting possibility, because differences among children in communicative competence are particularly acute at 24 months. Some caution is advised in interpreting this result, because comparison of the nonadoptive and adoptive siblings for this HOME factor, presented in the preceding section, did not suggest genetic influence.

The HOME yields few significant phenotypic correlations with noncognitive development such as temperament and behavioral problems. As mentioned earlier, the FES, which does correlate with temperament and behavioral problems, is not specific to each sibling. For these reasons, the CAP data do not permit further tests of the hypothesis of genetic mediation of environment–development relationships using the sibling adoption design. Another approach to the topic, described in the following section, is more general and more powerful.

CAP environment–offspring data

When environment–development relationships are analyzed using a parent–offspring adoption design, analyses are not limited to families with siblings, nor are they limited to finding genetic mediation of environment–development relationships that occurs because environmental measures reflect genetic differences between children in a family. Continuing with the example of books in the home, the sibling adoption design would find no evidence of genetic influence for this measure or for its relationship to children's IQ. However, in the parent–offspring adoption design, the relationship between books in the home and children's IQ could indicate genetic mediation. As Galton noted in 1875, in nonadoptive homes, in which parents share heredity as well as family environment with their children, relationships between environmental measures and measures of children's development can be mediated genetically via parental characteristics. That is, genetically influenced characteristics of the parents can be related to both the environmental measure and the measure of children's development. In adoptive homes, however, adoptive parents share only family environment with their adopted children in the absence of selective placement; for this reason, correlations between measures of environment and children's development in adoptive homes cannot be mediated genetically. Thus, if genes underlie relationships between measures of the home environment and children's development, environment–development correlations in nonadoptive homes will be greater than in adoptive homes. The greater the difference between the correlations in the nonadoptive and adoptive homes, the greater is the extent to which the environment–development correlation is mediated genetically. Unlike the twin and sibling designs, this design does not detect environmental responses to gene-based differences among children because responses of this type occur for adopted children as well as for nonadopted children.

A path model that describes the partitioning of phenotypic covariation between environmental measures and measures of behavioral development

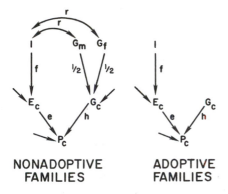

Figure 11.1. Model of genetic mediation of environment–development correlations in nonadoptive families and adoptive families. See text for explanation. (From Plomin, Loehlin, & DeFries, 1985. Reprinted with permission.)

into genetic and environmental components is shown in Figure 11.1. The path diagram elaborates the preceding discussion. That is, in nonadoptive families, correlations between environmental measures and measures of children's development can be mediated genetically as well as environmentally; in adoptive families, the correlation arises only for environmental reasons. More precisely, the child's phenotype P_c is assumed to be causally determined by its genotype G_c and by its environment E_c via genetic and environmental paths h and e; the residual arrow impinging on P_c allows for measurement error. The environmental measure I is assumed to be correlated to an extent r with mothers' and fathers' (unmeasured) genotypes G_m and G_f. For simplicity, r is assumed to be equal for mothers and fathers.

On the left side of Figure 11.1, it can be seen that the correlation between an environmental measure and children's development can occur in two ways in nonadoptive families: environmentally via the path *fe* or genetically via the parents' and child's genotypes, with a value of $0.5rh$ for the path through each parent and a combined value of rh for the genetic paths.

For adoptive families, depicted on the right side of Figure 11.1, the environmental measure I has only an environmental connection to the child's phenotype. In the absence of selective placement, the genotypes of the biological parents will not contribute to the correlation between environmental measures and the phenotype of the child. The environment–development correlation in adoptive families then simply takes on the value *fe*.

Thus, in nonadoptive families, the relationship between an environmental measure and children's behavior can be mediated genetically as well as environmentally – that is, $fe + rh$. In adoptive families, however, the correlation is represented by fe alone, because adoptive parents share family environment but not heredity with their adopted children. Therefore, the extent to which the correlation in nonadoptive families exceeds that in adoptive families can be attributed to genetic mediation of the relationship between environmental measures and measures of behavior. In other words, the environment–development correlation can be partitioned into an environmental and a genetic component. The phenotypic environment–development correlation in adoptive families directly estimates the environmental component of the correlation, and the difference between the correlations in the nonadoptive families and adoptive families estimates the genetic component. A multivariate extension of this model that includes three environmental measures and three behavioral measures has been developed (Thompson, Fulker, DeFries, & Plomin, 1986). Multivariate model fitting can provide simultaneous estimates of genetic and environmental influences for several environmental measures and several measures of development, taking into account covariances among the measures and providing an overall test of the model's fit.

Genetic effects on environment–development correlations in nonadoptive families are caused by passive genotype–environment correlations, described in Chapter 10. Reactive and active genotype–environment correlations could also contribute to correlations between environmental measures and children's development; however, it would do so in adoptive families as well as nonadoptive families. In this case, a correlation between an environmental measure and children's development in adoptive homes would no longer be purely environmental – it would contain a genetic component. Thus, the difference between environment–development correlations in nonadoptive and adoptive homes would be reduced and genetic influence on environment–development relationships would be underestimated in the presence of reactive and active genotype–environment correlations. Selective placement also biases the method against finding genetic mediation of associations between environmental and developmental measures. If adoptive parents are matched to biological parents of the adoptees, adoptive parents and adoptees will resemble each other genetically; environment–development relationships in adoptive homes will be mediated genetically to some extent, again leading to underestimates of genetic influence on associations between environmental measures and measures of development.

Another factor that biases the method against finding genetic mediation of environment–development relationships is genetic change from childhood to adulthood. As explained in Chapter 8, the genetic contribution to parent–offspring similarity is not really .5 as suggested by Figure 11.1; rather, it is the .5 coefficient of genetic relationship weighted by the product of the square roots of heritabilities in childhood and adulthood and the genetic correlation between childhood and adulthood. If the genetic correlation is low – that is, if substantial genetic change occurs from childhood to adulthood – parents' genetic contribution to their children's development could be quite low even when genetic factors are of considerable importance. Thus, unless genetic effects in childhood are substantially correlated with genetic effects in adulthood, it will be difficult to find environment–development correlations in nonadoptive families that exceed those in adoptive families.

Overestimates of the genetic component of environment–development relationships could occur if environmental variability is restricted in adoptive families. (As discussed in Chapter 10, variance of behavioral measures is expected to be lower for adopted children than for nonadopted children in the presence of passive genotype–environment correlation.) Reduced variance in environmental measures in adoptive families could restrict environment–development correlations in adoptive families and thus increase the difference between correlations in adoptive and nonadoptive families that is used to estimate the genetic component of environment–development relationships. However, this is an empirical issue: Variances of environmental measures in adoptive and nonadoptive families can be compared.

In summary, the comparison of environment–development associations in adoptive and nonadoptive homes provides a useful method of investigating genetic mediation of environmental influences. Although selective placement and genotype–environment correlation affect this approach, their effect is conservative in the sense that they make it more difficult to demonstrate genetic mediation. Variance differences in measures of adoptive and nonadoptive home environments are easily assessed. Thus, if environment–development correlations are greater in nonadoptive homes than in adoptive homes, it can reasonably be concluded that genes mediate relationships between environment and development to some extent. The greater the difference between the correlations in nonadoptive and adoptive homes, the greater the extent of genetic mediation.

Previous studies. The criterion for a relevant adoption study is that a correlation between an environmental measure and a measure of children's development is obtained in both adoptive and nonadoptive families, in the absence of marked selective placement or reduced variance in the adoptive families. Four studies meet these criteria, although they vary in degree of selective placement: Burks (1928); Freeman, Holzinger, and Mitchell (1928); Leahy (1935); and the Colorado Adoption Project.

The results of the first three studies consistently point to substantial genetic mediation of environment–IQ relationships in middle childhood and adolescence (see review in Plomin, Loehlin, & DeFries, 1985). For example, Burks's (1928) study included 200 adoptive families and 100 non-adoptive families with children from 5 to 14 years of age. For one measure of the home environment, the correlations with children's IQ were .42 in nonadoptive families and .21 in adoptive families; another environmental measure yielded correlations of .44 and .25, respectively. Although selective placement was substantial in the adoption study of Freeman et al. (1928), which included 40 nonadopted children and 185 adopted children ranging in age from 2 to 22 years, the correlation between a home index and IQ was .47 for nonadopted children and .32 for adopted children. Leahy's (1935) study of nearly 200 adoptive families and 200 nonadoptive families in which the children were from 5 to 14 years old yielded results similar to those of Burks. On average, for four environmental measures in Leahy's study, correlations with children's IQ were .46 in nonadoptive families and .16 in adoptive families.

The evidence from these studies is impressive in suggesting substantial genetic influence on the relationship between environmental measures and children's IQ, evidence that has previously gone unnoticed. Across these three studies, the average correlation between environmental measures and children's IQ is .45 in nonadoptive families and .18 in adoptive families. Nonetheless, these interesting findings raise several questions. Most notably, the fact that the environmental measures employed in these studies are imbued with socioeconomic status and parental education raises the question of whether similar results would be found for more proximal measures of the home environment. Because socioeconomic status, parental education, and parental IQ intercorrelate substantially and these distal environmental measures also correlate with children's IQ, some of the luster of the discovery of genetic influence fades – we already know that the relationship between parental IQ and children's IQ is influenced by heredity.

In addition to the question of whether more proximal measures of home environment also yield evidence of genetic mediation in their relationship to IQ, an important question concerns the specificity of these findings: Do some environmental measures show more genetic mediation than others? Another set of questions involves developmental issues: Can genetic mediation of environment–development relationships be found for measures other than IQ? Is genetic mediation stronger for some developmental measures than others? Finally, questions can be raised about age: Does genetic mediation of environment–development relationships change during development?

Infancy data from the Colorado Adoption Project. The concept of genetic mediation of environment–development relationships evolved because, in earlier analyses of CAP infancy data, correlations between environmental measures and developmental measures were consistently greater in nonadoptive families than in adoptive families (Plomin & DeFries, 1985a). In fact, stronger evidence for genetic influence emerged for environment–development relationships than for parent–offspring comparisons of presumably isomorphic behavioral traits. The design of the CAP is well suited for the exploration of this issue. Two major environmental measures – HOME (Caldwell & Bradley, 1978) and the FES (Moos & Moos, 1981) – have been employed in both adoptive and nonadoptive families, and a broad range of developmental assessments have been obtained for children at 1, 2, 3, and 4 years of age.

Furthermore, the assumptions of the model appear to be met. Selective placement is negligible in the CAP for educational and occupational status, cognition, and personality, as discussed in Chapter 4. As expected from the procedure in which nonadoptive families were matched to adoptive families, no significant mean or variance differences for educational attainment or occupational status were observed and no significant variance differences emerged for the HOME or FES. The third assumption concerns reactive and active genotype–environment correlation. Although we cannot rule out the possibility that the child's behavior has some influence on the HOME and FES measures, the correlations in adoptive families between these measures and children's development are quite low, which restricts the possible magnitude of such influences. That is, environment–development correlations should appear in adoptive homes if the environmental measure correlates with children's genetic propensities either because children actively create the correlation or because parents react to their children's propensities. Moreover, it should be remembered that the presence of reactive and active genotype–environment correlation is a conservative bias in that it makes it more difficult to find evidence of genetic mediation of environment–development relationships.

In order to reduce possible environment–development correlations to a manageable number, composites of the environmental measures and developmental measures in infancy were employed. Nonetheless, 113 correlations in nonadoptive families and 113 correlations in adoptive families constituted the basic data for these analyses (Plomin, Loehlin, & DeFries, 1985). Because genetic components of environment–development relationships cannot be assessed if no relationship exists between an environmental measure and a measure of development, 34 relationships were selected in which the correlation reached statistical significance in either adoptive or nonadoptive families. Of the 34 correlations, 28 yielded greater correlations in the nonadoptive families than in the adoptive families. Furthermore, the correlations in adoptive and nonadoptive families were significantly different in 12 comparisons; for all 12, the correlations in the nonadoptive families were greater than those in the adoptive families. For all 34 correlations, the mean correlation for nonadoptive families was .24; for adoptive families, the mean correlation was .09. This consistent pattern of greater correlations in the nonadoptive families than in the adoptive families suggests genetic involvement in relationships between environmental measures and major domains of infant development.

Genetic mediation is not limited to a particular domain of development nor to a particular environmental measure, although in general the HOME correlates with cognitive and language measures and the FES correlates with temperament and behavioral problems. For example, 24-month Bayley Mental Development Index (MDI) scores correlate .44 with the HOME general factor in nonadoptive families; in adoptive families, the correlation was .29. At 12 months, however, HOME–MDI correlations were low in both nonadoptive and adoptive families, as found in other studies (Gottfried, 1984); as discussed previously, genetic mediation of environment–development relationships cannot be assessed if no relationship exists between a particular environmental measure and a measure of infant development. The HOME correlated significantly with scores on the Sequenced Inventory of Communication Development (SICD) at 24 months and results similar to those for the 24-month MDI emerged: The HOME general factor correlated .50 with the SICD total score in nonadoptive families and .32 in adoptive families. A multivariate model-fitting analysis, including 2-year data for the HOME general factor, Bayley MDI, the SICD, and other measures, confirmed these results. Significant genetic influence was found for relationships between the HOME and MDI and between the HOME and SICD (Thompson et al., 1986).

The HOME suggested some specificity of genetic mediation: Two rotated factors of the HOME showed little or no evidence of genetic influence for MDI or SICD scores. These rotated HOME factors are Variety of Experience (essentially a Toys factor) and Maternal Involvement (maternal emotional involvement such as praising the child's qualities and conveying positive feeling when speaking of the child). At 24 months, the Variety of

Experience factor yielded correlations of .22 and .16 for the Bayley MDI in adoptive and nonadoptive families, respectively; correlations for the Maternal Involvement factor were .23 and .25. Thus, the pattern of correlations for these two HOME scales does not suggest genetic influence. Of the other two rotated HOME factors, one (Restriction-Punishment) yielded no significant correlations with cognitive development. The other rotated factor, Encouraging Developmental Advance (including items such as "mother consciously encourages developmental advance"), like the results for the HOME general factor on which these items load highly, suggested substantial genetic influence. The correlation with the Bayley MDI at 24 months was .44 in nonadoptive families, significantly greater than the correlation of .22 in adoptive families.

The infancy analyses also suggested some specificity within the cognitive domain. For factors derived from Bayley items, environmental correlations were generally higher in nonadoptive than in adoptive families; however, genetic mediation appeared to be stronger for verbal factors than for other factors. For example, the correlations for the HOME general factor in nonadoptive and adoptive families, respectively, were .34 and .26 for the Lexical factor and .36 and .19 for the Verbal (symbolic) factor. In contrast, the correlations for the Spatial factor were .19 and .15. This evidence suggesting genetic mediation of HOME–verbal relationships is consistent with the results mentioned earlier for the SICD measure of communicative competence.

For temperament and behavioral problems, genetic influences were not limited to any particular trait nor to a particular environmental measure. However, four significant differences between the nonadoptive and adoptive correlations involved the second-order FES Personal Growth factor. At 12 months of age, the age at which the FES was administered, Personal Growth correlated −.39 with Emotionality in the nonadoptive families and −.10 in the adoptive families; with Sociability, it correlated .34 and .16, respectively, in nonadoptive and adoptive families; with Soothability, the correlations were .41 and .06; and with Difficult Temperament, the correlations were −.32 and −.07. These measures of infant behavior intercorrelate in the range .32 to .58, and an equally weighted composite of the four measures correlated .49 with FES Personal Growth in the nonadoptive homes and .13 in the adoptive homes. These results suggest that an important aspect of genetic influence involves the relationship between familial "warmth" (cohesiveness and expressiveness) and infant "easiness' (low emotionality and difficultness and high sociability and soothability).

Thus, the CAP infancy data suggested some tentative answers to the questions raised earlier. Genetic mediation of environment–IQ relationships occurs for proximal environmental measures, not just for distal measures that primarily involve socioeconomic status (SES) and parental education. Evidence for environmental specificity also emerged. Although the HOME general factor and the Encouraging Developmental Advance factor show genetic mediation as they relate to cognitive development, two other HOME factors showed no genetic mediation. In terms of the question of domain specificity, genetic mediation does not appear to be limited to IQ; genetic mediation is also seen in the domains of language, temperament, and behavioral problems. In the latter two domains, however, genetic mediation appears to be especially concentrated in relationships involving familial warmth and infant easiness.

Another set of questions concerned developmental changes in the genetic mediation of environment–development relationships. In the cognitive realm, evidence for genetic mediation is stronger at 24 months than at 12 months; at 12 months, environment–cognition correlations are generally low, which makes it difficult to detect genetic mediation. For temperament and behavioral problems, it is difficult to compare correlations at 12 and 24 months because the environmental measure most likely to relate to these domains, the FES, was assessed at 12 but not 24 months.

Early childhood data from the Colorado Adoption Project. In early childhood, we expected that environment–development relationships would be stronger than in infancy and that this would provide an even better opportunity to assess genetic mediation of environment–development relationships. To the contrary, our analyses indicate that the HOME and FES in early childhood relate less strongly to outcomes in early childhood than they do in infancy, which increases the difficulty of decomposing environment–development relationships into their genetic and environmental components. The expectation that environment–development relationships increase in strength from infancy to early childhood lies in the common-sense notion that environmental effects are cumulative. In addition, nearly all studies show an increase in environment–IQ correlations from 1 to 2 years, and one might expect a continuation of this trend.

Moreover, some studies support this assumption. For example, results from a sample comparable to the CAP sample yielded a correlation of .15 between 15-month HOME and 18-month Bayley scores; the correlation between 39-month HOME and 42-month McCarthy general cognitive scores was .50 (Gottfried & Gottfried, 1984). Other studies indicate that HOME scores in infancy relate more strongly to IQ scores in early childhood than they do to IQ scores in infancy (Rutter, 1985).

CAP correlations between the HOME and IQ are presented in Table

Table 11.4. *HOME–IQ correlations in nonadoptive and adoptive families in the CAP*

HOME measure	Age	HOME–IQ correlation	
		Nonadoptive	Adoptive
General factor	1	.05	.12
	2	.42	.27
	3	.15	.11
	4	.16	.10
Toys	1	.07	.14
	2	.19	.16
	3	.10	.04
	4	.15	.09
Maternal Involvement	1	.07	.09
	2	.20	.26
	3	.17	.28
	4	.10	.02
Encouraging Developmental Advance	1	−.01	.09
	2	.41	.23
	3	.14	.23
Restriction-Punishment	1	−.08	−.07
	2	.02	−.06

11.4. As indicated by earlier CAP analyses and in accord with other studies, HOME–IQ correlations are low at 1 year in the full CAP sample and genetic influence is consequently negligible. At 2 years, however, HOME–IQ correlations are considerably greater and the correlation in nonadoptive families is significantly greater than the correlation in adoptive families. The HOME–IQ correlations plunge at 3 and 4 years, although the non-adoptive correlation continues to be about twice the size of the adoptive correlation. An attempt to model these relationships, incorporating parental IQ as well, suggests that in infancy the HOME reveals a direct environmental effect on children's IQ as well as indirect effects mediated via parental IQ. In early childhood, however, the weak relationship between the HOME and children's IQ may be due to genetic mediation via parental IQ (Rice, Fulker, DeFries, & Plomin, 1987).

The rotated HOME factors, also shown in Table 11.4, confirm the finding of environmental specificity in infancy in that the Toys factor and the Maternal Involvement factor do not show genetic mediation; for the Encouraging Developmental Advance factor, however, the correlation at 2 years is significantly greater in nonadoptive families than in adoptive families, similar to the results for the HOME general factor. At 3 and 4 years, correlations are low for these HOME factors.

It is noteworthy that parental education and SES yield results similar to those for the HOME because this finding suggests that these results are not due to some problem with the HOME assessment. For example, multiple correlations predicting offspring IQ from parental education and occupational status for nonadoptive and adoptive families are .20 and .16, respectively, at 1 year, .23 and .05 at 2 years, .22 and .19 at 3 years, and .16 and .12 at 4 years. The significant difference in correlations at 2, the lower correlations at 4, and the lack of evidence for genetic influence at the other years support the results that emerged for the HOME.

Although analyses of CAP measures other than IQ in early childhood are also hampered by the lack of strong relationships with environmental measures, some of the results are interesting. For example, at both 3 and 4 years, genetic influence is suggested for the relationship between the HOME and spatial ability, as measured by the CAP battery of specific cognitive abilities. The nonadoptive and adoptive correlations between the HOME general factor and spatial ability are .17 and −.04 at 3 years, a statistically significant difference, and .15 and −.02 at 4 years. Verbal ability also yields a significantly greater correlation with the HOME at 3 years in nonadoptive ($r = .17$) than in adoptive families ($r = .01$); however, the pattern of correlations at 4 years suggests no genetic influence (.17 in nonadoptive families and .21 in adoptive families). The SICD measure of communicative competence was administered at 2 and 3 years, and its correlations with the HOME are also consistent with the suggestion of genetic influence: At 2 years, HOME–SICD correlations in nonadoptive and adoptive families are .44 and .35, respectively; at 3, the correlations are .21 and .07.

Although the HOME was devised to assess the home environment relevant to cognitive development, we examined its relationship to temperament and behavioral problems. Again, correlations are weak but some are interesting. For example, the pattern of correlations in nonadoptive and adoptive homes for motor development in infancy, unlike mental development, suggests no genetic influence at either 1 or 2 years. At 1, HOME–motor correlations are .08 and .19 in nonadoptive and adoptive homes, respectively; at 2, the correlations are .14 and .29. At 3, an especially interesting result emerged for motor development: The HOME is positively related to gross motor development but negatively related to fine motor development in both types of family. Nonadoptive and adoptive HOME–motor correlation for gross motor development are .18 and .24, respectively; for fine motor development, the correlations are −.25 and −.32. Because nonadoptive correlations are not greater than adoptive correlations, these relationships are not due to genetically influenced characteristics of parents that are transmitted to their offspring, although it is possible that parents are responding to genetically influenced characteristics of their children.

Relationships between the HOME and behavioral problems appear to be mediated environmentally. For example, Difficult Temperament correlates negatively with the HOME Maternal Involvement factor in nonadoptive homes during the first three years: −.07, −.15, and −.18; in adoptive homes, the comparable correlations are −.09, −.05, −.14. Similarly, the relationship between the HOME factor of Restriction-Punishment − which is assessed only during infancy − and Difficult Temperament appears to be environmentally mediated; correlations are .09 and .13 in nonadoptive families at 1 and 2 years, respectively, and .15 and .27 in adoptive families. The HOME general factor correlated only −.06 with Difficult Temperament in nonadoptive families and −.01 in adoptive families on average across the four years. The HOME general factor and rotated factors at 4 years correlated near zero with Child Behavior Checklist (CBC) ratings of behavioral problems at 4.

The FES appears to be a more likely correlate of behavioral problems and temperament than does the HOME. Table 11.5 presents FES correlations for selected variables in nonadoptive and adoptive homes at 1 and 3 years, the years when the FES was administered. One of the most interesting results involves Difficult Temperament: At both 1 and 3 years, the FES Personal Growth factor (unlike the HOME correlations discussed earlier) yields significantly greater correlations with Difficult Temperament in nonadoptive families than in adoptive families; the correlations are negative in the sense that families higher in cohesiveness and expressiveness tend to have children who are less difficult temperamentally. This finding implies that genetic factors in parents mediate the relationship between greater cohesion and expressiveness in families and less general difficultness in children. As mentioned earlier, it is possible that the impact of heredity lies in parental perceptions. For example, optimism of parents or concerns about social desirability (if these traits are genetically influenced) might lead them to rate their families as "cohesive" and to rate their children as "easy." This interpretation would not diminish the importance of the finding; if true, it would imply that the FES Personal Growth taps genetically influenced characteristics of the parents that are genetically related to ratings of their children's difficultness. It is noteworthy that the same FES

Table 11.5. *Correlations between FES second-order factors and measures of development in nonadoptive and adoptive families in the CAP*

FES measure (age)	Child measure (age)	FES–development correlation	
		Nonadoptive	Adoptive
Personal Growth	CCTI Emotionality		
(1)	(1)	−.33	−.09
(3)	(3)	−.26	−.07
Personal Growth	CCTI Activity		
(1)	(1)	.17	.13
(3)	(3)	.06	.12
Personal Growth	CCTI Sociability		
(1)	(1)	.34	.13
(3)	(3)	.18	.11
Personal Growth	CCTI Attention Span		
(1)	(1)	.12	.11
(3)	(3)	.20	.15
Personal Growth	CCTI Soothability		
(1)	(1)	.39	.07
(3)	(3	.25	.07
Personal Growth	Difficult Temperament		
(1)	(1)	−.26	−.06
(3)	(3)	−.28	−.11
Personal Growth	Health		
(1)	(1)	−.17	−.07
(3)	(3)	−.11	−.02
Traditional Organization	Bayley MDI		
(1)	(1)	−.12	−.10
(1)	(2)	−.12	.00
Traditional Organization	Stanford–Binet IQ		
(3)	(3)	−.18	−.04
(3)	(3)	−.17	−.04

factor at 3 years is significantly related to specific problem behavior scores on the CBC at 4; however, this relationship appears to be mediated environmentally.

In terms of temperament, we examined relationships between the two second-order FES scales and scores on the Infant Behavior Record (IBR), the Colorado Childhood Temperament Inventory (CCTI), and the Behavioral Style Questionnaire (BSQ). The FES yields few significant correlations with the IBR at 1 year or the CAP modification of the IBR at 3 years. The fact that the FES correlates with parental ratings of other dimensions but not with the IBR raises the possibility that genetic mediation found in relationships between the FES and the former measures might be due to genetic factors involved in parental perceptions; just as likely, however, is the possibility that the IBR assesses behavior that is specific to the testing context. As indicated in Table 11.5, the FES Personal Growth factor correlates significantly with several parental ratings on the CCTI, and some of these associations appear to be mediated genetically to a substantial extent. The major example of genetic mediation involves familial "warmth" (FES Personal Growth) and infant "easiness" dimensions (Emotionality, Soothability, and Difficult Temperament). For each of these easiness dimensions, correlations with FES Personal Growth in nonadoptive families are significantly greater than correlations in adoptive families at both 1 and 3 years. This finding implies that parental perceptions of the warmth of their family are related to parental ratings of their children's easiness, not just for environmental reasons, but by way of genetically influenced characteristics of the parents that are transmitted hereditarily to their offspring.

Another trait, Sociability, shows significant genetic mediation of its relationship to FES Personal Growth at 1 but not at 3. Relationships between environmental measures and Activity and Attention Span are weaker and also suggest little genetic mediation.

Finally, the FES Personal Growth dimension is modestly related to ratings of children's health at 1 and 3 years; the greater correlations in nonadoptive than in adoptive families suggest that this relationship may be mediated genetically.

It is noteworthy that the other second-order FES factor, Traditional Organization, shows few relationships to personality. However, as indicated in Table 11.5, this FES scale is negatively related to IQ at 2, 3, and 4 years. Nonadoptive–adoptive comparisons suggest possible genetic influence. We explored this relationship further. The result for the constituent primary scales that comprise the second-order factor of Traditional Organization yielded similar results, especially Organization and Moral-Religious Emphasis. However, one primary scale showed particularly striking results: Correlations between Achievement Orientation and IQ in nonadoptive families were $-.27$ and $-.25$ at 3 and 4 years, respectively; in adoptive families, the correlations were $-.04$ and $-.04$. The differences in correlations between nonadoptive and adoptive families were smaller at 1 year ($-.06$ and $.00$) and at 2 years ($-.05$ and $.01$). The Achievement Orientation scale of the FES assesses the extent to which activities are cast into an achievement-oriented or competitive framework; its negative relationship to IQ in early childhood is mediated significantly by genetic factors in parents. This FES–IQ relationship may be due to passive genotype –environment correlation. One might suggest that the link is parental IQ;

for example, parents who are not as bright as others might try harder to achieve. However, as in our analyses of infancy data (Plomin & DeFries, 1985a), we find that obvious parental links, such as IQ in this case, are not responsible for genetic mediation.

In summary, some genetic mediation of environment–development relationships can be found during infancy and early childhood. For HOME–IQ relationships, genetic mediation increases sharply from 1 to 2 years and declines to a negligible level at 4. Relationships between the FES and children's temperament and behavioral problems also show some declines in genetic mediation from 1 to 3 years. Even more apparent than the decline in genetic mediation, however, is the decline in the phenotypic environment–development correlations in the nonadoptive families, most noticeably those between the HOME and cognitive and language development. The contemporaneous HOME–IQ correlations in nonadoptive families are .44 at 2 years, .24 at 3, and .14 at 4. It is possible that the CAP adaptations of the HOME at 3 and 4 years are at fault; alternatively, it may be that HOME–IQ relationships are in fact weaker in early childhood than in infancy. We favor the latter hypothesis because similar results were found for parental SES and education and for the FES, which suggests that the results are not limited to the HOME measures.

One reason for the decline of HOME–IQ correlations could be a reduction in genetic mediation of the HOME–IQ association (Pelton, Plomin, & DeFries, 1987). A developmental theory discussed in Chapter 10 (Scarr & McCartney, 1983) predicts decreasing genetic mediation of environment–development relationships from infancy to early childhood. The essence of the theory is that passive genotype–environment correlations, the type assessed in analyses of environment–development relationships, decline in importance, whereas the influence of reactive and active types are postulated to increase during development. Thus, the present results support the Scarr–McCartney theory in that genetic mediation of environment–development relationships – brought about by passive genotype–environment correlation – declines in importance from infancy to early childhood.

However, the CAP IQ results in early childhood conflict with results for older children in the early adoption studies of Burks, Freeman et al., and Leahy. In these studies, environmental measures correlated with children's IQ, and comparisons between correlations in adoptive and nonadoptive families suggested substantial genetic mediation of the environment–IQ relationship. Although the CAP results are similar to those of the older studies at 2 years, the environment–IQ correlations decline at 3 and 4 years, and negligible evidence of genetic mediation is found by 4 years. The conflict would disappear, however, if it were found that genetic mediation of environment–IQ relationships increases again when the CAP children enter the school years. If the CAP results for middle childhood do not conform to the older adoption studies, it is possible that the influence of passive genotype–environment correlation in families has diminished over the past 50 years due to such changes as television viewing and early childhood education outside the home. An alternative explanation is that the distal environmental measures used in the earlier studies are more highly correlated with parental IQ than are proximal measures such as the HOME.

Longitudinal analysis

The preceding section considered contemporaneous environment–development relationships. The possibility of genetic mediation of environment–development relationships, however, is just as relevant to longitudinal comparisons. Although developmentalists frequently interpret longitudinal environment–development associations in terms of environmental causation, longitudinal studies do not exclude the possibility of genetic mediation of environment–development relationships. For example, the HOME at 1 year of age predicts 3-year-old IQ better than it predicts 1-year-old IQ (Elardo & Bradley, 1981). This longitudinal environment–development relationship, however, does not imply that early environmental factors affect later IQ free of genetic mediation; parental behaviors indexed by the HOME might relate genetically to infant development at 3 years to a greater extent than to infant development at 1 year. Because the CAP is a longitudinal study, its data are useful for comparing longitudinal environment–development relationships in adoptive and nonadoptive families in order to explore the possibility of genetic mediation.

Because contemporaneous environment–development correlations in the CAP were low in early childhood, we were not optimistic that longitudinal correlations between environmental measures in infancy and developmental outcomes in early childhood would be of sufficient magnitude to permit the detection of genetic mediation. Nonetheless, in order to demonstrate this approach, we present longitudinal analyses of the CAP data using the two major approaches discussed in the preceding section in relation to contemporaneous environment–development associations: the sibling adoption design and the parent–offspring adoption design.

Sibling adoption design

The analysis of genetic and environmental components of covariance between two characters is directly relevant to the analysis of longitudinal covariance. In the preceding section, emphasis was placed on contemporaneous cross-correlations for adoptive and nonadoptive siblings – that is, environmental and developmental data for each sibling at the same age were employed. Rather than focusing on the phenotypic covariance between the HOME at each age and IQ at the same ages, one can apply the same technique to the analysis of longitudinal correlations. For example, genetic mediation of the relationship between the HOME at 12 months and IQ at 4 years can be assessed by comparing cross-correlations for adoptive and nonadoptive siblings, correlating the 12-month HOME score of each child with the 4-year IQ of the child's sibling.

Table 11.3 presents contemporaneous HOME–IQ cross-correlations for nonadoptive and adoptive siblings at each year. Despite the generally low phenotypic correlations between the HOME and IQ, some hints of genetic mediation were found. Table 11.6 presents longitudinal phenotypic correlations for nonadoptive siblings and cross-correlations for adoptive and nonadoptive siblings. In some cases, longitudinal correlations between the HOME and IQ are greater than contemporaneous correlations; in these cases, some evidence of genetic mediation emerges. For example, although the contemporaneous HOME–IQ phenotypic correlations are only .05 at 1 year and .16 at 4 years (from Table 11.3); the phenotypic correlation between HOME at 1 year and IQ at 4 years is .16, as shown in Table 11.6; from 2 to 4 years, the HOME–IQ correlation is .21. The longitudinal cross-correlation from the HOME at 1 year to IQ at 4 years for nonadoptive siblings is .24; the cross-correlation for adoptive siblings is − .02. The results for longitudinal comparisons at the other ages also suggest genetic influence, although the nonadoptive–adoptive differences are not statistically significant given the size of the sibling sample.

As in the analysis of contemporaneous HOME–IQ correlations, the results for the rotated HOME factor Encouraging Developmental Advance were similar to those for the HOME general factor. For example, as shown in Table 11.6, the average cross-correlations for nonadoptive and adoptive siblings are .27 and .07, respectively. Also similar to the contemporaneous analyses, phenotypic longitudinal correlations for the other rotated HOME factors are too low to permit meaningful analyses of genetic mediation of the longitudinal relationships.

The HOME also correlates longitudinally with the SICD, which was employed in the CAP at 2 and 3 years. As shown in Table 11.6, the 1-year HOME general factor correlates phenotypically .23 with the SICD at 2 years. The nonadoptive and adoptive sibling cross-correlations are .30 and .02, respectively. These results suggest that the longitudinal relationship between the HOME at 1 year and language development at 2 years

Table 11.6. *Longitudinal HOME–IQ phenotypic correlations for nonadopted children and longitudinal cross-correlations for nonadoptive and adoptive siblings in the CAP*

HOME measure (age)	Child measure (age)	Phenotypic correlation	Nonadoptive cross-correlation	Adoptive cross-correlation
General factor	Stanford–Binet IQ			
(1)	(3)	.15	.16	.00
(1)	(4)	.16	.24	−.02
(2)	(3)	.20	.32	.06
(2)	(4)	.21	.24	.13
Encouraging Developmental Advance	Stanford–Binet IQ			
(1)	(3)	.20	.13	.11
(1)	(4)	.22	.21	.00
(2)	(3)	.23	.36	.02
(2)	(4)	.23	.37	.15
General factor	SICD			
(1)	(2)	.23	.30	.02
(1)	(3)	.12	.16	.16
Encouraging Developmental Advance	SICD			
(1)	(2)	.22	.21	.09
(1)	(3)	.16	.12	.18

is mediated in part by genetic factors. Similar results occur for the HOME Encouraging Developmental Advance factor. However, neither HOME measure at 1 year shows genetic mediation in its relationship to 3-year SICD scores.

It is interesting that greater evidence for genetic mediation appears to emerge for longitudinal than for contemporaneous associations between the HOME and cognitive development. Ascertaining why this is so will require further research; the most immediate implication of these results is that longitudinal relationships between environmental measures and development outcomes cannot be assumed to be mediated environmentally; these data suggest that most of the association is genetically mediated.

Because the HOME scarcely correlates with noncognitive aspects of development such as temperament and because the FES is not specific to each sibling, the CAP sibling data provide no further tests of genetic mediation of environment–development relationships. However, the parent–offspring adoption design provides a more general approach to the question of genetic mediation of longitudinal relationships between environmental measures and developmental outcomes.

Parent–offspring adoption design

As explained earlier, the parent–offspring adoption design represents a more general approach to the analysis of environment–development associations than does the sibling adoption design. One advantage of the parent–offspring design is that it is not limited to families with adoptive and nonadoptive siblings. Nor is it limited to environmental measures sensitive to differences among children in a family. In this section, we examine longitudinal analyses based on the parent–offspring adoption design that parallel the contemporaneous analyses described earlier.

Contemporaneous correlations between the HOME and IQ are presented in Table 11.4. Even though the HOME is only modestly related to IQ, some evidence for genetic mediation was found. Longitudinal correlations between the HOME at 1 and 2 years and IQ at 3 and 4 years are presented in Table 11.7 separately for adoptive and nonadoptive families. As others have found (e.g., Gottfried, 1984), the HOME at 1 year predicts later IQ better than it predicts contemporaneous IQ. The CAP data indicate that the longitudinal prediction from 1-year HOME general factor scores to later IQ might involve genetic mediation in that the correlations for nonadoptive families exceed those for adoptive families, although not significantly so. The results for the HOME at 2 years, however, suggest no genetic mediation of later IQ, even though contemporaneous correla-

Table 11.7. *Longitudinal correlations between the HOME general factor and children's IQ in nonadoptive and adoptive families in the CAP*

HOME measure (age)	Nonadoptive		Adoptive	
	IQ (3)	IQ (4)	IQ (3)	IQ (4)
General factor				
(1)	.15	.16	.08	.06
(2)	.20	.21	.20	.23
Toys				
(1)	.02	.08	.03	.02
(2)	−.01	−.01	.04	.06
Maternal Involvement				
(1)	.00	−.02	.11	.11
(2)	.13	.13	.11	.16
Encouraging Developmental Advance				
(1)	.20	.22	.11	.07
(2)	.23	.23	.26	.28
Restriction-Punishment				
(1)	−.13	.00	−.04	−.08
(2)	−.05	−.02	−.17	−.08

tions between the HOME and IQ at 2 years suggested substantial genetic influence, as discussed earlier. As we have seen before, the rotated HOME factor Encouraging Developmental Advance yields results similar to those for the HOME general factor. The HOME Maternal Involvement factor at 2 appears to be modestly related to later IQ for environmental reasons. The other HOME factors show little relationship to later IQ. The complex results for the HOME might accurately reflect the inherent complexity of developmental transactions between environment and cognition; for example, parents' responses to their child change from one developmental phase to the next (Dunn & Plomin, 1986) and the processes involved in cognitive development change from infancy to early childhood. Clearly, the etiology of contemporaneous relationships can differ from the etiology of longitudinal relationships.

Concerning communicative development, analyses of contemporaneous HOME–SICD associations indicated significant genetic influence at 2 and 3 years. Longitudinal HOME–SICD associations yield results that are similar to those for IQ in two ways. First, genetic mediation is implicated by the 1-year HOME to the 3-year SICD (the nonadoptive and adoptive correlations are .23 and .12, respectively) but not to the 2-year SICD (.24 vs. .23). Second, the rotated HOME factor Encouraging Developmental Advance yields results similar to those for the HOME general factor: The nonadoptive and adoptive correlations are .27 and .22 between the HOME at 1 and the SICD at 2, and .26 and .16 between the HOME at 2 and the SICD at 3.

Longitudinal relationships between environmental measures and non-cognitive domains of development are generally weaker than those found for the contemporaneous relationships discussed earlier. The results for FES Personal Growth at 1 year and the "easiness" traits in later years are consistent with the evidence found for genetic mediation in contemporaneous comparisons. Correlations between FES Personal Growth at 1 year and Difficult Temperament in nonadoptive families are −.19 at 3 years and −.13 at 4 years and −.02 at 3 years and .00 at 4 years in adoptive families. Results for the other easiness traits were similar. For Soothability, correlations at 3 and 4 years were .26 and .26 in nonadoptive families and .02 and .07 in adoptive families. For Emotionality, correlations were −.29 and −.25 in nonadoptive families and −.07 and −.01 in adoptive families.

Of the many possible associations between FES scores at 1 year and later developmental outcomes, most were negligible. However, we shall mention two interesting relationships. The FES Personal Growth factor at 1 year appears to be environmentally related to behavioral problems at 4 years as measured by the CBC. At 4, correlations in nonadoptive and adoptive families are −.15 and −.21, respectively. Second, the FES Personal Growth factor at 1 year is modestly related to illness ratings at 3 and 4 years, and the data are consistent with hypothesis of genetic influence. At 3, correlations in nonadoptive and adoptive families are −.10 and .00, respectively, and at 4, the correlations are −.17 and .10. These results suggest that positive attitudes about family life in infancy are related to greater health of children at 3 and 4 years for genetic reasons. For example, it is possible that parents' health contributes to their positive attitudes about their family and is also genetically related to their children's health.

Another approach to the study of longitudinal relationships using the parent–offspring adoption design is to consider the joint effect of several environmental measures in predicting key outcome measures, an approach that recognizes the multivariate nature of environmental influences. Table 11.8 presents the results of multiple regressions in nonadoptive and adoptive families of several outcome variables on environmental measures (the 12-month HOME general factor, the two FES second-order factors assessed at 12 months, and parental SES and education). In overview, two points stand out. First, much of the variance of these outcome measures is not explained by environmental measures in either nonadoptive or adoptive families. Second, evidence of genetic mediation can be seen in that multiple correlations in nonadoptive families exceed those in adoptive fam-

Table 11.8. *Longitudinal multiple correlations of outcome measures in early childhood on environmental measures at 12 months in nonadoptive and adoptive families in the CAP*

Outcome measure	Nonadoptive multiple correlations		Adoptive multiple correlations	
	Year 3	Year 4	Year 3	Year 4
Stanford–Binet IQ	.42	.35	.27	.29
Verbal	.29	.37	.23	.21
Spatial	.17	.18	.11	.21
Perceptual Speed	.16	.09	.27	.26
Memory	.29	.24	.19	.04
Fine motor	.22	—	.22	—
Gross motor	.33	—	.31	—
CCTI Emotionality	.33	.32	.21	.14
CCTI Activity	.17	.17	.26	.21
CCTI Sociability	.22	.19	.19	.20
CCTI Attention Span	.17	.24	.25	.20
CCTI Soothability	.32	.34	.16	.14
Difficult Temperament	.28	.27	.15	.20
CBC behavioral problems	—	.30	—	.30

Note: The 12-month environmental measures employed in this analysis were the HOME general factor, the two second-order FES factors, and parental education and occupational status.

ilies. The difference in multiple correlations is greatest for IQ and for memory at 3 and 4 years. At 4 years, verbal ability indicates substantial genetic mediation, although at 3, evidence of genetic mediation is slight. Spatial ability shows no genetic mediation at either 3 or 4 years. The results for perceptual speed are odd in that environment–development multiple correlations are greater in adoptive than in nonadoptive families at 3 and 4 years.

No genetic mediation of longitudinal environment–development relationships is suggested for fine and gross motor development at 3 years, for CCTI temperament measures of Activity, Sociability, and Attention Span at 3 and 4, or for CBC behavioral problems at 4. However, the measures of Emotionality and Soothability indicate genetic influence at both years, as does the measure of Difficult Temperament, suggesting that genetic influence on the relationship between environmental variables and "easiness" dimensions emerges longitudinally as well as contemporaneously.

In summary, longitudinal associations between environmental measures and developmental outcomes can also be mediated genetically; indeed, longitudinal associations may even be influenced genetically to a greater extent than contemporaneous associations.

Discussion

This chapter provides an overview of a new direction for behavioral genetic research that could be referred to as the nature of nurture. The goal is to explore genetic effects on the variance of environmental measures and on the covariance between measures of environment and measures of development.

In terms of the first issue – genetic effects on environmental measures – what we need is a study of parenting of adult twins. This approach would uncover genetic influence on parenting to the extent that any characteristics of the parents are genetically related to the environmental measure and to the extent that heritable differences among their children affect the parents' scores on the environmental measure. Extant studies, however, involve twins as children; these studies are limited to genetic effects of the second type when objective measures of the environment are employed. When subjective measures are used, as is the case in nearly all previous studies, genetic influences will also arise if any genetically influenced characteristics of the respondents affect their perceptions of the environment. Research on subjective reports of twins concerning their parents' treatment has uncovered a fascinating finding: Parental affection appears to show genetic influence, whereas parental control does not.

The sibling adoption design of CAP provides the first analyses of this sort for objective environmental measures; environmental measures specific to each child can be correlated and compared for adoptive and non-adoptive siblings. The value of this method rests on the specificity of the environmental measures; in fact, environmental measures are rarely specific to each child in a family. Nonetheless, CAP results indicate genetic influence on the HOME in infancy and in early childhood. Videotaped observations of mothers' individual interactions with their children yield greater correlations for nonadoptive siblings than for adoptive siblings for affectionate behavior but not for controlling behavior.

The second, and even more important, theme of this chapter is that genetics can contribute to the covariation between environmental measures and measures of children's development. Two approaches were considered: twin and sibling adoption designs that compare environment–development cross-correlations, and a parent-offspring design that compares correlations between environmental measures and measures of development in adoptive and nonadoptive families. In CAP analyses in infancy and early childhood, both approaches yielded some evidence of genetic mediation of environment–development relationships. The parent–offspring design is more powerful in detecting genetic mediation in part because it is not limited to environmental measures that are specific to each child in the family. Genetic mediation was found primarily for the relationship between the HOME and cognitive measures such as IQ and language development and between FES "warmth" and children's temperamental "easiness." Genetic mediation of the relationship between the HOME and cognitive development appears to be due primarily to the HOME factor Encouraging Developmental Advance; two other HOME factors show no genetic mediation. Analyses of longitudinal associations between environmental measures in infancy and developmental outcomes in early childhood also indicate some genetic mediation.

Another direction for research is to identify parental and child characteristics that mediate genetic influence on environmental measures and on environment–development associations. It has been shown, for example, that the HOME and FES are related to parental personality and IQ and that young adults' perceptions of their rearing environment are related to the respondents' personality (Plomin, 1986a). It is likely, however, that traditional measures of personality and cognition do not entirely capture the genetically influenced concomitants of environmental measures in the intense, emotion-laden context of family relationships.

Concerning parental mediators of genetic influence on environment–development associations, all we know so far is that the answer is not obvious. For example, it has been assumed that the relationship between the HOME and infant Bayley scores in nonadoptive families is freed from genetic influence when parental IQ is partialed from the correlation between the HOME and Bayley scores (e.g., Gottfried & Gottfried, 1984). As in other studies, CAP analyses also indicate that partialing out parental IQ has little effect on the relationship between the HOME general factor and Bayley scores in nonadoptive families (Plomin & DeFries, 1985a). However, this lack of effect of parental IQ is also observed in adoptive families, which means that the correlations between the HOME and Bayley scores continue to be greater in nonadoptive families than in adoptive families even after the effects of parental IQ have been removed statistically. Thus, we are left with the intriguing notion that the parental characteristics responsible for genetic mediation of the HOME–Bayley relationship must be largely independent of the parents' IQ. Similar results are found for other domains of infant development in the CAP: Partialing out apparently equivalent parental behaviors has little effect on the magnitude of genetic mediation of environment–development associations.

Indeed, partialing out parental SES, education, IQ, specific cognitive abilities, and major dimensions of personality had little effect on the HOME–Bayley relationship in either nonadoptive or adoptive families; criteria to guide the search for parental factors that can explain genetic mediation of the HOME–IQ relationship have been suggested (Bergeman & Plomin, in press).

The major difficulty of studying genetic mediation of environment–development relationships is that the phenotypic relationships are relatively weak. Genetic mediation of environment–development relationships cannot be assessed unless environment–development relationships exist. Contrary to expectations, the CAP results indicate lower environment–development correlations in early childhood than in infancy. Although it is possible that this finding is due to a diminished role for passive genotype–environment correlation in early childhood, results from older adoption studies suggest that genetic mediation will again be observed, at least for environment–IQ relationships, when the CAP children reach middle childhood; however, it is also possible that the environmental measures employed in the older studies were more highly related to parental IQ than current environmental measures.

Finally, it should be mentioned that most of the research reported in this chapter – indeed, environmental research in general – focuses on environmental measures assessed between rather than within families. When the parent–offspring adoption design is employed, for example, an assessment of the home environment is correlated with children's development across families; that is, covariance is calculated between a score characterizing each family's environment and a developmental measure of one child in each family. This approach assumes that other children in the same families would experience a similar environment. However, one of the most important findings from behavioral genetic research is that environmental influences do not operate in this monolithic manner; whatever the relevant environmental factors may be, they do not make two children in the same family more similar than pairs of children picked at random from the population (for a review, see Plomin & Daniels, 1987). The critical question is, Why are children in the same family so different from one another?

To study this important "nonshared" category of environmental influence, new environmental measures will be needed, measures that assess environments specific to each child. That is, to the extent that an environmental instrument assesses experiences shared by two children in the same family, the measure is unlikely to assess environmental influences that affect development. Because nonshared environment is an important component of environmental variance, whereas shared environment is not, it is possible that measures of nonshared environment, as well as their relationship to development, are less subject to genetic mediation than are traditional environmental measures. Earlier in this chapter, we described research that developed a self-report instrument for assessing nonshared environment; only slight evidence for genetic influence on this measure was found (Daniels & Plomin, 1985).

Differential experiences of identical and fraternal twins or of adoptive and nonadoptive siblings can be examined in order to explore genetic influence on measures of nonshared environment. In addition, such differential experiences of twins or siblings can be related to differences in developmental outcomes in order to investigate genetic mediation of nonshared associations between environment and development. For example, in the CAP, we could have compared environmental differences for adoptive and nonadoptive siblings, and we could have related these environmental differences for siblings to differences in the siblings' outcomes. However, of the two environmental measures in the CAP, the FES is not at all specific to a particular child and the HOME is only somewhat specific. Because the HOME is shared to such a considerable extent by siblings in a family, sibling difference scores would consist primarily of error of measurement. The sibling analyses reported in this chapter relied on sibling correlations for the HOME and cross-correlations between the HOME and IQ and thus involve analyses of shared rather than nonshared environmental influence. The CAP ratings of videotapes of mother–child interaction are specific to each child; however, these analyses suggest that mothers generally behave quite consistently toward their two children when the children are observed at the same age. Nonetheless, siblings other than twins are not the same age, and mothers were not similar in their treatment of the same child across ages. This suggests that differences in maternal treatment may be a source of differential experience of children in a family – or that differential developmental functions of siblings elicit differences in maternal treatment; the CAP sample size of siblings with complete videotape data is not yet large enough for analyses of nonshared environment to be undertaken.

Because the bulk of environmental influences lie in the category of nonshared environment, further research on nurture – as well as research on the nature of nurture – should consider this important source of environmental influence.

12 Conclusions

In this chapter we step back from the numerous analyses described in previous chapters in order to gain some perspective on what we know and what we need to learn about the origins of individual differences during infancy and early childhood. As presaged in Chapter 1, the ratio of what is known to what is not known is small; however, the ratio is more impressive when we consider how few studies have addressed the issue of the origins of individual differences in infancy and childhood.

Principles

Rather than summarizing the preceding chapters, we have attempted to abstract some principles that outline what is known about nature and nurture in infancy and early childhood. In our book on infancy, several principles were drawn from the infancy results of the Colorado Adoption Project (Plomin & DeFries, 1985a). These principles involve some general points, such as the following. The etiology of individual differences in infancy includes heredity, variations in family environment are related to individual differences in infancy, and the relative extent of genetic and environmental influence varies for different characters. We have no doubt that these general principles hold for early childhood as well as for infancy.

One other general principle should be added to our earlier list: *Individual differences among children are substantial and reliable.* Throughout infancy and early childhood, the range of individual differences is impressive, which calls into question the usefulness of average descriptions of children's development at a particular age. Stanford–Binet IQ scores within the CAP vary from 84 to 139 after the lowest and highest IQs are eliminated. The range of scores for other aspects of development is even greater. For example, at 2 years, some children score eight times higher than other children on a measure of communicative competence, and at 3 years 11-fold differences are observed; total behavioral problem scores are in the

314

60s for some children and other children have scores of only 2. As discussed in Chapter 2, variation as well as central tendency must be explained, for five reasons: Individual differences are substantial, issues of greatest relevance to society are issues of individual differences, average differences between groups are relatively small compared with individual differences within groups, the description and explanation of average group differences bear no necessary relationship to those of individual differences, and questions concerning the origins of individual differences are more easily answered than questions about the etiology of average differences between groups. Moreover, interest in the etiology of individual differences is the premise for research in behavioral genetics, which, as discussed in Chapter 3, provides a general theory of the genetic and environmental origins of individual differences in behavior.

Other principles from our earlier book are more specific: Individual differences in infancy in cognitive and communicative development are genetically related to adult general cognitive ability, gender has a negligible impact on individual differences in infant development, and parent–offspring relationships at the extremes of the normal continuum are similar to those for behavior within the normal range. Although we did not examine the latter two issues systematically in early childhood, we would nonetheless include all three in a list of principles concerning the origins of individual differences in infancy and early childhood.

Three of the principles from our earlier book are germane to the topics of Chapter 9, 10, and 11: genotype–environment interaction, genotype–environment correlation, and genetic involvement in measures of the family environment. After discussing these issues, we turn to new principles that focus on the major theme of the present book: developmental change and continuity during infancy and early childhood.

The nature–nurture interface

Genetic and environmental influences on development generally coact in an additive manner

Interactions – genetic, environmental, and genotype–environment interactions – are easily posed but rarely documented. The hundreds of interaction analyses reported in Chapter 9 lead to the conclusion that when individual differences among children are related to environmental or genetic factors, the relationships are additive. In addition to genotype–environment interaction, which can be analyzed adequately only in the context of an adoption study, three other types of interaction were explored: interactions involving parent–offspring resemblance, interactions involving longitudinal changes in IQ, and temperament–environment interactions. Few significant interactions of any kind were found.

Another possible exception is the indirect evidence discussed in Chapter 6 that suggests that nonadditive genetic influence may be important for personality. Twin studies consistently find heritable influence for observational and parental ratings, whereas studies of first-degree relatives do not.

In our earlier book on infancy, we formulated two related principles that we did not examine extensively in early childhood. These principles appear to be safe predictions in early childhood as well as in infancy: Correlations between environmental measures and development are linear (e.g., environmental influences show no different relationship to development at the tails of the distribution), and parent–offspring relationships at the extremes of the normal continuum are similar to those for behavior within the normal range.

Genotype–environment correlation affects cognitive development

Comparisons between variances for adopted and nonadopted infants led us in our earlier book on infancy to suggest that genotype–environment correlations account for little variance, although we indicated that this is a weak test of passive genotype–environment correlations because of the large standard errors involved in variance comparisons. The present analyses of comparisons between variances for adopted and nonadopted infants, however, suggest that passive genotype–environment correlation affects infant mental development, that its influence declines by early childhood, and that its effect on other domains of development is negligible. Parent–offspring model fitting also indicates modest passive genotype–environment correlation for mental development but not for other domains.

Reactive and active forms of genotype–environment correlation may be of even greater importance for cognitive development. However, the environmental measures used in the CAP did not identify specific sources of genotype–environment correlation, as assessed by correlations between environmental measures in adoptive homes and IQ of biological mothers.

Heredity influences measures of the family environment

Labeling a measure "environmental" does not make it an environmental measure. Heredity can play a role in such measures via genetically influenced characteristics of parents and of children. It appears that genetic influences affect measures of parental warmth to a greater extent than parental control, especially when children's perceptions of their parents' treatment are assessed.

It should be noted that these analyses assess only a limited portion of possible genetic effects on environmental measures; a study of adult twins rearing their own families could assess more fully the extent of genetic influence on measures of the family environment. Sorely needed in this area are better measures of the family environment, especially measures that are specific to a single child.

Associations between environmental measures and development
in childhood are often mediated genetically

In CAP analyses in infancy and early childhood, two approaches were employed to assess the genetic contribution to the covariation between environmental measures and measures of children's development: sibling adoption designs, which compare environment–development cross-correlations, and the more powerful parent–offspring design, which compares correlations between environmental measures and measures of development in adoptive and nonadoptive families. Both approaches yielded some evidence of genetic mediation of environment–development associations. Genetic mediation was found especially for the relationship between the HOME and cognitive measures such as IQ and language development and between FES "warmth" and children's temperamental "easiness."

Genetic mediation of the relationship between the HOME and cognitive development appears to be due primarily to the HOME factor Encouraging Developmental Advance; two other HOME factors show no genetic mediation of their association with cognitive development.

Longitudinal associations between environmental measures
in infancy and development in early childhood are often
mediated genetically

Although longitudinal environment–development associations are often interpreted in terms of environmental causation, longitudinal comparisons do not rule out the possibility of genetic mediation. Results for the sibling adoption design suggest that genetic mediation may be greater for longitudinal than for contemporaneous associations between environmental measures and cognitive development. For example, the HOME at 1 year is scarcely related, phenotypically or genetically, to Bayley scores at 1 year. However, the HOME at 1 year yields a longitudinal cross-correlation of

.24 with IQ at 4 years for nonadoptive siblings; for adoptive siblings, the cross-correlations is − .02. The relationship between the HOME at 1 year and IQ at 4 years also shows genetic mediation in comparisons of HOME–IQ correlations in nonadoptive and adoptive families. As in the contemporaneous environment–development analyses described earlier, longitudinal associations between warmth of the family in infancy and later easiness of the child evidence genetic mediation.

Genetic mediation of environment–development associations is not to be found in traditional measures of parental characteristics

Parental characteristics responsible for the genetic mediation of environment–development relationships are largely independent of cognitive and personality traits that are usually assessed in developmental studies. For example, it has been assumed that the relationship between the HOME and infant Bayley scores in nonadoptive families is freed from genetic influence when parental IQ is partialed from the correlation between the HOME and Bayley scores. However, correlations between the HOME and Bayley scores continue to be greater in nonadoptive families than in adoptive families even after the effects of parental IQ have been removed. Indeed, partialing out parental measures such as socioeconomic status, education, IQ, specific cognitive abilities, and major dimensions of personality had little effect on the HOME–Bayley relationship in either nonadoptive or adoptive families. It is likely that traditional measures of cognitive ability and personality do not capture the genetically influenced concomitants of environmental measures in the intense, emotion-laden context of family relationships.

Developmental change and continuity during infancy and early childhood

Our goal is to begin a discussion and exploration of developmental change from an individual-differences perspective. Because of the novelty of these topics, our contribution consists to a greater extent of concepts than of conclusions. For example, we described three categories of developmental change – changes in variance, changes in covariance among variables (factor structures), and changes in age-to-age covariance – and we indicated that these three categories are relevant to both descriptive analyses (Chapter 5) and etiological analyses (Chapter 6). These categories are useful for organizing research on the topic of developmental change from an individual-differences perspective. Because so few data are available on these topics, however, only the broadest outlines of conclusions have begun to emerge. As a spur to research in this field, our conclusions are presented below, although they are more properly considered to be tentative hypotheses that require further verification.

Phenotypic variances are stable during infancy and early childhood

Phenotypic variance – as indexed by the coefficient of variation, which adjusts for mean differences – shows little change during infancy and early childhood. This is somewhat surprising because increases in variance might be expected as new processes affect traits and magnify differences among children; also, there is greater opportunity to observe differences among older children.

Factor structures change during infancy and early childhood for cognition but not for temperament

The amount of variance accounted for by an unrotated principal component does not change developmentally for cognition and temperament during infancy and early childhood; this finding is contrary to the orthogenetic hypothesis of developmental differentiation as viewed from the perspective of individual differences rather than average age changes. However, for cognitive development, the *nature* of factor structures changes, as indicated by changes in factor loadings in unrotated first principal components and in rotated factors. For example, the unrotated first principal component for cognitive items shows a dramatic increase in the prominence of language items from 1 to 2 years; also, although verbal items continue to dominate at 3 and 4 years, there is some indication that this general cognitive factor encompasses increasingly varied abilities by 4 years. At the same time, examination of rotated factor structures for Stanford–Binet items suggests that cognitive abilities begin to diverge during early childhood. In contrast, measures of temperament show little change in factor structure during infancy and early childhood.

Age-to-age stability increases from infancy to early childhood for IQ and for temperament

For both year-to-year correlations and long-term correlations from infancy and early childhood to later childhood and adulthood, IQ scores show linear increases in age-to-age stability during the first four years of life. As described in Chapter 5, IQ correlations from 1 to 2 years are about .40, and correlations from 2 to 3 years are about .50. Results of longitudinal studies from infancy to adulthood display a similar shift: Correlations to adulthood are .25 from 1 year, .40 from 2, .45 from 3, and .50 from 4. Not enough research has been conducted on other aspects of cognitive development to answer questions concerning developmental changes in age-to-age stability. For temperament, several dimensions show little change in stability; however, when changes in age-to-age stability occur, they nearly always increase rather than decrease.

Descriptive and etiological developmental phenomena often differ

Descriptive changes in variances, within-age covariances, and age-to-age covariance can differ from etiological changes. For example, although phenotypic variances for cognitive measures do not appear to change much during infancy and early childhood, heritabilities tend to increase. The most dramatic example of this point is that modest phenotypic stability for IQ from childhood to adulthood masks substantial child-to-adult genetic correlations. One implication of this principle is that etiological as well as descriptive approaches to developmental change are needed.

When heritability changes developmentally, it tends to increase

For height and weight, heritability increases during infancy, reaching high levels by early childhood. For cognitive development, twin data suggest that heritability increases about 5% per year, from 10% to 25% from 1 to 4 years, although limited data from the CAP sibling adoption design do not support this conclusion. Even at 4 years, the twin data indicate that heritability of IQ scores is only half that of later childhood, suggesting that increases in heritability continue into middle childhood. Increases in heritability are also seen for measures of verbal ability. For measures of temperament, the resolving power of extant research is not yet adequate to posit developmental trends in heritability. This conclusion concerning increasing heritability is particularly interesting because it goes against the prevailing but unexamined notion that experiential factors increasingly overwhelm genetic differences during the course of development.

Genetic sources of within-age covariances often change during infancy and early childhood

As described in Chapter 6, for height versus weight and for communicative versus cognitive development, genetic correlations appear to increase during infancy. For mental versus motor development and for expressive versus receptive communicative skills, genetic mediation of the phenotypic relationship decreases, suggesting genetic differentiation. Multivariate model-fitting analyses confirm the finding that cognitive and communicative development are highly correlated genetically and that temperament and cognitive ability are independent genetically.

Genetic continuity can be observed during childhood and from childhood to adulthood

One of the most surprising and important findings is that, despite generally modest phenotypic stability, genetic correlations during infancy and early childhood – and even from infancy and early childhood to adulthood – appear to be quite substantial for IQ as well as for height and weight. In other words, for these measures, genetic influences at one age correlate substantially with genetic influences at another age. For IQ, model-fitting analyses estimate genetic correlations to adulthood of .42, .61, .56, and .75 at 1, 2, 3, and 4 years, respectively, which suggests a trend toward increasing genetic correlations during infancy and early childhood.

Less genetic continuity is found for other variables such as specific cognitive abilities and temperament.

Genes produce change as well as continuity in development

One theme of this book is developmental change, and especially the role of genetics in change. To the extent that age-to-age genetic correlations are less than 1.0, genetic change is implied. Such is the case even for IQ; for most other traits, genetic change greatly prevails over continuity in year-to-year comparisons as well as in child-to-adult comparisons.

Developmental changes in variances and covariances are gradual, not sharp transitions

In terms of individual differences, developmental changes during infancy and early childhood are not marked and sudden as implied by the word "transition." In general, changes are gradual and linear for the major indices of individual differences – developmental changes in variances, within-age covariances among measures, and age-to-age covariance – as well as for genetic and environmental sources of such changes. One implication of this principle is that frequent testing may not be essential for longitudinal studies of origins of individual differences in infancy and early childhood.

Shared environmental influences increase in importance for IQ during infancy and early childhood

For IQ, adoptive sibling correlations increase during infancy and early childhood – from about .00 at 1 year to about .25 at 4 years – and correlations between adoptive parents and their adopted children also increase – from about .10 at 1 to about .20 at 4. These results suggest that shared environmental influences increase in importance during infancy and early environment.

Nonshared environmental influences are of primary importance for temperament

Adoptive-sibling correlations as well as correlations between adoptive parents and their adopted children are low for measures of temperament, indicating that shared environmental influences are relatively unimportant. Even though nonadditive genetic variance may be important for these traits, most of the phenotypic variance appears to be due to nonshared environmental influence.

Questions

Although some principles of developmental behavioral genetics have begun to emerge from our examination of infancy and early childhood, many more questions are raised than answers offered by this first look at these issues. Describing and explaining individual differences in development require much more research; as discussed in Chapter 2, questions concerning individual differences are both important and tractable. In broad outline, the questions that must be answered involve descriptions of change as well as continuity in individual differences and explanations of the origins of these individual differences. Developmentalists must not shy away from the study of developmental change; for example, the most important point of this book is that genetics can create change as well as continuity.

A list of specific questions that we wish to answer could be very long if we considered the description and explanation of individual differences in all of the major domains of behavioral development. Because of our interest in behavioral genetics, we focus on questions of explanation involving genetic and environmental etiologies rather than on other types of explanation such as the study of psychological processes that mediate developmental outcomes. In large part, our list of questions follows from the principles stated above; rather than emphasizing what we know about each of those issues, we now focus on what we do not know.

Is nonadditive genetic variance important in the area of personality development? It appears that twin studies consistently show substantial genetic influence on personality in infancy and early childhood, whereas studies of first-degree relatives suggest little genetic influence. Does nonadditive genetic variance occur more for some traits than others?

For IQ, have the sibling adoption data underestimated genetic influence in early childhood, in contrast to parent–offspring adoption data and twin data? Do twin studies greatly overestimate the shared-environment component of variance for IQ because of special perinatal twin effects?

Can we identify specific examples of genotype–environment interaction? Although the number of genotype–environment interactions that have emerged so far is not impressive, will other combinations of environmental measures, outcomes, and ages yield greater evidence of such interactions? To what extent does the theory of genotype–environment interaction proposed in Chapter 9 explain interaction for other combinations of environmental measures and measures of development?

Will Scarr and McCartney's developmental theory of genotype–environment correlation be confirmed? According to this theory, the importance of passive genotype–environment correlation decreases and that of active or reactive genotype–environment increases during childhood. So far, the results are in reasonably good agreement with this theory. Can specific sources of reactive genotype–environment correlation be identified?

What processes underlie genetic influence on environmental measures? Why do genetic factors affect perceptions of parental warmth but not perceptions of parental control? Are the results of subjective perceptions similar to those for objective observations? (If not, the results have implications for the source of genetic factors that impinge on the environmental measures.) Can measures of the environment be developed that are specific to each child in a family? (Such measures are needed to detect genetic influence on environmental measures using twin and sibling designs as well as to identify nonshared environmental influences.)

What processes are involved in the genetic mediation of environment–

development associations? Why is the association between IQ and the HOME factor Encouraging Developmental Advance genetically mediated, whereas other HOME factors such as Maternal Involvement do not show genetic mediation? What developmental processes are at work if, as suggested by longitudinal cross-correlations in the sibling adoption design, genetic mediation is greater for longitudinal environment–development relationships than for contemporaneous relationships? Is greater genetic mediation found when environment–development associations are stronger? (The major difficulty faced in attempts to study genetic mediation of environment–development associations is that the phenotypic associations are relatively weak; genetic mediation cannot be assessed unless environment–development relationships exist.)

Which aspects of cognitive development are genetically most predictive of adult intelligence? One of the most exciting findings is that genetic continuity from childhood to adulthood is substantial for cognitive ability, which leads to the question whether some aspects of cognitive development in childhood are more predictive of adult IQ than others. Our preliminary hypothesis is that genetic continuity is not mediated by any specific cognitive ability but rather by general cognitive ability.

Can child-to-adult genetic continuity be found for traits other than cognitive abilities? Parent–offspring and sibling data for domains other than cognitive abilities yield only slight evidence of genetic continuity from childhood to adulthood, although nonadditive genetic variance or measurement problems may be key, especially for personality. Do age-to-age genetic correlations generally increase during development?

Are there transitional periods of sharp genetic change from age to age for certain traits? Are genetic changes during one transition (such as the transition from infancy to early childhood) predictive of other transitions (such as the transition to middle childhood or to adolescence)? When do specific cognitive abilities differentiate genetically? Studies of identical and fraternal twins may be particularly valuable for assessing the etiology of spurts and lags in age-to-age comparisons.

What are the nonshared environmental factors that are of such great importance in the development of personality and psychopathology? To answer this question, we will need to study more than one child per family and to construct measures of the environment specific to each child that assess differential experiences of children in the same family.

We have attempted to formulate questions, concepts, and methods concerning the origins of individual differences in infancy and early childhood. Because our interest lies in the novel topic of developmental change, we have framed our questions in terms of descriptive and etiological changes in variances, within-age covariance, and age-to-age covariance for environmental measures and environment–development relationships as well as for behavioral measures. Data from the Colorado Adoption Project provide some tentative answers to some of these questions. However, it remains for future research, especially large-scale, longitudinal behavioral genetic studies, to provide definitive answers to these questions about nature and nurture during infancy and early childhood.

References

Achenbach, T. M., & Edelbrock, C. (1983). *Manual for the Child Behavior Checklist and Revised Child Behavior Profile*. Burlington: University of Vermont, Department of Psychology.

Anastasi, A. (1958). Heredity, environment, and the question "How?" *Psychological Review, 65*, 197–208.

Appelbaum, M. I., & McCall, R. B. (1983). Design and analysis in developmental psychology. In P. H. Mussen (Ed.), *Handbook of child psychology* (pp. 415–76). New York: Wiley.

Baker, L. A., DeFries, J. C., & Fulker, D. W. (1983). Longitudinal stability of cognitive ability in the Colorado Adoption Project. *Child Development, 54*, 290–7.

Baldwin, J. M. (1894). *The development of the child and of the race*. New York: Macmillan.

Baltes, P. B., Reese, H. W., & Lipsitt, L. P. (1980). Life-span developmental psychology. *Annual Review of Psychology, 31*, 65–110.

Barclay, J. R. (1983). A meta-analysis of temperament–treatment interactions with alternative learning and counseling treatments. *Developmental Review, 3*, 410–43.

Bateson, P. P. G. (1978). How does behavior develop? In P. P. G. Bateson & P. H. Klopfer (Eds.), *Perspectives in ethology* (pp. 55–73). New York: Plenum.

Bayley, N. (1949). Consistency and variability in the growth of intelligence from birth to eighteen years. *Journal of Genetic Psychology, 75*, 165–96.

    (1954). Some increasing parent–child similarities during the growth of children. *Journal of Educational Psychology, 45*, 1–21.

    (1969). *Manual for the Bayley Scales of Infant Development*. New York: Psychological Corp.

    (1970). Development of mental abilities. In P. H. Mussen (Ed.), *Carmichael's manual of child psychology* (pp. 1163–1210). New York: Wiley.

Beckwith, L. (1971). Relationships between attributes of mothers and their infants' IQ scores. *Child Development, 42*, 1083–97.

Bell, R. Q. (1968). A reinterpretation of the direction of effects in socialization. *Psychological Review, 75*, 81–95.

Bergeman, C. S., & Plomin, R. (in press). Parental mediators of the genetic relationship between home environment and infant mental development. *British Journal of Developmental Psychology*.

    (in press). Genotype–environment interaction. In J. Bruner & M. Bornstein (Eds.), *Interactions in child development*. New York: Academic Press.

Boomsma, D. I., & Molenaar, P. C. M. (1987). The genetic analysis of repeated measures. I: Simplex models. *Behavior Genetics, 17*, 111–24.

Bouchard, T. J., Jr., & McGue, M. (1981). Familial studies of intelligence: A review. *Science, 212*, 1055–9.

Brim, O. G., Jr., & Kagan, J. (1980). *Constancy and change in human development*. Cambridge, MA: Harvard University Press.

Broman, S. H., Nichols, P. L., & Kennedy, W. A. (1975). *Preschool IQ: Prenatal and early development correlates*. Hillsdale, NJ: Erlbaum.

Bulmer, M. G. (1970). *The biology of twinning*. New York: Oxford University Press.

Burks, B. (1928). The relative influence of nature and nurture upon mental development: A comparative study of foster parent–foster child resemblance and true parent–true child resemblance. *Twenty-Seventh Yearbook of the National Society for the Study of Education, P. 1*, 219–316.

Buss, A. H., & Plomin, R. (1975). *A temperament theory of personality development*. New York: Wiley-Interscience.

(1984). *Temperament: Early developing personality traits*. Hillsdale, NJ: Erlbaum.

Caldwell, B. M., & Bradley, R. H. (1978). *Home Observation for Measurement of the Environment*. Little Rock: University of Arkansas.

Cameron, J., Livson, N., & Bayley, N. (1967). Infant vocalizations and their relationship to mature intelligence. *Science, 157*, 331–3.

Casler, L. (1976). Maternal intelligence and institutionalized children's developmental quotients: A correlational study. *Developmental Psychology, 12*, 64–7.

Cattell, R. B. (1973). *Personality and mood by questionnaire*. San Francisco: Jossey-Bass.

(1982). *The inheritance of personality and ability*. New York: Academic Press.

Cattell, R. B., Eber, H., & Tatsuoka, M. M. (1970). *Handbook for the Sixteen Personality Factor Questionnaire (16PF)*. Champaign, IL: Institute for Personality and Ability Testing.

CERN (1977). *Minuit: A system for function minimization and analysis of parameter errors and correlations*. Geneva: CERN.

Chess, S., & Thomas, A. (1984). *Origins and evolution of behavior disorders: Infancy to early adult life*. New York: Brunner/Mazel.

Clarke, A. D. B., & Clarke, A. M. (1984). Constancy and change in the growth of human characteristics. *Journal of Child Psychology and Psychiatry, 25*, 191–210.

Coates, L., & Lewis, M. (1984). Early mother–infant interaction and infant cognitive status as predictors of school performance and cognitive behavior in six-year-olds. *Child Development, 55*, 1219–30.

Cohen, J. (1968). Multiple regression as a general data-analytic system. *Psychological Bulletin, 70*, 426–43.

(1977). *Statistical power analysis for the behavioral sciences*. New York: Academic Press.

Cohen, J., & Cohen, P. (1975). *Applied multiple regression/correlation analysis for the behavioral sciences*. New York: Halstead Press.

Corley, R. P. (1987). *Genetic and environmental continuity among measures of general cognitive ability in infancy, early childhood, and adulthood using combined parent–offspring and sibling data from the Colorado Adoption Project*. Unpublished doctoral dissertation, University of Colorado, Boulder.

Crockenberg, S. B. (1981). Infant irritability, mother responsiveness, and social support influences on the security of infant–mother attachment. *Child Development, 52*, 857–65.

Cronbach, L. J. (1957). The two disciplines of scientific psychology. *American Psychologist, 12*, 671–84.

Cronbach, L. J. (1987). Statistical tests for moderator variables: Flaws in analyses recently proposed. *Psychological Bulletin, 102*, 414–17.

Cronbach, L. J., & Snow, R. E. (1975). *Aptitudes and instructional methods: A handbook for research on interactions*. New York: Irvington.

Crow, J. F. (1986). *Basic concepts in population, quantitative, and evolutionary genetics*. New York: Freeman.

Crow, J. F., & Kimura, M. (1970). *An introduction to population genetics theory*. New York: Harper & Row.

Daniels, D., & Plomin, R. (1985). Differential experience of siblings in the same family. *Developmental Psychology, 21*, 747–60.

Daniels, D., Plomin, R., & Greenhalgh, J. (1984). Correlates of difficult temperament in infancy. *Child Development, 55*, 1184–94.

Darwin, C. (1958). *The origins of species by means of natural selection or the preservation of favoured races in the struggle for life* (Mentor edition). New York: New American Library of World Literature. (Original published in 1859.)

DeFries, J. C., & Fulker, D. W. (1986). Multivariate behavioral genetics and development: An overview. *Behavior Genetics, 16*, 1–10.

DeFries, J. C., & Plomin, R. (1978). Behavioral genetics. *Annual Review of Psychology, 29*, 473–515.

DeFries, J. C., Plomin, R., & LaBuda, M. C. (1987). Genetic stability of cognitive development from childhood to adulthood. *Developmental Psychology, 23*, 4–12.

DeFries, J. C., Vandenberg, S. G., McClearn, G. E., Kuse, A. R., Wilson, J. R., Ashton, G. C., & Johnson, R. C. (1974). Near identity of cognitive structure in two ethnic groups. *Science, 183*, 338–9.

Dewey, R. (1935). *Behavior development in infants: A survey of the literature on prenatal and postnatal activity, 1920–1934*. New York: Columbia University Press.

Dunn, J. F. (1986). Commentary: Issues for future research. In R. Plomin & J. F. Dunn (Eds.), *The study of temperament: Changes, continuities and challenges* (pp. 163–71). Hillsdale, NJ: Erlbaum.

Dunn, J. F., & Kendrick, C. (1982). *Siblings: Love, envy, and understanding*. London: Grant McIntyre.

Dunn, J. F., & Plomin, R. (1986). Determinants of maternal behavior toward three-year-old siblings. *British Journal of Developmental Psychology, 57*, 348–56.

Dunn, J. F., Plomin, R., & Daniels, D. (1986). Consistency and change in mothers' behavior towards young siblings. *Child Development, 57*, 348–56.

Dunn, J. F., Plomin, R., & Nettles, M. (1985). Consistency of mothers' behavior towards infant siblings. *Developmental Psychology, 21*, 1188–95.

Eaves, L. J., & Gale, J. S. (1974). A method for analyzing the genetic basis of covariation. *Behavior Genetics, 4*, 253–67.

Eaves, L. J., Long, J., & Heath, A. C. (1986). A theory of developmental change in quantitative phenotypes applied to cognitive development. *Behavior Genetics, 16*, 143–62.

Eichorn, D. H. (1969, August). *Developmental parallels in the growth of parents and their children*. Presidential address (Division 7) presented at the meeting of the American Psychological Association, Washington, DC.

Elardo, R., & Bradley, R. H. (1981). The Home Observation for Measurement of the Environment (HOME) Scale: A review of research. *Developmental Review, 1*, 113–45.

Elder, G. H., Jr. (1985). *Life course dynamics: Trajectories and transitions, 1968–1980*. Ithaca, NY: Cornell University Press.

Endler, N. S., & Magnusson, D. (1976). Toward an interactional psychology of personality. *Psychological Bulletin, 83*, 956–74.

Fagan, J. F., III (1985). A new look at infant intelligence. In D. K. Detterman (Ed.), *Current topics in human intelligence* (pp. 223–46). Norwood, NJ: Ablex.

Fagan, J. F., III, & McGrath, S. K. (1981). Infant recognition memory and later intelligence. *Intelligence, 5*, 121–30.

Fagan, J. F., III, & Singer, L. T. (1983). Infant recognition memory as a measure of intelligence. In. L. P. Lipsett (Ed.), *Advances in infancy research* (pp. 31–79). Norwood, NJ: Ablex.

Falconer, D. S. (1960). *Introduction to quantitative genetics*. New York: Ronald Press.

(1981). *Introduction to quantitative genetics*. New York; Longman.

Fisch, R. O., Bilek, M. K., Deinard, A. S., & Chang, P. N. (1976). Growth, behavioral, and psychologic measurements of adopted children: The influences of genetic and socioeconomic factors in a prospective study. *Behavioral Pediatrics, 89*, 494–500.

Fischbein, S. (1981). Heredity–environment influences on growth and development during adolescence. In L. Gedda, P. Parisi, & W. E. Nance (Eds.), *Progress in clinical and biological research: Twin research 3, Part B. Intelligence, personality, and development* (pp. 211–26). New York: Liss.

Fisher, R. A. (1918). The correlation between relatives on the supposition of Mendelian inheritance. *Transactions of the Royal Society of Edinburgh, 52*, 399–433.

Fox, M. M. (1979). *A longitudinal study of temperament in early childhood*. Unpublished doctoral dissertation, Temple University, Philadelphia.

Freeman, D. (1983). *Margaret Mead and Samoa: The making and unmaking of an anthropological myth*. Cambridge, MA: Harvard University Press.

Freeman, F. N., Holzinger, K. J., & Mitchell, B. (1928). The influence of environment on the intelligence, school achievement, and conduct of foster children. *Twenty-Seventh Yearbook of the National Society for the Study of Education, 27*, 103–217.

Fulker, D. W. (1981). The genetic and environmental architecture of psychoticism, extraversion and neuroticism. In H. J. Eysenck (Ed.), *A model for personality* (pp. 88–122). New York: Springer.

Fulker, D. W., Baker, L. A., & Bock, R. D. (1983). Estimating components of covariation using LISREL. *Data Analyst: Communications in Computer Data Analysis, 1*, 5–8.

Fulker, D. W., & DeFries, J. C. (1983). Genetic and environmental transmission in the Colorado Adoption Project: Path analysis. *British Journal of Mathematical and Statistical Psychology, 36*, 175–88.

Fulker, D. W., Plomin, R., Thompson, L. A., Phillips, K., Fagan, J. F., III, & Haith, M. M. (1987). *Rapid screening of infant predictors of adult IQ: A study of twins and their parents*. Manuscript submitted for publication.

Fuller, J. L., & Thompson, W. R. (1978). *Foundations of behavior genetics*. St. Louis, MO: Mosby.

Gadamer, H. G. (1975). *Truth and method*. Los Angeles & Berkeley: University of California Press.

Galton, F. (1875). The history of twins as a criterion of the relative powers of nature and nurture. *Journal of the Anthropological Institute, 6*, 391–406.

Garmezy, N., & Rutter, M. (1983). *Stress, coping, and development in children*. New York: McGraw-Hill.

Gholson, B., & Barker, B. (1985). Kuhn, Lakatos, and Laudan: Applications in the history of physics and psychology. *American Psychologist, 40*, 755–69.

Gottfried, A. W. (1984). *Home environment and early cognitive development: Longitudinal research*. New York: Academic Press.

Gottfried, A. W., & Brody, N. (1975). Interrelationships between and correlates of psychometric and Piagetian scales of sensorimotor intelligence. *Developmental Psychology, 11*, 379–87.

Gottfried, A. W., & Gottfried, A. E. (1984). Home environment and cognitive development in young children of middle-socioeconomic-status families. In A. W. Gottfried (Ed.), *Home environment and early cognitive development: Longitudinal research* (pp. 57–115). New York: Academic Press.

Gottlieb, G. (1983). The psychobiological aproach to developmental issues. In P. H. Mussen (Ed.), *Handbook of child psychology* (pp. 1–26). New York: Wiley.

Guilford, J. P., & Fruchter, B. (1973). *Fundamental statistics in psychology and education*. New York: McGraw-Hill.

Hardy-Brown, K. (1983). Universals and individual differences: Disentangling two approaches to the study of language acquisition. *Developmental Psychology, 19*, 610–24.

Hardy-Brown, K., & Plomin, R. (1985). Infant communicative development: Evidence from adoptive and biological families for genetic and environmental influences on rate differences. *Developmental Psychology, 21*, 378–85.

Hardy-Brown, K., Plomin, R., & DeFries, J. C. (1981). Genetic and environmental influences on rate of communicative development in the first year of life. *Developmental Psychology, 17*, 704–17.

Hauser, R. M., & Featherman, O. L. (1977). *The process of stratification: Trends and analysis*. New York: Academic Press.

Hay, D. A. (1985). *Essentials of behaviour genetics*. Oxford: Blackwell Scientific.

Hay, D. A., & O'Brien, P. J. (1983). The La Trobe Twin Study: A genetic approach to the structure and development of cognition in twin children. *Child Development, 54*, 317–30.

Hedrick, D. L., Prather, E. M., & Tobin, A. R. (1975). *Sequenced Inventory of Communication Development*. Seattle: University of Washington Press.

Heidegger, M. (1962). *Being and truth*. New York: Harper & Row.

Henderson, N. D. (1967). Prior treatment effects on open field behaviour of mice: A genetic analysis. *Animal Behaviour, 15*, 364–76.

  (1970). Genetic influences on the behavior of mice can be obscured by laboratory rearing. *Journal of Comparative and Physiological Psychology, 73*, 505–11.

  (1972). Relative effects of early rearing environment on discrimination learning in housemice. *Journal of Comparative and Physiological Psychology, 79*, 243–53.

Herrnstein, R. J. (1982, August). IQ testing and the media. *Atlantic Monthly*, pp. 68–74.

Hinde, R. A., & Bateson, P. P. G. (1984). Discontinuities versus continuities in behavioral development and the neglect of process. *International Journal of Behavioral Development, 7*, 129–43.

Honzik, M. P. (1938). The constancy of mental test performance during the preschool period. *Journal of Genetic Psychology, 52*, 285–97.

Honzik, M. P., Macfarlane, J. W., & Allen, L. (1948). Stability of mental test performance between 2 and 18 years. *Journal of Experimental Education, 17*, 309–22.

Hoopes, J. L. (1982). *Prediction in child development: A longitudinal study of adoptive and nonadoptive families*. New York: Child Welfare League of America.

Hunt, E. (1985). The correlates of intelligence. In D. K. Detterman (Ed.), *Current topics in human intelligence: Vol. 1. Research Methodology* (157–78). Norwood, NJ: Ablex.

Jacklin, C. N., & Maccoby, E. E. (1983). Issues of gender differentiation. In M. D. Levine, W. B. Carey, A. C. Crocker, & R. T. Gross (Eds.), *Developmental-behavioral pediatrics* (pp. 175–84). Philadelphia: Saunders.

James, W. (1890). *The principles of psychology*. New York: Holt.

Jencks, C. (1972). *Inequality: A reassessment of the effect of family and schooling in America*. New York: Harper & Row.

Jensen, A. R. (1976). The problem of genotype–environment correlation in the estimation of heritability from monozygotic and dizygotic twins. *Acta Geneticae Medicae et Gemellogiae, 25*, 86–99.

  (1980). *Bias in mental testing*. New York: Free Press.

Jessor, R. (1983). The stability of change: Psychosocial development from adolescence to young adulthood. In D. Magnusson & V. L. Allen (Eds.), *Human development: An interactional perspective* (pp. 321–41). New York: Academic Press.

Jinks, J. L., & Eaves, L. J. (1974). IQ and inequality. *Nature, 248*, 287–9.

Jinks, J. L., & Fulker, D. W. (1970). Comparison of the biometrical genetical, MAVA, and classical approaches to the analysis of human behavior. *Psychological Bulletin, 73*, 311–49.

Jöreskog, K. G., & Sörbom, D. (1976). *LISREL III: Estimation of linear structural equation systems by maximum likelihood methods.* Chicago: International Educational Service.

Kagan, J. (1971). *Change and continuity in infancy.* New York: Wiley.

Kagan, J., & Moss, H. A. (1962). *Birth to maturity: A study in psychological development.* New York: Wiley.

Kagan, J., Reznick, J. S., & Snidman, N. (1986). Temperamental inhibition in early childhood. In R. Plomin & J. F. Dunn (Eds.), *The study of temperament: Changes, continuities and challenges* (pp. 53–65). Hillsdale, NJ: Erlbaum.

King, W. L., & Seegmiller, B. (1973). Performance of 14 to 22-month old black, firstborn male infants on two tests of cognitive development. *Developmental Psychology, 8*, 317–26.

Kopp, C. B. (1983). Risk factors in development. In P. H. Mussen (Ed.), *Handbook of child psychology* (Vol. 2, pp. 1081–1188). New York: Wiley.

Kuhn, T. S. (1962). *The structure of scientific revolutions.* University of Chicago Press.

Kuse, A. R. (1977). *Familial resemblance for cognitive abilities estimated from two test batteries in Hawaii.* Unpublished doctoral dissertation, University of Colorado, Boulder.

LaBuda, M., DeFries, J. C., & Fulker, D. W. (1987). Genetic and environmental covariance structures among WISC-R subtests: A twin study. *Intelligence, 11*, 233–44.

LaBuda, M. C., DeFries, J. C., Plomin, R., & Fulker, D. W. (1986). Longitudinal stability of cognitive ability from infancy to early childhood: Genetic and environmental etiologies. *Child Development, 57*, 1142–50.

Lakatos, I. (1970). Falsification and the methodology of scientific research programs. In I. Lakatos & A. Musgrave (Eds.), *Criticism and the growth of knowledge* (pp. 91–196). Cambridge University Press.

   (1978). *The methodology of scientific research programs.* Cambridge University Press.

Laudan, L. (1981). *Science and hypothesis.* Boston: Reidel.

Leahy, A. M. (1935). Nature–nurture and intelligence. *Genetic Psychology Monographs, 17*, 236–308.

Lerner, R. M., Lerner, J. V., Windle, M., Hooker, K., Lenerz, K., & East, P. L. (1986). Children and adolescents in their contexts: Tests of a goodness of fit model. In R. Plomin & J. F. Dunn (Eds.), *The study of temperament: Changes, continuities and challenges* (pp. 99–114). Hillsdale, NJ: Erlbaum.

Levine, M. D., Carey, W. B., Crocker, A. C., & Gross, R. T. (1983). *Developmental–behavioral pediatrics.* Philadelphia: Saunders.

Lewis, M. (1983). On the nature of intelligence: Science or bias? In M. Lewis (Ed.), *Origins of intelligence: Infancy and early childhood* (pp. 1–24). New York: Plenum.

Lewis, M., Jaskir, J., & Enright, M. K. (1986). The development of mental abilities in infancy. *Intelligence, 10*, 331–54.

Lewis, M., & McGurk, H. (1972). The evaluation of infant intelligence: Infant intelligence scores – true or false? *178*, 1174–7.

Lewontin, R. C., Rose, S., & Kamin, L. J. (1984). *Not in our genes: Biology, ideology, and human nature.* New York: Pantheon.

Loehlin, J. C. (1978). Heredity–environment analyses of Jencks's IQ correlations. *Behavior Genetics, 8*, 415–36.

(1983). John Locke and behavior genetics. *Behavior Genetics, 13*, 117–21.

(1987). *Latent variable models: An introduction to factor, path, and structural analysis.* Hillsdale, NJ: Erlbaum.

Loehlin, J. C., & DeFries (1987). Genotype–environment correlation revisited. *Behavior Genetics, 17*, 263–78.

Loehlin, J. C., Horn, J. M., & Willerman, L. (1981). Personality resemblance in adoptive families. *Behavior Genetics, 11*, 309–30.

Loehlin, J. C., & Nichols, R. C. (1976). *Heredity, environment, and personality.* Austin: University of Texas Press.

Lykken, D. T. (1982). Research with twins: The concept of emergenesis. *Psychophysiology, 19*, 361–73.

Maccoby, E. E., & Jacklin, C. N. (1974). *The psychology of sex differences.* Stanford, CA: Stanford University Press.

(1983). The "person" characteristics of children and the family as environment. In D. Magnusson & V. Allen (Eds.), *Human development: An interactional perspective* (pp. 75–110). New York: Academic Press.

Mackenzie, B. (1985). Explaining race differences in IQ: The logic, the methodology, and the evidence. *American Psychologist, 39*, 1214–33.

Magnusson, D. (1985). Implications of an interactional paradigm for research on human development. *International Journal of Behavioral Development, 8*, 115–37.

(1988). *Individual development from an interactional perspective: A longitudinal study.* Hillsdale: NJ: Erlbaum.

(in press). Adult delinquency in the light of conduct and physiology at an early age. In D. Magnusson & A. Ohman (Eds.), *Psychopathology: An interactional perspective.* New York: Academic Press.

Magnusson, D., & Allen, V. L. (1983). An interactional perspective for human development. In D. Magnusson & V. L. Allen (Eds.), *Human development: An interactional perspective* (pp. 3–34). New York: Academic Press.

Magnusson, D., & Endler, N. S. (1977). *Personality at the crossroads: Current issues in interactional psychology.* Hillsdale, NJ: Erlbaum.

Mangan, G. (1982). *The biology of human conduct: East–West models of temperament and personality.* Elmsford, NY: Pergamon.

Matheny, A. P., Jr. (1980). Bayley's Infant Behavior Record: Behavioral components and twin analyses. *Child Development, 51*, 1157–67.

(1983). A longitudinal twin study of stability of components from Bayley's Infant Behavior Record. *Child Development, 54*, 356–60.

Matheny, A. P., Jr., & Wilson, R. S. (1981). Developmental tasks and rating scales for the laboratory assessment of infant temperament. *JSAS Catalog of Selected Documents in Psychology, 11*, 81–82.

Matheny, A. P., Jr., Wilson, R. S., & Nuss, S. N. (1984). Toddler temperament: Stability across settings and over ages. *Child Development, 55*, 1200–11.

Mayr, E. (1982). *The growth of biological thought.* Cambridge, MA: Harvard University Press.

McArdle, J. J. (1986). Latent variable growth within behavior genetic models. *Behavior Genetics, 16*, 163–200.

McCall, R. B. (1972). Similarity in developmental profile among related pairs of human infants. *Science, 178*, 1004–5.

(1977). Challenges to a science of developmental psychology. *Child Development, 48*, 333–44.

(1979). The development of intellectual functioning in infancy and the prediction of later IQ. In J. D. Osofsky (Ed.), *Handbook of infant development* (pp. 707–41). New York: Wiley-Interscience.

(1981). Nature–nurture and the two realms of development: A proposed integration with respect to mental development. *Child Development, 52,* 1–12.

(1983). A conceptual approach to early mental development. In M. Lewis (Ed.), *Origins of intelligence: Infancy and early childhood* (pp. 107–33). New York: Plenum.

McCall, R. B., Appelbaum, M. I., & Hogarty, P. S. (1973). Developmental changes in mental performance. *Monographs of the Society for Research in Child Development, 38,* 39–98.

McCall, R. B., Eichorn, D. H., & Hogarty, P. S. (1977). Transitions in early mental development. *Monographs of the Society for Research in Child Development, 42* (Whole No. 171).

McCall, R. B., Hogarty, P. S., & Hurlburt, N. (1972). Transitions in infant sensorimotor development and the prediction of childhood IQ. *American Psychologist, 27,* 728–48.

McCarthy, D. (1972). *McCarthy scales of children's abilities.* New York: Psychological Corp.

McDevitt, S. C. (1986). Continuity and discontinuity of temperament in infancy and early childhood: A psychometric perspective. In R. Plomin & J. F. Dunn (Eds.), *The study of temperament: Changes, continuities and challenges* (pp. 27–38). Hillsdale, NJ: Erlbaum.

McDevitt, S. C., & Carey, W. B. (1978). The measurement of temperament in 3–7 year old children. *Journal of Child Psychology and Psychiatry, 19,* 245–53.

McGue, M. (1983). Bivariate path analysis of plasma lipids. *Human Heredity, 33,* 145–52.

McNemar, Q. (1969). *Psychological statistics.* New York: Wiley.

Mead, M. (1928). *Coming of age in Samoa.* New York: Morrow.

Moore, T. (1967). Language and intelligenc: A longitudinal study of the first eight years: I. Patterns of development in boys and girls. *Human Development, 10,* 88–106.

Moos, R. H., & Moos, B. S. (1981). *Family Environment Scale manual.* Palo Alto, CA: Consulting Psychologists Press.

Moss, H. A., & Susman, E. J. (1980). Longitudinal study of personality development. In O. G. Brim, Jr., & J. Kagan (Eds.), *Constancy and change in human development* (pp. 530–95). Cambridge, MA: Harvard University Press.

Mueller, W. H. (1976). Parent–child correlations for stature and weight among school aged children: A review of 24 studies. *Human Biology, 48,* 379–97.

Mussen, P. H. (1983). *Handbook of child psychology.* New York: Wiley.

Neale, M. C., & Fulker, C. W. (1984). A bivariate path analysis of fear data on twins and their parents. *Acta Geneticae Medicae Gemellologiae, 33,* 273–86.

Nelson, K. (1981). Individual differences in language development: Implications for development and language. *Developmental Psychology, 17,* 170–87.

Nichols, P. L., & Broman, S. H. (1974). Familial resemblance in infant mental development. *Developmental Psychology, 10,* 442–6.

O'Brien, R. G. (1978). Robust techniques for testing heterogeneity of variance effects in factorial designs. *Psychometrika, 43,* 327–42.

Ozer, D. J. (1985). Correlation and the coefficient of determination. *Psychological Bulletin, 97,* 307–15.

Packer, M. J. (1985). Hermeneutic inquiry in the study of human conduct. *American Psychologist, 40,* 1081–93.

Pelton, P. A., Plomin, R., & DeFries, J. C. (1987). *Genetic mediation of environmental influences in early childhood.* Manuscript submitted for publication.

Plomin, R. (1986a). *Development, genetics and psychology.* Hillsdale, NJ: Erlbaum.

(1986b). Multivariate analysis and developmental behavioral genetics: Developmental change as well as continuity. *Behavior Genetics, 16,* 25–44.

(1988). The nature and nurture of cognitive abilities. In R. Sternberg (Ed.), *Advances in the psychology of human intelligence.* Hillsdale, NJ: Erlbaum.

Plomin, R., & Daniels, D. (1986). Genetics and shyness. In W. H. Jones, J. M. Cheek, & S. R. Briggs (Eds.). *A sourcebook on shyness: Research and treatment* (pp. 63–80). New York: Plenum.

   (1987). Why are children in the same family so different from each other? *Behavioral and Brain Sciences, 10*, 1–16.

Plomin, R., & DeFries, J. C. (1979). Multivariate behavioral genetic analysis of twin data on scholastic abilities. *Behavior Genetics, 9*, 505–17.

   (1980). Genetics and intelligence: Recent data. *Intelligence, 4*, 15–24.

   (1981). Multivariate behavioral genetics and development: Twin studies. In L. Gedda, P. Parisi, & W. E. Nance (Eds.), *Twin Research 3, Part B: Intelligence, personality and development* (pp. 25–33). New York: Liss.

   (1985a). *Origins of individual differences in infancy: The Colorado Adoption Project.* New York: Academic Press.

   (1985b). A parent–offspring adoption study of cognitive abilities in early childhood. *Intelligence, 9*, 341–56.

Plomin, R., DeFries, J. C., & Loehlin, J. C. (1977). Genotype–environment interaction and correlation in the analysis of human behavior. *Psychological Bulletin, 84*, 309–22.

Plomin, R., DeFries, J. C., & McClearn, G. E. (1980). *Behavioral genetics: A primer.* San Francisco: Freeman.

Plomin, R., & Dunn, J. F. (1986). *The study of temperament: Changes, continuities and challenges.* Hillsdale, NJ: Erlbaum.

Plomin, R., & Foch, T. T. (1981). Sex differences and individual differences. *Child Development, 52*, 383–5.

Plomin, R., Loehlin, J. C., & DeFries, J. C. (1985). Genetic and environmental components of "environmental" influences. *Developmental Psychology, 21*, 391–402.

Plomin, R., McClearn, G. E., Pedersen, N. L., Nesselroade, J. R., & Bergeman, C. S. (in press). Genetic influence on childhood family environment perceived retrospectively from the last half of the life span. *Developmental Psychology.*

Rao, D. C., Morton, N. E., & Yee, S. (1976). Resolution of cultural and biological inheritance by path analysis. *American Journal of Human Genetics, 28*, 228–42.

Reiss, A. J., Duncan, O. D., Hatt, P. K., & North, C. C. (1961). *Occupations and social status.* Glencoe, IL: Free Press.

Rice, T., Carey, G., DeFries, J. C., & Fulker, D. W. (in press). Multivariate path analysis of specific cognitive abilities in the Colorado Adoption Project: Alternative models of assortative mating. *Behavioral Genetics.*

Rice, T., Corley, R., Fulker, D. W., & Plomin, R. (1986). The development and validation of a test battery measuring specific cognitive abilities in four-year-old children. *Educational and Psychological Measurement, 46*, 699–708.

Rice, T., Fulker, D. W., & DeFries, J. C. (1986). Multivariate path analysis of specific cognitive abilities in the Colorado Adoption Project. *Behavior Genetics, 16*, 107–26.

Rice, T., Fulker, D. W., DeFries, J. C., & Plomin, R. (1987). *Path analysis of IQ during infancy and early childhood and an index of the home environment in the Colorado Adoption Project.* Manuscript submitted for publication.

Rice, T., Plomin, R., & DeFries, J. C. (1984). Development of hand preference in the Colorado Adoption Project. *Perceptual and Motor Skills, 58*, 683–9.

Rowe, D. C. (1981). Environmental and genetic influences on dimensions of perceived parenting: A twin study. *Developmental Psychology, 17*, 203–8.

   (1983). A biometrical analysis of perceptions of family environment: A study of twin and singleton sibling kinships. *Child Development, 54*, 416–23.

Rowe, D. C., & Plomin, R. (1977). Temperament in early childhood. *Journal of Personality Assessment, 41*, 150–6.

(1981). The importance of nonshared (E1) environmental influences in behavioral development. *Developmental Psychology, 17*, 517–31.

Rushton, J. P., Brainerd, C. J., & Pressley, M. (1983). Behavioral development and construct validity: The principle of aggregation. *Psychological Bulletin, 94*, 18–38.

Rutter, M. (1983). Statistical and personal interactions: Facets and perspectives. In D. Magnusson & V. L. Allen (Eds.), *Human development: An interactional perspective* (pp. 295–319). New York: Academic Press.

(1985). Family and school influences on cognitive development. *Journal of Child Psychology and Psychiatry, 26*, 683–704.

Rutter, M., & Garmezy, N. (1983). Developmental psychopathology. In P. H. Mussen (Ed.), *Handbook of child psychology* (pp. 775–911). New York: Wiley.

Scarr, S. (1983). An evolutionary perspective on infant intelligence. In M. Lewis (Ed.), *Origins of intelligence: Infancy and early childhood* (pp. 191–223). New York: Plenum.

Scarr, S., & McCartney, K. (1983). How people make their own environments: A theory of genotype → environment effects. *Child Development, 54*, 424–35.

Scarr, S., Webber, P. I., Weinberg, R. A., & Wittig, M. A. (1981). Personality resemblance among adolescents and their parents in biologically related and adoptive families. *Journal of Personality and Social Psychology, 40*, 885–98.

Scarr, S., & Weinberg, R. A. (1978). The influence of "family background" on intellectual attainment. *American Sociological Review, 43*, 674–92.

Singer, S., Corley, R., Guiffrida, C., & Plomin, R. (1984). The development and validation of a test battery to measure differentiated cognitive abilities in three-year-old children. *Educational and Psychological Measurement, 49*, 703–13.

Skinner, Q. (1985). *The return of grand theory in the human sciences.* Cambridge University Press.

Sklar, J., & Berkov, B. (1974). Abortion, illegitimacy, and the American birth rate. *Science, 185*, 909–15.

Skodak, M., & Skeels, H. M (1949). A final follow-up of one hundred adopted children. *Journal of Genetic Psychology, 75*, 85–125.

Snedecor, G. W., & Cochran, W. G. (1980). *Statistical methods.* Ames: Iowa State University Press.

Snygg, D. (1938). The relation between the intelligence of mothers and of their children living in foster homes. *Journal of Genetic Psychology, 52*, 401–6.

Sternberg, P. W., & Horritz, H. R. (1984). The genetic control of cell lineage during nematode development. *Annual Review of Genetics, 18*, 489–524.

Stott, L. H., & Ball, R. S. (1965). Evaluation of infant and preschool mental tests. *Monographs of the Society for Research in Child Development, 30* (Whole No. 101).

Tambs, K., Sundet, J. M., & Magnus, P. (1986). Genetic and environmental contributions to the covariation between the Wechsler Adult Intelligence Scale (WAIS) subtests: A study of twins. *Behavior Genetics, 16*, 475–91.

Tanner, J. M., Healy, M. J. R., Lockhart, R. D., Mackenzie, J. D., & Whitehouse, R. H. (1956). The prediction of adult body measurements from measurements taken each year from birth to 5 years. *Archives of Diseases in Childhood, 31*, 372–81.

Terman, L. M., & Merrill, M. A. (1973). *Stanford–Binet intelligence scale: 1972 norms edition.* Boston: Houghton Mifflin.

Thomas, A., & Chess, S. (1977). *Temperament and development.* New York: Brunner/Mazel.

(1986). The New York Longitudinal Study: From infancy to early adult life. In R. Plomin & J. F. Dunn (Eds.), *The study of temperament: Changes, continuities and challenges* (pp. 39–52). Hillsdale, NJ: Erlbaum.

Thompson, L. A., Fulker, D. W., DeFries, J. C., & Plomin, R. (1986). Multivariate genetic analysis of "environmental" influences on infant cognitive development. *British Journal of Developmental Psychology, 4*, 347–53.

Thompson, L. A., Fulker, D. W., DeFries, J. C., & Plomin, R. (1988). Multivariate analysis of cognitive and temperament measures in 24-month-old adoptive and nonadoptive sibling pairs. *Personality and Individual Differences 9*, 95–100.

Thorndike, R. L. (1940). Constancy of the IQ. *Psychological Bulletin, 37*, 167–87.

Tsuang, M. T., Crowe, R. R., Winokur, G., & Clancy, J. (1977, June). *Relatives of schizophrenics, manics, depressives and controls.* Paper presented at the 2nd International Conference on Schizophrenia, Rochester, NY.

Tuddenham, R. D., & Snyder, M. M. (1954). *Physical growth of California boys and girls from birth to eighteen years.* Los Angeles & Berkeley: University of California Press.

Underwood, B. J. (1975). Individual differences as a crucible in theory construction. *American Psychologist, 30*, 128–34.

Uzgiris, I. C. (1983). Organization of sensorimotor intelligence. In M. Lewis (Ed.), *Origins of intelligence: Infancy and early childhood* (pp. 135–90). New York: Plenum.

Uzgiris, I. C., & Hunt, J. M. (1975). *Assessment in infancy.* Urbana: University of Illinois Press.

Vogler, G. P. (1985). Multivariate path analysis of family resemblance. *Genetic Epidemiology, 2*, 35–53.

Vogler, G. P., & DeFries, J. C. (1985). Bivariate path analysis of familial resemblance for reading ability and symbol processing speed. *Behavior Genetics, 15*, 111–21.

Wachs, T. D. (1979). Proximal experience and early cognitive–intellectual development: The physical environment. *Merrill–Palmer Quarterly, 25*, 3–41.

(1985, April). *Organism–environment interaction.* Symposium at the Biennial Meeting of the Society for Research in Child Development, Baltimore, MD.

Wachs, T. D., & Gandour, N. J. (1983). Temperament, environment, and six-month cognitive–intellectual development: A test of the organismic specificity hypothesis. *International Journal of Behavioral Development, 6*, 135–52.

Wachs, T. D., & Gruen, G. (1982). *Early experience and human development.* New York: Plenum.

Wachs, T. D., & Hubert, N. (1981). Changes in the structure of cognitive–intellectual performance during the second year of life. *Infant Behavior and Development, 4*, 151–62.

Watt, N. F., Anthony, E. J., Wynne, L. C., & Rolf, J. E. (1984). *Children at risk for schizophrenia: A longitudinal perspective.* Cambridge University Press.

Wechsler, D. (1952). *Range of human capacities.* Baltimore, MD: William & Wilkins.

Werner, E. E., & Bayley, N. (1966). The reliability of Bayley's revised scale of mental and motor development during the first year of life. *Child Development, 37*, 39–50.

Werner, H. (1948). *Comparative psychology of mental development.* New York: International Universities Press.

Wilson, R. S. (1976). Concordance in physical growth for monozygotic and dizygotic twins. *Annals of Human Biology, 3*, 1–10.

(1977). Mental development in twins. In A. Oliverio (Ed.), *Genetics, environment and intelligence* (pp. 305–36). New York: Elsevier Science.

(1983). The Louisville Twin Study: Developmental synchronies in behavior. *Child Development, 54*, 298–316.

(1986). Continuity and change in cognitive ability profile. *Behavior Genetics, 16*, 45–60.

Wilson, R. S., Brown, A., & Matheny, A. P., Jr. (1971). Emergence and persistence of behavioral differences in twins. *Child Development, 42*, 1381–98.

Wilson, R. S., & Harpring, E. B. (1972). Mental and motor development in infant twins. *Developmental Psychology, 7*, 277–87.

Wilson, R. S., & Matheny, A. P., Jr. (1983). Assessment of temperament in infant twins. *Developmental Psychology, 19*, 172–83.

(1986). Behavior–genetics research in infant temperament: The Louisville Twin Study. In R. Plomin & J. F. Dunn (Eds.), *The study of temperament: Changes, continuities and challenges* (pp. 81–97). Hillsdale, NJ: Erlbaum.

Windle, M., Hooker, K., Lenerz, K., East, P. L., Lerner, J. V., & Lerner, R. M. (1986). Temperament, perceived competence, and depression in early and late adolescents. *Developmental Psychology, 22*, 384–92.

Windle, M., & Lerner, R. M. (1986). The "goodness of fit" model of temperament–context relations: Interaction or correlation? In J. V. Lerner & R. M. Lerner (Eds.), *Temperament and social interaction during infancy and childhood* (pp. 109–19). San Francisco: Jossey-Bass.

Winer, B. J. (1971). *Statistical principles in experimental design*. New York: Holt, Rinehart & Winston.

Wohlwill, J. F. (1973). *The study of behavioral development*. New York: Academic Press.

Wright, S. (1921). Correlation and causation. *Journal of Agricultural Research, 20*, 557–85.

(1931). Statistical methods in biology. *Journal of the American Statistical Association, 26*, 155–63.

(1978). *Evolution and the genetics of populations*. University of Chicago Press.

Yarrow, L. J., Goodwin, M. S., Manheimer, H., & Milowe, I. D. (1973). Infancy experiences and cognitive and personality development at ten years. In J. L. Stone, H. T. Smith, & L. B. Murphy (Eds.), *The competent infant: Research and commentary* (pp. 1274–81). New York: Basic Books.

Author index

339

Subject index